A Dragon's Head and a Serpent's Tail

CAMPAIGNS & COMMANDERS

GREGORY J. W. URWIN, SERIES EDITOR

A Dragon's Head and a Serpent's Tail

Ming China and the First Great East Asian War, 1592–1598

Kenneth M. Swope

University of Oklahoma Press : Norman

ALSO BY KENNETH M. SWOPE

(ed.) *Warfare in China since 1600* (Aldershot, England/Burlington, Vt., 2005)

Library of Congress Cataloging-in-Publication Data

Swope, Kenneth.
  A dragon's head and a serpent's tail : Ming China and the first Great East Asian war, 1592–1598 / Kenneth M. Swope.
      p. cm. — (Campaigns and commanders ; v. 20)
  Includes bibliographical references and index.
  ISBN 978-0-8061-4056-8 (hardcover : alk. paper) 1. Korea—History—Japanese Invasions, 1592–1598. 2. China—History, Military—960-1644. 3. Wanli, Emperor of China, 1563–1620—Military leadership. 4. China—History—Ming dynasty, 1368-1644. 5. Japan—History, Military—16th century. 6. East Asia—History, Military—16th century. 7. Korea—History—Japanese Invasions, 1592–1598—Sources. 8. China—History, Military—960-1644—Sources. 9. Japan—History, Military—16th century—Sources. 10. East Asia—History, Military—16th century—Sources. I. Title.
  DS913.43.S93 2009
  951'.026—dc22

                                                                        2009013808

A Dragon's Head and a Serpent's Tail: Ming China and the First Great East Asian War, 1592–1598 is volume 20 in the Campaigns and Commanders series.

The paper in this book meets the guidelines for permanence and durability of the Committee on Production Guidelines for Book Longevity of the Council on Library Resources, Inc. ∞

1 2 3 4 5 6 7 8 9 10

CONTENTS

ILLUSTRATIONS

FIGURES

MAPS

PREFACE

This book had its genesis in 1998 when I was a graduate student at the University of Michigan. As I was preparing to take my candidacy examinations, I remarked to Hitomi Tonomura, one of my committee members, that I found it odd that no one had yet written an English-language monograph on the Hideyoshi invasions of Korea.[1] Her response was, "Why don't you do it?" As someone with an interest in military history already, it made a good degree of sense.

But there was one problem. My major field of study was premodern Chinese history, and most of my academic training had been in Sinology. My primary advisor, Dr. Chang Chun-shu, was concerned that my dissertation focus should be primarily on China. That semester he offered a reading seminar in which I and other students could read primary sources in areas of our choosing. I decided to start reading primary Chinese sources dealing with the Ming response to the Japanese invasion with the aim of touching on the war as part of an examination of a broader picture of Ming military decline.

What I found, however, was surprising to say the least. The Ming intervention in Korea was the second of the so-called Three Great Campaigns of the Wanli Emperor (*Wanli san da zheng*). The first was the suppression of a troop mutiny in the northwest border city of Ningxia, where an erstwhile Mongol retainer named Pubei attempted to create a revitalized Mongol empire of sorts with steppe allies. The third campaign was the suppression of an aboriginal revolt in south-west China led by Yang Yinglong, a hereditary chieftain. Although denigrated by prominent historian Ray Huang as a "historiographical invention" of late Ming writers, a closer examination of the extant primary sources suggested that a more nuanced interpretation of these campaigns was in order.[2] This topic met with the blessing of my primary advisor, and a dissertation was born.

It did not take much reading of the primary sources for my preconceptions of the campaigns to change. While Huang argued that there was no basis for grouping these actions together, they in fact were conducted more or less simultaneously. So for the Ming state, they were all part of a grand strategic design. Court conferences concerning one campaign often made reference to the needs of the others, and many of the same commanders and soldiers served in one or more of them. Their successful prosecution involved the mobilization of hundreds of thousands of troops over great distances and in vastly different terrain. As any historian of early modern militaries knows, the ability to mobilize, equip, and supply such large forces over any distance suggests considerable military and bureaucratic skill. Moreover, far from portraying the Ming military as utterly incompetent and technologically backward, Korean and Japanese sources tend to state otherwise, especially regarding the power of Chinese firearms.

Furthermore, after reading thousands of pages of primary sources largely unexamined by scholars for centuries, I determined that Ming success in the Three Great Campaigns was actually part of a much larger general military revival from the 1570s through the first decade of the seventeenth century. Throughout these decades the Ming empire was militarily aggressive, even expansionistic, along all its frontiers, not only acting defensively but also willing to launch surgical strikes into Mongol lands to capture horses and other livestock and keep these nomadic enemies off balance. The government also encouraged Han Chinese settlement into frontier areas, a project that included the acculturation of aboriginal peoples, though sometimes with deleterious consequences.

The initiative for these reforms appears to be due to both favorable economic circumstances wrought by the lifting of a longtime ban on maritime trade in 1567, which allowed a massive influx of New World silver that stimulated a rapidly monetizing economy, and the visionary leadership of Grand Secretary Zhang Juzheng (1525–82), who served as

de-facto ruler of China from 1572 to 1582 and as tutor for the young
Wanli Emperor. Zhang was a firm believer in the importance of a strong
military. Zhang Haiying argues that all of his policy goals and administrative and economic reforms stemmed from a desire to improve the
military.[3] Primary sources suggest that the grand secretary passed these
values down to his protégé, who internalized them and sought to emulate
his former tutor even after Zhang's death and posthumous discrediting
(the result of factional politics).

Likewise, the primary sources suggest a revisionist interpretation of
Wanli and his reign. Standard accounts since the end of the Ming dynasty
have maintained that Wanli was greedy, lazy, petty, and petulant, content
to indulge himself in the pleasures of his concubines and ignore important affairs of state. In fact the authors of the *Official History of the Ming
Dynasty (Ming shi)* assert, "Therefore when discussing the fall of the
Ming dynasty, in reality its fall starts with Shenzong [Wanli]; certainly he
cannot be excused from blame." Later historians tended to repeat such
assertions uncritically, often influenced by an almost universally hostile
historiographic tradition toward Wanli.[4] This antagonism seems to stem
from the fact that the emperor (as will be seen in the following chapters) actively pursued his own vision for Ming China and frequently
patronized and defended military officials against charges leveled by their
civil counterparts, who otherwise wielded overwhelming influence in
late Ming government and society.[5]

My dissertation therefore went from an examination of the causes
of Ming military and political decline to a revisionist study of the Wanli
Emperor and his important role in overseeing the Ming military revival
of the late sixteenth century. It also led me to start thinking about East
Asian militaries in a comparative fashion and to consider examining
the Three Great Campaigns in light of contemporary developments
elsewhere. While unable to do much of this within the scope of the dissertation, many of these issues are treated in the following chapters.

The foremost aim of this book, then, is to present a narrative of
the First Great East Asian War for the broader community of military
historians. There are numerous articles and books that touch on various aspects of the war in English, but up to this point none of them
have made extensive use of primary and secondary sources produced
by the people and scholars of the three major belligerent states. This
book is based on my extensive and critical examination of Chinese and
Japanese secondary scholarship on the war (in their original languages)

and comparative reading and evaluation of the primary sources produced by all three sides (and generally written in classical Chinese). Although I do not read Korean, colleagues in the Korean academic community have been most helpful concerning the changing interpretations of the war in their country.

Nevertheless, the scope of this book is primarily from the Ming perspective and relies far more on Chinese sources than on those produced by Koreans or Japanese—to give full attention to the voluminous primary sources produced by all three sides would necessitate a much larger book. For example, a recent compilation of Korean primary source materials runs to an excess of thirty volumes and is by no means exhaustive. The Japanese literature, while perhaps not quite as extensive, is equally daunting. Chinese sources, in contrast, are much fewer in number and therefore easier to manage. Additionally, I am a specialist in the history of Ming China, and that is where my major scholarly interests lie.

I am also reasonably versed in the broader English-language debates concerning warfare in early modern Europe as represented by the likes of Geoffrey Parker, Jeremy Black, Mark C. Fissell, and Bert Hall. Therefore, within the spirit of this series, I will refer to works concerning European warfare and military practices throughout this book so as to highlight potential areas of interest for the reader. In particular I will devote much attention to technology, strategy, and tactics, examining how and why the war in Korea unfolded as it did and trying to determine how and why commanders made tactical decisions. This is actually an area of the war that has been relatively understudied even in Asian languages, for much previous scholarship has largely ignored discussion of logistics or battlefield conditions.

In the process of narrating the events of the war, I highlight the important role played by the Wanli Emperor in the Ming state and the continuing primacy of the empire in early modern East Asia, noting the implications for China's subsequent development. Additionally I look at conceptions of interstate relations in all three countries and the relationship between foreign and domestic politics, particularly as they pertained to military affairs. While scholars have often presumed intimate links between the military and Japanese politics due to the presence of the militarily oriented shogun governments from 1185 to 1868, similar relationships are often ignored or glossed over by historians of China and Korea, who are wont to accept the dismissive platitudes of centuries of moralizing Confucian officials. But as Peter Lorge notes:

"Effective generals were the most problematic figures in imperial China. . . . Generals were really the arbiters of dynastic fortune in ways that civil officials were not, since the only crises that threatened dynastic survival were military ones." Likewise, recent work by Eugene Park illuminates the importance of military officials in late Chosŏn Korea.[6] This observation may come as a surprise to some readers and again invites comparisons with Western Europe.

The book is organized as follows. Chapter 1 presents an overview of the broader context of Ming intervention in Korea, drawing attention to the problems of the late Ming military and the solutions devised by government officials. It also offers brief accounts of the other two military campaigns normally associated with the war in Korea, discussing how these events fit into Ming China's grand strategic vision and combined to make this the First Great East Asian War.

Chapter 2 covers the prelude to war, with the rise of Hideyoshi and the formulation of his grand plans for continental conquest. In addition to examining various theories concerning Hideyoshi's motivations and aims, this chapter includes background information on the state of affairs in Korea, briefly touching on earlier sixteenth-century conflicts between the three states, as well as Korean and Chinese assessments of the threat posed by the Japanese by the spring of 1592.

The third chapter treats the first seven months of the war, which witnessed a Japanese blitzkrieg that left the Korean king dazed and frightened on the Chinese border, begging the Ming to send military aid. But even as the Japanese armies were cutting a bloody swath through Korea's regular armed forces, guerrilla bands led by local officials or even Buddhist monks rallied to the defense of their homeland. By midsummer 1592 the Korean navy was also scoring important victories off Korea's south coast, stemming the Japanese tide, if not turning it entirely. Although a small Ming relief force was utterly decimated in late summer, the conflict was about to escalate.

Chapter 4 encompasses the full-scale Ming intervention of February 1593 through 1594. The first part chronicles the major battles of the first half of the year that resulted in the withdrawal of Japanese forces to a series of fortresses along Korea's southeast coast. The second part discusses conditions in the countryside and explores the factors behind the opening of peace negotiations. Special attention is devoted to the military circumstances surrounding the decision by both sides to open peace talks, for the actual military situation is often ignored by nationalistic scholars determined to find a scapegoat for failing to prosecute the war to an unequivocal victory.

The fifth chapter focuses primarily on the peace talks while also devoting attention to Korean military reforms. The discussion also looks at the factional politics at the Ming court in an attempt to trace the reasons for decisions made by Wanli and his advisers about investing Hideyoshi as king of Japan, a move bitterly opposed by China's Korean allies. The discussion also examines the Japanese occupation of and life in Korea during the war.

Chapter 6 picks up the story with Hideyoshi's rejection of Ming investiture and his decision to launch another full-scale invasion of the peninsula, this time with the primary aim of exacting revenge for his perceived humiliation. This second offensive was characterized by bitter siege warfare. The major sieges are discussed in great detail, with the aim of shedding light on early modern East Asian siege warfare within a comparative context. Also addressed are the naval battles that marked the climax of the war and ensured victory for the Sino-Korean allies.

Chapter 7 examines the aftermath and legacies of the war, lingering issues such as the repatriation of war captives, and the resumption of trade and diplomacy between Korea and Japan. It also addresses whether or not the war truly had a disabling effect on the late Ming state while considering some of the more fanciful notions concerning the conflict, including the idea that captured Japanese soldiers were critical in introducing modern firearms to China. Most importantly, the discussion focuses on how the allied victory contributed to continuing notions of the superiority of the Chinese tributary system of foreign relations and their further codification by the Ming's Manchu conquerors, to their great detriment, some two centuries later.

ACKNOWLEDGMENTS

As with any work of this length and scope, one invariably incurs a number of personal and professional debts and must rely on the knowledge, patience, and kindness of others. As the present book stems from my dissertation completed at the University of Michigan in 2001, I would first like to thank my dissertation committee members. Hitomi Tonomura first suggested I work on the war, and my primary advisor, Chang Chun-shu, encouraged me to expand my focus to include the Three Great Campaigns of the Wanli emperor. Ernest Young and David Rolston were dedicated readers who improved the flow and logic of the narrative immeasurably. John Whitmore continues to be a great friend and mentor who has impressed upon me the importance of taking a broader view of things. As the book project was in its earlier stages, I received a Summer Faculty Research Grant from Marist College and an Asia Library Travel Grant from the University of Michigan's Asia Library. I was also greatly aided by the library staff of the C. V. Starr Library of Columbia University and the interlibrary loan offices at Marist, which handled many requests for materials.

Once I relocated to Ball State University, I was fortunate enough to receive a New Faculty Summer Research Grant that afforded me the opportunity to spend three weeks in South Korea during the summer of 2005. Dr. Soo-heon Park, the dean of International Exchanges of our sister institution, Kyunghee University in Seoul, graciously put me up in a hotel in Insadong for the duration of my stay. The late James Palais put me in touch with one of his graduate students, Cheolbae Son, who provided transportation to and from the Seoul airport and arranged for me to give a guest lecture at Sungkyunkwan University, where I made many valuable acquaintances. Cheolbae also photo-copied many valuable primary sources for me. Kenneth Robinson was an expert tour guide and interpreter as we followed the course of the war from Seoul to Chinju to Yŏsu, enjoying many delicious meals and healthy amounts of Korean beer in the process. Ken also facilitated my access to archival collections in the Chinju National Museum, the National Library of Korea, the Kyujanggak Archives at Seoul National University, and Sogang University. He even went above and beyond the call of duty by copying materials I needed when he learned a col-lection would be closed during my visit. I would like to thank the staffs of all these fine institutions for their cordiality.

Adam Bohnet also stepped in to lead me on a quest for Ming remnants in Seoul's back alleys and bookshops. Prof. Chung Doo-hee graciously invited me to participate in the 2006 conference A Transnational History of the Imjin War, held in Tongyŏng, during which I had the opportunity to interact with prominent scholars on the war from all over the globe. My spirited exchanges with Prof. Han Myonggi have become the stuff of legends. Adam Bohnet, Nam-lin Hur, and Edward Shultz assisted me with interpreting the often rapid Japanese and Korean conversations at the conference.

A National Endowment for the Humanities Summer Stipend in 2006 provided me with the opportunity to begin writing the first drafts of the first two chapters. Jack Wills and Hitomi Tonomura deserve thanks for writing letters of support on my behalf for that grant. Ball State University matched the grant, allowing me to travel to other locations to gather materials. Diana Wen-ling Liu, head librarian of the East Asian Collection at Indiana University, has been invaluable in helping me locate items and even assigned Korean research assistants to help me transliterate Korean-language materials. Margaret Key of Indiana's East Asian Studies Center provided a travel grant to examine materials in the Lilly Library. The Lilly staff was fantastic, and I am grateful for their permission to reproduce photographs of images held in their collection. The National Palace Museum in Taibei, Taiwan, Republic of China, generously granted permission to use the official portrait of Wanli and several images from the Ming imperial procession scroll from their collection.

At Ball State my friends and colleagues in the History Department have been wonderfully supportive throughout the process. Chris Thompson and Jim Connolly helped me prepare grant applications, and Chris proved a wonderful source of advice on getting the manuscript out. My chair, Bruce Geelhoed, has been a great source of advice and support in negotiating the university bureaucracy and finding the funds needed for various endeavors. Kevin Smith and Abel Alves as assistant chairs helped create a more workable teaching schedule to facilitate completing my manuscript. Ken Hall has always been willing to read and comment on drafts, and our golf outings with Chuck Argo have convinced me that some things are simply beyond human control. Dinners at Thai Smile with Slava Dmitriev and Dave Ulbrich have provided welcome respites from the rigors of writing.

On a personal level I cannot thank my wife, Amy Hollaway, enough for all her love, support, encouragement, and advice over the years, particularly her understanding when I told her I needed "just a few more minutes" that then turned into hours. Amy also went above and beyond the call of spousal duty in following me around the world in pursuit of obscure sources and enduring endless discussions about Ming history. She also painstakingly read the entire manuscript, finding many contradictory or repetitious statements and passages. Finally, she sacrificed her own career for mine on more than one occasion, and I thank her for that. My family, particularly my parents and step-parents, have been more indirectly involved but always curious and supportive, wondering how it could possibly take so long to finish a simple book. As my niece Dana remarked, "You sure have a lot of studying to do!" Arthur Ling has been a great friend since graduate school and a wonderful sounding board. Michael Chiang read and commented on parts of the book in the draft stage. Ed Woell likewise provided insights and inspiration, having recently gone through the process himself. Jack Wills and Sun Laichen have also been invariably supportive as our paths have crossed over the past few years. David Robinson organized and hosted the Ming Court Culture Conference at Princeton in 2003, which helped sharpen my notions about Wanli's role as supreme commander of the Ming Empire. Thanks must also go to my many friends in the Chinese Military History Society for their friendship and support over the years, especially Peter Lorge and David Graff.

Greg Urwin, Chuck Rankin, and Steven Baker have been great editors to work with and have enthusiastically supported the project from its inception. Kevin Brock did a great job of copyediting an unwieldy manuscript. Michael Hradesky drew the maps. The photographs were taken by myself and by Amy Hollaway, who learned digital-photography skills especially for this project. Peter Blume, director of the Ball State University Museum of Art, purchased and granted me permission to reproduce the fabulous triptych image that graces the book's cover. Sherry Smith prepared the index. Please note that the interpretations and conclusions expressed herein are entirely my own and do not necessarily reflect those of any of the granting institutions listed above. If I have unwittingly forgotten anyone, you have my apologies and my thanks.

Kenneth M. Swope
Muncie, Indiana

Stylistic Conventions

All Chinese personal and place names are rendered in the pinyin system of Romanization without tone marks. For sake of consistency, this includes works published in Taiwan as well as their authors' names. The only exceptions to this rule are books published in English by Chinese authors who use variant forms of Romanization. Japanese names and terms are rendered in the standard Hepburn system. For Korean names and terms, I use the modified McCune-Reischauer system without hyphens between syllables for personal and place names. For Mongolian names and places, I use the system employed in *The Cambridge History of China* volumes. For places well known in the English-speaking world such as Tokyo and Pyongyang, long-vowel indicators are omitted. For translation of Chinese official titles into English, I follow Charles Hucker, *A Dictionary of Official Titles in Imperial China*. For converting lunar dates into their Western equivalents, I follow *A Sino-Western Calendar for Two Thousand Years, 1–2000 A.D.*, by Bi Zhongsan and Oyang Yi. Specific dates are generally rendered into their Western equivalents, but when a reference is made to a month (for example, the fourth month), this refers to the lunar month.

With respect to citing specific works, in general I cite them by the modern page numbers where possible. Otherwise citations are given by *juan* (chapter) and fascicle number within the *juan*. Because the works in question were usually printed on woodblocks, each page has two sides, hence the first side or face of page 12 of chapter 15 of a work is rendered 15, 12a. In the case of compiled materials such as Li Guangtao's *Chaoxian shiliao*, the original chapter and page numbers are generally included with the excerpt.

CHINESE WEIGHTS AND MEASURES

Chinese Unit	U.S. Equivalent		Metric Equivalent	
1 *fen*	0.141	inches	0.358	centimeters
1 *cun*	1.41	inches	3.581	centimeters
1 *chi* (linear)	14.1	inches	35.814	centimeters
1 *chi* (itinerary)	12.1	inches	30.734	centimeters
1 *zhang*	141	inches	3.581	meters
1 *bu*	60.5	inches	1.536	meters
1 *li*	1821.15	feet	0.555	kilometers
1 *mu*	0.16	acres	0.064	hectares
1 *qing*	16.16	acres	6.539	hectares
1 *liang* (tael)	1.327	ounces	37.62	grams
1 *qian* (cash)	0.1327	ounces	3.762	grams
1 *jin* (catty)	1.33	pounds	603.277	grams
1 *dan* (picul)*	133.33	pounds	60.477	kilograms
1 *shi* (stone)	160	pounds	72.574	kilograms
1 *sheng*	1.87	pints	1.031	liters
1 *dou*	2.34	gallons	10.31	liters

* The measures *dan* and *shi* were used interchangeably for grain weights for most of the Ming era, so I have decided to use the *dan* value throughout the book.

TIMELINE OF THE WAR

1592

May	Japanese land at Pusan
June	King Sŏnjo and his court flee Seoul
July	First appearance of "turtleboats" in battle; King Sŏnjo retreats to Ŭiju on Chinese border
August	Ming expeditionary force annihilated in Pyongyang
September	Rise of "Righteous Guerrillas" in Korean countryside
October	Shen Weijing and Konishi Yukinaga negotiate fifty-day truce
November	Li Rusong named supreme commander of Korea by Wanli; Song Yingchang named military-affairs commissioner by Wanli

1593

January	Ming relief forces arrive in Korea
February	Allied forces recapture Pyongyang and Kaesŏng; Battle of Pyŏkchegwan
March	Japanese retreat to Seoul
April	Japanese sue for peace
June	Chinese envoys go to Japan
July	Japanese massacre population of Chinju
Autumn	Most Japanese troops withdraw; Pusan perimeter established; most Chinese troops withdraw
November	King Sŏnjo returns to Seoul

1594

January–December
　　　　　　Inconclusive debates at Ming court over peace terms

1595

January　　　Japanese envoy Konishi Joan finally proceeds to Beijing
February　　　Wanli decides to invest Hideyoshi as "king of Japan"
Summer　　　Ming mission led by Li Zongcheng reaches Pusan

1596

May　　　　　Li Zongcheng abandons the envoys
July　　　　　Ming mission sets out for Japan
October　　　Ming envoys meet Hideyoshi, who rejects their "terms";
　　　　　　Hideyoshi orders second invasion of Korea under Katō
　　　　　　Kiyomasa

1597

February　　　Japanese ships land at Tongnae
Summer　　　Japanese advance; Yi Sunsin back in action at sea
September　Namwŏn falls
October　　　Allied victory at Chiksan; Yi Sunsin wins naval battle
　　　　　　at Myŏngyang

1598

January–February
　　　　　　Siege of Ulsan by allied forces
April　　　　　Japanese forces start to withdraw
Summer　　　Allies launch multipronged offensive
September　Hideyoshi dies; allied offensive continues as Japanese
　　　　　　withdraw
December　Battle of Noryang Straits marks end of war; Yi Sunsin
　　　　　　killed

A Dragon's Head and a Serpent's Tail

Official portrait of Emperor Wanli. *Courtesy
National Palace Museum, Taibei*

Introduction

The Unforgotten War

Tucked away in a back alley of Kyoto, largely ignored amid the temples, pagodas, castles, and teahouses, stands a curious monument to the cold, calculating callousness of war in early modern East Asia. Called "Kyoto's least mentioned and most-often-avoided tourist attraction" by one scholar, the Mimizuka (Mound of Ears) and children's playground actually contains what is left of thousands of severed and pickled Chinese and Korean noses sent back to Japan's overlord and instigator of the First Great East Asian War of 1592–98, Toyotomi Hideyoshi (1536–98). Because heads, the normal proof offered to gain rewards for one's deeds in battle in Japan, were too large and unwieldy to ship overseas, the Japanese resorted to severing the noses of slain foes and sending them home to satisfy the *kampaku*'s thirst for revenge against those who refused to accept his primacy in East Asia. Hideyoshi's men were assigned a quota of three Korean (or Chinese) noses per soldier. Although modern estimates vary, it is generally accepted that 100,000–200,000 noses eventually reached Japan, though some Koreans apparently survived the ordeal and spent the rest of their days without a nose.[1]

Hideyoshi ordered the Mimizuka established not far from the Grand Buddha he built to show his mercy toward the ghosts of his victims as well as to serve as an eternal testament to the prowess and glory of his loyal commanders. Its sheer size and the voluminous and detailed records of the number of heads, ears, and noses taken by Hideyoshi's lieutenants underscore the brutality of this conflict and provide clues to why its memory lingers in East Asia. The Mimizuka is the largest and best known but not the only such memorial, the others having been established by lesser lords in their own fiefs elsewhere in Japan.[2]

One would be hard pressed to find another four-hundred-year-old conflict anywhere in the world with as much contemporary visibility. Shrines, memorials, and statues to the heroes and battles of the war dot the Korean countryside, while in Japan some of its commanders were deified in the ensuing Tokugawa period. From 2004 to 2005 a yearlong bio-epic on the life of Adm. Yi Sunsin (1545–98), Korea's greatest national folk hero, whose exploits are credited with saving the country from destruction, aired on South Korean television. At one time in the 1970s, statues of Admiral Yi were placed in public schools all over the country, both to inspire patriotism and to demonstrate the government's steadfast resolve to defend the country against the communist threat from the north; one huge statue guards the approach to the president's house in Seoul. Strolling through the capital's many gift shops, one is inundated with pewter figurines of Yi and his famous turtleboats (kobuksŏn). You can even buy commemorative pewter shot glasses engraved with the admiral's likeness or packs of cigarettes bearing the image of a turtleboat.

A recent academic conference on the war held in the South Korean seaside town Tongyŏng, located near Admiral Yi's naval base at Hansan Island, attracted scholars from Korea, Japan, Europe, and North America.[3] The mayor of Tongyŏng greeted the attendees, who were feted with a series of receptions and banquets. One of Japan's largest daily newspapers, the *Asahi Shimbun*, sent multiple reporters and photographers to cover the gathering, which received two days of print coverage the following week. The fact that a four-century-old war would receive such extensive national media attention suggests the conflict's enduring significance and place in the public eye in both Korea and Japan.

The anniversary of the Mimizuka itself was commemorated in September 1997 in Kyoto with an academic symposium that also produced a conference volume. This symposium represents but one part of a much larger debate between Japanese and Korean scholars and citizens alike concerning the scale of the suffering inflicted by the Japanese upon Korea in the 1590s. In debates similar to those concerning the Japanese colonial era of the twentieth century, Koreans contend that Japanese textbooks have tended to gloss over the atrocities committed by Hideyoshi's troops and cloak Japan's actions by praising Hideyoshi for enshrining the spirits of the dead. With respect to the Mimizuka, Korean opinion has been divided. Some have suggested leveling the mound to erase its shameful memory, while others advocate repatriating the remains to Korea. But the Japanese government's position has been that because the mound is a national landmark, it should not be disturbed. Thus, in the words of journalist Nicholas Kristof, the Mimizuka underscores "the tensions and hostilities that still set the countries of East Asia against each other," and for many Koreans it serves as "a symbol of a Japanese brutishness that still lurks beneath the surface, waiting to explode."[4]

Although a seminal event in the region's history, the First Great East Asian War (as I prefer to call it) is barely known outside East Asia. Even in China it is far less understood or acknowledged than in Korea and Japan (for reasons discussed herein). The war's designation is even a subject of debate. In Korea it is generally referred to as the Imjin War, or *Imjin Waeran* ("the Japanese calamity of 1592," *imjin* being the designation for the year 1592, the Year of the Black Water Dragon in the Chinese sexagenary calendar then employed throughout East Asia). The Japanese generally call it *Hideyoshi no Chōsen shinryaku* (Hideyoshi's Invasion of Korea) or the *Bunroku-keichō no eki* (the Campaigns of 1592 and 1597). Japanese sources from the Tokugawa (1603–1868) and Meiji (1868–1912) eras often refer to the war as either the *Seikan* (Glorious Conquest of Korea) or the *Seibatsu* (Glorious Pacification of Korea). In China the war has been called the *yuan Chaoxian* (the Rescue of Korea) or the *dong zheng* (Eastern Expedition).

This war was the single largest military conflict in the world during the sixteenth century. The Japanese mobilized more than 150,000 troops for their first invasion in 1592 and more than 140,000 for their second major invasion in 1597. Ming China provided in excess of 40,000 troops to help Korea in 1592 and more than twice that many in 1597, even as hundreds of thousands of its soldiers were simultaneously engaged in quelling uprisings at home. Although the actual number of Koreans involved is difficult to estimate since many fought as guerrilla troops or assorted irregulars under the command of local elites or even Buddhist monks, tens of thousands of Korean combatants and the majority of the civilian population were directly involved in the war at one time or another.

Hostilities were not confined simply to Korea, China, and Japan. As Korean scholar Han Myŏnggi notes, this "was a world war encompassing all of East Asia." Prior to his invasion of Korea, Hideyoshi dispatched envoys to the surrounding states, hoping to persuade or bully their rulers into joining his enterprise. He also contacted Spanish and Portuguese officers, merchants, and clergy, then in the process of extending their own colonial holdings into East and South Asia.[5] While most ignored these entreaties or replied with artful diplomacy, some, like the kingdom of Ryukyu, were forced to assist him at least indirectly. But Siam and Ryukyu both allegedly contributed military support to the allied effort against Japan. The Chinese clearly saw Hideyoshi's gambit as an audacious attempt to usurp Ming (1368–1644) hegemony in East Asian commercial and diplomatic affairs and therefore responded to his challenge with appropriate military force.

The broad scope of this conflict has even prompted one Chinese scholar, Li Guangtao, to call this war the single greatest event in the history of East Asia. While that might be going too far, for these and other reasons, I prefer to call this conflict the First Great East Asian War, a designation that has met with no small amount of debate among scholars of East Asia in part because it evokes painful memories of Japanese expansionism in the modern era.[6] But it is precisely this connection that I draw attention to in the present work while avoiding (I hope) facile direct analogies or erroneous assertions about national predispositions to conquest or aggression. Given the tense state of affairs in Northeast Asia today, it seems imperative that we arrive at a deeper understanding of the historical backdrop to contemporary concerns as well as look at more positive historical ties. Unlike some writers, who maintain that the events of Japan's nineteenth- and twentieth-century expansionism had absolutely nothing to do with that nation's historical experience prior to the nineteenth century, I suggest that the explicit references to the war of the late sixteenth century by scholars, politicians, colonial overlords, and colonial victims in twentieth-century Korea and China testify to its continuing relevance.

As might be expected, all three states utilized contrasting memories of the war for their own nationalist purposes in the nineteenth and twentieth centuries. Meiji expansionists referred to "unfinished business" in Korea in planning Japan's ascent on the international geopolitical stage. In 1910, when Korea was formally annexed by the burgeoning Japanese empire, Terauchi Masatake, governor-general of Korea and future prime minister of Japan, noted that the annexation was the long-anticipated fulfillment of Hideyoshi's unfulfilled glorious enterprise (*igyō*). Japanese colonial rulers subsequently occupied and rebuilt some of their old castles from the sixteenth century, making them imperial administrative buildings.[7] Statues of Korean heroes and martyrs of the war were often knocked down or removed, sometimes even being replaced by those of Japanese generals.

Toyotomi Hideyoshi's castle at Osaka was rebuilt in 1931, the year that Japan initiated the conflicts that mushroomed into the Greater East Asian and Pacific War by invading Manchuria and creating the puppet state of Manchukuo. Today the castle houses an excellent museum of Sengoku-era (Warring States, 1467–1600) artifacts. Visitors can also watch video reenactments depicting Japanese armies cutting their way through Korea in the 1590s. (Of course videos and interactive displays from the Korean perspective can be found in most war-themed museums in South Korea.) Next to Osaka Castle is the Osaka City Museum, where the original document from Ming emperor Wanli (r. 1573–1620) investing Hideyoshi as king of Japan is held. Other monuments to Hideyoshi's greatness and influence on Japanese history can be found scattered throughout the Kyoto-Osaka area.

In China, memories of the war are less vivid, and for a variety of reasons, it has a much lower profile than in Korea or Japan. First, in the decades following the war, the Ming dynasty entered into its period of decline. Within twenty years, the Ming suffered its first major defeat at the hands of the upstart Latter Jin state, which would eventually become the Manchu Qing dynasty after conquering the Ming in 1644. The Qing, eager to justify their right to rule China, described the Ming regime as effete, decadent, and corrupt, concealing or ignoring evidence of Ming military prowess. Likewise late Ming and early Qing scholars, who were the heirs of a long tradition of factionalism in Chinese politics, blamed the imperial leadership and supposedly incompetent and selfish military commanders for the dynasty's fall. Because Emperor Wanli had little tolerance for their petty games and self-serving righteousness, he became one of the major scapegoats for the fall of the Ming dynasty, even though he had been honored in Korea with a sacrificial altar to his memory in Seoul.[8] Therefore contemporaries and seventeenth-century scholars glossed over his achievements, particularly his military exploits in the late sixteenth century, which constituted the high point of his reign. The scapegoating of Wanli has continued to the present day.

But with the renewal of Japanese aggression toward China in the nineteenth and twentieth centuries, Chinese interest in this war revived to some extent. Scholars such as Wang Chongwu and Li Guangtao wrote profusely documented articles and books on the subject.[9] The general tone of Li's works in particular is one of Ming military effectiveness and Chinese resourcefulness in the face of seemingly overwhelming Japanese military superiority. Whereas Japanese commentators both during the war and for centuries afterward tended to maintain that Japan's defeat was due to inferior numbers and Hideyoshi's untimely death, Li attempts to demonstrate that Ming military prowess, particularly the adept use of superior firearms, was the single-most important factor in driving the Japanese from the peninsula. Li's work also highlights the importance of Sino-Korean friendship and cooperation, asserting that there was no Korean request to which the Ming did not respond. By Li's estimation China sent 166,700 troops and 17 million *liang* (about six months' revenue for the entire Ming Empire) in silver and supplies to Korea.[10] The underlying message seems to be that Japanese aggression had been resisted once by Sino-Korean cooperation and could be again. Yet one should note that Li's work is suffused with considerable Sino-centrism despite its scholarly credibility. Regardless, these broad generalizations do not do justice to the full scope of debate surrounding the war in East Asia. Over the last three decades in particular, a plethora of works offering much less politicized and more nuanced interpretations of the war and its regional significance have emerged.

When UN forces approached the Yalu River in autumn 1950, those with a deeper understanding of Chinese history probably would have been more wary of possible Chinese intervention. The historical precedent of the Ming intervention was known to Mao and his generals, many of whom were keen students of history. Just like their Ming forebears, Mao and his commanders warned foreign forces not to cross the Yalu. And when the Chinese communists felt their border was threatened, just like the Ming in the 1590s, they decided to assert themselves and thereby establish their diplomatic and military primacy in East Asia. They would do the same in Vietnam (which incidentally was also the subject of Ming military intervention). Bruce Elleman has recently argued that the entire communist era in China should be regarded as the era of "imperial resurgence" with respect to military and political affairs as a confident China attempts to reassert its "rightful" place on the global stage.[11]

In addition to questioning the sixteenth-century war's relationship to events in the modern era, some scholars argue that calling this conflict the First Great East Asian War is inaccurate because of earlier wars

worthy of such an appellation. For example, the sixth and seventh centuries witnessed wide-ranging conflicts between the Sui (581–618) and
Tang (618–907) empires of China and the three Korean kingdoms of
Koguryŏ, Silla, and Paekche. The Sui dynasty invaded Koguryŏ, the
northernmost kingdom, three times in response to aggressive forays
into ostensibly Chinese territory. Although the last invasion in 617
resulted in at least a nominal Sui victory, it also contributed greatly to
domestic unrest at home and helped spark revolts that toppled the
regime in favor of the Tang dynasty, founded by a Sui general.[12]

The Tang then launched unsuccessful invasions in 645 and 647
that perhaps gave Koguryŏ the confidence to attack a Tang vassal state
in 655 and join with Paekche (the southwestern Korean kingdom) in
an invasion of Silla (the southeastern Korean kingdom). Silla appealed
for and received military assistance from the Tang. The Silla-Tang
allies defeated Paekche in relatively rapid fashion with combined land
(Silla) and sea (Tang) attacks. Paekche restorationists then contacted
the Japanese state of Yamato, which had maintained ties to Korea via
a shadowy and poorly understood regional confederation known as
the Kaya League, or Mimana. Despite Japanese reinforcements, the
Silla-Tang forces managed to crush Paekche by October 663 in a series
of engagements culminating in the famous Battle of the Paekchon
River.[13] They then turned their attention toward Koguryŏ, which they
subjugated, albeit temporarily, by 668. Not wishing to share this fate,
Silla supported a Koguryŏ restorationist movement, which the Tang
crushed by 674 before turning on their former Silla allies. While
sources differ on the outcomes of the resulting battles, eventually the
Chinese pulled back to what is now Manchuria and directed their
military attentions elsewhere, leaving Silla in control of virtually the
entire Korean peninsula.

Because these conflicts involved substantial military commitments
by several major polities in premodern East Asia, it is tempting to view
these events as an "East Asian World War." But this would be misleading.
First, these clashes took place over several decades and often just spilled
into one another as a result of internal and external factors. There was
never any grand design for overarching conquest by any one power, even
Tang China. And while events on the Korean peninsula certainly influenced developments in China and Japan, they did not fundamentally
alter subsequent historical developments, at least outside the peninsula.
The Tang Chinese continued to be an aggressive expansionist power,

and a stable Korean frontier afforded them the opportunity to concentrate on other military problems. Had they formally colonized Korea, the results may well have been more problematic for the Chinese, but the overall course of Tang history most likely would not have changed all that much. The war may have accelerated Japan's centralization process and contributed to the development of a more sophisticated state apparatus to oversee defenses against a possible continental invasion, but it was only "one link in a larger chain of events."[14]

More significant from the broader East Asian perspective, in the sixth century Japan was still a very peripheral player while in its earliest stages of state development. There was little awareness of what was happening on the continent and no real design on the part of any belligerent warlords to create or reshape some sort of international order—that is to say, their interests were local or regional in scope. None of the leaders of the states involved ever articulated a clear vision for international hegemony. Indeed, it may be anachronistic to expect any of them to have done so. But by the late sixteenth century, all East Asians, including the Japanese, were coming into much wider contact with traders, missionaries, and mercenaries from all over the globe, thus gaining an increasingly international perspective on the relationship between foreign trade and domestic power and authority. Such contacts also brought greater awareness of foreign resources and the potential they might have for legitimizing questionable rulers. This in turn could influence successful domestic conquerors to harbor wider ambitions, which is exactly what Hideyoshi did.

But what of the Mongol wars of the thirteenth century? The Mongol conquests tremendously influenced not only Asian but also world history. Although one cannot deny the organizational genius and charisma of men such as Chinggis and Khubilai Khan, it again seems that the Mongols lacked the overall planning and imperial vision of Hideyoshi. Chinggis Khan in particular seemed pulled along by events as much as he directed them. His underlying aims were not much more sophisticated than providing a continuing source of lands and booty for his ever-hungry followers. Perhaps if Chinggis had not died in 1227, some kind of overarching order might have been created. But with his death, his empire fragmented as did any unifying vision, if there was one. As a result the khanates established by Chinggis's descendants continued in their separate directions with varying levels of success, often troubled by internal discord.

✻

In contrast to the large conflicts of earlier eras, the war of the 1590s was explicitly waged for Asian hegemony. In his letters to foreign rulers inviting them to join, submit, or be crushed, Hideyoshi waxed poetic about the wonderful new political order he was going to create to replace that established by the Chinese.[15] He used every opportunity to demean the Chinese and their fighting prowess while extolling his own martial accomplishments and the superiority of Japanese civilization. He promised to extend the customs of the Japanese to distant lands and ensconce himself, interestingly, in the Chinese trading port of Ningbo, where he would direct the economic and political affairs of his massive new empire. In this way he established himself, for better or worse, as the first true Pan-Asian visionary, and at close reading, many of his statements sound eerily familiar to anyone who studies twentieth-century Japanese imperial expansion.

Hideyoshi's exploits, even if distorted and misconstrued, were the inspiration for later generations of expansionists. The opening lines to the English-language foreword of a Japanese work on the war published in 1936, a year before the massive invasion of China, are illuminating. Written by Hiroshi Ikeuchi and published by the prestigious Toyō Bunko, they encapsulate the valorization of Japan's imperialist enterprise in nineteenth- and twentieth-century nationalist scholarship.

> The war of Bunroku and Keichō (the last years of the sixteenth century), brilliant in history as the foreign expedition of Tayco-sama or Toyotomi Hideyoshi, the greatest hero of these days, was the one ambitious enterprise of his last years. Even as he achieved the tremendous task of unifying all the Japanese provinces, his fiery ambition remained still unsatisfied. Overwhelmed by an enthusiastic desire to conquer the Asiatic continent, he dispatched his troops to the Korean peninsula as a preliminary step in ful-filling his purpose of defeating the Ming dynasty. Unfortunately, however, his magnificent purpose was defeated by unforeseen adversities and being attacked by an illness, the great hero passed away before his monumental campaign was successfully carried out, and this failure of his expedition spelled one of the chief causes of the fall of the Toyotomi.[16]

As will be seen in the ensuing chapters, the Chinese and Koreans steadfastly rejected Hideyoshi's bombastic designs and berated him for his foolish ignorance of the proper diplomatic forms and protocols. Furthermore, Emperor Wanli picked up the gauntlet cast by Hideyoshi and tossed it back in his face with threats of million-man armies sent from China in addition to the combined military might of the Ming's other tributary states. Thus it was the comprehensiveness and grandiosity of Hideyoshi's vision that provoked such an impressive Ming military and diplomatic response. The Chinese simply could not countenance a challenge to their international hegemony.

Additionally the war provoked important institutional and military reforms in Korea that enabled the tottering Chosŏn dynasty to stabilize itself and last until the early twentieth century. Most notably these included the importation of Chinese training manuals and drilling techniques pioneered by the famous Ming general Qi Jiguang (1528–88).[17] In China the war is often blamed for hastening the fall of the Ming dynasty by virtue of forcing the empire to expend vast economic and military resources that thereby weakened its ability to fight the rising Manchu power in Northeast Asia, though the validity of such assertions is questionable.[18] Add the involvement of the other East and Southeast Asian states, and the designation "First Great East Asian War" seems warranted.

1

WILD FRONTIERS

Emperor Wanli and the Military Revival of the Ming, 1570–1610

In mid-April 1619 at the Battle of Sarhu, three of the four Ming columns sent against the forces of Nurhaci (1559–1619), the upstart khan of the nascent Latter Jin state, met destruction. Sarhu was located in Liaodong, a territory northeast of the Great Wall (and therefore outside China proper) long claimed by the Ming but rather lightly administered through a system of hereditary chieftains. Nurhaci was one of these chieftains and was considered loyal until he declared the establishment of a rival state in the northeast in 1616. Despite probable Ming involvement in the deaths of his father and grandfather, Nurhaci was an adopted son of the redoubtable Ming general Li Chengliang (1526–1618) and had even offered to send troops to aid Ming forces in ousting the Japanese from Korea in the 1590s.[1]

By 1619, however, the political and military situations had changed, and Nurhaci's Jurchens (later known as Manchus) were in the process of expanding their state and its influence just as the Ming empire was going into decline. As historian Ray Huang notes, "The Liao-tung Campaign of early 1619 brought to an end the Ming empire's unchallenged dominance in that region, while it raised the Manchus to the status of formidable rivals." Nurhaci defeated a Ming force of 100,000 with around 60,000 Jurchens by keeping his more mobile units together, while the Chinese divided their troops into four advance columns, which Nurhaci isolated and annihilated one by one. In doing so he made optimum use of his

Provinces of Ming China

superior knowledge of local terrain and weather conditions along with his army's superior mobility. The only Chinese field commander to survive was Li Rubo, son of Li Chengliang (and incidentally a veteran of the war in Korea). Questions unsurprisingly arose in Beijing, and Li was charged with both collusion and cowardice in battle, even though he actually received word to retreat from Supreme Commander Yang Hao (d. 1629) and was merely following orders when attacked. Rather than face these charges, Li Rubo hanged himself and was posthumously rehabilitated by Emperor Chongzhen (r. 1628–44).[2]

While most scholars recognize the seminal importance of Sarhu in the rise of the Manchus, far fewer recognize its importance in the broader scope of late Ming military developments. The battle is generally recounted as just one more nail (albeit a large one) in a Ming coffin that had been built over the previous several decades. Such an interpretation, however, is more a case of revisionist history rather than a sober assessment based on surviving primary sources. It was in the interest of the Manchus for Sarhu to cast a shadow over preceding Ming military accomplishments, making them look better and the Ming more corrupt and incompetent.[3] Although the Liaodong campaign was a debacle of colossal proportions, it is better viewed as the end of a five-decade era of Ming military rejuvenation and international intervention as opposed to another episode in the dynasty's decline.

In the fifty years prior to Sarhu, the Ming managed to make peace with the Mongols, intervened in border disputes in Burma on multiple occasions, launched destabilizing raids and surgical strikes into Jurchen and Mongol territories in the northeast and northwest, suppressed a major troop mutiny in the northwestern garrison city of Ningxia, sent tens of thousands of troops on two occasions to oust the Japanese from Korea, mobilized another 200,000 plus troops to crush an aboriginal uprising in Sichuan province in the southwest, and conducted numerous other smaller military actions against a variety of bandits and aboriginal groups. In the process the Ming maintained its political, military, and economic primacy in East Asia.

After the defeat at Sarhu, however, the increasingly factionalized Ming court engaged in endless rounds of scapegoating, finger-pointing, and partisan wrangling. Concerning the Liaodong campaign itself, among the fall guys was Yang Hao, the supreme civil commander of the expedition, who had been embroiled in controversy during his tenure as commissioner of Korean affairs in the 1590s. Accordingly, Yang's defeat was viewed as part of a pattern of failure by the Ming military during the previous decades. Accounts of Ming victories were dismissed as overblown attempts by eunuchs and their lackeys to curry favor with corrupt and shortsighted monarchs, while defeats were magnified by righteous literati circles to effect administrative changes that advanced their own interests. At the center of much of this controversy was Emperor Wanli, whose reign was the longest and one of the most controversial of the entire dynasty. Wanli has become synonymous with imperial lassitude and avarice, eunuch abuses, bureaucratic factionalism and infighting, military reverses, and general dynastic decline. Yet in spite of all his faults, or perhaps because of them, a number of biographical studies of this enigmatic ruler have appeared in Chinese in recent years. Unfortunately, with the exception of Fan Shuzhi's thorough and well-researched *Wanli zhuan,* most publications have remained wedded to the traditional interpretations. For example, historian Cao Guoqing calls Wanli "a muddleheaded emperor at the head of a rotten state."[4]

Western scholars of Wanli have echoed these sentiments, most being content to perpetuate common stereotypes of him as a selfish, disinterested profligate. Even the more sympathetic treatment of Ray Huang notes that Wanli "earned a reputation as the most venal and avaricious occupant of the imperial throne in history," a charge that could certainly be leveled at any number of Chinese monarchs. The influence of Huang's portrayal on subsequent scholars in the West is undeniable. As one prominent historian notes in a recent work, "It is almost superfluous to write at any length about the Wanli reign because it has been so effectively portrayed and analyzed in the writings of Ray Huang."[5]

But for all his faults, Wanli was very interested in and devoted to maintaining Ming military supremacy in Asia. Following in the footsteps of Zhang Juzheng, the emperor sought to curb the power of civil officials, limit the influence of factions, and generally circumvent the cumbersome bureaucracy by turning to prominent military officials and their families.[6] He viewed military affairs as one of the areas in which he could assert his will and did so fairly often, especially in the first three decades of his reign. Even toward the end of his reign, Wanli remained concerned about the growing Manchu threat and approved the release of funds and the dispatch of the aforementioned Ming expeditionary force to meet the Manchus in Liaodong in 1619. Although, as we have seen, the expedition was a disaster, it involved a number of military officials Wanli had patronized. Even in the wake of defeat, he sought to protect Li Rubo.

Before going into more detail concerning Wanli's political and military leadership, a few general observations about Chinese military culture and the Ming military establishment are in order. One of the pervasive myths is that Chinese dynasties, especially in the late imperial period, were staid Confucian bureaucracies that eschewed war. In imperial times it was in the interest of both the state and its official historians to hide the value or coercive effectiveness of warfare as a tool of politics. In modern times "it has been equally important to establish the historical reality that a weak or fragmented China is subject to exploitation or even conquest by foreigners."[7]

Thus, writing in the early twentieth century as China was in the process of being carved into spheres of influence by Western imperialists, scholar Lei Haizong contended that China possessed an "a-military culture" that had stifled creativity and social mobility since the Qin era (221–206 B.C.).[8] This resulted in an ossified governmental structure that made China vulnerable to foreign conquest. Conversely, early modern European visitors were initially impressed with China's civil bureaucracy, which seemed much more pacifistically inclined and cultured than contemporary European nobilities. Later, however, these same qualities encouraged predatory intentions on the part of some foreign expansionists.

Within the broader scope of Chinese history, native Han dynasties were generally perceived as less militarily inclined than their steppe-based counterparts and therefore more prone to defensive actions and isolationism with respect to foreign affairs. Generally smaller territorially than the "conquest dynasties," even modern historians have typically denigrated their martial prowess until very recently.[9] The Ming military, for example, has widely been decried as one of the weakest in the long history of imperial China. As historian Jacques Gernet, echoing the sentiments of the Jesuit Matteo Ricci (1552–1610) notes, the Ming armies were "the refuse dump of society and consisted of idlers, rascals, jailbirds, and highwaymen."[10] While the Ming military establishment certainly had its share of problems, such observations obscure the fact that the institution was a dynamic and vital component of the government for most of its existence, ensuring the overall peace and stability of the world's most populous empire for more than two and a half centuries. Ming officials continuously sought to improve the effectiveness of their forces while endeavoring to meet a bewildering variety of military challenges.

While the Ming period is often lauded as being one of the most stable and peaceful in all of Chinese history, historian Fan Zhongyi identifies some 275 large and small wars the Ming engaged in from 1368 to 1643, not counting the final wars of resistance against the Manchus. Iain Johnston likewise notes that there were on average 1.12 foreign wars per year during that period. Arguing that the empire was in fact a very aggressive military power, he finds that Ming actions were in accordance with the teachings of the *Seven Military Classics* of China, which

"share a preference for offensive strategies over static defensive and acco-
modationist options."[11]

Such activity necessitated constant advances in military technologies,
most notably in firearms. The Ming created firearms-training divisions
in the early fifteenth century and eagerly imported superior foreign
models in the sixteenth and seventeenth centuries. They used cannon
for attack and defense and for both mobile and stationary warfare. The
Chinese also made more limited use of a variety of muskets, some
domestically produced and others adapted from foreign designs such as
the Dutch-inspired "red barbarian cannon." Smaller firearms, however,
were seldom if ever used on horseback because of their general ineffec-
tiveness.[12] Ming forces also made extensive use of firearms on warships,
a practice that would serve them well in the fight against the Japanese.

According to Fan Zhongyi, the increased use of firearms was perhaps
the single-most important aspect of Ming military development as a step
toward a more modern style of warfare. Sun Laichen has gone further,
calling the Ming the world's first true gunpowder empire, making a
case for China being the primary exporter of this technology throughout Asia prior to 1500. He asserts that the Ming should be credited with
initiating the global "Military Revolution," countering claims made
by scholars in the West for its origins in early modern Europe. In support
Sun finds that as early as 1450, most Ming frontier units were equipped
with guns. In addition Chinese weapons had reached Europe in the late
1320s, around the same time gunpowder technologies reached Korea
and a few decades before these technologies reached Japan. The Ming also
pioneered tactical changes, utilizing volley fire as early as 1387 against
the Maw Shans in Burma. Thus, as Kenneth Chase has observed recently,
in many ways the Ming military was arguably more "modern" than its
Qing successor, though the latter made more adept use of cavalry in
conjunction with firearms.[13]

The extent of Ming military activity is also evidenced by the sheer
volume of military treatises, training manuals, and the like produced
during the dynasty. By one count an astounding 33 percent of all military texts produced in China date from that period.[14] The most impressive of these works include Mao Yuanyi's *Wubei zhi* [Encyclopedia of
Military Preparedness] of 1601, Zhao Shizhen's *Shenqi pu* [Treatise on
Firearms] of 1598, and Zheng Ruozeng's *Chouhai tubian* [Gazeteer of
Coastal Defense] of 1562. All these works include technical descriptions of the development and application of military technologies along

with illustrations and maps. Zheng also includes extensive descriptions of actual campaigns and battles, though others produced a plethora of works to chronicle specific wars or campaigns.

Training manuals produced by Ming general Qi Jiguang were disseminated to Korea. In them Qi gave detailed instructions in the use of small-group tactics, psychological warfare, and other "modern" techniques. Qi recognized that the hereditary military system used by the Ming up to his time was in dire need of revamping and therefore advocated the use of private soldiers with better pay rates and more systematized training. The general advocated training men in units, divisions, and formations and dividing them into strong and weak soldiers. He emphasized repetitive drilling, and his manuals contained extensive drawings of formations and discussions of drilling techniques far ahead of their time. Qi believed that by creating different types of small units and integrating them into larger companies, battalions, and armies, they could operate like ears, eyes, hands, and feet, thus constituting a whole military "body." He also stressed using different weapons together and favored utilizing different tactics depending upon terrain, skills, and weaponry.[15]

Qi realized that instilling courage and discipline in his men was paramount and that even getting men to fight at half their real ability could make an army unmatched on the battlefield. He even made extensive use of mythological creatures and fierce animals on banners to inspire and embolden his troops, who were generally of peasant stock. Placing an emphasis on training the heart over training the spirit, because the spirit comes from outside but the heart is the root of everything, Qi's instructions reflected his Confucian influences and may explain why his ideas also became popular in Korea, where such virtues were extolled to an even greater extent than in China.[16]

Another important development of the late Ming period was the transition from a hereditary to a largely mercenary army. The original reason for creating a hereditary military lay in the dynasty founder's desire to construct an idealized agrarian empire. He divided society into hereditary occupational classes, including the military. But within a few years the system started breaking down, and by 1500, Ming military strength may have been as low as 3 percent of prescribed levels in some garrisons, with desertion rates as high 85 percent in some areas despite numerous efforts by the government to ameliorate the problem.[17]

Organizationally, the largest unit of the Ming military was the guard (*wei*), which consisted of 5,600 men. Guards were divided into battalions (*suo*) of 1,120 men. Each battalion contained ten companies of 112 men. Each company had two platoons of 56 men, and each platoon typically had five squads comprised of 11 or 12 men. In terms of overall strength, military registers from the 1390s indicate an enrollment of approximately 1.3 million, a figure that rose to more than 2 million in the Yongle (1403–24) reign and to more than 3 million during the sixteenth century (though according to contemporary estimates from the 1570s, the actual number of troops was around 845,000). This number allegedly swelled to more than 4 million by the turn of the seventeenth century.[18]

Such a state of affairs would have distressed Hongwu (r. 1368–98) to no end. To him hereditary soldiers were to provide their own food via military farms (*tuntian*) and then rotate to training and military posts where needed. Ideally most troops would receive operational training in a variety of locales and weapons, and special-training divisions in the capital would provide elite training, most notably in firearms. This practice continued throughout the Ming period, with troops en route to Korea first going to Beijing for training under firearms drill instructors. Yet because of a bewildering number of factors—including corrupt officers who used their soldiers as construction gangs, oppressive and duplicitous officers, old or weak men hindering the training of younger recruits, and the improper observation of rotation schedules—the military capacity of the hereditary forces declined precipitously. Some have blamed the increasing reliance upon eunuchs in military decision-making and as the actual leaders of campaigns, while others point to the general trend of diluting military authority after the discovery of a treasonous plot by the prime minister during Hongwu's reign.[19]

Whatever the causes, from around 1450 to 1550, the Ming military experienced a decline in effectiveness that one scholar has called "unprecedented in Chinese history." Reports indicate that the Ming empire, which boasted a paper strength in excess of 3 million troops, could barely muster 30,000 cavalry for action against nomadic raiders, the majority of the capital armies being "old and weak lackeys of central government officials." This was despite a series of reforms that had been initiated in the late fifteenth century designed to update training and bring in younger, more vigorous soldiers.[20] Therefore, when the Mongol chieftain Altan Khan invaded in 1550, the minister of war could muster only about 60,000 troops, who then fled at the sight of the Mongols. The minister was executed.

This prompted Wang Bangrui, acting minister of personnel, to exclaim, "If our enemies can penetrate this deeply into our country, in terms of fighting and defending ourselves, we can say we have no army at all." Wang went on to note that the exhortations of many officials had been ignored and plans for reform deliberately thwarted. As Liew Foon Ming points out: "The lot of the Ming Ministers of War was precarious in a court divided into ambitious antagonistic factions who seemed to be in perpetual conflict stimulated more by personal interest rather than by differences of appearance in matters of policy. As a result, the more upright and conscientious men, who were often those with political insight and practical experiences of warfare, were either forced out of office to live secluded lives or became victims of power struggles for being too outspoken."[21]

Wang called for the dismissal of the offending officials and speedy military reorganization, to which Emperor Jiajing (r. 1522–66) assented. New training positions, albeit posts that still subordinated military officials to civilian oversight, were created. Many have pointed to the comparatively low status of military officers as one of the major factors behind the supposed martial incompetence of traditional Chinese empires. While the conditions for military professionalism, including the concentration of war-making power in the hands of the monarch, the standardization of war-making techniques, and military bureaucratization had all been present in China since the Song era (960–1279), the overwhelming influence of civil officials and the concomitant low prestige attached to military careers had retarded its growth. In specific reference to the Ming, Lynn Struve observes, "military might was not just controlled, it was stultified, military men were not just subordinated by civil officials, they were degraded . . . generals and soldiers were regarded with fear, suspicion, and distaste." Likewise Charles Hucker states, "Partly because of its hereditary character, but mostly because even the highest ranking officers were characteristically illiterate and untutored in Confucian proprieties, the military service enjoyed far less prestige than the civil service."[22]

Even as these institutional changes were being implemented, some officials began calling for wider recruitment of mercenaries, both to improve efficiency and to lighten the burden of military costs for local areas. It is interesting to consider this development in light of mercenary use elsewhere. As in Europe, some widely criticized the use of mercenaries, regarding them as cowardly, boastful, and ill-disciplined.[23] Ming officials often complained that such troops never trained, ignored all regulations, and frequently caused local problems, including riots. But others recognized that mercenaries, if properly trained and led, could be much more effective in battle than peasant conscripts. As in contemporary Europe, where the most effective fighting forces typically used mercenary Swiss infantry, if the state could afford them (and with the massive influx of foreign silver into China, the Ming could pay for such services), mercenaries constituted the more desirable option, though as was the case in Europe, they continued to serve alongside rural recruits and conscripts. Additionally, like other empires the Ming employed "martial minorities" as shock troops. Especially feared were the "wolf troops" (*lang bing*) of Guangxi province.[24]

In light of the deplorable state of the Ming military by the mid-1550s, its revival from 1570 to 1610 is truly remarkable. Over these several decades, in addition to besting a succession of domestic challengers, the Ming managed to defeat one of the most impressive military forces on the planet, the Japanese. Wanli was pivotal in making both policy and strategic decisions in these operations. His success was grounded in the appointment of competent military officers to key posts and in retaining them even when jealous civil rivals impeached them for trivial offenses. Wanli also repeatedly bestowed the ceremonial double-edged sword (*bao jian*) upon commanders in the field, giving them full authorization to do as they saw fit without having to memorialize the throne first. In doing this he was following the maxims set forth by military thinkers since ancient times, among them that commanders in the field should be invested with total authority as they are better equipped to deal with any situation that might arise.[25]

In marked contrast to standard portrayals that cast Wanli as irresolute, covetous, and self-indulgent, the emperor took an active interest in the action in Korea from the outset and made the decision to send troops and supplies. Countering a reputation for selfish venality, he repeatedly authorized the dispensation of extra funds from imperial coffers to provide extra rewards and supplies for troops in the field, a pattern he had established earlier in his reign.[26] Furthermore, he authorized the appointment of military officers to high posts formerly reserved solely for civil authorities, often over the protests of some of the most powerful officials in the empire.

This interest in military affairs stemmed from the tutelage of Zhang Juzheng, who served as the emperor's chief grand secretary (equivalent to the prime minister of the late Ming system) and teacher. Having lived through the terrifying Mongol raids of the 1550s and recognizing the still precarious state of affairs upon his ascension to authority in the late 1560s, Zhang's "purpose was to revive what he considered the spirit of the dynasty's founding emperor and to revitalize the dynasty's vital essence." Angering many of his contemporaries, Zhang made "enriching the state and strengthening the army" his paramount goals. According to one biographer, he was also a quiet admirer of the somewhat controversial philosophy of Legalism, which had proved instrumental in the creation of the Chinese empire in the third century B.C. This philosophy emphasized absolute obedience to the monarch and the state, which many of Zhang's contemporaries certainly found objectionable, believing that the emperor should serve as a figurehead under their guidance. For his part, Zhang charged such officials with being more concerned with "preserving ornateness" and decorum than with the practical business of government: "People these days haven't the brains to go beyond the prevailing trend. They just love to join in controversies. Like jealous prostitutes, they rush to embrace the opinion of the unthinking mob, mindful only of personal benefit and ignoring the effect on the country."[27]

Despite his appreciation for an ancient statist philosophy, Zhang was far from being a stodgy conservative and firmly believed in adapting to new circumstances, as evidenced by his staunch support for a monetarily based tax system (known as the Single Whip Reform). Additionally he revived the old military field system, strengthened border defenses in general, and tried to establish (even expand) a stable defensive perimeter, establishing a precedent Wanli would later emulate. Yet Zhang also had critics at all levels of government, many of whom charged that while preaching thrift, he himself lived a life of luxury and packed the government with his favorites. But with the backing of the young sovereign, the grand secretary was able to push through a number of reforms, most involving taxation, improving military efficiency, and strengthening the presence of the central government in local affairs. Some contemporary sources argued that he used his power solely for building up the sovereign power of the state, to some extent provoking the very dissent he hoped to quash.[28]

Thus despite his many concrete achievements, Zhang left a mixed legacy: "his policies and conduct did much to create the character of the Wanli Emperor" but also initiated the factional struggles that plagued Wanli's reign and contributed to the growth of inner-court, mostly eunuch, power at the expense of circulating officials.[29]

Nevertheless, even after Zhang's death, when many of his associates and protégés had been discredited and cashiered, several military officers he had appointed continued to enjoy the emperor's patronage and protection. This and other such actions improved Ming military morale to a level not witnessed since the mid-fifteenth century. They also helped start a new era in Han-Mongol relations, one in which the Ming were not always on the defensive, and helped encourage Wanli to adopt a more aggressive military posture generally. In addition, starting early in Wanli's reign, the government adopted a general policy whereby only officials with military experience received appointment to high posts in the Ministry of War.[30]

Border affairs was one area in which Wanli could exert his will to some degree. As modern historian Fan Shuzhi notes, when Wanli finally took the reins of power into his own hands, "he threw himself into border affairs and sought to reverse the static policies of his forebears with regards to the borders and make the army strong and fearsome once again." In the emperor's own words regarding a report of border raids by the Mongols: "We still shouldn't try to appease the nomads. They could be very ambitious and arrogant; there is no way to satisfy their appetite. It is still essential to build up our own strength so that the borderland is alertly safeguarded."[31]

As a result of Wanli's support, the Ming pursued a much more aggressive and reasonably successful frontier policy. During most of his reign, the empire was confronted with several military challenges simultaneously. But blessed with an unusually talented coterie of commanders, from about 1570 to 1610 the Ming military was probably at its strongest since the Yongle reign as the empire proved able not only to maintain internal security but also to project military force for political ends. It would never attain the same level of effectiveness again. Given that the Three Great Campaigns of 1592–1600 were the high point of Wanli's reign, it is worth discussing the other two operations briefly before proceeding to the war in Korea to gain a sense of the overall strategic situation of the late Ming empire.[32]

Historians often note that the Longqing and Wanli reigns were important for the history of Ming-Mongol relations. After the investiture of Altan Khan as *Shunyi wang* (obedient and righteous prince) in 1571 and the establishment of regular trade fairs, the situation remained generally calm along the northwestern frontiers as the Mongols ceased to be a military threat. Nonetheless, this obscures the fact that conflicts between the Ming and various Mongol tribes continued throughout the rest of the dynasty's history, sometimes involving tens of thousands of combatants on both sides. Such claims also ignore the third side of the Ming "peace triangle," military force. Throughout the last decades of the sixteenth century and into the seventeenth century, the Ming launched what can best be described as destabilizing surgical strikes into Mongol (and Manchu) territory, burning settlements, killing threatening leaders, and capturing valuable livestock. For example, a raid by Li Chengliang in 1591 resulted in the destruction of a Mongol encampment, with 280 Mongols slain and more than 1,000 scattered.[33] Actions like these were the brainchild of Zhang Juzheng and approved by Wanli.

Zhang afforded his frontier commanders great latitude in the completion of their duties and was willing to look the other way occasionally when those jealous of their achievements brought charges. An example of this can be seen in the case of Pubei (d. 1592), a Chahar Mongol who submitted to the Ming late in the Jiajing reign after being forced from his tribal lands as the result of a dispute. Pubei brought with him several hundred followers, who would become his core fighting force. While commentators at the time often pointed to this as an example of Pubei's inherent duplicity and indicative of his designs on power, such groups of "housemen," as they were called, were present in the retinues of most late Ming commanders and usually formed the elite backbones of Chinese armies.[34]

Within a decade Pubei rose to become regional military commissioner of Huamachi, near the strategically important garrison city of Ningxia. Further promotions and rewards from the court followed, and some officials began to complain that Pubei and his sons and associates were becoming unruly and difficult to control. Zhang brushed aside such objections, either because he trusted Pubei or perhaps because he feared upsetting him. Acting on Zhang's advice, Wanli refused to punish the Mongol, which accords well with the emperor's preference for results over accusations.[35]

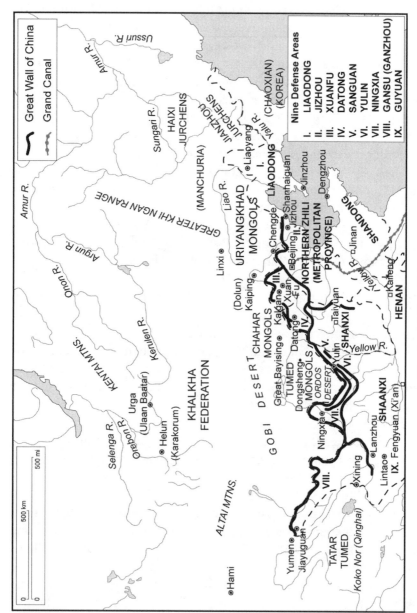

Northern Ming China

In 1589 Pubei was promoted to the post of regional vice commander of Ningxia, and his son, Bo Cheng'en, inherited his father's old position since he was also "fierce and warlike." By this point Pubei, who reportedly had as many as 3,000 personal retainers in his service, wanted to retire from active duty and pass his post onto his son. But the leading civil official in the region, Grand Coordinator Dang Xin, opposed such a transfer of power, fearing "the tail would grow too big to shake" and thus would present an imminent threat to the security of the frontier. During the next three years, Dang and Pubei clashed over a number of issues pertaining to military administration and military actions in the northwest, most notably Dang's refusal to send winter uniforms and extra rations for Pubei's troops, whom he considered to be private retainers and therefore not eligible for government support. Matters were exacerbated when Dang had Bo publicly flogged for attempting to steal another official's wife and ordered the arrest of Pubei's followers following their return from a campaign in the northwest.[36]

Surprisingly given their reputations, Pubei and his men endured these indignities and actually followed official protocol in seeking redress from the government, even sending a letter detailing the crimes of Dang. But this only angered Dang more and fed into his insecurities. Thus in the spring of 1592, Pubei found himself swept into a troop mutiny of the Ningxia garrison instigated by a Chinese officer named Liu Dongyang (though the rebellion is usually attributed to Pubei and his sons, most likely because of their Mongol ancestry). The mutineers killed Dang and a subordinate, burned and looted government offices in the city, and quickly seized some forty-seven outlying frontier fortresses. They demanded that the Ming government give them a free hand in the area or they would join forces with the Ordos Mongols to threaten the very existence of the dynasty.[37]

The rebellion was reported to the throne on April 19, 1592, by a Shaanxi surveillance official, who reported that the entire province was in an uproar and only a single official (Xiao Ruxun at Pingluo) was resisting the mutineers with any degree of success. Recognizing the gravity of the situation, Wanli immediately called for a meeting with Minister of War Shi Xing (d. 1597). They decided that the uprising needed to be settled quickly lest it engulf the entire northwest frontier. They issued an edict for the selection of 7,000 fearless men from Xuanda and Shanxi to come to the rescue. Wanli also offered his sympathy to the families of notable officials who had perished at the hands

of the mutineers. He then made a number of civil and military appointments, investing these officials with great temporary authority. The
most notable was that of Ma Gui, a prominent frontier general who
commanded a sizeable personal army.[38]

Meanwhile Wei Xueceng, supreme commander of the three border
regions and a civil official with a record of battling nomadic tribes, was
invested with full authority by the emperor and told to follow the
usual strategy of arresting the ringleaders and dispersing the rest of the
rebels. Wei acted quickly, dispatching commanders to key local strongholds and making sure the mutineers could not ensconce themselves
upon the south bank of the Yellow River. Within a few weeks the border
fortresses were retaken and only Ningxia remained in rebel hands.
Xiao Ruxun even managed to kill one of Pubei's sons with an arrow
during an ambush.[39]

Yet after these early victories, Wei complained that he lacked the
material and manpower to deal with the uprising and simply assumed
a defensive posture, inviting criticism from both the throne and more
hawkish officials. Many at court now had no confidence in his ability
to suppress the uprising, despite his prior record. At a court conference
Wanli and his advisers decided to use additional force before the situation grew more serious. Wei continued to press for a peaceful solution,
citing the safety of civilians trapped inside Ningxia. His most vocal
critic was a censor from Zhejiang, Mei Guozhen, who though a civil
jinshi degree holder, was very much in the vein of many of his contemporaries when it came to admiring martial deeds and qualities,
supposedly excelling at mounted archery as a youth.[40]

Over the next six weeks, government forces secured the outlying
areas but were unable to dislodge the mutineers from their fortified
bastion in Ningxia while continuing to be harried by columns of Mongol
cavalry joining the fight. Furious debates raged at court as to what exactly
should be done and how the Ming should counter the possibility of
large-scale Mongol involvement. In the fourth month the Ming assembled
their troops and mounted an assault against the city. They defeated a
rebel force estimated at 3,000 that was armed with fire carts and cannon,
recovering some one hundred military carts, and forcing many rebels
into a nearby lake, where they drowned. Several Ming commanders
pursued the enemy back toward the city's north gate, but they were
not adequately supported and suffered heavy losses.

Emboldened by this qualified success, the rebels urged a number of Mongol chieftains to raid nearby cities and cut Ming supply lines. Wei was forced to retreat, finding himself temporarily encircled by hostile forces. Many officials continued to be critical of his handling of imperial forces. Again it was Mei Guozhen who took the lead, saying, "If a renowned general assumes responsibility from Wei, then certainly his heroism will envelop the rebels like clouds and the garrisons can be defended [from further depredations] and they will only be able to retreat and shut themselves in [Ningxia]." Mei added that the emperor needed to be decisive, "there can be no victory in this national emergency if everyone waits in fear of your majesty's orders to arrive."[41]

Mei suggested appointing Li Chengliang, by this time the earl of Ningyuan, as military superintendent (*tidu*) of Ningxia because of his experience in leading troops in battle, especially against the Mongols, and his reputation as a military disciplinarian. Moreover, his sons Li Rusong, Li Rubo, and Li Ruzhen were all talented generals in their own right. His younger sons Li Ruzhang and Li Rumei had already earned distinction in the military, as had their cousin, Li Ruwu. The family was greatly feared and respected along the northern frontiers. Following the classic military maxims concerning the use of awe to impress one's foes, Mei hoped that their reputation alone would discourage the mutineers.[42]

His recommendation immediately sparked controversy. The Li family had made quite a few enemies over the years, both because of their great regional power in northeast China and because of their disdain for traditional Confucian sensibilities. In addition, they were tainted by their association with the now discredited Zhang Juzheng. Complicating matters further was the fact that the title of military superintendent theretofore had been reserved as a supplementary designation for civil grand coordinators, for it bestowed sweeping, albeit temporary, powers to deal with grave military threats. Wang Dewan, the supervising secretary for the Office of Scrutiny in the Ministry of War, opposed Li Chengliang's appointment on the grounds that the general was too distant (in Liaodong) and had already retired from active service—to give him a new post violated policy. Others argued that the Li were like wolves in temperament and simply could not be trusted with such an important assignment.[43]

Mei countered these arguments by replying, "Sometimes in order to keep the tiger at bay, you have to send in the wolves." He added that it was just this kind of savagery that would enable the Li to prevail. Besides, he continued, their authority would only be temporary. Mei concluded his entreaty to Wanli by stating, "If your majesty has any doubts, do not employ them, but if you employ them, do not have any doubts." Other officials also vouched for the Li family too. After considering both sides, Wanli decided that the suppression of the mutiny was paramount, appointing Li Chengliang as military superintendent, with Mei to accompany him as army inspecting censor for Ningxia. After all this Li Chengliang ended up not going on account of his advanced age (sixty-six) and the need for him in Liaodong in light of the rumored Japanese invasion of Korea. In his place his eldest son, Li Rusong, was appointed military superintendent of Ningxia and commander of Shaanxi in charge of suppressing the mutiny. Never before in the dynasty's history had a purely military officer been given such a title.[44]

Wanli offered to take up the spear and go to the front himself. As things turned out, he did not go to Ningxia, however, he did continue to closely monitor the affair from Beijing and issued a new call for brave volunteers to do their part even as he urged his superintendent to hasten to the front.[45] One of these volunteers was a censorial official named Ye Mengxiong. In answering Wanli's call for righteous officials to suppress the rebellion, Ye had vehemently asked to go to the front, saying he would take the pacification of the rebels as his personal responsibility.

Ye reached the nearby city of Lingzhou on July 14 along with some four hundred cannon and fire carts and a contingent of Miao troops from China's southwest.[46] The Ming divided their besieging forces into five armies, one for each cardinal gate, and a mobile corps under Ma Gui to catch any escapees and to deter relief columns. Two weeks after Ye's arrival, Pubei and his men sallied forth from the north gate and joined battle with Ma Gui. Although both sides sustained significant casualties, the Ming drove the mutineers back into the city with heavy cannon fire. Prior to this the rebels had attempted to get word to their Mongol allies to attack from the rear, which the latter refused.

The siege continued through the summer, with Li Rusong arriving at the end of July with Mei Guozhen, who complained about serious supply shortages. Soon after their arrival, Li and Mei hit the city walls with heavy cannon fire to no avail. On August 2 Li Ruzhang, Rusong's younger brother, tried to scale the walls but was repulsed. The next day Mobile Corps Commander Gong Zijing led Miao troops against the south gate, which Li Rusong sought to exploit by scaling the wall, but his men were turned back by a hail of arrows and cannonballs. Another assault that night failed, and the rebels started executing prisoners in retaliation. Meanwhile, as supplies in the city started running low, the inhabitants started dying in increasing numbers from wounds and starvation.[47] A few days later one of the rebel leaders explored the possibility of negotiations.

Meanwhile the Ming had learned of the Japanese invasion of Korea and their occupation of most of the peninsula. Wei Xueceng's policy of buying off the Mongols with titles and avoiding a lengthy struggle in Ningxia frustrated Wanli. The emperor continued to blast Wei, charging that he was always listening to the timid and the foolish and that his pacification plan was an incredible disgrace. Subsequently Wanli approved a plan put forth by Shi Xing that called for the construction of a dike around the city to flood out the rebels using water from a number of lakes and rivers, some nearly thirty miles away, if they refused to surrender. By late August, even as the water-assault plan was underway, Wanli tired of Wei, who continued to entertain thoughts of accepting the mutineers' surrender. Wei found himself impeached by a supervising censor, arrested by the Embroidered Uniform Guard (the equivalent of an imperial secret police), and returned to Beijing.[48]

Wei Xueceng was replaced by Ye Mengxiong, who was likewise invested with the authority of the double-edged sword. Ye in many ways was ideally suited for the command, given that in 1562 he had authored a treatise on warfare, the *Yunchou gangmu*, which featured extensive discussion of both incendiary and aquatic warfare, drawing on famous examples from throughout Chinese history. In Ye's words:

> I observe that water can be used to encroach and inundate, can be used to float and flow, can be used to sink and drown, can be used to encircle and besiege, and can be used to quench thirst. Thus those in antiquity who excelled in employing the army frequently relied upon the power of water to establish unorthodox achievements. The stupid must employ boats and vessels before they term it aquatic warfare, not knowing that if they fathomed its real meaning, prepared their implements, and took advantage of opportunities, aggressive warfare and unorthodox plans would all come out from it. What reliance must there be on boats and vessels?[49]

The dismissal of Wei Xueceng was tied to the situation in Korea. By late August, after the initial Ming expeditionary force of about 3,000 had been annihilated at Pyongyang, it was obvious they were going to have to intervene militarily to prevent a Japanese invasion of China if nothing else. As Li's forces constructed the dike around Ningxia, an official reported that the Japanese had already crossed the Taedong River in Korea and King Sŏnjo, then ensconced in the town of Ŭiju on the banks of the Yalu, was seeking permission to enter Liaodong with his court. Wanli told the king to sit tight and hold out for the time being while the Chinese court decided exactly how much help to give. The emperor appointed Song Yingchang (1530–1606) as military commissioner (*jinglue*) of Korea in September 1592. But the Ming knew they had to quell the unrest in Ningxia so that Li Rusong, who otherwise would have been stationed in Liaodong, could get back to the eastern border.[50]

Ye Mengxiong appointed a commander to oversee the flooding of Ningxia in August. By the twenty-third a dike 1,700 zhang (19,975 feet) long reportedly encircled the city. Pubei dispatched one of his adopted sons in the middle of the night to once again try and recruit help, but he was ambushed and killed along with twenty-nine of his men by Li's forces. Nonetheless, the mutineers continued to try and bribe the Mongol chieftain Bushugtu into joining them with gifts of gold and ceremonial robes. But Li dispatched Ma Gui and Dong Yiyuan to counter Bushugtu and sent another commander to secure Shapai Pass to the east. Although they lost one engagement, the Ming forced the Mongols to withdraw.[51]

By September 6 the water around the city walls was eight to nine feet deep. That night the rebel leaders set forth in small boats to try and break the dike, but they were forced back by the besiegers. A captive said that the situation in the city was desperate, the officers now eating horses and the commoners reduced to eating tree bark and dying in droves.[52] The next day 100 zhang (1,175 feet) of the dike southeast of the city collapsed. The officer in charge of that section was executed, and another rebel escape attempt in boats was turned back. The starving masses in the city were now begging the mutineers to surrender. On September 17 Mei Guozhen called for the defenders to open the gates so the Ming could minister to the populace but received no response. Five days later the mutineers attempted to break out with a cannon assault from atop the walls.

On September 25 the Mongol leader Jorightu, allegedly at the head of 18,000 cavalry, was stymied by the efforts of Li Rusong and others. The Mongols proceeded north of the city to the vicinity of Fort Zhangliang, where a fierce battle ranged from around dawn until noon. Li and Ma led the Ming counterattack, catching the enemy in an encircling maneuver. All told the Ming killed or captured 120 Mongols in this engagement, along with several horses and camels. More importantly, the mutineers now realized that help would not be arriving, and their morale ebbed as the water level outside the city rose. By October 12 water had brought the north wall down, and Ming units scaled the south wall with ropes and ladders.[53]

Seeing the soldiers enter the city, Bo Cheng'en was completely disheartened and pleaded with them to spare his life. The Ming sowed dissent among the surviving rebel leaders, getting them to kill or capture one another with false promises of clemency. Thereupon the Ming commanders led their units over the walls. Fires erupted in the north tower of the city, but the Bo clan remained at large. The next morning Bo surrendered himself to Yang Wen, but Pubei immolated himself before the Ming could apprehend him. They did, however, manage to recover his corpse for dismemberment and capture several of the other rebel leaders alive. In the winter of that year Wanli received congratulations from his officials for the victory at the Meridian Gate of the Forbidden City. Pubei and Bo Cheng'en were dismembered and the other rebel leaders were simply executed.[54] The Ningxia mutiny was crushed.

The commanders deemed responsible for the victory were showered with honors, Li Rusong being elevated to the post of supreme commander, Xiao Ruxun becoming a vice commissioner in chief with a hereditary post for one son, and Ye Mengxiong becoming censor in chief of the right with a post in the Embroidered Uniform Guard for one son. Many of the commanders and troops were ordered to hasten to Korea, including Li Rusong, who was now appointed supreme commander of the Eastern Expedition to chastise the Japanese. Wanli authorized the release of Wei Xueceng from prison, restoring his official rank, but Wei died at home in obscurity.[55]

The conduct of the Ningxia siege reveals a number of insights regarding the tactics and capabilities of the Ming military at the time. While detractors point to the length of time needed to quell the uprising, the Ming actually recaptured the outlying fortresses taken by the rebels relatively quickly. Ningxia itself was a fortified bastion of some

300,000 inhabitants, held by perhaps 30,000 rebel troops. The city had walls around twenty feet thick and thirty feet high. Pubei and his compatriots were the major military commanders in the region and had served for decades with distinction, so they were more capable than a typical peasant rebel in fomenting and perpetuating a military uprising. Likewise, whether or not one believes that their assistance for the mutineers was wholehearted, the Mongols put tens of thousands of cavalry into the field, necessitating serious countermeasures by Li. The fact that the Ming army could muster a force in excess of 40,000 to besiege the city, construct a massive dike for flooding it, and detail significant numbers to deter the Mongols, cut rebel supply lines, and intercept messengers was no small feat.

Critics have highlighted the weapons shortages and logistical difficulties experienced by the Ming. While there were shortages, these were eventually corrected. Government forces eventually brought hundreds of cannon to bear against the city and even constructed makeshift boats to launch water assaults across the pond they created. Part of the logistical problems stemmed from the decentralized nature of the Ming system, which placed the burden for supplies on local officials. Given the rapid spread of the uprising, it took time to get officials and supply lines in place, an issue compounded by the fact that they were operating against a distant frontier garrison. Likewise, Ming forces assembled from other distant frontier regions. Once the troops did arrive, Ming commanders made effective use of firearms, negotiation, mobile warfare (against the Mongols), and aquatic attack to attain victory. The officers and soldiers demonstrated courage and ingenuity, and many gained valuable experience that would serve them well the next year at Pyongyang.

The second of the Three Great Campaigns, the suppression of Miao chieftain Yang Yinglong in Bozhou in southwest China, proved the longest. This was a military problem that had vexed the Ming since 1587 and would not be completely solved until after the conclusion of the war in Korea. Yang's family had held positions of authority in the region since the Tang dynasty, the post of pacification commissioner (xuan wei shi) of Bozhou first bestowed upon the clan during the reign of Khubilai Khan (1260–94). The Yangs were not originally from the area, but over centuries of continued intermarriage and interaction with the locals, they came to identify themselves with the Miao and their interests.[56]

Throughout the Ming period, Bozhou was responsible for sending 2,500 shi (200 tons) of lumber and military supplies, including horses, to the Ming court every three years. It is possible that these exactions became more onerous over time, with at least one scholar suggesting that they led to the revolt. Yang Yinglong inherited his father's post in the Longqing period and initially earned much distinction fighting various aboriginals and Tibetans on behalf of the Ming. Like his counterpart Pubei in the north, Yang continually displayed his military prowess, being in the forefront of every battle, and honored obligations to the court by forwarding fine wood for public works and palace construction.[57]

Despite intimations that Yang was a potential threat, not to mention his run-ins with other local notables, the court stuck by its policy of rewarding frontier commanders who achieved concrete results. Accordingly he received rewards of gold and ceremonial clothing and was promoted to the rank of regional military commissioner (3a). According to surviving sources, however, these rewards were not enough to satisfy Yang's growing ambitions. Yang allegedly had a fierce disposition from birth and delighted in killing. He regarded most government troops as weak. Because Beijing always relied on locally recruited aboriginal forces to quell uprisings in the southwest, he became scornful of the Ming and disrespectful of their laws.[58] He also evinced imperial aspirations by creating eunuchs, abducting women to serve as "palace ladies," and setting himself up as an aboriginal sovereign of sorts.

It is unclear if the court would have acted against Yang had he just been accused of arrogant behavior and imperial pretensions, though it is certainly possible. It is also possible that these details were added to the sources later as further "evidence" of his villainy. Regardless, Yang entangled himself in a number of local power struggles and then threw in his lot with local Miao groups that resented Han intrusions into the area. Initial requests for assistance in quelling Yang's nascent rebellion were dismissed by central authorities on the grounds that Bozhou was a distant corner of the empire and there were more pressing matters at hand. Even the regional inspector of Shandong, Li Hualong (d. 1612), who would later command the Ming expeditionary force that crushed Yang, complained that he did not have time to investigate fully, arguing that Yang should be given the opportunity to redeem himself through meritorious service.[59] Nonetheless the court was already thinking about how to reorganize local administration, ordering the Ministry of War to investigate and make recommendations.

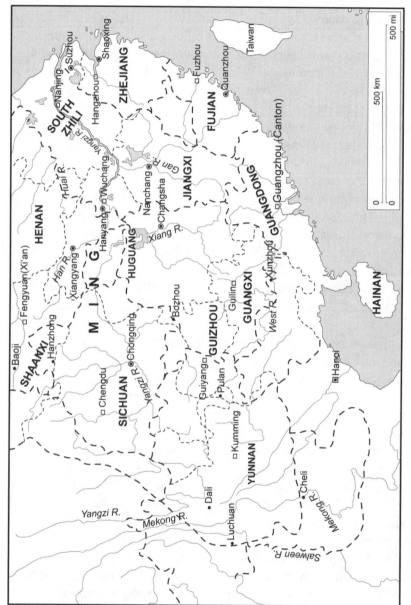

Southern Ming China

After a series of exchanges and to the surprise of many, Yang surrendered to authorities only to find himself sentenced to death. He managed to get his sentence commuted by promising to pay a hefty fine and offering to lead 5,000 troops to Korea to fight the Japanese. But his offer was not sincere, and once free he holed up in his mountain stronghold and rebelled again, looting and plundering a number of isolated prefectures and districts. In 1595 Yang was again brought to justice and again bought his way out of the death penalty. His son, Yang Chaodong, was given his hereditary post while another son was held in Chongqing as a guarantee of Yang Yinglong's good behavior. Considering the matter settled, Wanli promoted and rewarded the officials responsible for Yang's capitulation and once again turned his attention to matters in Korea. Within a year, however, Yang was back to his old tricks, raiding nearby provinces and claiming that he was the emperor of Bozhou. Over the next three years, he and approximately 100,000 Miao followers rampaged, settling old scores and creating a sense of fear and panic among the locals. Preoccupied with the Japanese threat, Wanli did little at this time other than to issue assurances that Yang's rebellion was relatively contained. But in early 1599 he moved to crush the revolt.[60]

At this time the emperor authorized further appointments and approved a counteroffensive against Yang. An embarrassing defeat prompted Wanli to appoint Guo Zizhang (1543–1618), one of the more notable officials of the era, to the post of pacification commissioner of Sichuan. Li Hualong was elevated to the post of vice minister of war and placed in charge of the military affairs of Sichuan, Huguang, and Guizhou.[61] Wanli then ordered the distinguished commanders of the Korean campaign to travel with all due haste to Sichuan. Arriving on the scene in July 1599, Li solicited cash and troops from all over the empire. The struggle against the rebels continued through the rest of the year, with the rebels at one point gaining the upper hand and striking at the important cities of Chongqing and Chengdu. The emperor intervened again, depriving some civil officers of all posts and demoting them to the status of commoners while bestowing the double-edged sword of authority upon Li.[62]

A veteran of many frontier wars, Li had a reputation as a fair-minded official who worked well with both civil and military colleagues. He had worked closely in fact with Li Rumei in Liaodong prior to his appointment in Sichuan. Together he and Guo Zizhang labored tirelessly, mobilizing Han and aboriginal troops and erecting defensive works around lands claimed by Yang. Li Hualong was a master planner, continually sending memorials to the Ministry of War requesting more troops and supplies and carefully calculating the costs of weapons, equipment, and provisions. He also was eager to have more experienced commanders at the front, complaining, "Sichuan not only has no troops, it also lacks even one person versed in military affairs."[63] Taking his vested authority to heart, Li issued a number of commands to local authorities calling for the creation of local defense forces and demanding that all troops in the region observe the strictest discipline to avoid undue hardship on the local populace.

Wanli told the Ministry of War to recruit troops from Shaanxi, Gansu, Yansui, and Zhejiang to quell the rebellion. He also issued a decree addressing Yang's revolt and his crimes. In this document he accused Yang of violating the principles of Heaven and turning his back on the kindness of the Ming, recounting all of Yang's heinous deeds. The emperor also charged that Yang and his allies were responsible for the deaths of more than 100,000 people, and threatened the rebels with a force of 500,000 men. Now Yang's atrocities were known all over the empire, and he had cut himself off even from his ancestors. Wanli further warned Yang's family and associates that they too would die with him for taking part in his dastardly deeds. The Miao rebels were offered a chance to live if they killed Yang and his top lieutenants, and he warned other allies that Yang was untrustworthy and might turn on them at any time. After all, reasoned the emperor, Yang regarded all their lands as his own, and he would freely sacrifice any of them to save himself. Wanli reminded his subjects that when one person rebelled, according to the law, all relatives within nine degrees of kinship were held responsible. The emperor finished his entreaty by stating: "If you kill Yang and his associates, things can return to the way they were before. Heaven will bestow its riches upon you and look upon you as it did before. There can be good fortune, or there can be disaster. The choice is yours."[64]

In the tenth month of 1599, the court ordered Li Hualong to go to Chongqing and begin mobilizing the forces from Sichuan, Huguang, and Guizhou. Wanli communicated with local aboriginal officials to secure their assistance in putting down the uprising. Upon his arrival from Korea, the redoubtable Liu Ting, whose family had a long relationship with the Yangs, was summoned to Li's office and lectured on the importance of loyalty to the state. Liu's presence was important to morale, for he and his father had served along the southwestern frontier for decades. As Li put it, "In the palaces and among the common people alike, there is no one who has not heard of Big Sword Liu." Liu pledged to do his utmost for the Ming, vowing to "eat the flesh and sleep on the hide" of Yang Yinglong.[65]

The end of 1599 and the first month of 1600 were filled with skirmishes between the rebels and government contingents, which continued to arrive from all over the empire. Wanli's influence on the selection of officials and recruitment of troops is apparent. The emperor personally selected many of the civil and military officials and used his influence to keep the latter out of trouble when others cast suspicion on their activities during the campaign (for example, charges of bribery against Liu Ting). The final Ming army reportedly numbered some 240,000 and included troops from all over the empire as well as surrendered Japanese units captured in Korea. Each commander and each army inspecting censor received a ceremonial sword and full field-command authority from Li Hualong, who addressed the assembled officers in a stirring speech at Chongqing in late February.[66]

On March 1, 1600, government forces embarked upon an eight-pronged assault. They battled the rebels in the jungles and ravines for nearly four months before encircling Yang at his isolated stronghold of Hailongtun. In the end the rebels were crushed and Yang immolated himself. Government records indicate that the Ming killed 22,687 rebels, captured another 1,124 rebels and their followers, took 5,539 noncombatant prisoners of war, obtained the surrender of 126,211 Miao, freed 1,614 prisoners, and captured 767 head of livestock and 4,444 weapons. Wanli declared the victory the verdict of Heaven and offered a tax amnesty for the regions affected by the rebellion. He later attend the ritual dismemberment of the surviving prisoners in January 1601.[67]

In the wake of the empire's victory in Bozhou, the Ming could be seen to be amid its renaissance, having defeated three formidable enemies simultaneously on three geographically distant frontiers. For all his failures in other areas, Wanli had good reason to feel pride in his military accomplishments during the 1590s. Indeed, in the decade following Bozhou, the Ming continued to pursue military actions with a fair degree of success, especially in the southwest, where a series of minor uprisings, caused in part by the disruptions of Yang's revolt, were successively quelled, paving the way for further Han settlement.[68] Likewise, Ma Gui and others continued to keep order along the northwestern frontier.

Despite the partisan struggles that subsequently engulfed his court and bureaucracy, the emperor continued to patronize his favorite military officials. But as they died off and military affairs, except for the Manchu threat, became less pressing, Wanli even lost interest in punishing those who angered him. He managed to rouse himself somewhat for the Liaodong campaign, involving many of his old favorites, including Yang Hao, Liu Ting, and Li Rubo. Even after Li Rubo's suicide, Wanli still appointed his younger brother, Li Ruzhen, to the family post in Liaodong in 1619, demonstrating his loyalty to the Li clan.[69] By this time it may have been clear that the military capabilities of the late sixteenth century were a thing of the past. Rather than attempting cooperation to re-create these successes, Ming officialdom became even more divided, with no official capable of uniting the bickering factions ever emerging.

2

DARK SAILS ON THE HORIZON

Prelude to War

What age has not been plagued by barbarian troubles?
—Cho Kyŏngnam

The long-term consequences of the First Great East Asian War are hard to overstate. Ming troops remained in Korea, several of whom actually stayed behind after Chinese forces left and raised families with Korean wives. The memory of Ming aid was used to solicit Korean assistance against the Manchus in the 1630s. Even after the fall of the dynasty in 1644, Koreans continued to use the Ming calendar in private communications and wore Ming ceremonial robes, even when on tribute missions to the Qing. After the Qing came to power, Koreans viewed themselves as the last bastion of Confucian civilization, which became for them a source of authority. King Hyŏjong (r. 1649–59) even dreamed of leading a northern expedition to punish the Qing and restore the Ming. Nevertheless, for the remainder of the Chosŏn period, they concealed symbols of Ming loyalty when Qing envoys visited. Before turning to the war itself, the relationship between the three countries, described as "an inseparable trinity" by one prominent scholar, prior to the outbreak of hostilities in 1592 is important to establish. Based on centuries of interaction, all three belligerents had firmly entrenched notions about one another, both positive and negative.[1]

Tumen River

Najin

Kyŏngsŏng ■

HAMGYŎNG

Yalu River

Pukch'ong
■

PYŎNGAN

Hamhŭng
●

■ Anju

Pyongyang
●

■ Hwangju

TONGHAE

HWANGHAE

KANGWŎN

● Haeju

Ongjin ▲

KYŎNGGI

Kyodong ▲

Kangnŭng
●

Ullŭng Island

Seoul
●

Wŏnju
●

HWANGHAE

Ch'ŏngju

CH'UNGCH'ŎNG ■

Poryŏng ▲

Kongju
●

KYŎNGSANG

Chŏnju
●

Taegu
●

Ulsan ■

CHŎLLA

Chinju
■

Tongnae
▲

Kwangju ●

Sunch'ŏn
▲

Pusan
●

Kangjin
■

Kosŏng
▲

Haenam ▲

0   80 km

Chosŏn Korea

Despite their geographic proximity and shared cultures, the three states often endured strained relationships marred by ignorance and distrust. Some of these feelings lingered from early rivalries between the states, including the supposed punitive expedition of the Japanese empress Jingū to Korea around 250 A.D. and the wars of the Sui-Tang eras.[2] The Japanese could point to the two failed invasions of Japan in 1274 and 1281, when the Mongols impressed into service Koreans and Chinese to assist them. Problems later arose between China and Japan over issues of trade, piracy, and investiture as the imperial pretensions of Hongwu and Yongle clashed with the aspirations of the Ashikaga shoguns, who sought Chinese trade and recognition after their own civil wars of 1336–92. Nevertheless, official Sino-Japanese trade continued until the mid-sixteenth century, and unofficial trade persisted thereafter until the Ming lifted maritime prohibitions. Despite their occasional disagreements, Japan maintained closer contacts with Korea than with any other state throughout its history.[3]

The Koreans were faithful tributary vassals of the Ming from even before the founding of the Chosŏn dynasty in 1392. Korea ranked first in the Ming hierarchy of tributary states, a distinction of pride for Koreans. Indeed they "saw their relationship to China as more than a political arrangement; it was a confirmation of their membership in Confucian civilization." For example, the foreword to an account of the war written in the seventeenth century exclaims: "Since ancient times China and Korea have enjoyed friendly relations akin to those of elder and younger brothers. They share both history and culture and have thus prospered together." Still the relationship was definitely one of a superior and an inferior, with the Koreans often forced to submit to humiliating Chinese requests for eunuchs, palace maids, and concubines.[4]

Nevertheless, Koreans did derive significant benefits in the way of material goods and cultural exchanges. From the time he ascended the throne and "gave" Korea its independence from Chinese rule, Hongwu sought to cultivate good relations with his neighbor, though the relationship was strained by the Korean civil war, which resulted in the establishment of the Chosŏn dynasty, and by frequent misunderstandings on the part of the Ming emperor concerning improperly deferential memorials. Until the late 1380s the peninsula was still threatened by the Mongols, who claimed sovereignty there. At this time Gen. Yi Sŏnggye (1355–1405; r. 1392–98), founder of the Yi dynasty, seized power after turning his army against the capital (Kaesŏng) rather than leading an expedition into China at the behest of an anti-Ming faction at the Korean court. Yet the Ming were disturbed by the fact that Yi was a usurper, fearing that recognizing his position and legitimizing his title for the purposes of tribute trade would imply a tacit acceptance of his methods. Moreover, they suspected the Koreans of sponsoring Jurchen raids in the northeast, and as the Ming were still in the process of consolidating their hold over the empire, this posed no small threat in their eyes.[5]

Finally, however, Korea received the designation Chosŏn (Chaoxian in Chinese) for the new kingdom when Yi's government dispatched an emissary to the Ming court in 1392 offering condolences for the death of Hongwu's heir apparent and requesting a name for their newly established state. Despite this recognition of the new regime, Hongwu never referred to his neighbor king by anything other than temporary titles. When both rulers died in 1398, the door was opened for smoother relations, especially under the vigorously expansive Emperor Yongle, who was said to be a great aficionado of Korean food and women (and may have even been part Korean himself).[6]

Thus after the conclusion of a civil war in China (resulting in Yongle's reign) and Yi's consolidation of power in Korea, relations between the two countries became much more amicable and mutually profitable. The Koreans sent an average of three to seven tribute missions to China every year, bearing gifts such as gold; silver; woven mats; leopard, tiger, and sea-otter skins; white silk; various types of dyed cloth; hemp; pearls and other precious items made with pearls; paper; calligraphy brushes; and ginseng. Horses were supposed to be sent every three years. In addition there were periodic requests for cattle, more horses, weapon-making materials, tea, pepper, grain, slaves (including women), and eunuchs.[7]

Despite the sometimes onerous nature of these obligations, Koreans generally were eager to maintain ties with imperial China. Although trade envoys received rather low salaries, they would bring extra items with them to barter and sell at considerable profit, including ginseng, paper, furs, and brushes, returning with Chinese products unavailable at home. Likewise, the Korean court was eager for the gifts bestowed upon them by the Ming, especially items of Chinese culture. Ming emperors provided their Korean tributaries all manner of lavish gifts, including dragon robes, jeweled belts, musical instruments, royal costumes, ornaments, silks, jade, and Chinese medicines.[8] Most important, though, were Chinese books, including the classics, histories, treatises, and literature of all kinds, which had the greatest influence on Korean high culture and society. In particular, Chinese legal texts provided the basis for the law code and penal statutes of the Chosŏn dynasty. Korea's close proximity reinforced relations with China and resulted in its receiving more impressive gifts from the Ming than other tributary states, solidifying its favored status.

The Ming also sent embassies to Korea. Almost always the Chinese followed a land route to Seoul (unlike the Koreans, who sometime traveled by sea), where special hostels provided them entertainment and a comfortable, dedicated residence awaited them just inside the south gate. Their purposes included announcing imperial succession or the naming of an heir apparent, conveying edicts and rescripts, making requisitions for tribute, bestowing instructions from the Ming Ministry of Rites, conferring patents of investiture on newly enthroned Korean kings, or simply investigating the state of affairs. Ming embassies were less frequent than their counterparts, the greatest number taking place during Yongle's reign, when peaceful relations between the two countries were being established, and during Hideyoshi's invasion, to help coordinate military efforts against the Japanese. These missions were not always jovial affairs, for the Chinese often behaved arrogantly, flaunting their authority and power.[9]

The Koreans also maintained tributary relationships with neighboring states, adapting the practice from the Chinese and situating "Chinese, Japanese, Jurchen and Ryukyuan elites in hierarchical and egalitarian relationships with the king of Chosŏn." Thus Kenneth Robinson has argued that "there were multiple models for organizing and ordering maritime and overland interaction, multiple centers of diplomacy, multiple hierarchies of diplomatic interaction, and multiple conceptions of rulership, siting emperors, sovereigns, and shoguns at centers of world orders."[10] Nevertheless the Chinese tributary order was preeminent and recognized as such by the other Asian states, which is why Hideyoshi sought to supplant the Ming, thus creating a new system under Japanese domination, rather than merely enhancing Japan's position in a lesser order.

An important (and by Western scholars, neglected) aspect of the Sino-Korean relationship was their military alliance. Even before Hideyoshi's invasion, China and Korea made efforts to help one another deal with common military problems. While the Mongols were one common enemy, their threat had largely dissipated on the eve of the founding of the Chosŏn dynasty thanks to Ming efforts in the northeast. The Jurchen tribes, though, presented a more enduring problem. Both the Ming and the Yi sought to maintain peace along their borders, which meant obtaining some sort of loyalty from the Jurchen chieftains. These local strongmen in turn played off the Chinese and the Koreans against one another, pledging loyalty to one in order to gain titles and gifts, then using that leverage to exact gifts from the other. But Korea could not match the resources of China, and most of Jurchen leaders became local military commanders for the Ming. Regardless, they continued to raid both Chinese and Korean towns. For their part the Koreans extended their formal control of territory along the Yalu River by establishing defense commanderies.[11] But it was joint Sino-Korean military operations that often managed to cripple and divide Jurchen leadership and bring a reasonable amount of stability to the borderlands.

Another common enemy was piracy, which was endemic to East Asia throughout the early modern period. References to Japanese pirates in Korea occur as early as 414, with extensive Japanese piracy recorded in the thirteenth century. Although abating after the Mongol conquest of China and Korea, it returned in the mid-fourteenth century, when uprisings in China challenged Mongol rule and the Japanese found themselves embroiled in a bitter civil war. The Ashikaga shoguns were in no position to check these raids, and massive numbers of Japanese pirates despoiled the Korean coast, even assaulting cities such as Kaesŏng and Pyongyang. These attacks also spilled over into China and became a major source of friction between the early Ming emperors and the Ashikaga shoguns. Both the Chinese and the Koreans sent embassies to Japan demanding that the bakufu bring the pirates under control. These initial entreaties were ignored, partly because the Ashikaga did not yet have full control over their own country. The Chinese fortified their coastal areas and subsequently adopted an aggressive policy of expansion under Yongle. The Koreans also strengthened their defenses and even carried out offensive operations against pirate bases in Tsushima. Finally in 1419 the Chinese ambushed and annihilated a large pirate fleet off the coast of Liaodong; that same year the Koreans launched an unsuccessful raid against Tsushima.[12]

These actions did not end piracy but did curtail it for well over a century. The Koreans at the same time adopted a policy of investing pirate chieftains or their sponsors, generally the daimyo of the coastal prefectures of Kyushu and Tsushima, with Korean titles and copper seals, allowing them to trade at Korean ports. The Sō family of Tsushima, who would later play a prominent role in the Japanese invasion, were the greatest benefactors of this arrangement. According to an agreement concluded in 1443 and known as the Kakitsu treaty (for the Japanese reign name for 1441–44), the Sō were responsible for verifying the cargoes and intent of all Korean-bound vessels, which were required to stop at checkpoints on Tsushima—any crew without paperwork from the Sō could be regarded as pirates. In exchange the family could sponsor fifty vessels a year in addition to sending other ships on special missions, would receive a substantial stipend from the Korean government, and could levy duties and fees upon the ships and the cargoes passing through their checkpoints. This made the Sō wealthy and influential, and piracy diminished along the Korean coast.[13]

China and Korea both restricted legitimate Japanese trade. Under an agreement reached between Ashikaga Yoshimitsu (1358–1408), an enthusiastic patron of the arts who greatly admired Chinese culture, and the Ming, the Japanese were permitted to trade only at the port city of Ningbo. Yongle also granted Yoshimitsu the title "king of Japan," which earned him a poor reputation among some nationalistic Japanese but provided the necessary benefits of trade to restore his depleted coffers. The accord also allowed the Japanese to send missions to China under a license system, with the Ashikaga bakufu given a monopoly over the trade, and both sides maintaining matching tallies to ensure the legitimacy of missions. In exchange for these trading privileges, Yoshimitsu promised to stamp out piracy. Japanese tribute items included horses, swords, armor, ink slabs, fans, folding screens, and sulphur. The Chinese in turn sent silver, copper coins, brocades, silks, jade, pearls, incense, scented woods, fine furniture, and classical texts. Chinese coins even became the medium of exchange in Japan.[14] This trade flourished until the 1450s, when conditions in both countries became increasingly unfavorable. Armed clashes occurred in Ningbo in 1523, and the trade was officially discontinued in 1548. When Japan sought to resume this commerce, Korea offered significant and effective opposition, which became a stated reason for the invasion of the peninsula in the 1590s.

Despite the arrangement with the Sō family, the Koreans still dealt very circumspectly with the Japanese. They put severe restrictions on the number of envoys allowed to travel to Seoul, the number of Japanese ships allowed to trade in their ports, and the number of places where these vessels could call. Nevertheless upward of two hundred Japanese ships a year landed at Pusan, Chinhae, and Ulsan, where the Japanese maintained hundreds of residential households and even Buddhist temples. A great deal of legitimate trade occurred in these enclaves as Japanese copper, lead, and sulphur was exchanged for Korean textile goods, luxury and artistic items, and Buddhist scriptures. But substantial smuggling also took place in which the Japanese drained away a large amount of Korea's cotton production, something Korean kings could not abide since cotton constituted the primary medium of exchange. Finally in the early sixteenth century, the Koreans adopted a policy of strictly enforcing the terms of the trade agreement. A message to the Sō demanded the suppression of piracy and careful validation of all would-be trading vessels. This led to Japanese riots in the three trading ports, which forced the Korean military to crack down and kill nearly 300 Japanese. After this the kingdom severed relations with the Sō, though they resumed just two years later and continued until the invasion. But the arrangement was increasingly marred by incidents of piracy and the presence of "imposter" families, such as the Hatakeyama, who insinuated themselves into the Korean-Japanese trading network with varying degrees of success in the fifteenth and sixteenth centuries.[15]

Given the explosion of international trade with the arrival of the European traders in the sixteenth century, piracy unsurprisingly made a comeback during this period. In addition to increased goods traffic, as much as half of all the precious metals mined in the New World ended up in Chinese coffers. As historian Marius Jansen has observed, "much of the activity we have parochially thought of as 'the expansion of Europe' was the European participation in the expansion of East Asia." With Ming military strength at an all-time low and the Japanese entering the full throes of a civil war that would last until the end of the century, many enterprising Chinese, Japanese, and Koreans took to the high seas to seek their fortunes. Chinese and Korean sources generally refer to these marauders as Japanese, or dwarf, pirates (wokou), but in actuality nationals of all three countries in addition to freebooters from Southeast Asia and even Africa engaged in this era of piracy. These raids, whether attributable to the Japanese or not, became a major source of tension between the three countries and were foremost in the minds of all three belligerents at the start of the war in Korea. By the late Ming period, earlier views of the Japanese as sagacious monks gave way to the Japanese being seen as "shadowy demons" who "created a deep-seated sense of fear and loathing in the hearts of the Chinese people."[16] Hideyoshi himself later seized upon these perceptions, using them to rationalize the ease by which he could subdue the Koreans and the Chinese. Yet when confronted by the Japanese onslaught in the 1590s, the Sino-Korean allies quickly adopted the military tactics that had proved successful against the pirates in the 1560s and sought to recruit men who had seen service in these earlier campaigns.

Thus the relationship between China, Korea, and Japan was complex and multilayered. There were elements of fear and distrust on all sides, yet there was also the very real desire for trade and commerce. Additionally the literati of Korea and Japan were versed in the Chinese classics, with both states modeling elements of their government and laws after the Chinese. The Japanese believed that whatever the military weakness of Korea and China, they were still repositories of culture and wealth. Buddhism, for example, traveled to Japan via Korea, after its initial transmission to China from India, and Buddhist monks often served as the primary intermediaries between the three belligerents.[17] Even though Japan's political institutions were rather different from those of the Ming by the late sixteenth century, there was an implicit acknowledgement of the Chinese roots of Japan's imperial system and a recognition by Hideyoshi that he needed to conquer China and claim its mandate for himself to assume preeminence in Asia. The Koreans and Chinese, though, remained aloof in their dealings with Japan, not recognizing the very real danger posed by its new ruler.

Therefore, when examining reasons for the outbreak of the war, the importance of imperial pretensions is essential. It is taken for granted when discussing European history that countries routinely clashed for reasons of pride and jealousy, yet many scholars seem either to accept the Chinese world order and its tributary system uncritically or to dismiss it as mere construct. Hideyoshi's full ambitions could never be realized if he did not conquer the Ming, for he could not bear to suffer the existence of a ruler with greater pretensions to authority than his own. Not only does this suggest a rejection or ignorance of the Chinese conception of the world, but it also supports the idea that other states in Asia could have imperial pretensions as great as those of the Chinese. The Koreans, for example, exhibited their own ethnocentric consciousness toward Japan, the Jurchens, and the Ryukyus as part of their own version of the Ming-centered world, even asserting their kingdom as the ideological center of Asia after the fall of the Ming.[18]

In early modern East Asia such ideological claims were articulated within the context of the Sinocentric world order as a matter of survival, but these states had considerable room for independent action so long as regional order and peace did not suffer. China's neighbors, realizing the benefits of a good relationship with the Ming empire, decided to "play the game" and try to turn the system to their advantage. But the proliferation of studies on China's regional relations that emphasize more agency on the part of its tributary vassals has obscured this understanding.[19]

The influence of Chinese culture and its formative role in shaping national consciousness in East Asia is important. Korea certainly had a sense of its place in the world with respect to China. Koreans had long enjoyed much closer relations with China than Japan and had far more direct and peaceful contact with their imperial neighbor, despite occasional misunderstandings. As a result of these contacts and the prolonged general peace in East Asia, the Korean upper class came to realize the Chinese scholar-literati ideal perhaps even more than the Chinese themselves, ironically falling prey to the same kinds of factional divisions that rent Ming society. These divisions would prove critical in the early stages of Hideyoshi's invasion.

Of course, one must also consider the character of the war's architect, Toyotomi Hideyoshi. Hideyoshi has been called the most extraordinary and significant political figure of the sixteenth century as well as the single-most-important individual in the history of Japan. His rise to power from humble origins as the son of a farmer and part-time soldier to apprentice page for Imagawa Yoshimoto to sandal bearer and eventually chief deputy of Oda Nobunaga (1534–82) is well chronicled, and his exploits exemplify the sixteenth century in Japan, known as the age of *gekokujō*, meaning the overthrow of the superior by the socially inferior and of lords by their vassals. After the death of his master, Hideyoshi became the hegemon of Japan, unifying the country under one sovereign for the first time in over a century. Despite his failure to conquer Korea, he has remained one of the most revered figures in Japanese history. Temples, shrines, and memorials to Hideyoshi and his exploits still dot the Japanese countryside.[20]

Like many national heroes of humble origins, Hideyoshi himself later concocted all manner of stories explaining his rise to power and his possible divine origins. From as early as 1577, according to some sources, he evinced a desire to conquer China and the other countries of Asia. In one of the wilder rumors current at the time, some maintained that Hideyoshi was actually a Chinese from Zhejiang who had fled to Japan after a brush with the law, taking a Japanese wife and adopting her surname, and determined to conquer China in order to exact revenge. Fictional works published in China later in the Ming period even cast Hideyoshi as the reincarnation of an evil flood dragon. He clearly saw himself as a man of destiny, one whose virtue would illuminate the four seas.[21]

Hideyoshi was the second of the so-called Three Unifiers of sixteenth-century Japan. He rose to high position under Oda Nobunaga and succeeded him in 1582 after another vassal, Akechi Mitsuhide (1526–82), cornered Nobunaga and forced him to commit seppuku. Mitsuhide lived barely two weeks after his coup, for Hideyoshi soon mustered enough troops to crush his rival at the Battle of Yamazaki. After this engagement Hideyoshi went about the business of defeating or co-opting his remaining military rivals and establishing a new government in Japan, one that was federalist in its makeup but legitimized by the authority of the imperial family, who bestowed high titles upon Hideyoshi, including kampaku (imperial regent) in 1585 and taikō (retired imperial regent) in 1591. Because of his humble birth, Hideyoshi could not attain the title of shogun, but by 1590 he had brought all of Japan under his rule and was poised to take the next step in his path to glory.[22]

As the unification of Japan moved closer to becoming a reality, Hideyoshi began articulating his plans for future conquests. He first publicly announced his desire to invade China in ninth month of 1585, and in 1586 he repeated this to one of his vassals, Mōri Terumoto (1553–1625). Later that year he told Jesuit Luis Frois that he wished to conquer Korea and China because no Japanese ruler before him had ever undertaken such an expedition. He also apparently inquired about obtaining warships from European powers via the good offices of the Jesuits but learned that war was not the brotherhood's primary business, conversion of the masses being a higher priority. Hideyoshi apparently intimated that he might facilitate this goal, though as demonstrated by his later prohibition of Christianity, this was an empty gesture.[23]

Despite this rebuff, Hideyoshi was confident of success. Armed with arquebus guns introduced by the Portuguese and cannon imported from China, he figured that he had more than enough firepower to attain his objectives. Moreover he had heard that the Chinese feared the Japanese like tigers and would run in fear as soon as they saw Japanese warriors. Hideyoshi planned on using Chinese guides to lead his forces from Fujian and Zhejiang provinces to Beijing and using Korean guides to approach the Ming capital from the north.[24] Hideyoshi promised all his successful generals territory in this new empire. Those who did not contribute to this great enterprise were to be punished.

Nevertheless, despite all his domestic successes, Hideyoshi was still very insecure and wary of his fellow daimyo, with their distinguished lineages and potentially threatening military power. Hideyoshi himself had fewer direct vassals than many of the most powerful lords in Japan, so he had to rely upon both the symbolically important legitimation conferred by the imperial family and on foreign trade, which would give him access to goods denied other daimyo, particularly superior weapons. In order to distinguish himself further from his rivals and underline his position as the supreme authority, he sent emissaries to neighboring Asian states, including the Philippines, Thailand, the Ryukyus, Taiwan, and Korea (and even Portugal), seeking tribute and recognition of his status as the legitimate ruler of Japan. While officials in many of these states were at least cautiously respectful, the Koreans openly questioned Hideyoshi's rank and status and steadfastly refused to treat him as the equal of the king of Korea. Indeed, when his first ambassadors arrived in Korea, officials there had no idea who Hideyoshi was or from whence he came. They regarded the shogun as the equal of their king or perhaps slightly inferior, and they knew that Hideyoshi, whatever his other titles might be, was not the shogun of Japan. To their eyes he was nothing more than an upstart who had usurped power from the Minamoto line.[25]

It is evident from the contents of a letter Hideyoshi sent to his wife during his early negotiations with the Koreans in 1587 that he craved international recognition and glory, writing: "As the king of Korea is sending acknowledgement of my rule, a messenger must be sent to Tsushima with all due haste. Now that which I have desired all my life is within reach. For certainly my rule shall be extended to the land of the Tang [China]."[26]

Diplomatic feelers had been sent to Korea even before Hideyoshi's assumption of Oda Nobunaga's mantle. The abbot of Shōfukuji Temple in Hakata, Keitetsu Genso, who would later serve as one of the primary Japanese diplomats during the war, visited Korea at least three times during the 1580s. Such missions are understandable if one accepts the notion that Nobunaga himself had planned on invading China after unifying Japan, as suggested in some sources.[27] In 1586 Hideyoshi instructed Sō Yoshishige and his son, Yoshitoshi (1568–1615), the daimyo of Tsushima, to send envoys to the Koreans informing them of his plans, asking them to act as guides, and requesting assistance for Japanese forces in their invasion of China. The Sō were understandably opposed when they heard of these plans and sought to change his mind, arguing that it would be a mistake to throw away two hundred years of friendship. Unconvinced, Hideyoshi reiterated that the king of Korea should come to Japan to pay his respects. In these early meetings the Koreans were adamant about the Japanese making the sea lanes safe and remanding several wanted pirates before considering entering into any kind of formal diplomatic relations with Hideyoshi's government.[28]

The first envoy dispatched was Yutani (Tachibana) Yasuhiro. During his visit, Yasuhiro allegedly insulted his hosts by first belittling the size of their spears and then by remarking upon the soft lifestyle of Korean officials. He later compounded these mistakes by behaving outrageously at a royal banquet, then warning his Korean translator: "Your country will not last long. Having already lost the sense of order and discipline, how can you expect to survive?" According to Japanese sources, in addition to trying to persuade Korea to submit to Hideyoshi's requests, Yasuhiro also was instructed to learn as much as he could about the peninsula's geography and defenses. While some ministers were concerned about the possibility of an invasion, others advised King Sŏnjo that the Japanese were bluffing. In the end the Koreans declined to respond affirmatively to the request.[29]

Hideyoshi was livid when he learned of this decision—not only did he kill his own envoy but also executed the man's entire family. He then dispatched twenty-six boats to ply the waters around Korea and search for the strengths and weaknesses in its defenses. Korean troops on land and at sea were timid in these encounters and fled before the Japanese. Only commander Yi Taewŏn dared come forth in battle, and he was killed when his boat sank. The Koreans were shaken by these attacks and started looking into making improvements to their coastal defenses, though military problems along the northern frontier necessitated the allocation of precious resources there as well. To compensate, some peasants were conscripted to begin repairs of mountain fortresses, causing no small amount of popular disgruntlement.[30] Some Korean commanders lied and said that when they went forth to meet the Japanese, the enemy had already fled. Late in 1587 Hideyoshi dispatched another envoy to enquire at the Korean court, but again there was no response.

Yet another envoy went to Seoul in 1588 to obtain a positive response from the court. Hideyoshi was furious the Koreans had not yet paid their respects to him by sending an envoy, prince, or even the king himself to Japan. Sō Yoshitoshi, perhaps eager to avoid disrupting the trade that was so lucrative for his clan, offered to go first to discuss matters with the Korean king and give him another chance to send an envoy before the Japanese launched a full-scale invasion. Thus he and Genso went to Seoul in the third month of 1589 to meet with Yi Tŏkhyŏng. They tried to get him to persuade Sŏnjo to send an envoy to Hideyoshi or even go pay his respects in person. Remembering the recent attacks by pirates, some of whom were allegedly working with Koreans living as fugitives in Japan, the court demanded the repatriation of these traitors first before they would even consider sending their own envoys to Japan. Yoshitoshi thought this would not be a problem and sent his own agent to Japan to retrieve these outlaws. A few months later some men were brought forth and executed before the king, though it is doubtful that these individuals were actually guilty.[31]

Nonetheless, Sŏnjo was so pleased that he held a royal banquet in honor of the Japanese envoys. At this meeting Yoshitoshi presented the Koreans with Japanese guns and swords, and the king gave him a horse from his own stable, though nothing more was decided. At this time Minister of Rites Yu Sŏngnyong (1542–1607) suggested coming to some sort of peace agreement with Japan, but he was opposed by others in the court. Late in 1589 some Koreans in the south reported that the Japanese might be mobilizing for war. These officials estimated they could turn back an invasion, albeit with heavy losses, but they were understandably perturbed by such rumors. Some favored alerting the Chinese immediately, though that suggestion was ignored, while others speculated that the Japanese were just using these threats to exact trade concessions. In December 1589 Minister Cho Hŏn sent a memorial to the court saying that he was certain the Japanese were planning an attack. Cho allegedly foretold the invasion at a banquet, saying, "Whoever eats with me tonight will die, for the Japanese are coming with 200,000 troops next year."[32] This worried some in the court, but no one dared utter a word to rouse the king from his revelry.

Moreover, Korea had virtually no generals capable of leading an army as a result of the prolonged peace, and the kingdom's most able ministers typically found themselves on the outside looking in as a result of factional politics. The serious factional rivalries of the Chosŏn era generally began about 1575 and derived from academic and doctrinal differences concerning the interpretation of Confucian teachings as well as connections between official families and the king's maternal relatives. The losers of power struggles often retreated to remote Confucian academies, where they trained disciples who bided their time for new power plays.[33]

Sŏnjo had ascended the throne as a minor under a regency, so he appointed scholars to prominent posts to counter the influence of his maternal relatives, who controlled the regency. Eventually two major factions, the Easterners and the Westerners (their names deriving from the location of their respective power bases in Seoul), coalesced. The Easterners were the younger progressive scholars in favor of extending the king's power, whereas the Westerners were generally the more conservative defenders of the interests of the king's maternal in-laws, the leader of the faction at one point being the brother of the Queen Dowager. The Westerners' power waned when the Queen Dowager died. But after becoming the dominant faction at court, the Easterners later split into Northern and Southern subfactions. This split eventually resulted in the rebellion of Chŏng Yŏrip in 1589, which saw the purge of seventy Easterners from government. In addition to purely academic or concrete policy disputes, petty personal incidents, such as a furor over one official taking a commoner as a concubine, became fodder for factional alignments. Paying no attention to real issues, officials often simply aligned themselves along partisan lines to curry favor with their superiors in hopes of landing a coveted government post. As a result of this unhappy situation, when Cho Hŏn voiced his concerns about the Japanese, he was accused of treachery and charged with wanting to stir up trouble among the people.[34]

This was the state of affairs in May 1590, when the Koreans finally decided to send Hwang Yungil (1536–ca. 1600) and Kim Sŏngil (1538–93) as envoys to Pusan to negotiate with the Japanese. Hwang was a Westerner and Kim, designated chief envoy, an Easterner. They boarded a ship bound for Tsushima on June 1, staying on the island for more than a month before heading on to Iki Island and finally arriving in Kyoto in August. Hideyoshi at that time was on campaign, so the envoys had to await his return. But this was not the first indignity they had suffered. When they first got to Tsushima, the Koreans were treated discourteously in their eyes, for Sō Yoshitoshi's retainers had brought him into a banquet hall in a palanquin, then Sō proceeded to sit in an elevated position. This infuriated Kim Sŏngil, who stormed out, exclaiming, "These barbarians really have no sense of propriety and cannot distinguish between higher and lower officials."[35]

Such distinctions were crucial, for "in the Chinese world order the seating arrangement was one of the most important diplomatic protocols symbolizing the status and relationship between states." By sitting in an elevated position, Yoshitoshi was blatantly flaunting Japan's superiority. Even worse from the Korean standpoint, as Kim exclaimed, Tsushima had formerly paid tribute to Korea, so they considered the Japanese living there as occupiers. Yoshitoshi blamed his retainers for their ignorance of diplomatic protocol and executed them, presenting their severed heads to his guests and apologizing profusely. From that point on the Japanese dreaded Kim and treated him with the utmost respect.[36]

The envoys stayed in Japan for several months, housed in the Daito-kuji Temple in rather austere conditions and served bland and demeaning food. Nevertheless, they presented their hosts with goods that included Portuguese cannons, maps of Ming territory, silks, tiger skins, medicinal herbs, fruit, rice, and gold. Kim and Hwang also bore a letter from their king with them in which he expressed his congratulations to the new overlord of Japan and explained that he himself was unable to come in person because of the great distances involved. The king also said he desired to maintain happy and cordial relations with Japan.[37]

Hideyoshi himself finally met with the Koreans in the twelfth month of 1590, having made them wait while he finished the siege of Odawara Castle. During the campaign Hideyoshi allegedly visited the shrine of the war god Hachiman and addressed the statue of Minamoto Yoritomo, Japan's first shogun: "You took all the power under heaven and you and I are the only ones who have been able to do this. But you were born of high descent while I am sprung from the peasants. But as for me, after conquering all the empire, I intend to conquer China. What do you think of that?" Seeking to impress the visitors with his majesty, he regaled them with tales of his divine birth. Eschewing the mistake made by his vassal, he sat in an honored position facing the south and gave the emissaries wine as he discussed his greatness and expressed his desire to establish friendly relations with Korea. The envoys were not impressed. They later reported that Hideyoshi was "short and ugly with a dark complexion and the overall appearance of a monkey, though his bright, piercing eyes looked right through people." He wore a black silk hat during the audience as he sat flanked by samurai. Kim Sŏngil was angry that Hideyoshi did not address the letter from Sŏnjo immediately, while Hwang was afraid of him and feared that war was imminent. The Koreans were perturbed that the wine they were served was both mediocre and in unglazed cups and that the only food provided consisted of rice cakes. Matters degenerated still further when the now tipsy Hideyoshi departed the audience but soon returned with his infant son, who proceeded to urinate on him, delighting the taikō and disgusting his guests.[38] The envoys were not granted another audience with Hideyoshi, who apparently believed the sole reason for their presence was to pay homage to him.

Greatly offended by his behavior, the Koreans continued to stall and promised Hideyoshi nothing. Feeling he had the upper hand, Hideyoshi offered them just four hundred ounces of silver each and a few other gifts for the lesser attendants. Although they asked for a letter to take back to their king, he initially refused, saying he had no time to write one.[39] They waited at the port of Sakai and eventually received a letter that was clearly intended to impress the Koreans with Hideyoshi's overwhelming power.

> Whenever and against whomever I have waged war, the victory has always been mine. The lands and districts invaded by me have always been conquered. Now our empire has entered upon a period of peace and prosperity, and the people are enjoying a benevolent rule. Lonely old men and forlorn widows are all well provided for. Both the national wealth and that of individuals has been so greatly augmented that it is unparalleled in our history. Since the nation's founding, our empire has never before witnessed such glory as that of our imperial court and such splendor as that of our imperial capital. However, human life in this world is brief. . . . I am not willing to spend the remaining years of my life in the land of my birth. According to my idea, the empire that I would create should not be separated by mountains

and seas, but should include them all. In starting my conquest, I plan that our forces should proceed to the country of the Great Ming and compel the people there to adopt our customs and manners. Then that vast country, consisting of more than four hundred provinces, would enjoy our imperial protection and benevolence for millions of years to come. I have in mind a plan of conquest which shall surely be carried to a successful ending. Your kingdom has taken the lead among the continental states by sending an envoy to our court, thus showing reverence to our throne. You have acted in accordance with the wise saying of the ancients that one who has foresight and is humble and cautious will always be free from grief and worry. . . . You, King of Korea, are hereby instructed to join us when we proceed to [the country of the] Great Ming at the head of all your fighting men. You may thereby further renew your pledge of service due to us as a neighboring state. Our sole desire is to have our glorious name revered in the three countries [of China, Korea, and Japan].[40]

The Korean envoys were understandably concerned about Hideyoshi's threats. They first tried to tone down the language of his letter, especially the way in which he addressed their monarch—though they agreed that Hideyoshi was certainly a great general, he was not the king of Japan and therefore in no position to order Sŏnjo to do anything. Genso tried to reassure them that no harm would come to Korea if they acted in accordance with Hideyoshi's wishes, but he refused to alter the text of the letter. Questioned about the talks upon returning home, Kim Sŏngil still did not believe the Japanese would mobilize troops against China and Korea, stating: "Hideyoshi looks like a rat. We need not fear him." He added that Japan was in no position to attack anyway, and even if they did, "Korea can defend itself without any doubts." Kim even suggested that Japanese envoys probably would soon arrive to apologize for their diplomatic gaffes. This response infuriated Hwang Yungil, who said Hideyoshi's bright eyes showed he understood people and was a man of vision and determination. He believed a disaster was nigh. Unfortunately, Hwang was both a member of the Western Faction and a military official, so his warnings were overshadowed by Kim's reassurances.[41]

Later, when pressed further by Yu Sŏngnyong, Kim Sŏngil admitted, "I think that it is certainly possible the Japanese will invade, but I explained things this way primarily in order to avoid creating a wide-spread panic."[42] This revelation prompted other officials to taunt and belittle Kim, some even calling for his execution. But the Koreans continued to defy Hideyoshi. Sŏnjo sent this reply to the Japanese leader that read in part:

> You stated in your letter that you were planning on invading the supreme state [China] and requested that our kingdom join you in your military undertaking. This demand was most unexpected. We cannot even understand how you have dared to plan such an undertaking and to make such a request of us. . . . The relation of ruler and subject has been strictly observed between the supreme state and our kingdom. . . . Our two countries have always kept each other informed of all national events and affairs. Each has given ready assistance when the other has suffered calamity or has been in trouble. Our two countries have acted as a single family, maintaining the relationship of father and son as well as that of ruler and subject. This inseparable relationship between the Middle Kingdom and our kingdom is well known throughout the world. . . . We shall certainly not desert our lord and father country and join with a neighboring state in her unjust and unwise military undertaking. Moreover, to invade another state is an act of which men of culture and intellectual attainments should feel ashamed. . . . We would conclude this letter by saying that your proposed undertaking is the most reckless, imprudent, and daring of any of which we have ever heard.[43]

Genso and Sō Yoshitoshi continued to keep the lines of communication open, hoping to forestall disaster. But two further missions sent by the Sō proved unable to elicit a positive response. Genso admitted that an invasion was likely because Japan had still not forgotten that Korea had joined the Mongols in invading the islands some three hundred years earlier. Yoshitoshi stressed that refusal to help the Japanese would result in the needless deaths of countless civilians.[44]

On the Korean side Cho Hŏn, who was also a Westerner by affiliation, continued to predict an invasion and called for reforms, even suggesting that Korea attack Japan first. His words were not entirely ignored, for an official named Kim Su was sent to reinforce the defenses of Kyŏngsang province. Other officials were dispatched to Chŏlla and Ch'ungch'ŏng with instructions to secure and stockpile weapons and rebuild town and fortress walls. Even more significantly, an officer named Yi Sunsin was promoted to the rank of naval commander of Left Chŏlla province. Yi was known as a brave officer and a skilled archer who had distinguished himself in campaigns along the northern frontier but had run afoul of jealous rivals before being rehabilitated by his childhood friend, Yu Sŏngnyong.[45] Nonetheless, many officials simply consoled themselves by comparing Japan unfavorably to China in terms of size, wealth, and military potential.

In Japan Hideyoshi attempted to boost his troops' morale prior to the invasion. He told them that since the Japanese had invaded Nanjing in the 1560s with a mere three hundred men, imagine how much easier it would be now with his myriads. He assured them that the Chinese "fear Japanese like tigers," proclaiming that "our troops will cut through them like a fine blade hacks through bamboo." In another statement he said: "The Japanese will overrun the Ming like water washing over sand. . . . There is no city we cannot take, no country we cannot conquer." He crowed that he would personally ride at the head of half a million troops to sweep all before him with myriad weapons and mounts.[46]

In a later meeting on Tsushima, the Koreans reiterated that they would not allow the Japanese to pass freely through their country on the way to China. They added that a Japanese invasion of China would be "like a bee trying to sting a tortoise through its shell." But the Japanese continued to be befuddled by unclear and contradictory Korean letters sent by members of both prominent court factions. In April 1591 another Japanese delegation went to Seoul in hopes of persuading Sŏnjo to come around. In a secret meeting Genso told Kim Sŏngil of Hideyoshi's mounting anger at Korea's refusal and of his continued determination to attack the Ming. Drunk at the time, Genso confided that the Japanese were invading because they desired trade, which had been severed for too long by the Chinese. He added that if they would just let the Japanese pass through their country, there would be no problems. He reminded Kim that the Ming "trembled in fear of the Japanese who are like tigers and will chop through Korea like bamboo if they hinder Hideyoshi's invasion of the Ming."[47] Kim still thought it was nothing more than a grand scheme, and he did not relate the conversation to his fellow officials.

Apparently Kim and other Easterners operated under the assumption that those with strong interests in the trade between Japan and Korea would be able to avert hostilities. They also deliberated whether or not to report the news to China. Those opposed to this argued that "China will certainly laugh at us for this foolishness and Japan will certainly be furious," reasoning too that China already knew what was transpiring because of widespread trading contact with Japan. In fact the Ming had gotten word from a trader in the Ryukyus indicating that an invasion of China was imminent and that the Koreans were acting as guides. Yu Sŏngnyong reported that although Hideyoshi was certainly violent and unrestrained, he would never be able to pull off a full-scale assault on Korea, so there was no need to fear him or alert China.[48]

This reluctance to inform the Ming about possible Japanese action for fear of possible reprisals speaks volumes about the relationship between the two states. In his letter to Wanli, Sŏnjo proclaimed: "China is the parent country. Our country and Japan are foreign countries of equal status; we are like children. If you say that we are children with regards to China as the parent, then my country is the filial child and Japan is the evil child."[49] Regardless, Chinese officials twice visited Korea in 1591 to investigate matters.

In July 1591 Sō Yoshitoshi again went to Pusan to report that the Japanese were mustering an army to attack the Ming but Korea could still avert disaster if they allow the army safe passage. When this was conveyed to the king, he still did not believe it. After working more than ten days, Yoshitoshi left Pusan in disgust. He returned to Japan and presented his lord with a map of Korea. Hideyoshi decided that since the Koreans refused to act as his vanguard, they would be the first to feel his wrath. He and his top advisors agreed that the army would go first and Hideyoshi himself would follow later. His military headquarters were set up at Nagoya, in Hizen province on Kyushu, under the supervision of Kuroda Nagamasa. A great market established outside the city soon boasted the highest rice prices in all of Japan. Hundreds of boats were hastily built to ferry troops and supplies and rations were requisitioned from daimyo all over Japan. Hideyoshi planned on landing the vanguard in the first month of 1592, with the main body following in the second and third months.[50]

In late 1591 the Japanese executed a Korean envoy to impress the Koreans of their seriousness. Hideyoshi then sent letters to the rulers of the Ryukyus and other states of the south seas, informing them that they were now under Japanese rule.[51] He again boasted that he could subdue the Ming within a year, his swords cleaving through his adversaries "as if they were cutting bamboo." The new king of the Ryukyus, Shō Nei, did not want to abandon China but feared antagonizing the Japanese, so in 1590 he had sent a delegation to Japan, which delighted Hideyoshi and stroked his imperial pretensions. He informed Shō Nei that the Ryukyus would need to supply troops for the invasion. The king protested that his country was too poor and unversed in war, so Hideyoshi said that it need only supply rations for 7,500 troops for ten months, or 11,250 piculs (750 tons) of grain.[52]

After learning of Hideyoshi's plan, Shō Nei immediately sent word to the Ming. But he was not the only one. In June or July 1591, a Chinese trader captured by the Japanese managed to send an assistant with news of the invasion to Zhejiang, warning the Chinese that 100,000 Japanese were to set out in the first month of the next year. Pacification Commissioner Zhao Canlu (d. 1609) reported the information to the court, saying the Japanese were gathering supplies and mustering troops for an invasion. Upon hearing this news in late 1591, Wanli ordered the Ministry of War to reinforce coastal defenses. In the eighth month of 1591, Chinese representatives from Liaodong sent a letter to Korean officials after receiving the report from Zhejiang. Two months later the Koreans sent another official to Beijing to report the news of the Japanese threat. Early in 1592 an official named Song Yingchang suggested training troops to meet a possible Japanese invasion, and the Ministry of War promised to look into the matter. In the second month of 1592, the ministry reported that they had news the Japanese were indeed planning to attack China. Wanli warned the military that the Japanese were crafty and ordered the strengthening of coastal defenses and the investigation of the situation in Korea.[53]

Meanwhile, Japanese spies went forth to report on Korea and China and procure maps. Specific orders went out to daimyo all over Japan as to the number of troops and supplies they were to amass for the invasion. Any who failed to supply troops or supplies would be investigated. Hideyoshi's master plan called for 1 million troops under 150 generals. A good portion of the men raised were farmers or fishermen, perhaps not as well trained or loyal as Hideyoshi might have liked, but the mobilization of commoners to fight was certainly not out of line. Further demands for three years' worth of grain were issued to the surrounding countries in December 1591. He also reiterated his request for ships and guns via missionaries living in Japan, his implication of supporting Christianity belying his stated desire of uniting the three great traditions of Shinto, Buddhism, and Confucianism under his benevolent rule.[54]

Hideyoshi instructed his commanders that once in Korea, they were to construct fortresses, to rule as they would their domains in Japan, and to refrain from plundering the countryside. Battle assignments were distributed early in 1592. Mōri Terumoto was to secure Kyŏngsang province in the southeast; Kobayakawa Takakage (1532–96) was to take Chŏlla province in the southwest; Ukita Hideie (d. 1662), Chungchŏng province; Konishi Yukinaga and Sō Yoshitoshi were to take the western provinces nearest to China; and Katō Kiyomasa, the eastern provinces north of Kyŏngsang. The three grand generals would be Konishi Yukinaga, Katō Kiyomasa, and Sō Yoshitoshi.

Hideyoshi's motives and goals for invading Korea were diverse (and debatable). As can be seen from the negotiations with the Koreans, some Japanese have maintained that all Hideyoshi desired was the resumption of trade with China. He was very cognizant of the value of foreign trade in helping maintain his preeminent military position in Japan, an insight he had gained from Nobunaga. Therefore it appears that Hideyoshi hoped to create a new East Asian trade order with himself supplanting China at the apex. One can infer from the demands he would later present to the Ming that trade was possibly the most important goal of his enterprise, though publicly he perhaps could not admit this. Hideyoshi may have viewed the war and the creation of new trading opportunities as the means to solve some of his domestic economic problems by linking trade in Asia through Japanese ports, Osaka and Kyoto in particular.[55]

Etsuko Hae-jin Kang notes that Hideyoshi recognized the connection between political hegemony and foreign trade within the broader East Asian context. He suggests that Hideyoshi believed that restoring legitimate foreign trade was the first step in gaining a general monopoly over all commerce, and by extension regional political hegemony. But he "failed to perceive that other Asian states had a thoroughly dissimilar ideological and political makeup and, more importantly, he lacked insight into the foundations of the Chinese world order which was based on the concepts of Confucianism."[56] This led to his defiant rejection of the Sinocentric world order and his attempt to create a new one of his making.

In addition to economic motives, Hideyoshi craved recognition and homage from foreign rulers. This goal should not be trivialized. As Mary Elizabeth Berry points out, Hideyoshi was understandably proud of his accomplishments and impressed with the power and technology of the European empires that Japan was encountering for the first time. The best way to become like them in his eyes was to conquer the great empires of Asia. This would fulfill the needs of merchants and traders who wanted to compete internationally, solve conflicts among rival daimyo, solidify the unification regime, and restore national pride.[57] In the process Japan would replace China as the center of the East Asian world. Moreover, while some of Hideyoshi's statements to foreign rulers are overbearing to the point of laughter, it seems likely that he, like so many great conquerors, truly believed in his destiny and ability to overcome all odds.

James Murdoch suggests that Hideyoshi both wanted to prevent domestic unrest and was angry at Korea for not sending at least a prince to recognize his subjugation and unification of Japan. Other scholars have examined the notion of using the campaign to divert the energies of restless warriors and assert his authority. As George Elison puts it, "It is clear that one of Hideyoshi's principal aims in invading the mainland was to demonstrate the unassailable power of Japan's national hegemon."[58] In addition to just diverting their military energy, he drained his daimyo's coffers and depleted their natural resources by forcing them to build his castle at Nagoya and supply provisions for the armies.

These arguments build upon traditional interpretations of the war. The seventeenth-century *Chōsen seibatsuki*, by Hori Kyōan, presents Hideyoshi's decision to invade the Asian mainland as a natural outgrowth of his personality and ambitions. The *Taikō-ki*, a somewhat romanticized biography of Hideyoshi by his personal physician, maintains that he wanted to "extend his peace" and its benefits to all the peoples of Asia. By contrast a Korean account from the seventeenth century simply notes that the greedy Japanese leader desired to "swallow up the entire world." But late Ming author Xu Guangqi, who had lived in Shanghai during the war, believed that what motivated the Japanese to invade Korea was "the desire to assume Korea's tributary status with China and therefore take advantage of the tribute trade that this status allowed." Xu's contemporary Zhuge Yuansheng favored the explanation that Hideyoshi sought land for his vassals.[59]

Tokugawa commentators offered three reasons for the invasion: first, Hideyoshi liked war and leading troops in battle; second, he wanted to weaken potentially powerful rivals and exhaust their fighting strength; and third, because relations between Japan and China had been strained for so long, he desired to restore them once and for all by simple conquest. Meiji historians offered three more reasons, adding that Hideyoshi first, wanted to continue Japan's development and therefore needed to acquire the resources of other countries; second, wanted to encourage trade and possibly control it; and third, was merely continuing the policies of Oda Nobunaga by seeking to meld Japan, Korea, and China into one great empire.[60] This final explanation was especially popular in Japan's period of imperialist expansion as reflected in the works of Yoshi S. Kuno and Nakamura Tokugoro.

Modern scholars have tended to emphasize economic and domestic political factors, downplaying Hideyoshi's desire for glory. It is possible that he saw conquest as the only way to reward his vassals, for land was becoming scarce in Japan. Samuel Hawley notes, "Hideyoshi's vassals became accustomed to his generosity; they came to regard ever greater land holdings and incomes as their just reward for serving him." By the late 1580s, the potential for bestowing these rewards in Japan was diminishing, so new fiefs needed to be acquired overseas. This suggestion is born out by the fact that Hideyoshi did seek to extend the baku-han feudal structure to Korea. The key to his power lay in control of agricultural resources via the daimyo, and Korea represented an important new resource base. This is suggested by the fact that Hideyoshi was eager for Korean agricultural and mineral production, even slaves, to be sent to him.[61]

The invasion was also a means by which he could keep pressure on the daimyo, removing the dangerous ones to a safe distance and allowing for the strengthening of his own authority at home. Some therefore suggest that the war itself was mere pretext for imposing a stricter institutional framework on the home islands.[62] When the Ming were conquered and the Japanese emperor established in Beijing as Hideyoshi wished, his own family's power in Japan might be made more secure. This assertion could well be contended, however, because he used the Japanese imperial family to legitimize and sanction his own rule and if they were removed, the other daimyo might be less willing to acknowledge the symbolic authority of the throne. The idea that Hideyoshi wanted to make sure he retained preeminence in Japan is supported by the fact that he sent to Korea loyal generals who were clearly his underlings.

Chinese scholar Zheng Liangsheng has ascribed five major motives to Hideyoshi for the invasion: cementing his own greatness in the annals of East Asian history by creating one great Asian empire, keeping Japan at peace by reorganizing its troops and lords, keeping his troops occupied and out of trouble, making up for Japan's lack of resources by acquiring them from abroad, and monopolizing the benefits of foreign trade to ensure his own superiority within Japan. Samuel Dukhae Kim concurs, adding that Hideyoshi may have wished to remove the Christian daimyo from Japan as part of his overall goal of excising Christianity from his country.[63] Given that many of the daimyo sent to Korea were indeed Christians, such a scenario is plausible.

Related to these reasons was Hideyoshi's expressed desire to extend Japan's "divine country" system overseas. In his study of Tokugawa ideology, Herman Ooms has noted how Hideyoshi, emulating the precedent of Nobunaga, created a stage for himself to dispense *tendo* (the Way of Heaven). Therefore, he appropriated a great degree of Shinto and Buddhist symbolism prior to the invasion, portraying himself as an instrument of heaven and holding numerous ceremonies at shrines of the war god Hachiman, who was connected to Empress Jingū, the legendary conqueror of Korea. Invoking Shinto theology to justify foreign conquest and domestic pacification, he made the invasion of Korea "an exercise in *kulturpolitik:* the realization of a unity that is already there and calls out for implementation." Hideyoshi considered it his responsibility to maintain proper hierarchies within the East Asian cultural sphere and sought to make the notion of *shinkoku* (Divine Land) synonymous with Japan. Therefore, because he gave his authority an explicit religious base, Hideyoshi should not be dismissed as merely an irresponsible megalomaniac. Thus, Shōsaku Takagi has remarked that the campaign "was intended to bring *mukuri kukuri* (demons and monsters) within the framework of general peace and make them tributaries of the divine nation."[64]

The desire to gain control of foreign trade and create a new international order to supplant the Ming were Hideyoshi's main motivations. While some of the other reasons outlined above played roles in his decision, they were subordinated to these two primary objectives. As Li Guangtao notes, it is difficult to figure out Hideyoshi's real intentions because he had been so flexible in his approaches to problems during his rise to power. Had the Koreans sent a prince or their king to pay homage to him in the first place, the entire invasion may well have been avoided.[65] But Hideyoshi had a chip on his shoulder and when the Koreans knocked it off, he felt compelled to act. Yet it must be remembered that in the Korean world order, Hideyoshi, an upstart warlord, was not the equal of their king and he did not deserve recognition as such. Hideyoshi felt that he had been disparaged by both Wanli and Sŏnjo, not realizing perhaps that China and Korea were as ignorant of the Japanese political situation as he was of theirs. All they knew was that he was neither king, nor emperor, nor shogun and was therefore unworthy of their recognition.

At any rate Hideyoshi was supremely confident of victory and drew up detailed plans for his conquest. The Japanese emperor would be ensconced in Beijing. The ten prefectures around the capital would be set aside for maintaining the Japanese royal family. Hideyoshi's heir would be established as *kampaku* of the new empire in China while another daimyo would assume that title in Japan. Hideyoshi himself would assume the role of retired regent and tend to affairs from Ningbo, the port to which Japanese traders had previously been confined, which lends credence to the theory that his primary motive was to monopolize foreign trade.[66] The other military leaders were to extend their holdings by further conquests in Asia. Hideyoshi's initial plan called for him to go over after Korea was subdued and personally direct the subjugation of China. But (as will be seen below) a confluence of factors prevented him from ever going to Korea in person.

The invasion forces assembled at Osaka. Hideyoshi boasted of all the tribute he was receiving and repeated his claim that he would raise an army 1 million strong for the invasion of China. Arms would include 50,000 polearms, 100,000 great beheading swords, 100,000 spears and axes, 100,000 chopping swords, 500,000 long swords, and 300,000 arquebuses. Soldiers were expected to supply their own three-foot-long great swords.[67] These figures, however, were no more than wishful thinking. While sources differ somewhat on the exact disposition of the initial invasion force, the generally accepted figures put the total number of land troops at around 160,000 men, with perhaps another 140,000 or so mobilized as reserves. Estimates place the total fighting strength of Japan at the time at 563,000, a staggering figure given the country's small size and total population of perhaps 12 million. Contemporary

European armies rarely exceeded 40,000 men, and even 30,000 was by no means the norm.[68]

The makeup and leadership of the forces were as follows:[69]

Commander(s)	Number of Troops
Konishi Yukinaga & Sō Yoshitoshi	18,700
Katō Kiyomasa	22,800
Kuroda Nagamasa & Ōtomo Yoshimasa	11,000
Shimazu Yoshihiro	14,000
Fukushima Masanori & others	25,100
Kobayakawa Takakage & others	15,700
Mōri Terumoto	30,000
Ukita Hideie	10,000
Hidekatsu & Hosokawa families	11,500
Kuki Yoshitaka (naval forces)	9,200
Total	168,000

The rates of requisition varied by location in Japan. The heaviest burdens, about six men per one hundred *koku* of rice yield, fell upon the daimyo of Kyushu.[70] The daimyo of Western Honshu averaged around five men per one hundred koku, while those of central Honshu and Shikoku supplied approximately four men per hundred koku on average. Other regions had lower rates of just two to three soldiers per hundred koku. Sailors were conscripted from fishing villages along the Inland Sea and on Kyushu at the rate of about ten sailors per one hundred households. Still, it is important to consider these figures only as general guidelines because Hideyoshi both granted partial exemptions to favorites and put greater pressure for requisitions upon those whose loyalty was unquestioned. While some peasants certainly absconded, there is a record of only one vassal who actively resisted the call to battle; he was killed for his disobedience. Hideyoshi anticipated swelling his ranks during his advance with conscripted Koreans. This was the largest fighting force ever mustered in Japan up to this time under the command of a single leader. More importantly, in addition to their vast numbers, many of these troops were seasoned veterans. As James Murdoch puts it, "In the practical sphere of war and of administration it is questionable whether any contemporary state was so rich in talent as was the Japan of Hideyoshi."[71]

As in all his military endeavors, the taikō took great pains to ensure he had the best commanders. His trust in Konishi Yukinaga and Katō Kiyomasa was based on their many years of loyal service and skill. It is said that Konishi had enjoyed reading military texts from an early age and was a masterful planner of campaigns and an articulate diplomat. In addition to these qualities, he had traveled abroad with his father and was well versed in foreign affairs. Even though he and Katō Kiyomasa did not like one another as a result of a previous dispute, Hideyoshi assigned them joint command because they were his two best generals. In contrast to Konishi, Katō was the son of a blacksmith and a flamboyant hothead who wore elaborate crowns and sported a growth of whiskers. He was extremely aggressive in battle and had no concern for his personal safety. Not only were these two men different in character but also clashed on the matter of religion, Konishi being a Christian convert and Katō an ardent Buddhist devotee of the Nichiren sect.[72] Their rivalry would play a significant role in both the war itself and the peace negotiations.

By way of comparison, Korea in 1592 could not possibly have been more of a David to Japan's Goliath. Again drawing from the vivid description of Murdoch, Korea was governed by a class of nobles, "leisured and learned indeed, but effeminate and generally destitute of practical ability in everything except venal intrigue, in which they were extremely proficient. . . . [E]ven with the enemy sweeping the country with fire and sword, the filthy cabals still went on." As for the Korean army, it "was more of a mob than anything else," a sentiment echoed by Stephen Turnbull, who similarly observes, "no country can have been less fitted to face the might of Japan than was Korea in 1592." Horace Underwood comes to a similar conclusion, saying that "although cannon were introduced in 1389, the Japanese invasion two hundred years later in 1592 found the Koreans without any kinds of guns for their infantry and thus at so terrible a disadvantage against the Japanese land forces."[73]

By the 1550s the quality of Korean military examinations had declined precipitously, and officials became increasingly concerned about the lack of military talent. Corruption and factionalism had undercut the exams themselves, and once men were enrolled in the military, there was virtually no distinction made between army and navy service, with special training for naval troops left to individual commanders. By the 1580s everyone who took the military examinations was passed and sent off to battle the Jurchens in the north. Even the best commanders had trouble training and disciplining their recruits as evidenced by Yi Sunsin, who later remarked that he preferred commanding men at sea to land troops because sailors had nowhere to run. Given this state of affairs, arriving at an estimate of Korean military strength is problematic. Projections of the number of men in the navy vary from around 26,000 to over 100,000, but, as was the case in China, many of these were literally paper tigers.[74] Of some two hundred defense posts set up under the Chosŏn dynasty to this point, only thirty-three were large permanent works, and even these were generally understaffed.

While these generalizations do have some merit, historians should be cautioned against accepting them uncritically. The accepted wisdom is that Korea was in a marked state of unpreparedness in 1592, crippled by bureaucratic factionalism and softened militarily by two centuries of peace.[75] Moreover, Sŏnjo is portrayed in traditional accounts of the war as a morally degenerate king who idled his time away with women and wine, placed his trust in incompetents, and fled like a coward as his people were put to the sword. These characterizations are challenged, though, by both primary sources and recent secondary literature. Gari Ledyard has argued that Sŏnjo was in fact a diligent and concerned monarch throughout the invasion.[76] When his country was imperiled, he worked from dawn until late in the night and constantly met with his officials to devise strategy and rally the populace.

Likewise, while the Koreans may well have been woefully unprepared for Hideyoshi's invasion, they did not behave quite like the proverbial ostrich with their heads in the ground. As soon as Kim Ungnam, Korea's emissary to Ryukyu, reported developments there, Seoul embarked upon a program of new military appointments and repairing of defenses. Korea's two foremost military commanders, Sin Ip (1546–1592) and Yi Il, were dispatched to the north and south respectively to inspect defenses and check guard registers, weapons supplies, stores, and the like. Unfortunately, being overconfident of their own prowess, Sin and Yi did little other than order more weapons for the garrisons, though Sin also ordered many locals beaten for dereliction of duty.[77]

On May 11, 1592, Sin, Yi, and other high officials gathered at Yu Sŏngnyong's residence to discuss war preparations. Yu suggested that matters were looking bleaker by the day, even the cries of birds outside the palace heralding disaster, but Sin was unperturbed. Having made his reputation battling fierce Jurchen tribesmen, Sin had a fairly low opinion of the Japanese and their martial abilities. He noted that they were short and could therefore be easily bested in hand-to-hand combat by Koreans. When Yu noted that the Japanese possessed large numbers of muskets with great range, Sin replied that they were poor shots anyhow. Again Yu expressed his misgivings about Korea's preparedness, arguing that two hundred years of peace had rendered the country ill-equipped for war and urged crash recruitment and training programs. Sin remained nonplussed and maintained his faith in Korea's sturdy cavalry, which had helped him gain repeated victories in his frontier campaigns.[78]

But many other Korean military commanders had no illusions about their ability to withstand an invasion. Several officers warned that simply strengthening walls and defensive works would not be enough, for the Japanese could fly through these with ease. An example of the incompetence of these new preparations can be seen in the construction of fortress walls that were actually too long to defend with the manpower at hand. Training more locals would not be enough to stem the tide of a Japanese advance. Unfortunately there were not enough competent officers, nor did they have enough political clout, to effect a speedy rejuvenation of Korea's armed forces. Kyŏngsang province's military governor, for example, was said to be old and cowardly, and though some suggested that he be replaced by Yi Il, the proposal was rejected because Yi was stationed in the capital region, which was deemed more important. Kim Sŏngil eventually assumed the post.[79]

Part of the reason the government allowed military administration to decline was a fear of mutinies. Factional affiliations also came into play. For example, in 1583 Yi Yulgok, then minister of war, had recommended the creation of a permanent 100,000-man standing army, with 10,000 soldiers to be stationed in each province and 20,000 in the capital. But as Yi was a member of the Western faction, his proposal was summarily rejected on the grounds that maintaining such a large army would harm the livelihood of the people. Recruiting was another problem. Technically all men from the ages of fifteen to sixty were eligible for military service, but the yangban elites were exempt and others could buy exemptions. Recruitment difficulties were exacerbated by a series of crop failures and epidemics necessitating greater than usual levels of taxation and labor conscription for public-works projects in the years prior to the war. Popular rebellions had forced many residents to take up banditry. Add to this slavery rates as high as

30 percent, and it is easy to see that the Korean populace was not necessarily inclined to follow government directives in the early 1590s.[80]

Military organization in Chosŏn Korea was complex, with capital armies and commanders, one to three army and naval commands in every province, and multiple commands in strategically important provinces. Typically one of these posts was concurrently held by a civil commander, who acted as a provincial governor-general. Garrison troops, consisting of permanent regular soldiers, labor battalions, and sailors, fell under the army and navy commands of each province. Army garrison soldiers were the most numerous, with the majority consisting of peasant conscripts who farmed when not on duty, not unlike their Ming counterparts. While in addition to provincial forces there initially had been central-government forces and capital armies, these units were merged in the middle dynasty years, creating a garrison command structure centered on fortified points and staffed almost entirely by conscript soldiers. The state also maintained a system of postal relay stations and beacon fires for military emergencies.[81]

But even though there was an impressive system of military garrisons and defense installations in name, many did not actually exist, a situation mirrored by the Ming. One estimate suggests that despite a paper strength of some 200,000 men, only a few thousand Koreans could be considered combat-worthy veterans as of 1592. Furthermore, when a crisis occurred, generals were dispatched to take command of undisciplined and leaderless armies. As a result ill-trained forces stationed in distant areas often had to face the enemy's vanguard without adequate leadership. New military regulations drawn up at various times during Yi rule to remedy these defects in the military system were neither fully adopted nor maintained for any appreciable length of time. Too much was left in the hands of subordinate commanders, who varied widely in initiative and talent. Therefore, when news of the Japanese invasion spread, Korea was unprepared, and its leaders reacted quickly and haphazardly.[82]

Surprisingly, the Japanese actually were concerned, receiving word that Korea was raising troops and making some effort to strengthen its defenses. Yi Sunsin in particular is said to have thrown himself into his work, repairing fortress walls, testing cannons, stockpiling gunpowder, and even laying cables and chains underwater to protect harbors. When Yu Sŏngnyong questioned Sin Ip about whether or not the Japanese would have an easy time invading, Sin confessed that he did

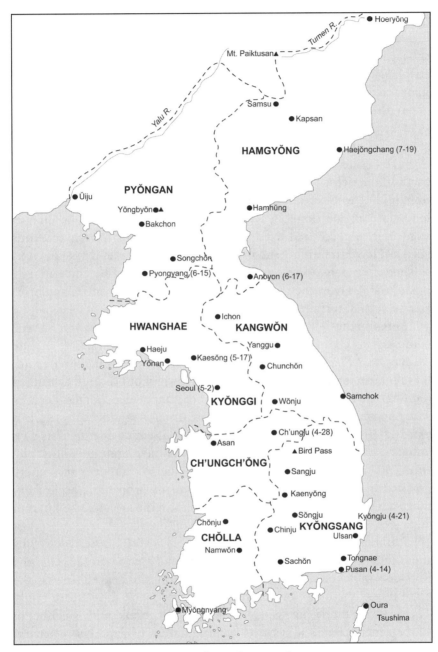

Korean Defense Commands

not yet have sufficient information to make a determination.[83] Yu sent him back out, cautioning that even though they were short in stature, the Japanese and their muskets should not be taken lightly. Defenses still needed to be upgraded according to Yu, but Sin, who was a brave man and disdained cowards, paid little heed to his sage advice.

With respect to arms, the Koreans had virtually no firearms other than artillery pieces mounted on ships and the few that they had received as gifts from the Japanese. Their weaponry consisted primarily of spiked clubs, short double-edged swords, bows, various spears, and battle flails, which were a favorite of cavalry units. The flail was a round, hard wooden stick, painted red and approximately 1.5 meters long, with an additional heavier piece at the end, attached by links of iron chain, and covered with heavy nails or knobs.[84] Korean polearms such as glaives (reclining moon knives), battle rakes, and pikes as well as shock weapons were fairly similar to those used by the Chinese, unsurprising given the fact that both faced similar enemies and operated in similar terrain.

Korean bows were outstanding, with a range of some 450 meters, compared to about 300 meters for Japanese great bows. These were composite reflex bows fashioned of mulberry wood, bamboo, water buffalo horn, and cow sinew and used a variety of missiles, including flaming arrows and darts augmented with gunpowder charges. Archery was one of the few martial pursuits normally practiced by Korea's yangban elites, "the one token of martial skill which ever held its own among a people who for thousands of years have preferred silks, pictures, poems, and music." There are frequent references to archery practice in the wartime diaries of Yi Sunsin, who built an archery range across an inlet at Hansan Island to train his men for the kinds of distances they would encounter fighting on the seas.[85]

Although they rarely used firearms as field artillery, instead deploying them mostly on ships and to a lesser extent atop fortress walls, the Koreans employed five major types of cannon; the heaven's mark, the earth mark, the black mark, the yellow mark, and the victory mark. The heaven's mark gun weighed 300–450 kilograms, with a caliber of 12–17 centimeters and a barrel approximately two meters in length. The smaller yellow mark cannon weighed 60–80 kilograms and had a caliber of 6–7 centimeters and a one-meter barrel. Black and earth mark cannon were slightly smaller than this on average. Victory mark cannon had calibers of approximately 2.5 centimeters with a total length around

26–62 centimeters. They also used other types of projectile weapons, including mortars, primitive time bombs, flaming arrows, fascinating multiple-arrow launchers called *hwacha,* and a device called the "flying thunderbolt," which consisted of a hollow iron ball packed with gunpowder and weighed a whopping 530 catties (or jin; 320 kilograms).[86]

Korean officers and cavalry wore reinforced coats over chainmail and simple helmets. Officers often wore bright color sashes. Ordinary soldiers wore lamellar armor of white or gray, if they wore any armor at all—often their dress consisted of little more than quilted or padded armor, possibly with a shield of bamboo or metal. Naval crews wore sea-blue uniforms with black felt hats and used swords, spears, tridents, battle axes, maces, scythes, grappling hooks, or iron chains in combat.[87]

The Korean navy ostensibly consisted of 600–800 ships for active warfare and coastal patrols in addition to auxiliary vessels, though a more reasonable estimate suggest a total naval strength of about 250 units. The largest-class vessels were approximately twenty-five meters in length with a beam of nine meters. Underwood relates that a first-class Korean man-of-war, known as a *panoksŏn,* "was probably not less than seventy feet overall in length and probably went up to about one hundred feet with a beam of about one-third the length. . . . Along the sides were heavy bulwarks of thick planking loopholed for archery and fitted with ports for small cannon. On some vessels shields were hung along these bulwarks." The most remarkable Korean warships of course were the famous turtleboats, or *kobuksŏn,* which were supposedly reinforced with iron plates and spikes across the deck to prevent boarding and lined with cannon across the bulwarks. A turtle's head at the fore of the boat was supposedly filled with a combination of sulphur and salpeter that spewed blinding smoke to confuse the enemy.[88]

As for Japanese weapons and tactics, the first image that generally springs to mind is the archetypal samurai warrior brandishing his deadly katana. Although Japanese swords were better, longer, and sharper than their Chinese and Korean counterparts, with the exception of the Battle of Pyŏkchegwan in 1593, it is hard to say that swords alone made much of a difference through the course of the war. Far more important were arquebus guns, which had played an important role in the unification of Japan and facilitated the general transformation of the Japanese military over the course of the sixteenth century.[89] Although models from the Chinese arrived earlier, the generally accepted date for the introduction of Western-style arquebuses to Japan is 1543, when Portguese sailors landed on the small island of Tanegashima. Swordsmiths soon began copying these models. Moreover, the firearm's introduction would exert a profound influence on the subsequent course of Japanese history. Put briefly, guns and spears were easier to use than samurai swords and bows, peasant conscripts were cheaper than elite warriors and, when used properly, just as effective on the battlefield as their superior numbers generally offset the superior skills of samurai. Used in conjunction with small numbers of elite cavalry combined with infantry, armies of peasants equipped with guns and spears and utilizing tactics of volley fire, as pioneered by Nobunaga, constituted a truly formidable fighting force.[90]

Indeed the number of mounted troops sent to Korea was rather low, though the number of guns sent was particularly telling. To use one illustrative example, the Hachisuka family's 1,328 soldiers brought 314 guns, 53 helmets, and 213 suits of armor with them. The ratio of approximately one-third of all Japanese troops possessing firearms held true across the board and is roughly comparable to Ming ratios, though the Chinese preferred heavier artillery. Arquebuses had an effective range of perhaps 300 meters but were rarely used beyond 200 and considered most effective at about 50 meters. Because the guns were cumbersome to reload, units of arquebusiers were normally accompanied by archers and pikemen, and they were considered more dangerous at greater distances. The Sino-Korean allies recognized this and sought to adopt tactics that emphasized rapid advance between volleys. The Japanese also possessed cannon for siege warfare but seem to have taken relatively few of these to Korea, judging from their relative absence in accounts. Those taken seem to have been fairly portable. One medium-sized gun used at the siege of Namwŏn in 1597 had a range of 500 meters and was specifically designed to be fired from horseback.[91]

Japanese foot soldiers generally fought with great spears or pikes and long swords, the former being used in tandem with archers and arquebusiers. Cavalry units bore similar weapons. The superior reach of Japanese swords and spears was frequently commented upon by Chinese and Korean soldiers, resulting in the greater rotation of southern Chinese troops, trained in the famous anti-wokou methods of Ming general Qi Jiguang, into the field. The favored Japanese battlefield tactic was to fire an arquebus volley and then close rapidly, perhaps with archery cover. As the war dragged on, however, they came to utilize ambush tactics, disdaining set-piece battles in which they might by outclassed by superior Chinese heavy artillery.

Japanese great bows were about 2.5 meters in length and 2–3 centimeters thick. They shot shafts of 1.5 meters and used a variety of different arrows for signalling, piercing armor, and the like. An archer usually carried two to three dozen arrows. Although their range was perhaps as great as 300 meters at their outer limit, they were most effective inside 30 meters.[92] Significantly, Chinese and Korean sources make little mention of this aspect of Japanese military technology, undoubtedly satisfied with the superiority of their own bows and crossbows.

Defensively, the Japanese boasted the best armor of any of the belligerents. Japanese armor was often lamellar, reinforced with iron plates and complemented with a helm. They rarely used shields except in siege warfare, when large target shields might be erected on battlefields. Commanders were noted for their magnificent armor, which was understandably quite intimidating to the Koreans as many Japanese lords outfitted themselves with helms and masks fashioned after demons or other mythological creatures. Commander Ii Naomasa clad an entire unit in red armor, earning them the moniker "Red Devils." Date Masamune supposedly outfitted his units with spectacular gold-lacquered helmets and red-shafted spears exceeding five meters in length.[93] Many other commanders became well known in Korea by either their colorful battle crests, or *mon,* or their distinctive armor, helmets, or weapons. Numerous examples of such items, most notably the great sun helm and cross-bladed spear of Katō Kiyomasa, still grace museums and private collections.

The one area where the Japanese found themselves at a distinct disadvantage was naval technology. They had three main types of vessels, none of which were as seaworthy as those of the Sino-Korean allies. The largest, known as *yasutaka,* were veritable floating castles, surmounted by a large observation tower atop which the fleet commander sat and commanded the action. The other two vessels were smaller oared ships, but neither was particularly well armored.[94] Although they sometimes carried small cannon onboard, the preferred Japanese tactic was to close with enemy boats and grapple, hoping to make use of their superior hand-to-hand fighting skills. This left them particularly vulnerable to the Chinese and Koreans, who used much larger cannon on their boats and preferred to blow their opposition out of the water from a distance.

Indeed Hideyoshi seems to have envisioned his navy as merely a transportation battalion. Even later in the war after he had issued orders for the improvement of his navy, the invaders enjoyed only limited success at sea. The resultant logistical difficulties proved to be one of the major factors behind the eventual Japanese defeat.

As for the Ming, they boasted the greatest array of armaments, no doubt due to China's greater size and geographic diversity. They had also inherited an enormous body of military knowledge and managed to combine very ancient weapons, such as trebuchets and other siege devices, with the latest in firearms technologies. For example, the grand general cannon (*da jiangjun pao*) had a range of approximately 450 meters. The crouching tiger cannon (*hucun pao*) would be used to great effect in the Siege of Pyongyang in 1593. Measuring approximately sixty centimeters and weighing thirty-six catties, this weapon fired a spray shot of up to one hundred small projectiles. The Portuguese-derived *folangji*, a type of culverin, had been introduced in 1523 and was regularly used on Ming ships. A typical Fujianese warship of the late sixteenth century carried one heavy cannon, one mortar, six culverins, three falconets, and sixty firelances, easily outclassing anything the Japanese put to sea.[95]

On the seas the Ming deployed an array of effective warships. The *meng chong* was a large vessel equipped with powerful crossbows for attack and defense. The *lou chuan* was a three-decked boat similar to Japanese flagships, while the *haigu*, or partridge boat, had a large aft section resembling a bird's tail. The best Ming warships were constructed in the southern provinces of Guangdong and Fujian from reinforced pine and ironwood. The larger boats carried upward of one hundred sailors and were outfitted with catapults and cannon. Smaller oared vessels were used with the larger warships as they were faster and could pursue enemies into shallows, rivers, and mud flats. Still another boat, called the "falcon boat," bore a striking resemblance to Korea's turtleboats.[96] Others featured arquebusiers and were used for eradicating coastal pirates.

For land warfare, in addition to the firearms and siege weapons mentioned above, the Ming used a dazzling array of polearms, swords, bows, crossbows, clubs, spears, and martial-arts weapons such as military rakes. Ming swords included both curved blades and shorter double-edged straight blades. Military rakes were 2 meters in length and used to unseat enemy riders and hook and grab enemy weapons. Ming halberds were as long as 4.5 meters, fashioned of bamboo, and topped with steel tips. They were favored as distance weapons to counter the Japanese katana. Ming clubs were up to 2 meters in length and often outfitted with steel heads or spikes.[97]

Large crossbows, or ballistae, were favored in siege warfare, some of them launching multiple bolts at once. Repeating crossbows functioned as primitive machine guns, offering suppressive cover. The Ming also made extensive use of fire arrows and assorted hybrid weapons featuring projectiles augmented with gunpowder charges. These included the "mother gun," which consisted of three guns lashed together, and the "rapid spear," which was a combination spear and firearm 2 meters in length with a thirty-centimeter tip and two barrels, often carried by cavalry. For armor their soldiers generally wore red coats over studded leather or quilted armor with metal studs. The men used bamboo, wooden, and iron shields and often wore helms. Shields included both large varieties for siege or missile defense and smaller varieties were paired with swords. In terms of geographic composition of forces, northern units tended to be cavalry that carried short slashing swords and short composite bows, the latter having a range of about 150 meters. Southerners tended to be infantry but preferred polearms. The Ming used both large and small firearms, preferring the former, and endeavored to attain a level of at least 30 percent firearms capability in their units. These weapons were often transported on carts with their own operators; the long distance cannon (*wei yuan pao*), for example, a gun 2 meters in length and weighing 120 catties, required three men to operate.[98]

The First Great East Asian War serves as a wonderful case study for examining the applications of firearms technology in the early modern world. While the Japanese specialized in hand-held weapons and light artillery, the Chinese and Koreans possessed larger cannon and superior naval technologies.[99] The war's conduct also emphasizes the important role played by logistics and how the different bureaucracies of China, Korea, and Japan managed warfare, providing several interesting bases of comparison with contemporary Europe. Finally it also highlights the relationship between war and society in the early modern world, for both the Japanese and the Ming came to ravage the hapless Korean populace, adding insult to the injustices done to them by their own government.

Ming imperial procession (detail). *Courtesy National Palace Museum, Taibei*

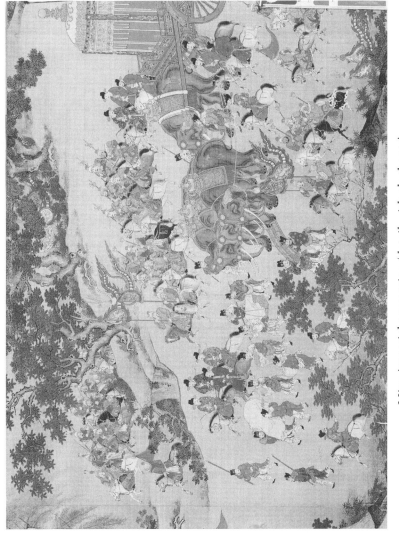

Ming imperial procession (detail with elephants).
Courtesy National Palace Museum, Taibei

馬箭

Mounted warrior. From *Chouhai tubian. Photo courtesy Amy J. Hollaway*

Archery range at Yi Sunsin's headquarters. *Author's collection*

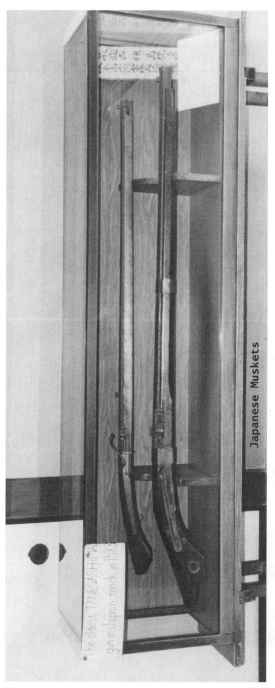

Japanese arquebuses. *Photograph courtesy Amy J. Hollaway*

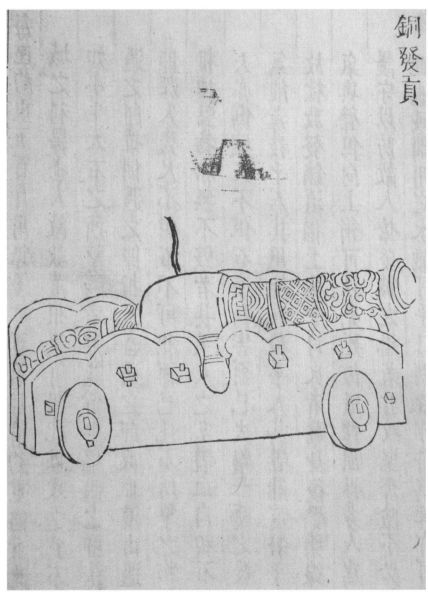

Ming cannon. From *Chouhai tubian. Photograph courtesy Amy J. Hollaway*

The Japanese in battle. From *Chōsen seibatsuki*.

3

A DRAGON'S HEAD

The Japanese Onslaught, May–December 1592

Hideyoshi distributed his battle orders around the time his castle at Nagoya was completed in the third lunar month of 1592. His new bastion was to be the staging ground for his massive army and would provide a fitting stage for the public spectacle he planned as he launched what he hoped would be the crowning achievement, literally and figuratively, of what had already been a most remarkable life. He presented his commanders with a map of Korea, each assigned provinces by color, the intent being that they would first subdue, then later survey and administer, the regions assigned to them.[1] The first division was scheduled to set forth from Nagoya on the first day of the third lunar month under the overall command of Konishi Yukinaga.

Commoners gathered to view Hideyoshi as he traveled from Osaka to Nagoya to see off the troops. Colorful flags waved in the breeze, and the shiny armor and weapons of the soldiers dazzled all who looked on. When he finally arrived at Nagoya, Hideyoshi stoked the troops' battle lust with another bombastic speech, telling them how weak their foes were and how much glory they would earn. There was also a religious dimension to the proceedings, as Matsura Shigenobu climbed atop the raised deck of his ship and bowed toward the statue of the war god Hachiman at the nearby Iwashimizu Shrine. Guns were fired, and his followers gave three great war cries. Sitting resplendent in his campaign attire, Shigenobu likened the expedition to Empress Jingū's mythical

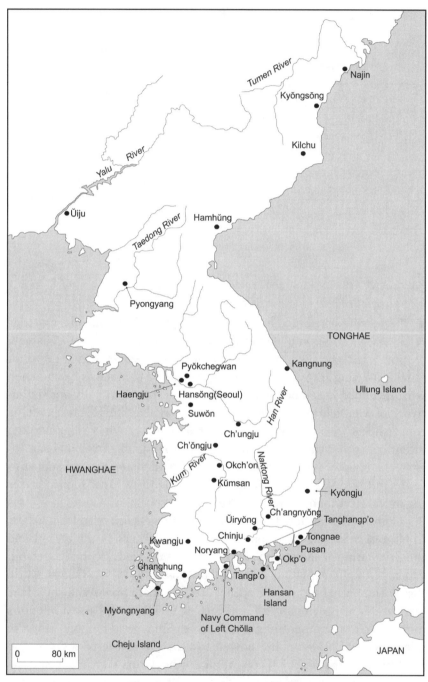

First Japanese Invasion, 1592–93

conquest of Korea. Hideyoshi was apparently delighted to hear his name linked with so august a personage. At the sound of a gong, the sails fluttered, and the vessels launched in unison, firing flaming arrows into the sky to mark their departure.[2] According to one account, the warships made waves like a pod of great whales. The armada first went to Tsushima, where final preparations were made and additional contingents raised, possibly including Koreans impressed into service by the Sō, who apparently had difficulty raising the 5,000 men required of them.[3]

Meanwhile, the Koreans continued their haphazard reform efforts as rumors of war continued to spread across the countryside. In some areas local officials surveyed and stockpiled food, water, and military supplies. Some also inspected mountain fortresses (sansóng) and made limited efforts to repair their walls. Buddhist monks were even enlisted in hauling stores to bolster the readiness of these strongpoints.[4]

As was the case in China, the usual method of dealing with major military threats was to evacuate the local populace to walled fortresses in the mountains, a strategy known as "clear the fields and strengthen the walls." Fortress walls were actually rather low, but because they were usually built on steep slopes, they presented formidable defensive works. Several weeks' or even months' worth of supplies could be stored inside. Such strongholds had served the Koreans well during previous invasions, most notably when the Mongols attacked during the thirteenth century. On the negative side, however, they still constituted a passive rather than an active defense measure. If the state evacuated most of its populace to these isolated posts, a determined invader could simply bypass them and seize more vulnerable cities, which could well be undermanned or even empty. Plus, widespread discontent over what many perceived as onerous exactions meant that few practical improvements actually occurred.[5]

The initial Japanese force under Konishi Yukinaga and Sō Yoshitoshi landed at Pusan in some 700 ships on May 23, 1592. In the vivid hyperbole of a popular Korean folktale about the war: "the sun's rays dimmed, the air filled with death, waves touched the sky, black clouds covered the water as they approached. Countless thousands of Japanese ships covered the ocean, their three-tiered masts wrapped with blue awnings, the beat of drums and battle cries shaking the waves as they came."[6]

There were supposedly 20,000 Korean troops stationed at Pusan. Chǒng Pal, the Korean commander, came forth to fight, but fearing his forces would be cut off, he effected a retreat to the city. Sō led the assault upon Pusan proper. Despite being surrounded by attackers, Chŏng, clad in his black scaled-leather armor for which the Japanese referred to him as "the black general," fought valiantly, supposedly leaving a pile of bodies around himself as he rallied his men. The fighting was especially fierce at the city's south gate, where an old veteran and his men rained arrows down upon the invaders, forcing them to turn their attentions to the north gate after sustaining heavy casualties.[7]

Sō's men subsequently took positions on the mountain behind the city and fired down upon the Koreans within, creating a breach in the northern defenses. The retreating defenders failed to maintain their ranks and were cut down easily by the Japanese. According to some Japanese sources, 8,500 Koreans were killed and 200 captured in the fighting, though the chronicles of the Matsura provide a lower figure of 1,200 dead and many captured.[8] Chŏng Pal was among those who died in the fighting; the body of his concubine, who apparently committed suicide, was found beside his corpse. Afterward a Japanese general said to the survivors, "Amongst the generals of your honorable country, the black-garbed general of Pusan was the most valiant."[9]

Simultaneously, Konishi moved to isolate the naval fortress near the harbor, which was defended by 6,000 troops. He first feigned a retreat, then returned and attacked in the middle of the night, taking the stronghold. Konishi claimed as many as 30,000 heads were taken in these initial battles, but that figure is certainly inflated.[10]

Meanwhile Japanese commander Tōdō Takatora took Tang Island, as Katō Yoshiaki led Japanese forces in a night attack that sunk forty Korean ships. Nevertheless the Japanese suffered heavy losses in these naval engagements from Korean arrows and cannon fire. While fighting was spirited in the coastal regions, farther inland the Koreans generally just shot once from their bows and retreated. As the Japanese continued to capture and destroy Korean ships, Wŏn Kyun (d. 1597), one of the naval officers of Kyŏngsang province, led his boats to Hansan Island to the southwest. Feeling the situation was tenuous even there, though, he retreated without joining battle, much like naval commander Pak Hong, whose men simply abandoned their posts and fled, scuttling many ships in the process. From Pusan Konishi and Sō headed north to take the city of Sŏsaengpo, killing its commander too in battle.[11]

Kuroda Nagamasa and the other commanders arrived the day after the initial landing. Kuroda quickly moved to seize Kimhae, which was defended both by land and sea, with upward of 14,000 troops. The

Japanese defeated the naval forces easily and peppered the city with their gunfire. Kuroda split his arquebusiers into two wings and advanced steadily, concentrating their fire in turn on one area until the defenders fell back.[12] The city's commander fled the scene, abandoning his 10,000 troops to the slaughter. The next day the combined forces of Sō and Konishi reached the fortress of Tongnae, a fortified hill just to the north of Pusan.

Upon hearing of the fall of Pusan, Yi Kak, another Korean commander, rushed east to Tongnae to assist Song Sanghyŏn in its defense, but he did not arrive in time as the forces he tried to assemble scattered, with only twenty staying with him. Song, despite being a civil official, had always been fond of military drills and pursuits and already had earned a great reputation by the age of twenty, holding successively higher posts that culminated in the governorship of Tongnae. Now he directed 20,000 poorly trained, ill-equipped men in the defense of the city from atop the south gate. Konishi's forces reached Tongnae just two days after the fall of Pusan. He called for Song to surrender and be spared, but the Korean refused, responding, "It is easy for me to die, but difficult for me to let you pass." The invaders attempted to parley again and became livid when he again refused. But Song remained calm, bowing to the north and lamenting that he could no longer honor his parents. When the young commander realized that he could not win, he cast off his armor and went to his quarters to compose a farewell letter to his father.[13]

Although the defenders held out for twelve hours, they were defeated, and 3,000 more Koreans were killed and 500 others captured. The Japanese were so impressed with Song's valor that they built a gold-plated coffin for him and his wife outside the city walls, also erecting a placard in his honor. They even executed a soldier accused of torturing Song prior to his death. For their part, the Korean government saw to it that tales of Song's loyalty spread far and wide as an example worthy of emulation. When Tongnae fell, the women inside were forced to entertain the Japanese troops, and its stores and riches were plundered and sent back to Japan along with letters to Hideyoshi proclaiming these easy triumphs. Sō's men also used captives as guides.[14]

At this point Korean resistance began to crumble altogether. Kim Su was near Chinju at the time and galloped back to defend the city and rally resistance throughout the region. Yi Il was designated touring pacification commissioner as a number of other appointments were hastily made in desperate hope of slowing down the invaders. But the

Japanese quickly seized Yangsan on May 26 as the Koreans again chose flight over resistance. Kim Su, who had been en route from Chinju to Yangsan, rerouted himself to Miryang, posting public-evacuation notices in many local districts. Retreating Korean forces burned military supplies and rations before fleeing into the mountains. Some commanders even ordered their troops to massacre other Korean soldiers for real or imagined slights.[15]

Advancing toward Kimhae, the Japanese were confronted by District Magistrate Sŏ Yewŏn, who resolved to defend the city, personally taking charge of the south gate. The invaders countered by cutting down stalks of barley around the city, using them to fill the moats and create natural ramps. After heavy fighting, another Korean commander fled in the middle of the night, and Sŏ soon followed suit. Miryang fell too, and the invaders raced toward Sŏngju. That post's commander, Cho Taegŏn, also fled in the middle of the night. Stymied by a lack of boats from crossing rivers to engage his foes, Kim Sŏngil was impeached for his failure to realize the true nature of the Japanese threat.[16]

Katō Kiyomasa seized the port of Ungchŏn on May 27 and then advanced inland toward Taegu, finding only empty, burned out stores when his men reached that city. He then moved east to Kyŏngju, killing 3,000–4,000 more in taking the city on May 31. Even commanders such as Yi Kak fled (after evacuating his concubine to safety), prompting Yu Sŏngnyong to observe that the Koreans scattered "without even one soldier daring to stand and face the enemy."[17] Yi No lamented that "whereas in ancient times soldiers would fight a hundred battles, suffer a hundred defeats and still come back for more, . . . nowadays the soldiers all scatter to save their lives and I don't know of one who suffered the hardship of death." In a later defeat at Yong'in, Japanese swords "cut through Korean defenders like hemp," and their leaders dazzled Korean commanders with their skillful coordination of infantry and cavalry using battle fans for communication.[18] Looking ahead, Konishi Yukinaga asked about the defenses of Ch'ungju, a strategic defensive point to the northwest. He was told that the city was well defended, held by a brave general and 60,000–70,000 skilled troops. Therefore Konishi decided to wait until he had marshaled all his forces and secured all the vital positions along the coast. But his men found the roads empty, for all Korean soldiers and civilians in the vicinity had already fled.

Nonetheless, there were those who still believed Korean armor and defenses could withstand Japanese swords and spears. Following the views of Sin Ip, others still felt that superior Korean height and better defensive strategies, when augmented by sufficient numbers, would provide the chance to draw in the enemy, surround them, and annihilate them in a single decisive battle. When Sŏnjo asked for more concrete plans, the king received no reply, though some suggested using natural defenses like the Han River to make their stand and augment it with more defense works. Finally, Yi Il resolved to set forth from the capital with 300 crack troops. But he was disgusted to find that his "crack troops" were made up of new recruits, young Confucian scholars who showed up to take the military examinations with pens and brushes, and lowly officers. Yi ended up departing with but sixty archers, though he optimistically anticipated raising 4,000 more soldiers en route to Sangju.[19]

Sin Ip also vowed to stop the invaders. When the king pointed out that reports thus far indicated the enemy was formidable indeed, Sin brushed aside this information, contending that he could still crush them in the proper environment and with surprise. Fearful of a rapid Japanese advance, Sŏnjo bestowed the double-edged sword of authority upon Sin and sent him in the direction of the strategically important Choryŏng (Bird) Pass, the main route to Seoul. The king felt both heartened and worried as Sin appeared before him in fine clothes on the eve of his departure.[20] Sin set forth on the twenty-first day of the fourth lunar month, just six days after the initial Japanese landing.

Sŏnjo gave orders to make a stand at Sangju, but as Yi traveled the countryside in search of recruits, he did not see even one person on the empty roads. By the time Yi reached Sangju, the local military commissioner had already fled, so he was forced to assemble a ragtag army of several hundred inexperienced peasants, who had been enticed out of hiding in the mountains only by Yi's opening up the food stores of Sangju. He organized these men into cavalry and infantry forces, sending the latter into the forests around the city to set up an ambush. Yi had reports that the Japanese troops were very close but did not believe them, even executing one informant for lying.[21]

The Japanese soon surrounded the nearby fortress of Kaenyŏng to the south. Yi arrayed his men in battle formation. People knew the enemy was close, but they feared to speak up, given what had happened to the other informant. Several Japanese scouts emerged from the forest and turned back. Soon after the Koreans saw plumes of smoke rising in the air. Yi dispatched a man to investigate, but he was shot by a Japanese soldier hiding under a bridge with an arquebus. As he fell off his horse, the Korean was beheaded and the enemy got away. The battle was joined shortly thereafter as the Japanese opened fire and Konishi moved his forces to encircle the Koreans. Yi had his men respond with arrows, but again they proved ineffective. The Japanese standards flapped in the breeze as they easily outmaneuvered their poorly trained foes. Yi decided to retreat north, but as he turned to leave, discipline, such as it was, crumbled. He got on his horse and fled, barely escaping with his life as the defeat turned into a rout, with 300 Koreans perishing.[22] Yi ditched his horse to effect his escape and staggered into Bird Pass bruised and bloody, with just a few men under his command.

One report from the battlefield exclaimed: "The enemy we faced today could be called immortal soldiers. Normal men can't stand up to them in battle." When news of Yi Il's defeat reached Seoul, residents grew very restless. To quell their misgivings, Yi Yangwŏn was appointed grand general in charge of defending the capital. Kim Myŏngwŏn was named grand marshal with orders to reinforce defenses along all routes to Seoul. The king was already making plans to flee the capital, but the Koreans heard that the Japanese were interested in negotiating, the meeting to be held at Ch'ungju, about halfway between Seoul and Sangju. Yi Tŏkhyŏng was sent to negotiate on behalf of Korea, but while en route he learned that his envoy had been killed by Katō Kiyomasa and Ch'ungju had already fallen to the invaders, so he turned around and eventually fled to Pyongyang. Despite the defeat at Ch'ungju, the king and his advisers still hoped they might be able to slow the Japanese enough to allow Ming troops time to mobilize and arrive. They issued a call to arms for all provinces to dispatch troops immediately for the defense of the capital. Meanwhile Yi Wŏn'ik was made censor in chief of Pyŏngan province in the northwest and Ch'oe Hungwŏn was made touring censor in chief of Hwanghae. The navy, which at this time was under the overall command of Wŏn Kyun, was also called into action.[23]

Some officials clamored for the king to evacuate north. Yu Sŏngnyong, however, firmly belived that the king should not abandon his capital, calling for the impeachment of anyone who suggested as much. Dozens of officials gathered outside the palace weeping and imploring him to stay. At this juncture Sŏnjo was still of a mind to stand and fight, feeling it was his responsibility to defend the ancestral altars and palaces. He suggested dispensing more funds from the treasuries to procure weapons and entice volunteers. Nevertheless, Sŏnjo lamented that most people had already fled anyhow (there were supposedly 7,000 still in Seoul), so there was no one left to fight. He added that because everyone had self-ishly pursued his own interests, the entire kingdom was now undone. Sŏnjo named his second son, Yi Hon, also known as the Kwanghaegun, his heir apparent and instructed him to rally support in the countryside.[24]

After defeating Yi at Sangju, the Japanese continued their advance toward Ch'ungju, which lay just to the north of Choryŏng Pass. But instead of meeting the Japanese at the pass, which would have been relatively easy to defend, Sin Ip decided to try and lure the enemy into the flatlands around Ch'ungju, where he hoped his cavalry could catch them in a vise and crush them with their battle flails and halberds. He ordered Yi Il and his other commanders to array their forces around the valley. Despite the amazing success of the Japanese in the first stages of the war, Sin still believed they were too short to be capable fighters. In addition, he was not impressed with their guns, which he deemed inaccurate and unreliable.[25]

One of his aides suggested laying an ambush in the pass and catching the Japanese in a crossfire. Sin rejected his proposal, saying the invaders would just withdraw and regroup, then added: "The enemy are foot soldiers and we are cavalry. If we go forth and meet them on the open plain with our iron cavalry, how can we not be victorious?" At this junc-ture Yi joined in as well: "The enemy we are facing is much stronger than the northern barbarians. Now it would be suicide to engage them on an open plain. I can see almost no chance for victory. We should take care to defend all strategic approaches to the capital." Sin was furious and replied: "You're nothing more than the general of a defeated army. You deserve to be put to death for your cowardly military blunders, but you've been allowed to live for the time being. Just wait and watch; when the enemy attacks, I'll achieve victory and you'll be able to atone for your failures." Much like his Chinese counterparts later in the war, Sin seriously underestimated the capabilities of the Japanese soldiers, possibly because his primary battle experience had been cavalry warfare along the northern frontier. Moreover Sin was outnumbered, having about 16,000 troops under his command compared with at least 19,000 on the Japanese side, though some accounts claim upward of 60,000 Japanese troops were present.[26]

As if this was not bad enough, Sin, like Yi, did not listen to his intelligence reports. An advance scout reported that the Japanese army was close, but Sin did not believe him and had the man executed so his report would not undermine morale. Since contradictory reports were coming in, the troops did not know exactly where the enemy was, and fear and uncertainty began to spread through the camp. Sin also made the mistake of arraying his forces with their backs to the Han River, though at least one modern scholar believes this may have been because he wanted to ensure the men could not flee, following a maxim put forth in many ancient Chinese military classics. One of Sin's subordinates, the same man who had favored defending the pass, wrote a letter to his son as the battle was about to be joined, lamenting the fate of the brave youths about to sacrifice their lives.[27]

The Japanese split their forces and entered the valley from all sides "like the wind and the rain." The combined force of their arquebuses and cannon shook the earth as several outlying towers quickly surrendered to the Japanese. Sin saw that he was in danger of being surrounded, so he led his men in a desperate charge against the enemy lines. But the Koreans encountered great difficulties maneuvering their horses through the muddy rice paddies in the valley. Sin and his lieutenants nonetheless fought fiercely, launching arrows into the oncoming ranks as blood streamed down their arms. According to one Japanese source, in the middle of the night Konishi employed a "flaming ox attack" (attaching burning reeds to the tails of oxen that then were sent forward to create havoc), and the Korean lines broke. Sin tried to rally his forces and break out of the encirclement, but failing in this, he plunged his horse into the river and committed suicide. He gave orders to escape to his lieutenant, who merely shot back, "How can I fear death?" With that he was enveloped in a crush of bodies. In addition to Sin, some 3,000 of his men died, either being cut down by the Japanese or drowning in the rivers. Yi managed to escape with his life. Another 100 Koreans were captured, and the city of Ch'ungju fell on June 7. According to the *Taikō-ki*, this was accomplished by a contingent of ninja who accompanied Konishi Yukinaga's forces. The ninja allegedly snuck into the city in the middle of the night and started fires, panicking those inside and affording the troops outside a chance to get close and breach the walls. Ch'ungju was one of the critical battles of the war, for a Korean victory at this point might well have checked the initial Japanese advance.[28]

Two days later a few survivors straggled into Seoul with news of the debacle. With the defeat of its two most prominent generals, all of Korea was thrown into panic. Some Japanese commanders allegedly

traveled dozens of miles without seeing a single person. The ease of
the Japanese advance actually worried Hideyoshi and his advisors. He
did not want Yukinaga to overextend himself, especially in the event
that the Ming entered the fray. The Japanese commanders held a conference at Ch'ungju to determine their next course of action, deciding
to take advantage of the momentum they had already built up and
continue toward Seoul. The commanders disagreed, however, over
how to proceed and who should be in the vanguard. Konishi argued
that he had fought the toughest battles and penetrated deepest into
Korea on his own, while Katō belittled these achievements and said
that he owed his position solely to family connections. Katō also made
light of Konishi's merchant ancestry. Finally, another commander
stepped between the two and said: "His majesty [Hideyoshi] appointed
both of you to be the vanguard leaders of his forces. His thoughts in
this regard were certainly penetrating and without fault. But now you
two are fighting like tigers. This can only help the enemy and hurt us.
Killing one another will only exacerbate things."[29] They were both
shamed by these words and stopped their quarreling, drinking together
in their tents that night.

As the Japanese held their council of war, the Korean king and his
court were having a conference of their own. They were divided as to
what to do, some advocating flight from Seoul, and others pointing out
that such an action would certainly cause the king to lose the hearts of
the masses. In addition to this, abandoning the ancestral altars in the
city would result in a loss of face. While plans called for a force of 30,000
troops to be mustered to defend the capital, barely 7,000 remained, and
many of these were already fleeing without waiting for the king's command.[30] Sŏnjo continued to hope that Korea's natural defenses might be
enough to stem the tide of the Japanese advance, and they might have
had they been used properly. But Yi advised that there was no way Seoul
could be held, and given the fact that he had seen the enemy firsthand,
his opinion was significant.

King Sŏnjo and his court agreed to flee to Pyongyang, where they
hoped to hold out until the Ming arrived. The weeping king and his
courtiers could not even look at one another when they made this
decision. As Sŏnjo had just designated Kwanghaegun his heir apparent
and sent him south, he sent his other two sons, Imhae and Sunhwa, to
the northeast. He and his officials hoped the princes could galvanize

resistance and give people hope. Imhae was sent to Hamgyŏng province in the northeast, while Sunhwa was sent to Kangwŏn, the province east of Seoul, though he later joined Imhae in the northeast.[31]

The capital had been nearly empty for days. Sŏnjo wept bitterly, saying: "For two hundred years We have resided here and nourished the state. But now for lack of a single loyal minister or righteous scholar, matters have come to this!" The people of Seoul allegedly hurled insults and garbage at the king and his retinue as they fled the city, shouting: "Our government has abandoned us! Now who can we rely on for our lives?" Rioters looted stores and burned government records, most notably those of slaves and criminals.[32] An official was detailed to defend the king's retreat and hold the capital as long as possible. Some of the few troops who actually answered the king's summons merely joined in the looting and then fled. Palaces and treasuries were also ransacked, as were the homes of civil and military officials.

It was already the fourth drum of the night when the royal procession left the city. Yi Hangbok (1553–1618) led the way with a torch through the pouring rain, which drenched the king's resplendent dragon robes. Looking back, the fleeing group of perhaps one hundred officials could see their flaming capital lighting the night sky. They staggered on for two hours before reaching Tongp'o station, Sŏnjo declaring, "The people have abandoned me!" By the time they reached the station, most local officials had already fled. The group was finally met by a retinue of a few hundred troops and perhaps fifty to sixty mounts, with insufficient rations for even this few.[33]

But while the king's plight was dire indeed, it paled in comparison to the depredations inflicted upon the common people by the Japanese invaders. Fortunately from the perspective of the historian, because so many Korean yangban lived in the countryside either as officials or because they had fallen prey to factional strife, many war diaries detailing daily life during the invasion survive. Perhaps the most illuminating of these is Ŏ Hŭimun's *Swaemirok*, which translates as "Record of a Wandering Refugee" and is derived from an allusion to a poem found in an ancient Chinese book of poetry, the *Shijing*. Although a yangban, Ŏ had never passed the civil-service examinations but still managed to enjoy a decent living from landholdings scattered across southwest Korea. Starting in late 1591, he began visiting his possessions to oversee the agricultural harvest by his slaves and to visit friends and relatives, many of whom were officials.[34] He kept a fairly detailed diary, most likely as a means of imposing some order upon a traumatic existence that otherwise seemed beyond his control. By reading his diary, one can follow his travails as he seeks aid from friends and family and nervously receives scattered bits of news about the war, providing a fascinating and often disturbing local perspective.

In the diary's early pages, Ŏ records spending most of his time drinking with friends, going to moon-viewing parties, and visiting ancient Buddhist temples. But the specter of war is evidenced in references to military requisitions and preparations. As the war begins, he had just finished visiting his youngest sister in Yŏng'am and was staying with his brother-in-law, Yi Pin, the magistrate of Changsu in North Chŏlla province. Upon receiving word of the Japanese invasion, many of Ŏ's friends and associates were hastily recalled to Seoul. Even worse, Ŏ was separated from his family in the capital and, as conditions deteriorated, could not learn if his relatives were still alive. He dispatched two servants, but because there was widespread looting and plundering by escaped slaves as well as government troops, they could gain no real information, learning only that the city had been ordered shut up even though the monarch himself had fled. Ŏ lamented that the king and his ministers had not worked together to prevent the Japanese desecration of the royal family's sacred ancestral tablets.[35] Likewise he hoped that if his relatives still lived, they had managed to save their own ancestral tablets so they could continue their filial sacrifices. He also criticized Sŏnjo for his craven abandonment of his subjects, comparing the king's flight unfavorably to that of Chinese rulers in the past.[36]

The diary is marked by Ŏ's personal reflections on the trauma of war. Early on, as he envisioned his wife and elderly mother huddled in the mountains somewhere, Ŏ states that he finally understood the pain of those tortured by war as recorded in the histories. Turning his attentions toward the military situation, he blamed the lack of adequate preparations the previous year for hastening Japan's advance. But more importantly, he observes, "even if the walls themselves are tall, castles alone are not castles. It is the people who are the bulwark." But because of Sin Ip's inept leadership and misplaced notion that he could simply overawe the enemy, all had been lost. Because Sin was too strict in his imposition of military discipline, the people had all fled. Ŏ feared that no one had the righteousness of old and without official leadership, the people were lost. As for the military registers, it was widely known that many of the names on the list were false and the lists had been neglected for quite some time. And with "all of the so-called commanders running for their own lives, how could the hearts of the common people be stabilized?" Presaging actions throughout Korea, Ŏ suggested having local officials raise armies of *ŭibyŏng*, or righteous troops, to resist the invaders since the country's decentralized military system was so unreliable.[37] He believed that a Korean restoration was possible if regular government forces acted in concert with such groups.

But even as reports of minor victories by land forces and more significant naval triumphs were trickling in, Ŏ had word of Korean troops mutinying and plundering military-supply depots for their own use. Other Koreans defected to the invaders and served them as guides and spies.[38] Even the vaunted archery skills of Korean soldiers seemed to no avail. More and more of the populace were simply melting into the forests, valleys, and hills.

It also became obvious that the invaders were interested in more than just obtaining free passage to China; they desired the human resources of Korea as well. Ŏ notes: "I have heard that the Japanese have taken young beautiful women from official families in Kyŏngsang and loaded them onto five boats. Before sending them to their country, they combed their hair and put on powder and black eyeliner; if they refused to do so [their captors] became enraged. Because they all feared death, they followed these instructions. In actuality these women had all already been raped. Those who had not been considered desirable were then repeatedly gang-raped, which is even more bitterly heart-rending."[39] Gen. Kim Sŏnggye had personally heard the following account from an escaped captive:

> At the previous day's Battle of Kŭmsan a woman was captured by the Japanese and she was taken into a grain storehouse. After the battle was over, she came out and begged for her life. They asked her where she was from but she clammed up and would not speak. But it later turned out that she was the concubine of a native of Sŏngju. But the ferocious bandits had no sense of propriety and when she tried to escape with her mother-in-law she was captured by the bandits and they quickly took her inside and gang-raped her repeatedly. She could not bear her shame and wanted to die, but was unable. Whether her mother-in-law lived or died I do not know. She was clothed only in a torn dress wrapped around her waist, with no underwear. When our soldiers lifted her dress and looked at her, they saw that her

nether regions were so swollen that she could barely walk. What cruelty! What cruelty! Someone from this district who followed the army personally saw this and related the story.[40]

Similar sentiments are expressed in another wartime account, Yi T'akyŏng's *Chŏngmannok* [An Account of Quelling the Barbarians]. Yi was an army inspector who worked under Kim Su, so he provides interesting local details from a military perspective. Like Ŏ, Yi is plagued by hunger and nightmares, constantly fretting about the fate of his aged mother. He describes his shame and disgust at Korean officials who offered up their daughters as prizes to Japanese generals in exchange for safety and appointments.[41]

But as bad as things seemed to be going for the Koreans, they had not lost hope yet. With proper equipment and good deployment under competent leaders, there still seemed to be a chance to blunt the enemy's advance. Officials early on seemed to have seized upon the idea of using small, mobile guerrilla units to harass the Japanese rear and cut supply lines. The redoubtable Kwak Chaeu (1552–1617), who raised the first guerrilla force on the peninsula, was said to have started with just four men. Together they burned three Japanese ships and quickly saw their reputation grow. Because he always wore red armor, allegedly dyed from the menstrual blood of Korean virgins, Kwak became known as the "Red General." Despite his dashing reputation, he was generally circumspect in his military operations and avoided engaging the enemy when conditions were not favorable, unlike many of his peers. In these early probing attacks, Kwak was able to observe Japanese tactics firsthand and discern some of their weaknesses. For example, he realized that the slow rate of fire of Japanese arquebuses made the enemy susceptible to good bows or crossbows, and he stressed that a combination of mobile harassment and reliance upon walled fortresses could serve Korea well. Because they never knew when he would attack, the Japanese came to dread the guerrillas and feared going into the mountains to loot and pillage. They claimed he was too fast and elusive on his white horse. In leading his men Kwak used drums and signals like the Japanese to coordinate their actions. He also urged them to simply kill the enemy and not waste time taking heads for rewards.[42]

Unfortunately, his exploits also made him many enemies at court, who feared he was insubordinate.[43] Kwak angrily burned orders that attempted to limit the scope of his operations. He also discounted the allegations of those who criticized his actions without knowing the true military situation, arguing correctly that officials in distant cities had little real knowledge of conditions in the occupied countryside.[44] While not always effective, guerrilla exploits had their value. Such operations were critical to morale early in the war and encouraged the common people and local officials alike when the situation looked bleak. Significantly, many guerrilla leaders became popular in part because they were not identified with the central government. But it did not take long for the court to tap into the reservoir of good will created by another type of local force, the righteous armies, with whom joint operations would be conducted through the fall of 1592.

Within a month the Japanese landings, the court began dispatching circular letters urging the people to unite in resisting the invaders. These were apparently transmitted from both the court-in-exile and the princes and regional military commanders. The letters are generally similar in content, detailing the various indignations inflicted by the Japanese and expressing confidence that the people will be moved to righteous and loyal action. For example, one circular issued to the Confucian scholars of Chŏnju stated that "the island bandits have despoiled the ancestral altars and are carving up twelve generations of achievement like they are fileting a fish." Although the court had been reduced to ashes, the letter continues, "all is not lost, for much territory and ample military resources remain in Korean hands." Officials were sure that if "the people could unite with one mind, the present defeatist attitude could be reversed and victory could still be achieved." After all, "the people of the province [Chŏlla] were like fathers and brothers to one another and should demonstrate their loyalty to the ruling house. Youths were to take up arms to personally avenge the deaths of their parents and the desecration of their ancestors' resting places. If the young men take the vanguard position, they would soon have the force of a raging torrent and there would be no way the enemy could resist them. As long as people put public good before private interests, all their goals could be realized." Another call to arms stressed that "it did not matter if one were a civil or military official, slave, monk, or even petty functionary, all who loved their country should join in the resistance."[45]

While Koreans attempted to rally, the Japanese moved to attack Seoul from two directions. Katō Kiyomasa took the shorter southern approach, which was protected by the Han River, while Konishi Yukinaga's contingent took the longer but less-well-defended approach from

Kwak Chaeu   Names of Guerilla leaders

Hoeryŏng

Chŏng Munbu
Kyŏngsŏng ●

Yu Eungsu
Hamhŭng ●

Yujŏng
Hyujŏng

● Pyongyang
● Chunghwa
● Hwangju **Hwang Hasu**
● Pongsan **Kim Mansu**
● Haeju

● Pyŏkchegwan
Kanghwa ● Seoul
Kwŏn Yul
● Suwŏn

● Chuksan
● Ch'ungju
● Asan
● Ch'ŏngju
● Kŏngju

Cho Hŏn ●
Yongkyu Kŭmsan ● Kaenyŏng
● Chŏnju ● Songju

Kim Ch'ŏnil
Namwŏn   **Kwak Chaeu**
Ko Kyŏngmyŏng Chinju ● Uiryŏng
● Kwangju   ● Tongnae
● Sachŏn ● Pusan

Eastern Sea

Yellow Sea

Tsushima

Iki

Chejudo

Kyushu

Guerrilla Activity, 1592–98

103

the east. A garrison had been left behind to defend the city, but as Katō approached, Kim Myŏngwŏn's men panicked and threw all the garrison's weapons into the Han. Yi Yangwŏn, who had been detailed to defend the city, also fled. When other officials got word of the Japanese approach, they told the commoners to hide in the mountains, where they would then be on their own with regards to defense.

Konishi's forces reached a nearly deserted Seoul, still burning from the riots, on June 11, prying their way in through a floodgate in the city's east wall. The Japanese were astounded to find the city gates undefended upon their arrival and suspected a trap, Konishi noting how defensible the city was. He entered through the city's great east gate, while Katō came in via the south gate, having had his men build makeshift rafts to cross the Han. The Japanese reportedly laughed as they entered the capital, saying: "Korea can be called a country without people. Her mountain passes have no soldiers. And great rivers have no defenders." Still, they remained cautious and camped outside the first night in the shadow of Seoul's great, undefended walls. When the troops finally entered the city, they looted the king's palaces and ravaged what remained of its populace.[46]

Japanese commanders then decided to divide their forces so as to occupy all of Korea as fast as possible. Katō would strike east and secure Kangwŏn and Hamgyŏng provinces while Kuroda Nagamasa and Konishi pursued the king and his court toward the Chinese border. Once the situation was stable, Kuroda would administer Hwanghae province and Konishi would control Pyŏngan province. Katō would be in charge of Hamgyŏng. Kobayakawa Takakage would govern the area around Kaesŏng, while Mōri Yoshinari would have Kangwŏn province. Kuroda would be raised to the rank of overseer of Korea and the Japanese commanders would start collecting taxes.[47]

Corpses soon filled Seoul as the Japanese initially sought to intimidate the populace. But before long, molesting the locals was strictly forbidden, and the occupiers tried to return the city to some sense of normalcy. Men were encouraged to return to agriculture and women to sericulture. A proclamation promulgated in the countryside around Seoul said that since the king had already fled and abandoned his people anyhow, they should just return to their homes and occupations and accommodate their new masters.[48]

Having received victory reports in the middle of the fifth month, Hideyoshi was ecstatic. He replied that he was soon going to Korea in person and that his generals should prepare a residence for him. It seemed that conquering Asia was going to be even easier than envisioned. From his planned trade capital based in the Chinese port city of Ningbo, Hideyoshi would then direct the conquest of India. He also sent a letter to his designated heir, Hidetsugu, telling him to be prepared to move overseas by the following year. Hideyoshi also started making arrangements for the appointment of an executive council to govern Japan when he went to the Asian mainland. But while it seems that the taikō himself really did plan on going to Korea soon, his advisors were divided. Some, like Ishida Mitsunari, supported his going to the front. Others, such as Maeda Toshiie and Tokugawa Ieyasu, opposed it. Hideyoshi initially postponed his visit on the grounds that the autumn weather would make the overseas passage perilous and scheduled his arrival in Korea for the third lunar month of 1593.[49]

He also sent a series of letters to his commanders in Korea with detailed instructions on administrative matters, assuming that the population would be easily persuaded to accept Japanese-style feudalism. As it turned out, the quotas he envisioned were unrealistic, and because so many Koreans fled into the mountains and forests, full productivity could never be realized. Soon thereafter he would receive less-heartening reports about Japanese naval defeats, but Hideyoshi remained consoled by missives from the likes of Kobayakawa Takakage, who would tell him in midsummer that Korea was all but pacified. He also apparently reveled in tales attributing Japanese successes to the favor of Hachiman, for it legitimized the divine sanction he claimed.[50]

But because the Japanese had advanced so fast, they had overextended their lines and left far too few troops behind to garrison captured towns. Even as the Japanese occupied Seoul, Korean armies under Kim Sŏngil and Yi Kwang were coming up from the south, though they pulled back before attacking. Kwak Chaeu commenced raiding coastal and riverine areas in the southeast. Although Kim drew criticism from some, they soon realized that the best strategy at this point was to set ambushes in forested mountains. Many officials also noted that proclaiming a possible Chinese intervention on their side could also embolden the populace.[51]

The day the Japanese entered the capital, King Sŏnjo and his bedraggled followers reached Kaesŏng. By then the city was already deserted. Upon hearing of the cowardice of Yi Yangwŏn, the king dismissed him and replaced him with Yu Sŏngnyong. Meanwhile Yi Kwang, the touring censor of Chŏlla province, had reportedly mustered some 70,000 troops whom he had hoped to lead north but had disbanded when he heard that Seoul had already fallen. Kwŏn Yul and Pak Kwangon amassed some 50,000 troops and attacked the Japanese at Yong'in, just south of Seoul. The defenders repulsed the initial assault and rushed forth as the Koreans withdrew, inflicting heavy losses. Kwŏn and Pak were routed the next day. Simultaneously, heavy fighting took place between the cities of Chinju and Sachŏn, with the Koreans scoring some victories and setting the stage for what would be a series of battles in the fall.[52]

Once in Kaesŏng, the king convened a council of war. Yi Hangbok, who was first royal secretary at the time, said: "There is no one here who can bail us out of this situation. The only thing we can do at this point is to send a letter to the Ming, begging them to send a relief army. That is what we must do first." Third State Councilor Yun Tusu (1553–1601) said that if the Koreans could make a stand at the Imjin River, that might buy them enough time to rally troops to retake the peninsula. He had great confidence in the sturdy men and mounts of northern Korea to help turn the tide of the war. Yun was also concerned about the damage that a Ming relief army might do to Korea, for these forces often had large Mongol contingents that enjoyed an unenviable reputation for savagery.[53]

At this point some even contemplated fleeing to China or perhaps to the more rugged terrain of northeast Korea. Yu Sŏngnyong stepped in and warned, "If your majesty steps even one foot outside of Korea, then the kingdom will no longer be yours." After much debate, Yi's point of view won out, and the Koreans decided to seek more substantial military aid from the Ming but not flee the country altogether. Inexplicably, given his earlier failures, Kim Myŏngwŏn was entrusted with overseeing the defense of the Imjin River. Yun was placed in command of a motley army of a few hundred at Kaesŏng as the king apologized for his crimes before a group of officials assembled at the city's south gate.[54] In making these and other appointments, the king now evinced a preference for Westerners, with the notable exception of Yu. Fearing the Japanese were closing in already, Sŏnjo fled Kaesŏng in the middle of the night on June 14, reaching Pyongyang on June 17.

Japanese forces under Konishi Yukinaga and Sō Yoshitoshi arrived at the south bank of the Imjin six days later. They were initially stymied because the Koreans had burned all the boats on that side of the river. The Japanese withdrew after an exchange of fire and sent emissaries to the Korean camp, ostensibly to discuss peace but in actuality to get a better look at Korean defenses. The chief envoy explained that the Japanese had no quarrel with Korea; their fight was with the Ming. He added that "the exterminator of Korea is Korea herself," further stating that if the Koreans came to terms, then the Japanese would enter into peace negotiations with the Ming, withdraw their armies from Korea, and allow the king to return to Seoul.[55] The Koreans answered that because of all the bloodshed, there could be no peace talks. Konishi dispatched another representative on June 25, but the Koreans refused to give personal audience to one of such lowly station. Receiving no further response after three days, the Japanese burned their riverside defenses and effected a false retreat, hoping to ascertain the location of fords from the anticipated Korean pursuit.

Kim Myŏngwŏn correctly guessed the enemy's purpose but could not restrain the other Korean commanders, who were eager for revenge. They led their troops across the river and straight into an ambush in the mountains. The Koreans were forced back to the river as once again their weapons proved no match for the katana. Kim could only watch helplessly from the north bank of the Imjin as the overaggressive Koreans and their commanders were either cut down on land or drowned in the river. The Japanese finally crossed the Imjin on June 27, capturing fifty boats in the process. The Koreans tried to stop them but were scattered by cannon fire. At the forefront of this battle were the Matsura, who claimed some 230 heads.[56]

Hideyoshi gave the order to send more troops to Korea on July 11, believing that Ming relief columns were on the way. Another 60,000 soldiers were readied for action. He was very concerned that his commanders should take care to secure all strategic sites and link up their camps so they could provide mutual assistance and support. He also wanted Korea quelled so that its resources could be efficiently exploited. At the time the largest Japanese camps were strung out from Ch'ungju north to Wŏnju and west toward Seoul. Hideyoshi stressed keeping supply lines open and ordered the bolstering of city defenses for possible sieges with cannons and more bows and arrows for the garrisons. The system he anticipated would never be fully realized. For one, the Koreans continued to attack major Japanese strongholds in the south, even winning a few minor engagements.[57] More significantly, after the initial shock of the invasion, the Japanese soon found themselves under almost constant attack by locally raised ŭibyŏng.

These forces were typically organized and led by local officials or Buddhist monks, the latter-led units called *sungbyŏng*. It might seem odd to find monks so heavily involved in martial activities, but it was certainly not unknown in East Asia, as seen both in the sōhei of Japan and the famed Shaolin monks of China. During the Hideyoshi invasions, Korean monk-soldiers were motivated both by patriotism and—perhaps more importantly—by the desire to improve their social position, which had sunk to its lowest level in history. Some monasteries had even been converted into stables, and monks regularly served as common laborers for the state.[58] Desperate for military aid from any quarter, King Sŏnjo summoned the monk Hyujŏng to his court-in-exile in Ŭiju in June, asking him to rally the kingdom's monks and appointing him national leader of all monk-soldiers (*toch'ongsŏp*). In his manifesto to the monks, Hyujŏng stressed loyalty to king and state, reminding them that Buddhist law is to save the world. He also attacked the civil officials for their factionalism and even criticized the military establishment for seeking aid from China. Toward the end of his exhortation, Hyujŏng said: "Only our monk-soldiers are able to save the country and deliver the people. You have been training day and night to rise above life and death. You are not burdened with families. Bodhisattvas will give you protection."[59]

His words had some effect, for more than 8,000 monks enlisted from June to December 1592. But they wanted a pledge from the king to restore their lost certifications and other privileges in exchange for their service. Although their requests were contested by some court officials, Sŏnjo eventually honored his agreement through a series of measures later in the war that, among other things, granted formal recognition to two major Buddhist sects. Monk recruitment efforts even included novice boys and girls and bore the greatest fruit in provinces where anti-Buddhist discrimination had been harshest.[60]

Exactly how many Korean guerrillas were operating at any given time is difficult to determine, though one scholar estimates the number at just over 22,000. They came from all ranks and classes of local society and were primarily concerned with protecting their families, property, and villages, though their regional loyalties gradually developed into larger loyalties to the king.[61] Like their monk counterparts, these volunteers also would agitate for exemptions from state exactions such as corvee.

Ŏ Hŭimun suggested that these small units operated best when led by local Confucian scholars and staffed entirely by volunteers, for they then fought together with one mind. He advised that each district attempt to supply the men with two horses, five bows, and nine hundred arrows. Yet contrary to popular literature on the subject, these bands did not spring from an innate sense of righteous indignation on the part of local populations or officials. In fact the government issued a number of directives to local officials to actively raise militia to harass the Japanese. These units soon became an important adjunct to conventional forces, as noted by communications discussing their use in operations designed to cut supply lines and to force the Japanese to commit more troops to the defense of certain areas like Seoul, which was increasingly infiltrated by Korean spies. In July 1592, for example, Kim Ch'ŏnil led some 15,000 ŭibyŏng in an assault on the capital but was forced to pull back to Sunan due to a lack of adequate weapons and supplies.[62]

The court tried to encourage greater enlistment in the military by promising high rewards and pay for service and distributing relief to refugees. In every district through which the king and his retinue passed, officials went out to recruit more men. Kwŏn Yul issued a nationwide call to arms on August 3. In it he also put forth a plan for restoring the country to Korean rule, calling for the defense of key points, the mobilization of additional regular troops, the organization of the righteous guerrilla armies, and use of combined land and sea forces to catch the Japanese "like fish in a trap." Kwŏn hoped victories would improve morale and render the enemy's position increasingly untenable.[63]

Nonetheless, many Korean officials fled into the mountains, burying their seals of office. The Japanese would go into the highlands and fire their guns, attempting to flush the Koreans from their hideouts like animals. Former officials helped one another in finding refuge and in spreading news of the war's progress. Although he managed to bury his family's spirit tablets and other valuables, Ŏ Hŭimun wrote of retreating deeper into the mountains beyond the roads, hacking his way through branches, and needing to stop and rest every ten steps. He and his servants eventually came to a series of caves with icy springs that had once been Buddhist grottoes. Because the structures had long since decayed, no one knew of the place, so the group outfitted it as a refuge, putting a roof of boughs over the cave entry. From here Ŏ would dispatch servants to determine Japanese troop movements. Eventually other refugees, slaves, and maidservants joined them. Because the nights were wet and chilly, Ŏ sent his servants to retrieve buried garments from one of his residences, apparently learning in the process that the Japanese were pulling back from the district. Rumors of an impending Ming counteroffensive were already circulating throughout southern Korea by midsummer, possibly influencing these troop movements.⁶⁴

Kim Sŏngil continued to attempt to rally the populace in the southeast and was infuriated to hear reports of Koreans harming other Koreans or aiding and abetting the Japanese. The mountain roads were drenched in blood, and all the homes were empty, according to Yi No, one of Kim's subordinates, whose diary of the war, *Yongsa ilgi*, is another valuable primary source. There were also grave concerns about the number of Korean civilians taken as captives by the Japanese. Reports stated that Korean natives were in fact the main suppliers of women for Japanese officers. Former officials also were especially valued as they could provide detailed information about government and local resources and possibly serve as administrators for the occupation, which apparently more than a few did. In response to such stories, Kim issued a proclamation excoriating people for rejecting the beneficence of the state and ancestral altars, noting that some did not take life and death lightly but sought to honor their responsibilities: "If the masses followed their example, could not everyone recover their old homes and lifestyles?"⁶⁵

Back at the court-in-exile, Sŏnjo's ministers maintained that their best chance lay in relying on superior Korean archery and guerrilla tactics, for it was apparent that their infantry could not stand up to the Japanese. They also advocated using locally raised units of ŭibyŏng and guerrillas led by local officials, for the people knew and trusted these men. But the greatest problems they faced were training and supplying these would-be peasant fighters. New recruits were now given crash courses in archery and military tactics. Despite the fact that Korea's best generals were already dead, officials argued that the widespread raising of fearless men would transform Korea's military and shift the balance of power. They also had a reasonable grasp of what kinds of supplies were procurable from the northern districts and repeatedly emphasized the importance of maintaining control over the Hŏnam region, Korea's south and southwest, which constituted the kingdom's major breadbasket. But good news arrived with Wŏn Kyun's report that he had sunk thirty Japanese ships.⁶⁶ More significantly from Sŏnjo's perspective, Ming envoys finally arrived to investigate the situation in Korea.

The court had dispatched an envoy to request assistance from the Ming as soon as the Japanese landed. Around the time Konishi and Sō advanced from Seoul to Kaesŏng, the pacification commissioner of Liaodong, Hao Jie, sent a report to the Ming Ministry of War stating that

Korea's situation was already critical. He said: "The Japanese bandits have reached the Taedong River so the Korean monarch and his ministers wish to escape and I fear the king and his soldiers will enter Liaodong. To prevent them would not be benevolent, but to receive them would be to invite trouble." Hao added that the invaders put everything to the torch, including hapless civilians.[67]

Wanli acted quickly upon receiving the report and ordered the officials of coastal Liaodong and Shandong to begin training for battle. The emperor knew that Korea's military was quite weak and that the king had already retreated as far as Pyongyang. He asked the Ministry of War to submit proposals and opinions regarding the situation. Because resistance had crumbled so fast, some Chinese believed the Koreans were actually in league with the Japanese. Wanli dispatched officials to Pyongyang to discern whether or not these suspicions had any substance. After meeting with Sŏnjo, these envoys were convinced of the sincerity of Korea's request and requested Wanli to send troops. The emperor resolved to send forces to Korea "without the least hesitation," but he was in a difficult position militarily because his best troops were committed to putting down Pubei's revolt in Ningxia. Thus at this point all he could do was tell the Korean king to rally his troops and fight fiercely, assuring him that Ming troops would be dispatched as soon as possible. In his letter to Sŏnjo, Wanli declared: "The Japanese have overrun Korea and I sympathize with the king's desire to flee. Relief troops have already been dispatched so I order you and the high ministers of your country to gather troops for a stout defense until you can come up with a plan for recovering your country. How, then, can you remain in fear of extermination?"[68]

Meanwhile the supervising secretary of the Ministry of War, Xu Honggang, suggested sending one civil and one military official to Korea to serve as military commissioners in charge of exterminating the Japanese. The civil official would be given the title *jinglue* and the military would be *zongdu*, and they would be considered equals in terms of power. This plan would be adopted later in the year. In addition to this suggestion, the commander of Xuanda, Xiao Daheng, memorialized that he had already assembled 16,000 troops to go to the aid of Korea but needed 100,000 liang of silver to support them. His request was promptly approved.[69]

With the defeat of Korean forces along the Imjin River, the king and his court grew increasingly restless. They contemplated retreating farther north to Ŭiju, a town on the Yalu River, the border with China. The king also discussed leaving Korea altogether and seeking refuge in China, either in Liaodong or perhaps even in Beijing. Sŏnjo said he felt caught like a fish on a hook. At this point, though, a number of ministers stepped in and urged him to remain steadfast and at least stay within Korea's borders lest he lose everything. Upon hearing that Japanese spies were caught in the forest east of the city, the king decided to flee Pyongyang. Some officials, like Yun Tusu, feared that abandoning Pyongyang would ruin the entire defense operation, for the court would lose its toehold in the country in addition to abandoning still more sacred altars and temples. Many wept as the royal carriage prepared to depart the city. The angry residents supposedly shouted, "You've abandoned us and left us for dead!"[70]

After the court left Pyongyang, Yi Tŏkhyŏng met with the Japanese commanders on a boat in the Taedong River. The meeting was actually rather cordial, as Yi chatted and drank wine with the enemy commanders. The Japanese reiterated their explanation that they had only invaded because Korea refused to join them in attacking the Ming and expressed their desire to come to some sort of arrangement. If the Koreans backed down, the Japanese would stop their looting and pillaging. Yi explained that only after the Japanese withdrew their troops would the Koreans negotiate.[71]

Yi Il, Kim Myŏngwŏn, Yi Wŏn'ik, and Yun Tusu were left behind to defend the Taedong as the king headed for Ŭiju. Sō Yoshitoshi fell back and waited for Kuroda Nagamasa to arrive with reinforcements. That night several thousand Japanese massed along the south bank of the river. Approximately 3,000–4,000 Koreans occupied Pyongyang at first, but many fled upon seeing the size of the enemy forces. The Japanese placed their guns along the south bank of the river and set up camps behind them. Kim could see the enemy from atop the walls of the city and ordered Ko Ŏnbaek to lead a daring night raid against the Japanese. This raid was initially successful, throwing the Japanese ranks into confusion and killing one hundred Japanese and capturing 133 horses. Thirty more Japanese drowned in the river as they tried to pursue the withdrawing Koreans. After this residents of an island in the river panicked and ran away. Yi ordered several dozen men to advance to the island and from there shoot at the enemy, but the troops were fearful and initially refused, advancing only after he threatened to decapitate one of them. By this time the Japanese were already approaching the shore, but using their bows, the Koreans managed to drive them back.[72]

Sō Yoshitoshi was sorely pressed and killed several men himself in this clash. Another Korean raiding party was routed, though, when Kuroda Nagamasa and his men joined the fight. Many retreating raiders drowned in the river, and those manning the boats simply bolted without waiting for the fellows. The Japanese were able to cross eventually, in part because the river was low due to lack of rainfall, and they inflicted significant casualties. The Koreans were now so panicked that they did not shoot even one arrow as the Japanese forded the river. The invaders approached the city hesitantly, not sure of what was going on within the walls. But once again Kim Myŏngwŏn abandoned his weapons, throwing them into the river, and deserted his position. The Japanese entered a nearly uninhabited Pyongyang on July 20, recovering over 100,000 piculs (6,667 tons) of grain and military supplies in the process.[73]

The king continued his flight toward the Chinese border, desperately trying to raise troops to stall the Japanese and cover his escape. He was generally unsuccessful. When the court decided to abandon Pyongyang, according to one account the mountain paths were full of men and women, young and old, fleeing for their lives. The high ministers wondered openly if their ancestors and the people of Korea would forgive them. When the king and his entourage reached the town of Anju, they were greeted by just a handful of officials, the rest of the people having hidden in the mountains. Sŏnjo issued orders to the crown prince to assume all responsibilities of the monarch. Konishi Yukinaga and Kuroda Nagamasa smelled royal blood and continued their hot pursuit of Sŏnjo. The Koreans finally managed to slow down the Japanese by wounding Kuroda in battle.[74]

By this time the northern populace was in tumult, raiding storehouses, slaughtering animals, and fleeing into the mountains. Other northwestern cities fell easily as the roads remained opened and uncontested. Isolated Korean attacks kept the Japanese off balance but did not inflict serious casualties upon them. The king again evinced his desire to flee to China but was again dissuaded by Yu Sŏngnyong. Others voiced their encouragement as well, saying the people and troops of the areas around Pyongyang were made of tougher stuff than their counterparts at Seoul—surely these sturdy folk could hold out until the Chinese arrived. But Korean officials were troubled by not knowing what was happening in the rest of the country.[75]

Reaching Ŭiju, the beleaguered monarch wept, bowed toward the west, and composed a poem: "The affairs of state cloud even the golden sun. Who can make them right?" Yu correctly realized that the best strategy for the Koreans at this point would be to capitalize on Japan's astounding success. Even the Japanese had not anticipated cutting through the peninsula so fast, and their lines were seriously overextended. Yu recognized this and advocated a number of simultaneous attacks by land and sea at points all along the Japanese lines of supply to relieve pressure on the king in Ŭiju. Meanwhile Yi Tŏkhyŏng was sent on a fast horse to China to apprise the Ming of events and speed their relief. Although this was the apex of their power in Korea, the Japanese knew as well as the Koreans that their position was tenuous. Japanese commanders held no doubts that the Ming were going to respond. Moreover, despite Hideyoshi's boasts to the contrary, the Japanese appear to have had a healthy respect for Ming military prowess. Perhaps had they known about Ningxia, Japanese commanders might have agitated for a quick advance into China.[76] As it was, they simply tried to consolidate their immense gains and waited for the Ming to arrive.

One thing the Japanese did not anticipate was the surprising naval prowess of the Koreans under Adm. Yi Sunsin. Often compared to his British contemporary Sir Francis Drake, Yi stands out as one of the greatest figures in Korean history. He is portrayed as an infallible hero, one whose greatness was foretold even when he was still in the womb. Yi reportedly liked to mimic battles as a youth, and even though he possessed superior literary talent and would have been a great Confucian scholar, he always preferred the sword to the pen. His loyalty, valor, and filial piety were considered above reproach. But not all the primary sources treat Yi in such a hagiographic fashion. Later Korean writers, however, tend to dismiss less-glowing accounts of Yi as being the result of factional disagreements, ignoring the fact that by doing so they themselves are guilty of similarly biased historiography.[77]

Yi Sunsin received separate reports from Wŏn Kyun and Pak Hong on May 25 informing him that the Japanese had landed at Pusan. Yi immediately wrote an urgent letter to the king, telling him of the situation and outlining his plan of action, which was no more than putting all coastal forces on alert and conscripting more men. Hearing that the Japanese "were occupying our large coastal fortresses one after another, and breaking deep into our heartland," he proclaimed that "my heart is rent with anger and grief. Now is the time for all loyal minded subjects to offer themselves courageously to the state in order to wash out this national disgrace."[78]

The admiral was temporarily held in place by the fact that he had not received an official order to attack. Yi advised, "As the enemy is boasting of his numerical strength of five hundred vessels, we must make surprise attacks on them, displaying our martial spirit and shooting power in order to strike deep terror into their hearts and make them tremble before us."[79] He felt that the forces under his command were too scattered and thus too weak and thus ordered all local officials to bring their ships to his naval base, situated in a key area between Chŏlla and Kyŏngsang provinces. Soon thereafter Yi received a letter from Wŏn Kyun relating the news that his own station had fallen and that he lacked the strength to oppose the invaders. Yi sought help from Namhae, but that city had already fallen, as one of Yi's men reported:

Namhae has become a deserted town—not a human soul in the government buildings or private houses, no smoke in the chimneys, warehouses and armory doors flung open, with food grain scattered and weapons stolen. When I asked the remaining door-keeper what the matter was, he answered that when the enemy attack became imminent, the soldiers in town, hearing shouts of "enemy coming," all ran away, preceded by the magistrate and the commandant, who have disappeared and cannot be found. There was another man who ran out from the south gate, carrying a bag of rice and a bunch of arrows on his back. This man gave me some arrows.[80]

The admiral lambasted his cowardly land counterparts and ordered that all stores be burned if they were abandoned so at least to keep them out of enemy hands. Yi also gave orders to tighten military discipline and execute military fugitives. He and Wŏn Kyun finally sailed out together to meet the Japanese fleet on June 9 with some eighty-five vessels. Yi rounded up other local forces and their ships, and the combined forces sailed at dawn on June 16 to meet Japanese units under Tōdō Takatora at Okpo in the islands off the southeastern coast of Korea, not far from Angolpo. The battle was a resounding Korean victory. Yi reported that the Japanese "threw their stores overboard and jumped into the water to swim to the shore, dying in blood, while the survivors scattered over the rocky cliffs, creeping away to save their lives." His fleet destroyed twenty-six Japanese ships. Afterward "the flames and smoke on the sea covered the skies while the fleeing Japanese hordes scurried into the forests with shrieks of fear."[81]

Over the next few days, Yi and his commanders continued to harry the Japanese, sinking dozens more ships and forcing other crews to abandon their boats altogether and flee inland. Yi was moved by the refugees he encountered and ordered relief distributed as widely as possible. Many refugees also provided valuable information concerning enemy positions. Yi and Wŏn learned at this time that King Sŏnjo was evacuating to the northwest, an act that filled the admiral with sorrow and indignation. In his reports to the court, Yi listed the items recovered from Japanese ships, including rice, bows and arrows, clothing, red-black armor, iron helmets, horse manes, gold crowns, golden fleece, feather dress, feather brooms, shell trumpets, a variety of curious jeweled items, battering rams, iron-studded ropes, and guns.[82] He forwarded some of the items, along with some Japanese ears, to the court for inspection.

Yi then returned to base to allow his men time to rest and recuperate. He engaged the Japanese again on July 8, meeting the enemy near Sachŏn. Looking up at the cliffs above the fortress, Yi could see hundreds of Japanese soldiers stretched out like a long snake from eleven boats moored by the shore. With the tides going out, he realized that his vessels could not get in close to use artillery, so he resolved to feign a retreat and try to lure the Japanese out to sea. Wŏn wanted to engage the enemy immediately as they put out in pursuit of the Koreans, but Yi held him back until the time was right. According to the admiral's account: "I ordered all the captains to dash forward all at once; our ships poured down arrows and cannon balls like a hailstorm. They crushed the enemy, forcing him to scatter and flee in all directions. Those hit by the arrows alone numbered by the hundreds, and countless heads of the enemy were cut off." Yi was shot in the shoulder during this battle, the bullet allegedly penetrating two inches into his flesh. Undaunted, he continued to direct the battle to its successful conclusion. When the engagement was over, he had the bullet removed, acting as if nothing had happened.[83]

Yi then led his fleet southeast to Tangpo to engage the Japanese fleet there under Cmdr. Kurushima Michiyuki, who rode in a high chair on an ornate flagship, making him a visible and inviting target. The Japanese vessels were gathered close to shore in a small harbor and

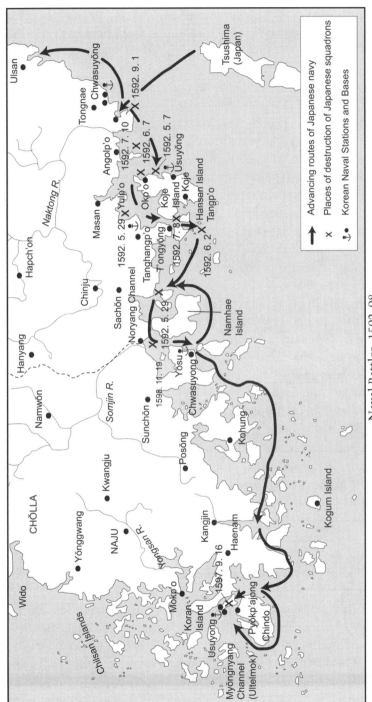

Naval Battles, 1592–98

Legend:

↑ Advancing routes of Japanese navy

X Places of destruction of Japanese squadrons

⚓ Korean Naval Stations and Bases

Map labels:

Tsushima (Japan)

Ulsan

Chwasuyŏng

Tongnae

X 1592. 9. 1

Angolp'o

1592. 7. 10

X 1592. 6. 7

1592. 5. 7

Usuyŏng

Koje

Masan

Yulp'o

Okp'o X

Koje Island

Hansan Island

Tangp'o

Naktong R.

Hapch'ŏn

Chinju

Sach'ŏn

Tanghangp'o

T'ongyŏng

1592. 5. 29

1592. 7. 8

1592. 6. 2

Noryang Channel

Namhae Island

Hanyang

Sŏmjin R.

X 1592. 5. 29

1598. 11. 19

Yŏsu ⚓

Chwasuyŏng

Namwŏn

Sunch'ŏn

Posŏng

Kohŭng

CHŎLLA

Kwangju

NAJU

Yŏnggwang

Yŏngsan R.

Kangjin

Haenam

Kogum Island

Wido

Chilsan Islands

Mokp'o

Koran Island

Usuyŏng ⚓

1597. 9. 16

Pyŏkp'ajŏng

Chindo

Usuyŏng ⚓

Myŏngnyang Channel (Ultelmok)

117

amid a number of islets. The consequent battle is especially notable because it marked the first use of the famed turtleboats against the Japanese.[84] Yi himself left this account of the turtleboat in action:

> Previously, foreseeing the Japanese invasion, I had had a Turtle Ship specially built with a dragon's head, from whose mouth we could fire our cannons, and with iron spikes on its back to pierce the enemy's feet when they tried to board. Because it is in the shape of a turtle, our men can look out from inside, but the enemy cannot look in from outside. It moves so swiftly that it can plunge into the midst of even many hundreds of enemy vessels in any weather to attack them with cannon balls and flame throwers. In this voyage our Flying Squadron Captain rode this Turtle Ship in the very van of the fleet. I commanded the Turtle Ship to dart into the enemy formation and to shoot the guns "Heaven, Black, Earth, and Yellow," which it did. Then the Japanese robbers poured down fire like hail from their positions on the mountains, at the foot of the hill and on the boats. In the midst of the battle, I plainly saw that some Korean traitors, mixed in with the enemy's rank and file, also shot at us. This made me very angry. I ordered my oarsmen to row my Flag-Ship at top speed, and dashed to the foremost front, hammering the enemy vessels; then my officers and ships' captains rallied around me and hurled cannon balls, long arrows, winged arrows, fire arrows, and other death dealing missiles from big guns "Heaven and Earth," while our battle cries shook the land and sea. Finally shrieks and death agonies were heard from the enemy vessels as their warriors fell dead or ran away with the wounded on their shoulders in countless numbers. The survivors pulled further up the hill and dared not come forward to fight.[85]

Yi wanted to pursue the Japanese inland, but he was apprehensive about their numbers and did not want to suffer serious losses in the dark forest after gaining another important victory at sea. The admiral suffered yet another flesh wound during this battle. Kurushima died, though sources differ as to whether he was killed and beheaded by the Koreans or if he committed seppuku. Some twenty-one additional Japanese vessels were sunk at a nearby wharf the next day, the turtleboats again inflicting the majority of the damage. The Korean fleet proceeded to Tanghangpo, where they faced twenty-six Japanese vessels of varying size. Given what had happened in the previous few days, Yi did not want to give the enemy the opportunity to flee to the shore. Therefore, after an initial exchange of fire, he effected another false retreat, which lured the Japanese farther out into the bay, allowing the Koreans to encircle them. All but one of the Japanese vessels were sunk, and many crewmen were cut down as they tried to escape to shore. A number of Japanese made it to the last warship and with it tried to escape the next day, only to be smashed by the Koreans. According to Yi's report, the commander of this vessel sustained ten arrow wounds before falling dead. The Koreans recovered military lists, armor, spears, swords, bows, gun barrels, tiger skins, and horse saddles from the wreckage.[86]

Korean success in these battles rested in the superior firepower and maneuverability of the turtleboat. Although still a point of debate, according to most modern reconstructions, a turtleboat was about 35 meters long, with a 9-meter beam, and measured about 2.5 meters from bottom to deck. Bulwarks on each side were fitted with ports for guns and cannon. The turtle's head was about 1.5 meters long and 1 meter wide and filled with a combination of sulfur and saltpeter, which when mixed produced a smokescreen. The vessel contained twenty-four cabins, five of which were used for powder magazines, arms, and gear; the rest were used for sailors. It had ten oars to a side and probably carried forty or more cannon, one or two heavier pieces, fire arrows, and assorted bombs and incendiaries to be thrown by the crew.[87]

But it was not just the turtleboat that outperformed Japanese naval vessels. The square sails used by the Japanese were not nearly as effective as Chinese and Korean fore-and-aft sail designs, making them far more maneuverable than their counterparts. The diversity and sophistication of the kingdom's naval defenses, at least on paper, is a testament to the importance Koreans had always placed on the sea for their livelihood. It also speaks to the peaceful relations Korea had long enjoyed with Ming China. Because the Chinese posed no active military threat, there was scant need for Korea to outfit and equip a massive army. They therefore only maintained land forces sufficient to deal with the relatively minor threat posed by the Jurchen tribes of Manchuria.

As Yoshi S. Kuno observes with respect to the Japanese, "On land they fought like tigers but on the sea, when engaged in naval battles with the Koreans, they could fight no better than a tiger could fight in the water against a shark."[88] But Hideyoshi needed to secure the sea lanes to transport supplies and troops if his invasion was to succeed. Thus other Japanese naval commanders, Kuki Yoshitaka, Katō Yoshiaki, and Wakizaka Yasuharu, hastened to Pusan and prepared to deal a death blow to the Korean navy. They started by sending small probing missions through the waters along the southern and southeastern coasts. The main fleet then sailed into the narrow straits of Kyŏnnaeryang, hoping to catch the Koreans off guard. Unknown to them, however, the Yi Sunsin had anchored his fleet at Tangpo, just on the other side of an isthmus. A cow herder reported the presence of the Japanese fleet riding at anchor, and the next morning, August 14, 1592, the Koreans moved out for a fateful battle.

In light of what had happened to other Japanese naval commanders, it is puzzling how Wakizaka Yasuharu and his cohorts made the same mistakes at the Battle of Hansan Island. Two possible explanations are their general lack of experience in naval matters and the lack of a unified naval command. According to Yi's account, the Koreans found some eighty-two Japanese vessels lined up in a long row, but the channel was so narrow and rocky that the Korean ships could not close in to engage them. The admiral again adopted the tactic of feigning a retreat to draw the enemy out into the open bay. This time, however, Yi ordered his men to array their ships in his famous "Crane Wing Formation," whereby the Korean fleet turned and flanked the mass of Japanese ships that set out in pursuit and annihilated them. The exact figures vary according to the account, but Yi reported that only fourteen Japanese warships escaped destruction. About four hundred Japanese managed to make it ashore and escape into the hills, the weary Koreans deciding not to chase them. This engagement, called the "Salamis of Korea" by Park Yune-hee, was crucial in denying the Japanese control of the seas and in bolstering Korean morale. Yi followed his great victory by engaging another fleet of forty-two Japanese ships at the port of Angolpo. This time the Japanese refused to be lured out to sea, so Yi had to divide his men into small assault parties to attack the enemy vessels. In the end the Japanese lost virtually all their ships and suffered heavy casualties, while the Koreans did not lose a single boat, though more than one hundred Koreans were killed or wounded in the battle. The Koreans took more than 250 enemy heads and captured considerable numbers of weapons and provisions.[89]

Emboldened by these victories, Yi resolved to lead a direct assault on the enemy position at Pusan. The Japanese, meanwhile, had greatly increased the size of their navy but confined its activities to either transporting supplies from the homeland or conducting night raids on isolated Korean villages, being loathe to engage the Korean navy in direct combat. Yi first withdrew to his base at Yŏsu and remained busy training and strengthening his navy. By the time he sailed for Pusan on September 29, his fleet numbered some 166 warships. Yi was joined at sea by another fleet led by Wŏn Kyun. They soon learned that nearly 500 Japanese ships were anchored in Pusan's harbor. The combined Korean fleets smashed four Japanese vessels in the vanguard and then sailed into the harbor, guns blazing. They were met by a furious counter-attack, which included men raining arrows, musketballs, and cannonballs down on the ships from the surrounding hills. More than 100 Japanese vessels were sunk, and countless Japanese were killed. Yi related that his men were so busy destroying enemy boats that they had no time to cut off enemy heads. Again the admiral decided not to pursue the fleeing Japanese on land because the Koreans had no horses and the fortifications at Pusan, which he described as being like a beehive, were particularly formidable. Yi observed that many enemy vessels appeared to be heading south. He considered destroying all these survivors but decided against it, fearing the Japanese would wreak even greater devastation on the Korean people if their escape route was cut off. The admiral decided to wait for a major land offensive to drive the enemy out.[90]

Yi fell back to his base on October 6 and devoted himself to support duties for the duration of the winter. His memorials include a number of references to the king's detached palace at Ŭiju as he forwarded weapons, paper, grain, and other items to the court, in addition to progress reports on the war. These items were transported by land and by sea, the latter indicating that Yi's military operations had indeed helped the Koreans a great deal by allowing them to maintain naval supply lines and pre-venting the Japanese from doing the same. Yi also enlisted the aid of monk-soldiers and commissioned them to garrison local fortresses and take up the battle against the Japanese on land.[91]

Back in Pyongyang, Konishi Yukinaga told his generals that he was ready to cross the Yalu. He even sent Sŏnjo a letter in which he stated: "I know you are a great king. How is it that matters have come to this?" But by this time Sŏnjo had learned that the Ming were alarmed by the news of Japan's rapid advance and were preparing a punitive expedition. This force of course was meant not only to protect its tributary state but also to

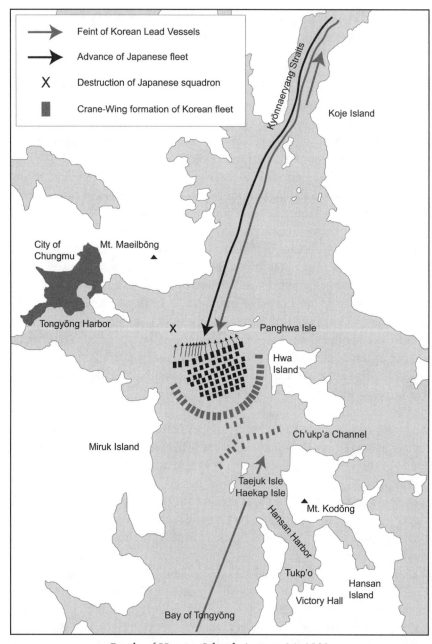

Battle of Hansan Island, August 14, 1592

defend its own border. As Song Yingchang adroitly pointed out at the time, "In defending Korea, we are really just looking out for ourselves."[92] Still, modern scholars are mistaken to cynically underestimate the importance of the tributary relationship and Ming feelings of obligation toward Korea. Chinese officials demonstrated their anger that the Japanese did not realize that the Ming defense umbrella extended not only over Korea but also over Ryukyu and the island countries of the south seas.

The Koreans initially asked for 100,000 Ming troops. While recognizing that Korea was strategically important and had to be defended, the Chinese were in no position to send that many troops at the time. First, most of the better Ming units and commanders were still battling Pubei in Ningxia. Second, despite the amazing success of the invasion to this point and the depredations the wokou had inflicted on the Ming earlier in the century, the Chinese had little regard for Japan's military capabilities. The Ming did not think they would need 100,000 troops to drive the Japanese out of Korea. Therefore they decided on a stopgap measure, dispatching the vice commander of Liaoyang, Zu Chengxun, and Mobile Corps Commander Shi Ru at the head of a mere 3,000 troops to investigate the situation around Pyongyang and drive the invaders out of the city if possible. Zu was a veteran commander with a long record of achievement earned battling the Jurchens and the Mongols along the northern frontiers.[93] He had nothing but contempt for the Japanese and figured that even his small force would be enough to oust them from Pyongyang.

The first Ming response was to send 20,000 liang of silver to help pay for soldiers and supplies. They also ordered Luo Shangzhi to lead 3,000 southern troops to guard the Yalu and detailed Zha Dashou to patrol the area with 3,000 additional infantry. Ceremonial garments were sent to Sŏnjo, presumably to allow him to maintain himself in some semblance of state while in exile. More importantly, weapons, including firearms, were also sent to the Korean court-in-exile. Yi Tŏkhyŏng then went to the quarters of Hao Jie and implored him for help, refusing to leave until Hao pledged to send 5,000 troops to the aid of Korea.[94]

Shi Ru led a force of 1,029 men and 1,093 mounts into Korea on July 23, 1592, as the vanguard of Zu Chengxun's command. When Zu arrived at the head of an additional 1,319 men and 1,529 mounts, he consulted with Yu Sŏngnyong, who told him the districts around Ŭiju could support an army of 10,000 for one month. Zu reassured Yu, telling him:

"Certainly we will come to the aid of our small neighbor. China and Korea are as close as lips and teeth." Morale improved markedly at the sight of the Chinese commander and his troops, though the Koreans were disappointed at the size of the relief column. Zu estimated that the Ming could wipe out and expel the Japanese in one decisive battle, boasting that a million Japanese could not stand up to the force the Chinese could muster. Yu suggested detailing a Korean general to guide the expeditionary force to Pyongyang. He hoped the Ming would be able to link up with loyalist forces in the vicinity, and when they captured Pyongyang, that they would also capture the supplies and equipment there, enabling the allies to launch a counteroffensive. Zu was warned that the Japanese possessed firearms in abundance, but he remained unconcerned. Over wine the night before taking his men into battle, Zu said, "Certainly Heaven will favor me with a great victory."[95] Shi and Guo Mengzheng led 1,000 men to scout ahead. Finding nothing, they waited for Zu's column to catch up.

Zu made a sacrifice to heaven, saying that he would certainly see the Japanese commander there, and advanced toward Pyongyang in three columns on August 22. The Chinese were ignorant of the terrain but pushed on confidently. Zu and Shi Ru found the gates of Pyongyang wide open. Despite the oppressive gloom of dawn and heedless of danger, the Ming galloped through the Seven Star Gate, only to be caught in a wicked crossfire from Japanese arquebusiers perched in the towers and tall buildings, emerging "like ghosts in the night." The vanguard of 300 troops, led by Shi, fought bravely but were confronted with overwhelming numbers. Compounding matters for the Chinese, rain fell very hard that day, and their horses could not maneuver in the city's narrow, muddy streets. The attackers and their mounts were riddled with bullets and arrows. Some sources state that barely a few dozen of the 3,000 Chinese survived. Shi was killed by one of the Matsura retainers, and Zu barely escaped with his life, the Japanese pursuing the defeated Ming for ten li (nearly four miles).[96]

Upon his return to Ŭiju, Zu contended that he had killed many Japanese, but the outcome had not been favorable. He went back to Liaodong to await the arrival of more troops and to report his defeat to the throne. Some Koreans, however, thought that Zu was frightened by his defeat and wanted nothing more to do with the Japanese. Both sides pointed fingers, the Koreans accusing the Chinese of overconfidence and poor planning, and the Chinese accusing the Koreans of cowardice. Zu complained that he was frustrated by poor visibility that greatly hindered his ability to direct the fighting. As for the mud and rain, Korean observers claimed that some of the horses sank to their stomachs in the city streets. Zu pledged to attack again as soon as more troops arrived, particularly southern troops, who had firearms and were skilled in battling the Japanese as a result of Qi Jiguang's training methods. He consoled the Koreans by saying that 6,000 southern troops armed with guns were already on their way.[97] Oddly enough, the Japanese were shaken by the battle as well, for they correctly assumed it was but the first probing action. They did very little raiding in the vicinity of Pyongyang after the attack, though Japanese atrocities continued elsewhere.

Wanli and his court were shocked and alarmed by the news. But there were still some doves at the court who argued against Ming intervention, using the example of their failed involvement in Vietnam some two centuries earlier. Others, however, contended that the present situation was far different. First, Korea was friendly. Second, the peninsula was much closer, only 1,200 li (413 miles) from the Yalu to Seoul. A large army could be supplied and reinforced by both land and sea, and supplies could reach the front in just three to four days. Siding with the hawks and expressing his indignation at Korea's plight, the emperor resolved to send troops immediately, encouraging Sŏnjo to steel his resolve and not lightly cast aside what his ancestors had bequeathed to him. Assuming his role as "the earthly ruler who possesses Heaven's Mandate and commands the myriad barbarians," Wanli promised that he would mobilize other tributary states like Siam, the Philippines, and the Ryukyus to help Korea. Together they would supply some 100,000 troops that, when combined with those of the Ming, would hit the Japanese "with the force of Mount Tai."[98]

In deciding to send military aid to Korea, Emperor Wanli was both fulfilling his role as the tributary father in his relationship with King Sŏnjo (and the Japanese for that matter) and asserting his military and political primacy in Asia. Indeed Wanli "outstripped his ministers in initiative" and "acted quickly to maintain authority and discipline" in the face of partisan bickering by his court. The emperor's promise of mobilizing military aid from faraway Siam and other states, despite the fact that he would later reject such aid when it was proffered, can be viewed as a pointed and direct rejoinder to Hideyoshi's own boastful claims that he had compelled the world to join his cause.[99] These conclusions are born out by Wanli's own words in an imperial decree he issued concerning military aid for Korea:

For generations you have been our Eastern neighbor and you have always been docile and obedient. Your gentry take pleasure in learning and culture. I heard that your nearby land had been invaded and was being plundered by the rapacious Japanese villains and that your capital city has been looted and Pyongyang has been occupied, forcing your people to scatter near and far and I was deeply disturbed. And now Your Majesty has fled for the Western coast and is seeking refuge among the rustics. You must now focus your attention to the task at hand strengthen your resolve. For, as soon as I heard the news yesterday, I ordered the border officials to begin mobilizing troops to come to your aid. I will also dispatch a high civil and a high military official to act in concert. They will assemble 70,000 crack troops from the various defense commands around Liaoyang, which will be sent forth to assist you in chastising the [Japanese] bandits and in conjunction with your own country's men, they will catch the enemy in a vise and annihilate them. Furthermore, I have issued imperial commands to the tributary kings of the myriad states in all directions so that they too can assist in helping with this nasty business. I have also issued an order to the various coastal garrisons of the southeast and promulgated an edict to countries such as Siam and Ryukyu to assemble an army of 100,000 to join us in attacking Japan and dislodge them from their nests. . . . Now Your Highness must focus upon maintaining what your ancestors have bequeathed to you. How can you just lightly cast it all away? Now you must exert all your energy in the business of saving your state and restoring its prestige and you should order all your civil and military officials and ordinary people to likewise exert themselves to the utmost. For if Your Majesty's mind is open and you rectify your past transgressions, then you will be able to recover the territory that you have lost. The masses will face this calamity out of filiality to their father, and the ministers of your country, recognizing your righteousness, will certainly all look up to you. Your Majesty will thereby regain the respect you once had.[100]

This passage is one of the clearest articulations of the Ming imperial perception of the Japanese invasion and its larger ramifications. It also provides much insight into Wanli's state of mind and personal agendas. Other memorials and letters to Sŏnjo find Wanli sermonizing on the debilitating evils of factionalism and royal corruption and laziness, the very things he himself was often charged with facilitating. But in Korea Wanli could easily be seen in the role of savior, a role he may well have enjoyed. According to Sin Kyŏng's account, when King Sŏnjo summoned his officials to the riverbank and read Wanli's words, they all cried tears of joy.[101]

This is not to suggest that there was no element of self-interest involved. The Ming also were concerned about their own coastal security and how best to bolster their own territorial defenses. Censor Peng Haogu recommended attacking the Japanese in Korea, arguing that fighting them along China's coasts was only the second-best alternative, and waiting for them to get into China itself was equivalent to no plan at all. Other officials, recalling the wokou raids of the 1550s and 1560s, warned that China's southeast coast must be protected at all costs. Some advocated intercepting the Japanese at sea, echoing the sentiments of commanders from the marauder era. Others were in favor of land-based operations or even arming peasants on offshore islands to serve as a first line of defense. Officials also disagreed over whether local troops or mercenaries recruited from elsewhere should be used, cost and effectiveness again being among the variables considered.[102]

Regardless of the strategic question of where to fight the Japanese, officials did discuss or institute specific coastal-defense measures. Watchtowers would be erected every three li (one mile) along the coast to guard against incursions. Each would have a lookout platform and house twenty soldiers. Ten volunteers would be recruited from each local district for shore-patrol duty. Two cannon were to be placed every li along the coastline, with a company of men to guard and operate them, six men per fifty being assigned to such duty. Other men were to be given separate responsibilities for maintaining equipment, signal fires, and the like. Coast watchers would use smoke signals in the event the enemy was sighted. Stoneworks were to be improved to make more effective use of cannon in defensive roles, though as most towers would be constructed of wood, defense officials assumed that the localities could shoulder the burdens of cost. Firearms training and distribution was also considered critical. Ideally 50 percent of all Ming units would

have guns. Officials also pointed out that the Japanese would have difficulty landing on China's rocky coasts and that superior Chinese cannon,
such as the grand general, the crouching tiger, or the caitiff exterminator,
could be used to devastating effect in such environs, provided that production was stepped up and the artillery could be deployed. This last
was especially crucial because many officials recognized the skill of
the Japanese as swordsmen and doubted that local militia could resist
them in close-quarters combat on land.[103]

Tianjin, the port city for Beijing, was the linchpin of the Ming
northern coastal defenses. An interlocking network of armies totaling
18,000 troops would be stationed at key points, with about 3,000 others
operating as mobile reserves. Although they were more expensive as
mercenaries, southern troops were considered better at fighting the
Japanese and were thus in high demand. The coordinator of northern
coastal defenses, Yang Hao, requested additional funds and mounts to
maintain supply lines and to ensure that his troops received their pay
in a timely fashion.[104]

Demonstrating the Ming penchant for bureaucratic specificity, all
items were to be made to prescribed standards and with certain materials. For example, elm, willow, and locust trees were specified for the
construction of military carts. Even plank width was noted. Such carts
were also supposed to be reinforced with iron. Bamboo spears and hard
ironwood cudgels were to be shipped north from southern regions.
Ming memorials even contained detailed formulas for the best composition of gunpowder.[105]

There were some in China who still suspected the Koreans of being
in league with the Japanese, but as Sŏnjo said, "If we are acting as guides
for the Japanese, then how come our three capitals are in the hands of the
invaders?" Shi Xing wanted to go to the front himself as commander, but
Wanli would have none of it, appointing Song Yingchang as military
commissioner of Jizhen, Baoding, and Liaodong in October and ordering
him to begin preparations for a major punitive expedition. The emperor
also put a bounty of 10,000 liang of silver on the heads of Hideyoshi and
Keitetsu Genso and smaller bounties, along with hereditary military
titles of nobility, to be bestowed upon anyone who took the heads of
other Japanese commanders.[106]

Song was to proceed to Liaodong at once with Wu Weizhong and
3,000 southern troops along with 10,000 Liaodong soldiers. Another
26,000 troops were to be raised from other northern-defense commands

Coastal Ming China

and still more from more-distant provinces. For the short term the Ming would send two divisions of crack troops with weapons and supplies, though the Koreans were expected to help with arming, supplying, and especially feeding the soldiers. As was his style, Wanli vested Song with sweeping power to act when and how he saw fit.[107]

Song took his assignment very seriously, calling for the troops to immediately begin constructing 360 military carts. He estimated that he would need 72,000 cannon of various types, 27,000 bows and cross-bows, thousands of shields of varying sizes, several million arrows and crossbow bolts, and as much gunpowder and bullets as possible. Soon thereafter Song requested another 200,000 liang of silver to buy mounts and issued production orders to factories in Tianjin, Yongping, and Liaodong for more transport carts, large mobile cannon, small cannon, reliable field pieces, crossbows, blankets and covers, crossbow bolts, bullets, and various and sundry other military supplies. He pressured Shi Xing when men and materials did not arrive in a timely fashion.[108]

One is struck by the emphasis placed upon logistics and the acumen of Chinese and Korean bureaucrats in estimating such things as transport times and wastage rates.[109] In his requests Song included suggestions for transportation routes, cost estimates, and observations about the relative wealth and poverty of different parts of the empire pertaining to their ability to raise and deliver supplies. He also stressed local interests. In asking for supplies from the northeast region of Dengzhou, for example, Song emphasized the gravity of the situation, the national-interest angle, and the proximity of the region to Korea.[110] The decentralized nature of the Ming accounting system meant that multiple government agencies were responsible for procuring supplies and equipment for military operations. Even soldiers' pay was allocated from both the Ministries of Revenue and War.

But while Song continued to receive promises of men and materiel, their actual arrival was another matter. Song himself was partly to blame, for he stressed pacing the troops so they would not be exhausted upon their arrival at the front. Arrangements were made to quarter different units in various garrisons as they traveled across China, with some being detailed to specific locales for specialized training in things like firearms tactics or coastal warfare. There were also efforts to bring the empire's best commanders to the theater so they could train troops upon their arrival. Song continued to badger his counterparts to hasten their efforts to get their men into position for the projected winter offensive, hoping to achieve a troop strength of just under 50,000.[111]

Despite his considerable efforts, Song came under fire from impatient colleagues. He submitted his resignation in response to the charges of one, Guo Shi. Wanli forcefully rejected the resignation, reprimanding both officials in the process:

> As for you, Song Yingchang, you have already accepted the order to become Military Commissioner [of Korea], but now on account of one word from Guo Shi, you think you can avoid your prior responsibilities. Who will then take responsibility for defending our coasts and borders? Are a few meaningless words enough to make you shirk your responsibilities to the Court? What will become of discipline under the state if no one takes his assignments seriously? The situation with the Japanese is paramount. You, Song Yingchang, must be ready to move today. The nine ministers and supervising secretaries here [in Beijing] have proven unable to reach an accord; from now on there is no need to debate this further. In selfishly harboring his own schemes Guo Shi has unnecessarily hampered the affairs of state, so he is hereby demoted and sent to the frontier. Anyone else who wishes to add another gratuitous remark to this confusion will be sent off with him.[112]

But the appointment of Song Yingchang would not be the most fateful decision made at this time. At the request of Shi Xing, an obscure trader named Shen Weijing (fl. 1540–97) was named envoy to the Japanese in the ninth month of 1592. Shen was a native of Zhejiang whose parents happened to live next door to the parents of Shi Xing's wife. When the court issued a call for men of talent to rise to the challenge of defending Korea, Shen sent a letter to Shi offering his services. As a result Shi recommended Shen, giving him the rank of a mobile corps commander (youji jiangjun). Shen's qualifications included fluency in Japanese and experience in fighting the wokou during the 1560s. He had joined the military at a young age and, according to one source, had also served in the capital armies, becoming fascinated with and skilled in the use of firearms. It was this interest that allowed him to make the acquaintance of Shi's father-in-law, who also had an interest in firearms.

Shen reportedly cut an imposing figure, despite his advanced age of over seventy, and was a smooth talker, though many felt that he was duplicitous and untrustworthy. Upon receiving his appointment, Shen requested additional funds so he could buy python robes to present to his Japanese counterparts.[113] He was also provided a small retinue of attendants to make an impression upon the Japanese.

Before meeting with the Japanese, Shen went to consult with King Sŏnjo in Ŭiju. He comforted the Koreans upon his arrival, saying Wanli had already mobilized 700,000 men and mounts to come to their nation's rescue. The king asked that 6,000–7,000 troops be sent immediately. Shen answered that he must first meet with Konishi Yukinaga, adding: "Although your country has been our loyal vassal, you do not understand the art of war. Therefore you press for assistance. But mobilizing troops along the road to war is not easy and moreover, the troops coming from Liaodong to do battle are short on bows and arrows so we must manufacture more." The king said he only knew that if the Japanese realized the Ming were coming in force, they would not dare venture out from Pyongyang. Shen soothed him again by informing him of the 3,000 southern troops already beyond Shanhaiguan and just seventy li (24 miles) from Korea, adding that China would not sleep until Korea was freed. Shen then had tea and played chess with the Korean monarch.[114]

It is said that in his initial meeting with the Japanese, Shen impressed them with his fearlessness and haughty bearing, galloping into Pyongyang without fear. He threatened Konishi with a million-man army, to which the Japanese commander replied, "The Koreans have prevented us from reestablishing trade relations and raised troops to hinder us, so we invaded them." Genso maintained that trade was their main desire— there was no reason for hostility between China and Japan. Undaunted, Shen told the Japanese to evacuate and wait for orders from the Ming, for this was their territory. Konishi produced a map and said, "This is clearly Korea." Shen responded: "For a long time they have received our imperial commands and therefore they have many palaces (meaning they enjoy prosperity); though this may be Korea's land, it still borders the superior kingdom. Therefore you may not stay here."[115]

Konishi continued to maintain that Japan simply wanted to restore her old relationship with China but made the mistake of using the term *heqin*, which implied a marriage relationship between Hideyoshi and Wanli. Furthermore, he reiterated the fact that the Japanese did not want to relinquish any territory they currently held, offering to divide

Korea between China and Japan. At this point Shen allegedly said: "We can come back with an army of tens of thousands. What do we have to fear from the likes of you?"[116]

Despite these harsh words, after brief negotiations and an exchange of gifts, they settled on a fifty-day truce that confined the Japanese to within ten li (about 3.5 miles) of Pyongyang and kept the Koreans at least ten li away from the city. Shen reported that the Japanese would return the captured territory if they could be allowed to reestablish tribute-trade relations with China. This was not really the case. Konishi offered to divide Korea at the Taedong River, giving the Chinese everything north of the river and the Japanese the rest, the portion of the peninsula they occupied at the time. Shen also dispatched one of his attendants, a relative by the name of Shen Jiawang, to the Japanese camp, ostensibly to assist in the talks but in actuality to spy on them. Jiawang reportedly was treated well by the Japanese, spending most of his time feasting and drinking with the commanders. Even so, when the fifty days concluded on November 23, 1592, and no Chinese reply had been received, Konishi became suspicious and ordered his men to start bolstering Pyongyang's defenses in anticipation of an attack.[117]

As the Korean navy was smashing the Japanese in the south, conditions were also becoming more difficult for the invaders on land, especially in the northeastern province of Hamgyŏng. Katō Kiyomasa had been entrusted with the conquest of this region after the fall of Seoul. He left Kaesŏng in July with Nabeshima Naoshige and Sagara Nagatsune, taking a number of Koreans along as guides.[118] He had been warned that the weather in that part of the country was always nasty and that the Korean commander in charge of defending the province still led a number of well-armed troops. The Japanese encountered little resistance until they reached the town of Haejŏngchang, the location of an important grain warehouse.

Haejŏngchang was defended by Han Kukham, commander of the province's six garrisons. He assembled an army of seasoned veterans to resist the invaders. When the two sides joined battle, the Koreans initially had the better of it, their cavalry forcing the Japanese to retreat into the warehouse. While some of his subordinates called for a tactical withdrawal during the night, Han decided to press the attack. Katō's men formed barricades with grain bags to resist the stones and arrows of the Koreans. The approach to the warehouse was narrow, and the Koreans were forced to attack in massed formation, making them easy targets for Japanese guns. Three hundred Japanese sallied forth, eventually forcing Han to retreat to a nearby mountain, from whence he planned to launch another assault the next morning.[119]

When dawn finally came, the area around the mountain was shrouded in fog. Katō led his men out of the warehouse in a bold assault that caught the Koreans completely by surprise. He left an opening in his lines that the enemy naturally headed toward as the battle got ugly. But this ruse only led the Koreans to a swamp, where they were massacred by the Japanese, though Han was able to make his escape to the north. Shortly after this, on August 28, Katō reached the town of Hoeryŏng, where Princes Imhae and Sunhwa had been trying to rally popular support. Unfortunately for them, the town was used by the court as a penal colony to exile political enemies, so the locals were not inclined to aid the royals. Korean collaborators revealed the princes' location to Katō, whose men captured them virtually without a fight. In addition to the princes, a number of high officials and court ladies fell into Japanese hands. Han was also apprehended and brought to the commander in fetters. All would become bargaining chips in the peace negotiations later in the war. In fact as soon as Katō captured the princes, he sent word to Konishi Yukinaga asking him to inform Sŏnjo of the situation, but the news only strengthened his desire to resist. The report of course also reached Hideyoshi, along with thirty silver pieces from the captured Tanch'ŏn mines.[120]

Katō then decided to take advantage of his proximity to the border to test his mettle against the fearsome Jurchens. Using local guides, he crossed the Tumen River and entered Manchuria early in the eighth month with about 8,500 troops. In one clash the Jurchens were driven back by rain, causing the chronicler of Katō's Korean exploits to declare this a testament to Japan being the land of the gods (shinkoku). Although his men supposedly acquitted themselves well and won a couple of skirmishes, he decided to return to Korea because his forces were sorely outnumbered. Katō even ordered that no heads be brought back, probably because he was harassed during his retreat to Hamgyŏng province, though he claimed killing more than 8,000 Jurchens.[121]

As Katō was trying to bring order to Hamgyŏng and collect taxes to support his troops, he received a directive from Hideyoshi ordering him to attack the Ming. He wanted to join forces with Konishi, but the northwestern province of Pyŏngan was not yet pacified. Furthermore, the roads leading west were not firmly under Japanese control, and a lone army would be very vulnerable to ambush. Therefore Katō decided to return to Japan personally with his royal captives, detailing 20,000 troops to remain behind to garrison Hamgyŏng. He left Myŏngchŏn in the hands of Korean collaborators and moved south to join other Japanese commanders. This may not have been the best course of action, for fierce resistance movements were mushrooming throughout Hamgyŏng. In the eleventh month, for example, Chŏng Munbu amassed a force of 7,000 men to attack the 1,500-man Japanese garrison at Kilchu and managed to cut off Haejŏngchang. Other uprisings followed, and although most were suppressed by the Japanese, they caused serious difficulties. This forced Katō to devote much effort to improving fortifications and requisitioning more supplies from elsewhere rather than simply extracting resources from the locals as he had anticipated.[122] By early 1593 Chŏng and his men had managed to drive the occupiers out of Haejŏngchang and Kilchu.

Back in the south, the Battle of Ch'ŏngju in early September 1592 marked one of the first engagements in which the monk-soldiers played a major role, with forces under the monk Yŏnggyu joining those of Cho Hŏn, Kim Ch'ŏnil, and Ko Kyŏngmyŏng. The armies of Cho and Yŏnggyu, which numbered just over 3,000 men, encircled the city on September 5. The monk-soldiers attacked the north and east gates, while Cho's men assailed the west gate. Initially driven back, the attackers lit fires in the forested hills around the city that night to present the illusion of much greater numbers. Convinced of the untenable nature of their position, the Japanese withdrew. Victories such as this prompted Ŏ Hŭimun to exclaim: "I have heard that the monk-soldiers do not fear death. Thus they advance but never retreat. Therefore if these monks are made our vanguard, we should certainly win."[123]

Closer to Seoul, the Battle of Ungch'i in mid-August again pitted Japanese muskets against Korean arrows. The Korean commander, Yi Punam, erected wooden palisades at the top of a hill and protected them with archers. After much fighting, the Japanese blasted their way through the pass. But the Koreans erected battle standards in the hills to trick the enemy into thinking reinforcements were en route. Fearing they would be flanked, the Japanese pulled back toward Kŭmsan. Kwŏn Yul then ambushed the Japanese at Ich'i in August, and other commanders in the south maintained the pressure, together forcing the Japanese to pull back farther and reinforce a few key strongholds. The victory at Ich'i also prevented the invaders from maintaining an unbroken supply line across the peninsula from coast to coast. It also demonstrated that despite earlier reverses, Korean commanders were not afraid to engage the enemy again.[124]

After his victory at Ch'ŏngju, Cho Hŏn was eager for more. Against the advice of his allies, he decided to lead a mere 700 volunteers against a Japanese host of perhaps 10,000 men under Kobayakawa Takakage at Kŭmsan, recently reinforced by the troops beaten at Ich'i. In fact Ko Kyŏngmyŏng and his sons all perished in a similarly lopsided assault on Kŭmsan the previous month. When reminded of the futility of such an attack, Cho angrily retorted, "I have but one life to give and that is all!" In the end Yŏnggyu also decided to follow Cho, though Kwŏn Yul refused to join in the endeavor. Seeing the enemy approach, the Japanese sallied forth and encircled the Koreans before they could form their battle lines. As the situation deteriorated, one of Cho's subordinates asked him if a retreat should be ordered. At this Cho reportedly laughed and said, "The true hero has no regard for his own death at the hands of the enemy and certainly does not look to avoid it."[125] With that he waded into the thick of the fray, where he was cut down; a subordinate retrieved his corpse for a proper burial. The Koreans were totally annihilated by the Japanese.

Despite debacles such as this, inspiring local forces to stage similar actions was the motivation behind sending the princes around the countryside. Prince Kwanghae issued frequent proclamations wherein appeals to the memory of ancestors were bolstered by concrete rewards of titles and cash for killing Japanese. Victory memorials sent to the court at Ŭiju were often accompanied by bags of severed Japanese ears. People were encouraged to engage in support operations even if they feared combat.[126] The court also stressed the importance of developing reliable intelligence networks to keep tabs on enemy troop movements.

While they could not take on the Japanese in large-scale battles, guerrilla units knew the local terrain and proved masterful in setting ambushes and severing supply lines. They often lured small groups of Japanese soldiers into forest clearings or tiny valleys where the Koreans could slaughter them. Japanese commander Mōri Terumoto reported on such actions in a letter: "The Koreans regard us in the same light as pirates. Therefore, they retreat to the mountains where they ambush the Japanese, especially when the latter happen to pass in small numbers." As a result the Japanese generally traveled about the countryside only in relatively large, well-armed bands and otherwise spent most of their time holed up in captured cities and fortresses. They also built a number of new fortifications, mostly with coerced Korean labor, in which to house their troops.[127]

Certainly the more the populace resisted, the more harsh and onerous Japanese exactions became. There were widespread reports of women shipped to Tsushima en masse, many of whom committed suicide to avoid being violated by their captors. Additional women were shipped to Seoul or other locations to serve as laborers, entertainers, or concubines. Still more Koreans were forced to gather snakes for the Japanese, who supposedly enjoyed eating snake soup for its reputed medicinal value. One escaped female prisoner told Korean officials that the Japanese valued snakes like pearls.[128]

At this time most Koreans were still unsure as to the real state of affairs in their country, and all sorts of wild rumors gained currency. When Sŏnjo inquired about the number of Japanese troops in Korea, estimates ranged from as high as 320,000 to as low as 80,000. Enemy numbers in the vicinity of Pyongyang were projected at anywhere from 1,000 to nearly 50,000, though most figured the number to be between 10,000 and 20,000. When the Ming-Korean push to dislodge them in the fall of 1592 failed, it became obvious that the Japanese were going to stay through the winter. Traversing the countryside in late 1592, Ŏ Hŭimun reported finding little besides torched homes and enslaved Koreans, though he at least managed to finally reunite with his wife.[129] With winter coming on, even those who still lived were likely to succumb to cold or starvation.

Word had it that the Japanese planned an invasion of Liaodong for the second month of 1593, though this rumor may have been designed to spur the Chinese into faster action. The Ming knew that the Japanese soldiers in Pyongyang were already running low on food and supplies and that those who left the safety of the walls to forage frequently fell prey to roving bandits or Korean loyalists.[130] Korean ministers requested Chinese weapons and instructors to help train their troops to better fight the Japanese. Sŏnjo himself openly questioned Japan's desire for peace and called it nothing more than a delaying tactic.

The mobilization process was by no means easy for the Ming. There were problems from the beginning, including trouble recruiting troops and keeping order among those they did enlist. Soldiers preyed upon commoners, taking their food and occupying their homes. Fights frequently broke out between northern and southern troops and their commanders, a problem that would plague the Ming throughout the Korean campaign. When one of his grand secretaries begged to resign on account of his mother's illness, Wanli replied, "With the Japanese troubles in the east and [Pubei] in the west which require diligent effort day and night, how could a minister just sit by and watch?" The emperor's calls were not unanswered. In October Chang Jujing, an official in Zhejiang, memorialized that some eighty-two boats, 1,500 troops, 3,600 assorted firearms and weapons, 6,000 jin (nearly 4 tons) of incendiaries, and 8,200 liang of cash and supplies were on the way.[131] Still, Song Yingchang had not mustered many of his troops yet, and there were rumors that the Japanese were preparing to strike across the Yalu. Many officials suggested merely building up Chinese forces along the border to deter any incursion rather than launching an ill-planned and ill-prepared offensive. Thus an initial 13,000 troops were stationed along the Yalu, divided equally between infantry and cavalry. In addition, more supplies rushed into Liaodong to feed and equip these new recruits.

As soon as Pubei's mutiny was put down, Li Rusong and other notable commanders involved left for Korea. Li was made supreme commander of the Eastern Expedition to Chastise the Japanese and concurrently superintendent of military affairs for Jizhen, Liaodong, Baoding, and Shandong. Upon receiving his appointment, Li reportedly said, "I accept the responsibility of Grand General whose duty is to crush the Japanese and restore the country [of Korea]." His assistants added, "To move a forest you have to do a lot of cutting," likewise accepting their assignments. Li requested extra funds to pay the troops and more supplies to help his men combat the bitter cold. In order to boost morale, Wanli announced that 100,000 liang of silver would be distributed for special rewards after the Japanese were defeated.[132]

While the Ming prepared to intervene on the peninsula, some Koreans collaborated with the Japanese as they began implementing their occupation policy. As stated above, Hideyoshi had issued instructions to his generals as early as the first month of 1592 concerning the administration of Korea. Occupation forces were to refrain from looting or pillaging while military governors maintained taxes at a low level, suitable for the upkeep of the invaders but not so high as to provoke insurrection. Hideyoshi seemed to take for granted that the Koreans would naturally embrace his enlightened rule over that of the debauched Yi dynasty. He later instructed his generals to return all captured peasants to their homes and even distribute famine relief for those who needed it. Efforts

were made to teach Japanese language and customs to the Koreans and
"in general by good treatment and conciliatory propaganda to persuade
them to consider themselves part of Japan."[133]

Although some Koreans were forced into combat or to guide Japanese
forces, the line between unwilling accomplice and active collaborator
was often hazy. The Japanese found more than a few willing Koreans to
help them administer and collect taxes. These individuals were given
special privileges and rights denied other Koreans and richly rewarded
for offering information on guerrilla units and loyalist forces.[134] But
those who resisted the occupation forces were publicly executed, their
bodies left to rot in the open. Actions such as this only intensified the
force of Korean resistance, which in turn impelled the Japanese to take
still harsher measures.

The natives may also have been increasingly less inclined to side
with the invaders because regular government forces were finally managing to gain some victories on land to complement those earned at sea.
Sŏngju was threatened by late September 1592, and Kwak Chaeu kept
the pressure on in the southeast. An assault on Kyŏngju by Pak Chin
was turned back initially. But Pak countered by using a delayed-action
bomb that killed thirty Japanese soldiers who came forward to inspect it
after it landed within the city. This convinced the garrison to pull back
to Sŏsaengpo on the coast. The recapture of Kyŏngju was both symbolic
and strategic, for the Japanese left considerable stores behind. Additionally, Korean guerrillas were buoyed by the expectation of Ming aid by
land and sea and rumors that Pyongyang had already fallen into Chinese
hands. Adding to this were reports from captured soldiers that the Japanese were already running low on supplies. Nevertheless, Korean triumphs
were scattered, and many captured soldiers and civilians continued to be
shipped out to Tsushima and Japan proper.[135]

The Japanese had hoped to use strategically important Chinju as a
major transportation node for their forces in the south. They pursued a
Korean commander named Yu Chŏng'in toward the city and then cut
him off. Yu asked Chinju's commander to let him in, but Kim Simin
refused because he did not want to compromise his defenses. This refusal
earned the approval of Kwak Chaeu, who remarked: "This is a good plan
for saving the city. The people of Chinju are fortunate."[136]

The ensuing Battle of Chinju would be one of the signal Korean
victories in the entire war and featured the creative tactics of Korean commander Kim Simin. Kim aware of the Japanese prowess with firearms,

had 170 guns mounted on the city walls. Although one of his subordinates wanted to sally forth, Kim knew he was outnumbered but held a strong defensive position on a hill with a river to one side. The Japanese, led by Hosokawa Tadaoki, encircled the city and then attacked in force, attempting to scale the walls with bamboo siege ladders. The defenders rained stones, arrows, cannonballs, and boiling water upon them, repulsing their assaults. Kim and his wife personally distributed food and wine to the defending troops. At night the commander dispatched runners to seek aid from other quarters. These men soon returned with bundles of arrows, improving the garrison's morale.[137]

But the siege continued. The Japanese next attempted to erect siege towers high enough for arquebusiers to fire into the city. The defenders countered with axes, rocks, guns, mortars, and spears to forestall their construction. Even women joined in the city's defense. Amid all of this, Kwak Chaeu arrived to aid the garrison. Although he had barely one hundred troops, Kwak's men arrayed themselves in the forested hills around the city, lighting pine torches and blowing into conch shells to give the illusion of greater numbers. Kwak also shouted that he would be joined by all the righteous soldiers of Chŏlla the next day. The Chinju defenders were eventually joined by some 2,500 additional guerrillas, bolstering morale within the city still further.[138]

The Japanese decided to launch one final assault on the evening of November 12, hitting the northern and eastern gates with arquebus fire. Although running low on ammunition, the Koreans resisted valiantly, and at the key moment, Kim Sŏngil arrived with more ammunition and supplies, sailing up the Nam River to the side of the fortress. Kim himself came out of the northern gate to lead the defense and received a mortal wound to the left side of his head. Rains helped cover the Japanese withdrawal soon afterward. The defenders had held out for six days, 3,800 troops and civilians against a Japanese force five times that size, inflicting massive casualties and retaining control of the grain-rich province of Chŏlla through the winter. The Koreans claimed that 2,600 Japanese were killed at Chinju, the ground covered with blood and bodies piled high outside the city walls.[139]

Meanwhile, Korean resistance elsewhere was gaining steam. The castle of Yŏnan, located between Haeju and Kaesŏng, was successfully defended by dropping burning pine torches on Kuroda Nagamasa's attacking troops, who tried to build a makeshift ramp of sticks, grass, and lumber to enter the castle. The Japanese onslaught lasted four days and nights before Kuroda withdrew on October 5. Kwŏn Yul occupied Toksan Castle near Seoul and supposedly deterred a Japanese attack by pouring buckets of rice over his horses in view of the attackers. The rice resembled water from afar and convinced the Japanese that Kwŏn had ample water supplies to withstand a protracted siege. In November Wŏn Ho led 1,000 Koreans against the forces of Shimazu Tadatsune at the fortress of Ch'unchŏn. Although isolated and outnumbered, Shimazu told his men, "We must take ten for every one we lose." The Japanese burst out of the castle and drove the Koreans back, taking seventy heads, but did not engage in further offensive action.[140]

Despite these generally positive developments, King Sŏnjo urged his commanders to be cautious and not expend their food supplies before the Ming forces arrived. Eager for retribution, many local commanders ignored such directives. Remnants of Cho Hŏn's armies raided Japanese camps across the south, and Wŏn Kyun's brother attempted to dislodge the Japanese from Yong'in, near Seoul. Meanwhile, supplies from China started pouring into Ŭiju by land and sea, and Ming officials began arriving as well, finding warm welcomes from their Korean hosts.[141]

Some 6,000 troops now protected the king at Ŭiju, though there were doubts as to how long these men could be supported by the available supplies. Declaring that he wished to make a drinking vessel of Konishi Yukinaga's skull and a drumskin of Keitetsu Genso's flesh, the king intimated that he himself might take the field against the enemy. Loyalist movements broke out in several Korean cities, including Seoul. According to Yu Sŏngnyong, when men died resisting the Japanese, they were replaced by their sons, and some resistors acquired formidable reputations among the enemy. Although most of these uprisings were crushed rather easily, they gave the Koreans heart and depleted Japanese forces.[142] For some time one force in the south even isolated the Japanese stronghold of Wŏnju, until the Korean commander in charge of the operation was killed in an ambush. The court tried to direct such uprisings, even ordering the populace to bring in their farming implements so they could be turned into weapons.

Meanwhile, the Chinese force being assembled for Korea's relief consisted largely of cavalry and military carts with cannon mounted on them. Given what had happened to the initial Chinese expeditionary force, the Ming had decided to wait until winter froze the ground before sending further troops, for it would be much easier to maneuver on frozen ground than in the mud. In the meantime, troops continued to arrive and train under commanders assembled at Shanhaiguan under the overall direction of Song Yingchang. By the end of the tenth month of 1592, about 30,000 men along with mounts and three months' supply of food had been gathered in Liaodong. The target number was just under 75,000 troops. In a report from December, Song told Shi Xing that in his estimation 100,000 troops could get the job done in two months, but with the forces he had on hand, the campaign could end up taking a year or more.[143] Song was directed to take his troops to Ŭiju and on to Pyongyang, recruiting and training additional men as he advanced.

Shen Weijing continued to play the role of diplomat, hustling back and forth between the Chinese, Japanese, and Korean camps. While Shen kept everyone talking, he also continued to engender fear and distrust. The Koreans questioned China's commitment to them because Shen confided to Kim Myŏngwŏn while having tea: "Making peace is our number one priority. I do not know if it will be possible to force a decision by attacking the enemy." But Korean misgivings were allayed somewhat when they heard of the appointment of Li Rusong as supreme military commander of the Eastern Expedition.[144]

In a memorial from Ming official Liu Huangshang, the Koreans learned that Song Yingchang was a master planner, "whose mind could not even be fathomed by ghosts or spirits," and Li Rusong had earned his valorous reputation in a hundred battles, displaying "the ferocity of the generals of yore." Additionally, Rusong was the eldest son of China's most renowned general, Li Chengliang, and was currently the toast of Beijing as a result of the reputation he gained in suppressing the mutiny of Liu Dongyang and Pubei. Plus the Li family had its origins in Korea. Beyond personnel, Liu Huangshang also stressed the range and power of Ming cannon compared to Japanese arquebuses.[145]

An imperial communication from Wanli to Sŏnjo reiterated the closeness of Sino-Korean culture and related that the Son of Heaven "boiled with rage upon hearing of Korea's plight and ordered the Ministry of War to appoint an official [Song Yingchang] to take charge of affairs and lead an army of retribution." Wanli had bestowed the double-edged sword of authority upon Song, and soon his soldiers would engage the Japanese. Plus, in addition to the warships coming from Guangdong and Fujian, Wanli continued to promise help from Thailand and Ryukyu. Song added other tributaries such as Hami and Annam to this list because "all were under the protection and guidance of the sage ruler of

China who soothes and pacifies the four seas, brings tranquility to the barbarians, and stands alone in his abundance of virtue." The Japanese had good reason to fear the troops from Xuanda and Shanxi alone, Wanli declared, who would soon cross the Yalu "with dragon-like prancing and tiger-like steps" and hit the invaders "with the force of roaring thunder and crushing winds."[146]

Song, however, was not quite so confident. He fretted that his troops were ill-equipped, particularly their armor and winter clothing. Careful instructions were issued as to the distribution of supplies among units, even cooking pots. All soldiers with guns were expected to have five hundred bullets, though Song complained about a lack of firearms and the fact that the units brought in from all over the empire would have little chance to train together before going on campaign. In a report to Shi Xing from late November, Song estimated that it would take seven days for the troops to travel from Shanhaiguan to Liaoyang. Once there they were to undergo accelerated training, particularly in firearms. On the positive side, Liaoyang was open enough to be a good area to muster a large host, though the area's ability to support such an army was questionable. For this reason Song decided to ship provisions by sea from Shandong in addition to overland routes. He estimated that it would require 90,000 piculs (6,000 tons) of food to maintain 100,000 men and mounts for two months.[147]

Even with the onset of winter, the Ming were still concerned with bolstering China's coastal defenses. All the islands within a 500-li (172-mile) radius of Dagu and Tianjin were to erect defenses and keep watches. Each defense post kept several dozen torches for signaling. The islands were to have boats that could be manned by commoners, who were otherwise expected to till their fields. Each house was to have a drum that could be struck to rouse the village to arms. And each locale was to select the most upright, brave, and trustworthy men to act as squad commanders and lead the stalwarts of the region. The method was expected to raise some 7,000 marines and two hundred boats.[148] Regular troops were to be dispatched from Nanjing to assist local militia in readying cannon for use against any marauders who approached the coast. It was believed that creating an interlocked system of sea and land defenses would deter the Japanese.

Noting that the Japanese were not particularly adept at naval warfare, Song emphasized the need for China to build more large warships.

Styles from Fujian were deemed the best, followed by a number of other midsized galleys and oared vessels for shallow-water duties. The Ministry of War was ordered to bring all these kinds of vessels north at once; if they lacked sufficient numbers, they were to request the Ministry of Works build them. Forty boats were requested from the area of Nanzhili. Other localities also supplied boats for conversion into military vessels. For example, in Tianjin and northern areas, salt and fishing boats would be requisitioned for government use. Such craft could be used for their intended purpose on most days but operate as spy vessels if needed. Song also asked Wanli to order Zheijiang and Nanzhili provinces to supply one hundred more large galleys and the Ministry of Works to provide funding for additional smaller rowboats. He cautioned that larger boats were tough to operate in windy conditions and required lots of men to sail them, so fewer numbers of these should be constructed. Song estimated needing a total of 17,000 sailors and figured some of these could be recruited from among fishermen or salt-boat workers. In terms of total numbers, he wanted more than twenty-four hundred smaller boats and a few hundred larger vessels.[149]

Song also addressed a number of practical matters pertaining to naval combat. He observed that high winds and rough waters made sailors sick and dizzy and made fighting onboard difficult. It was also essential that ship captains be aware of currents and shoals. In fighting the Japanese, he suggested using long spears and erecting bamboo screens on deck to counter muskets and katana. For offense he advised using smoke to blind the enemy and fire arrows to burn their ships. Three-barreled guns, Portuguese-style *folangji*, and rapid-fire guns were to be mounted on ships too. Larger boats were supposed to carry crouching tiger cannon, caitiff exterminators, and grand general cannon. Mastheads would have signal flags. Song explained that the intent of having such well-armed vessels was to overawe the enemy so that they would not even dare to engage Chinese warships, thereby minimizing casualties.[150]

Contingency plans were also made should the Japanese slip past coastal defenses and actually invade the Chinese mainland. One called for intercepting them in mud flats or right on shore. To aid in this, all the watchtowers in the environs of Tianjin were to be furnished with various types of cannon. Rows of caltrops and iron spikes were to be strewn on the ground around these installations in case of assault; Song noted that he had already placed orders for caltrops, iron stakes, and saltpeter.

Finally, iron chains might be strung underwater across harbors, as Yi Sun-sin had done in Korea. Inland, drums and beacons could be used to create overlapping early warning networks that would resemble the spokes of a wheel. Existing city walls would be reinforced and bamboo palisades raised in areas that did not already have stouter defensive works. Moats would be dug out as well. Fire carts and defensive weapons would be distributed among the populace. Villagers were instructed to store extra water and firewood within the safety of city walls. Song noted that such measures inland would have the added purpose of aiding locals resist raids by native bandits. The most ambitious plan called for erecting a defensive wall two zhang (23.5 feet) in height stretching some 180 li (62 miles) from Dagu to Zhengjiagou. Song figured 30,000 men could build such a barrier in just one month.[151]

Even though an estimated 18,000 troops had been detailed to defend Tianjin and its environs, officials remained concerned about the potential vulnerability of the capital. Therefore Song requested stationing an assistant regional commander and 3,000–4,000 troops at Tangtou to be ready to respond to any threat. Likewise, he placed Liaodong on constant alert for raiders from Tsushima. The ultimate plan was to have 40,000–50,000 troops guarding the northeastern port cities. The Ming were worried that if Korea should fall, the people of Liaodong "would not be able to sleep in peace for even one night."[152]

Learning from the mistakes made at Pyongyang, in a communiqué to Ming generals, Song stressed the need to know the whole situation in Korea prior to advancing too deeply. He told them accurate information and adaptability in the field would greatly facilitate operations. To this end Song made sure that advance scouts and translators were sent ahead to confer with the Koreans. He also expressed to the generals his misgivings that too many of his troops were cavalry, concerned that the terrain of Korea was better suited to infantry and Chinese cavalry swords lacked the reach of Japanese katana. Therefore Song recommended using troops from the south, infantry units that fought with glaives and bamboo halberds. But because the southern provinces were so far away, he was resigned to relying on the northern cavalry available. Song reminded his commanders that the Japanese were adept at the use of muskets, but beyond eighty paces (about 320 feet) these weapons were not very effective. He also warned them that the Japanese were ferocious warriors who never retreated. Song suggested that using ambushes or stealing their livestock or supplies might be a good way to weaken enemy morale before battle. And once engaged, he stressed speed in battle, emphasizing that the tactics of Sun Wu and Sunzi for the use of different cavalry units could prove quite efficacious.[153]

A memorial sent to the throne on December 21, 1592, reported the Ming had assembled about 40,000 troops, 20,000 mounts, and about two months' worth of food and fodder. Other Korean records also refer to 40,000–50,000 seasoned troops under the banner of the Jurchen chieftain Nurhaci in Liaodong. The presence of these forces, they believed, would dissuade the Japanese from attempting to flank the Koreans at Ŭiju. But Nurhaci himself apparently took no part in the skirmishes against the Japanese the previous autumn, however, he repeatedly made overtures to the Ming, offering to lead troops to aid their cause against Japan. (Recent scholarship suggests that rather than taking advantage of the conflict to expand his own power in Manchuria, Nurhaci behaved circumspectly toward his Chinese and Korean neighbors, unsure of what their war with Japan might bring him.)[154]

The Chinese and the Koreans were very worried with ensuring adequate supplies and weapons for their armies. After conferring with Yun Tusu, Song explained in a letter to the Koreans his overall strategy but emphasized what the Ming expected of their ally. He stated that the Koreans would need to provide food supplies for 50,000 troops and their mounts for several months. He suggested that they establish military farms to furnish the necessary foodstuffs requested that they provide the Ming with maps of Pyongyang, Seoul, and other key sites. The Koreans also must appoint an official, who would initially be posted at Ŭiju, to oversee requisition and transportation of food and fodder for all allied troops, mounts, and draft animals. Civilians from all walks of life were to be enlisted in groups of five to ten to act as intelligence agents, providing information on local conditions to the advancing army. Finally, the Korean government was to start recruiting and training regular troops.[155]

But Song was most concerned about supplies and armaments. He requested another 18,000 liang of silver for the construction of 220 more grand-general cannon, half of which would remain in Beijing. Units still lacking firearms would be prioritized in receiving the new guns. He also asked that any extra cannons in the capital's arsenals be sent to the front at once. Song even recommended using private merchants and their vessels to facilitate faster delivery of supplies.[156] The emperor ordered that all such requests be expedited.

In his articles pertaining to military discipline, Song gave strict orders for the soldiers not to harm either the Chinese or the Korean people or their livestock or other animals. "Korea's land is our land. The Korean people are our children," he explained. "Therefore anyone who harms any Korean man or woman will be apprehended and executed." He told the soldiers that they must pay for everything they want and ordered his officers to prevent merchants and others from following the armies in hopes of making money. Decapitation was the penalty for refusing to advance or disobeying the orders of a superior. Anyone ravishing a Korean woman would also be executed, as would deserters or anyone who abandoned supplies or mounts. If a commander allowed his drummer to flee, the whole company would be executed. Anyone caught stealing water would receive one hundred lashes. In a more positive vein, Song also restated the bounties put on the heads of the Japanese leaders and the rewards for valiant service.[157]

Zhang Sanwei, a Ming official from Liaodong, was sent ahead to oversee food and supplies for the advancing armies. Korean officials briefed him on the status of the resistance movement, offering the suggestion that the monk-soldiers could be useful in intelligence-gathering activities. Qian Shizhen and Wu Weizhong, at the head of 5,000 troops, were the first Ming commanders of the Eastern Expedition to cross the Yalu. The main Ming army numbered approximately 44,000 men under some sixty commanders.[158] Yang Yuan led the Army of the Center; Zhang Shijue commanded the Army of the Right; and Li Rubo, Rusong's younger brother, commanded the Army of the Left. While the majority of the troops were northern cavalry, there were contingents of southern infantry in addition to fierce aboriginals from China's southwest. Even valiant Shaolin monks reportedly joined the expedition. Li Rumei, another of Rusong's brothers, was placed in charge of anti-Japanese efforts at Ŭiju.

Equipped with all manner of weapons and wearing different styles of armor, the Chinese must have made quite an impression upon the Koreans who greeted their arrival. The artillery train must have been stunning as well, for the Ming brought more than 2,000 cannon of various sizes transported on carts or on the backs of draft animals. Huge quantities of gunpowder, arrows, polearms, spears, caltrops, fuses, shields, whips, cudgels, axes, swords, and other weapons and munitions were also hauled across the frigid plains of Liaodong.[159] Although their allies were initially a bit disappointed by the size of the force, the Ming generals quelled Korean misgivings by assuring them that more than 100,000 additional troops were still on the way from more-distant parts of the empire.

Reportedly, as Li Rusong and his troops reached the border of Korea, the sky and water were both the same color; and as the men gazed at the mist-shrouded peaks of Korea, Liu Huangshang said heroically, "Behold the territory of thine ancestors!"[160] As Li prepared to cross the river, someone composed the following poem:

> Lightning flashed as the general set out
> His white horse had a golden saddle, embroidered in crimson
>   and knotted with jade
> From atop his mount he stares out at the clouds toward the
>   heavens
> Taking up his spear, he pointed toward the sun and tucked in
>   his chest with a flourish
> Surely among all the enemy, there are none who can match his
>   bravery
> Or the tiger awesomeness of his troops
> The drums thunder as the troops head east across the Yalu.[161]

Seeing the Ming troops arrive, the Koreans supposedly lost all fear. The king himself came forth to meet Li, saying: "The August Emperor's benevolence is great indeed! Upon seeing your greatness in person I can only receive your orders as your humble neighbor." Li replied, "You flatter me." Li was then given a number of gifts, including clothing, bows, and arrows.[162] He then sent to Yu Sŏngnyong a fan inscribed with a poem, which read:

> Upon hearing that our neighbor was in trouble
> I crossed the river, leading my army under starlight
> Our sage emperor is anxious for the news every day
> And his humble servant would not enjoy wine even at night
> The spring and the Great Bear make me lion-hearted
> The bones of the tricky Japanese will ache with fear
> Let me speak of nothing but victory even in jokes
> I am always on a horse, even in my dreams.[163]

In greeting Sŏnjo, Song Yingchang again emphasized the closeness of China and Korea and the Ming emperor's role as ruler of all under heaven. He predicted Seoul would be retaken in three months, with the rest of the country soon thereafter. He also told the king that the Chinese would withdraw as soon as the country was restored (contradicting the claims of some later Korean writers that the Ming intended to annex the peninsula). The allies then turned to the business of discussing their strategy for the impending assault recovery of Pyongyang. Spies reported upward of 10,000 Japanese in that city and 20,000 in Seoul, with untold numbers hunkered down in fortified castles around the country.[164]

Meanwhile, just a couple of weeks earlier, a number of Japanese commanders had assembled in Kaesŏng to discuss peace options. Kuroda Nagamasa had managed to requisition 20,000 piculs (1,333 tons) of supplies from Hwanghae, but overall the invaders' position was becoming more precarious. Commanders in the north especially were eager for transfers of divisions from Pusan and further reinforcements from the homeland. Disease, starvation, and resistance activities were taking their toll. While some estimates suggest that more than 160,000 Japanese troops garrisoned Korea as of the end of 1592, others maintain that anywhere from one-third to two-thirds of the original invasion force were dead by the spring of 1593.[165] Regardless, generals were already being brought back from Hamgyŏng, and whatever satisfaction Hideyoshi might have felt at the time, it was clear to many of his commanders in the field that the tide might soon turn. The Year of the Black Water Dragon had been a good one for the Japanese. The year of the serpent would not prove nearly as fortuitous.

4

A Serpent's Tail

The Rescue of Korea, 1593–94

Li Rusong's arrival had been preceded by that of Wu Weizhong, who led 3,000 troops across the Yalu, accompanied by Qian Shizhen, who led 2,000 men. Although the Ming hoped to assemble a force of 70,000 men, the number of troops mustered was slightly more than half that number. Wanli made another promise to King Sŏnjo, telling him that in addition to Chinese troops, he had issued a call for troops from the Philippines and the Ryukyus, and reassuring him that all of Korea's territory would be recovered for the king. The Ming Ministry of War reiterated the prices on the heads of Hideyoshi, the "evil monk" Keitetsu Genso, Konishi Yukinaga, Sō Yoshitoshi, and the other Japanese commanders.[1]

Addressing Korean concerns about the size and makeup of the relief force, Song Yingchang bragged: "Our army is like the wind and the rain. In the morning we will cross the Yalu and by evening we will have smashed the enemy." Despite his confident tone, Song was upset, lamenting that of the roughly 36,000 men in his command, "so many of these are weak and unfit for service that my crack troops barely exceed 20,000."[2]

Upon their arrival, the Ming commanders became angry with the Koreans for not telling them that Shen had continued to negotiate with and send gifts to the Japanese. Li Rusong in particular took an immediate disliking to Shen and wished to kill him on the spot for his insolence. He and the others maintained that Shen's talks were not held on the orders of the court and Shen had acted beyond his authority when he treated with the enemy. Shen retorted that he had been given full authority by Shi Xing.[3]

Chinese commanders held meetings with their Korean counterparts and with Shen Weijing. Among other things they discussed the importance of striking fast and deploying troops armed with firearms in key spots to prevent the enemy from again advancing once dislodged from their current positions. The Ming requested detailed information on waterborne transportation nodes. Their leaders tried to establish trade rates for silks and other items-in-kind since Korea's monetary economy was ill-developed, the Chinese asking that a Korean overseer be appointed to facilitate such exchanges. The Ming also emphasized that they did not intend to remain in Korea more than six months, their objective being to drive the Japanese out and restore the king to his throne.[4]

Friction developed between Li Rusong and Song Yingchang. Korean sources relate that Li was arrogant and disdainful of Song because the latter was merely a civil official. Additionally, Li identified Song with the peace party associated with Shi Xing and Shen. Indeed, Li's official biographers relate that he affected an air of arrogance and disdain for civil officials, feeling his job was to lead the army and not to dress or behave in a courtly manner, even when around high-ranking officials. Ironically, Song himself also distrusted Shen and would later be a vehement opponent of Shi's peace policies.[5]

Still, the Chinese decided to take advantage of the relationship Shen had cultivated with Konishi, and they instructed him to continue talks so as to lull the Japanese into a false sense of security. Li Yingshi, an assistant commander, is credited with suggesting that Shen be dispatched to the enemy camp with a false letter of investiture. Song and Li Rusong both thought this was a good plan and sent a military commander, Zha Dashou, ahead, promising that Shen would soon be on hand to conclude negotiations. Shen's initial directive from Song was to tell the Japanese that if they wanted tribute trade, they would have to withdraw all the way to Pusan to await the imperial command, but this stance was apparently softened to fool the enemy into coming to negotiate.[6] Genso was delighted upon hearing that peace was nigh, composing a poem that read:

The land of the rising sun has made peace, subduing China,
And the whole world is now one family
The signs of joy risen in our land melt the snow outside
Though still a little early, the flowers of peace are gorgeous.[7]

Meanwhile, Song reiterated the Chinese pledge to liberate all of
Korea, while Li Rusong dispatched Luo Shangzhi and other commanders
to scout the terrain and establish advance camps. Li was upset with the
lack of discipline among his troops, and he also had 400 old or weak
men dismissed. The Koreans expressed concerns about transporting
supplies along snowy roads, but these were dismissed by the Chinese.
But they also reminded the Chinese of their failure to listen to Korean
advice the previous year and warned them of the efficacy of Japanese
firearms, at which Li responded: "Japanese weapons have a range of a
few hundred paces while my great cannon have a range of five to six li.
How can we not be victorious?" Li also accepted a detailed map of
Pyongyang and its environs from Yu Sŏngnyong. Despite his earlier
humiliations, Yi Il was placed in overall command of Korean forces
in the vicinity, which numbered perhaps 20,000 men. The Chinese
had large numbers of cannon, and together the allies had amassed
four months' rations by this time.[8]

Li warned his subordinates to be ready for stiff Japanese resistance
and took measures to make his forces most effective. He distributed
his cannon equally among his units and ordered that they be carefully
guarded. Applying strict military discipline, he directed his officers to
behead any man who fled during combat. His plan was to surround
Pyongyang and open up on the city from all four sides, creating havoc
with smoke and fire. He reminded them that the key to countering
Japanese muskets was to rush the enemy after they fired but before they
had time to reload. Fire arrows could be used to help illuminate the
area during night combat. Any retreating from the city were to be forced
into the Taedong; those who did not drown could be cut down by troops
stationed along the riverbank. When entering the city itself, ordinary
soldiers were to be killed and enemy commanders captured alive.[9] Genso
and Konishi Yukinaga were considered the most important leaders and
were to be taken alive as useful captives in any subsequent peace talks.

Planners estimated that a mere 10,000 troops would be able to
retake Seoul after Pyongyang was liberated. Echoing Hideyoshi's own

words to his troops, Ming official Liu Huangshang predicted that the Chinese would take Pyongyang in one swift stroke, thereby rousing the rest of the country to take the capital with the ease that a knife cuts through bamboo. Liu added, "My country's fierce troops are like tigers or bears and no enemy can stand up to our great cannon that have a range of 1,000 paces." Song Yingchang was as eager as Li to attack the enemy, for he believed continued negotiations would only benefit the Japanese. Intelligence obtained from Korean spies suggested that as many as 30,000 Japanese might be hunkered down in Pyongyang, with two to three times that number elsewhere in Korea.[10]

The Chinese sent a message to Konishi Yukinaga, promising a grand ceremony outside Pyongyang for the two sides to formally sign a peace agreement hammered out the previous year.[11] They then set up an ambush at the meeting site in hopes of surprising Konishi and Genso. Unsuspecting, the Japanese commander sent an envoy with just twenty guards (as requested by the Chinese) to meet with his Ming counterparts on February 4, 1593. As the Japanese approached the pre-arranged meeting site, the Chinese, led by Li Ning, burst from hiding and tried to capture the Japanese messenger. His escort fought off the assailants, however, and three men managed to escape; fifteen others were killed and three taken alive. The captives divulged that a Japanese reinforcements were en route to Pyongyang.[12] Konishi was shaken by the news, but now alerted to the real intentions of the Ming, he returned to Pyongyang to ready his troops. He also dispatched his houseman, Konishi Joan, who would later serve as the Japanese envoy to the Ming court, to meet with Li Rusong to find out why the Chinese tried to capture him. Joan was turned away.

The allied troops burned incense for good luck as they set forth from Ŭiju. Proceeding with caution, the army first camped at Anju and sent scouts ahead to uncover ambushes. Advance detachments skirmished with the enemy, inflicting minor casualties. In another skirmish in the forests north of Pyongyang, fifteen horses were captured and dozens of Japanese were slain. The allied forces reached the outskirts of the city on the evening of February 6. Early the next morning Konishi tried to parley with Li Rubo, offering to negotiate within the city, but Li refused to take the bait. That night some 800 Japanese came forth, flags waving and blades flashing, to attack Li's camp, but they were turned back by the alert Ming troops, who relied primarily on fire arrows for their defense. Li then feigned a retreat and enticed a small number of Japanese to emerge from the main gates of the city, killing thirty in the ensuing skirmish.[13]

As the allied commanders deployed their forces, Konishi was still with the detachment outside the city on Moranbong Hill. On February 5 the monk commander Hyujŏng moved 4,200 men from Pophŭng Monastery to Iwangni, north of Moranbong; they attacked the Japanese entrenched there the next day. The allies tried to keep Konishi trapped, but he was rescued by Sō Yoshitoshi, who turned back an assault led by Wu Weizhong. The allied commanders were frustrated that they had again let Konishi slip through their hands, but they still felt confident that they could take the city with their heavy guns. Li Rusong selected a few crack troops to attempt a probing assault that evening, but heavy Japanese fire forced them to withdraw.[14]

Li was most concerned about overcoming Pyongyang's natural defenses, for the city was bordered by the Taedong River on the south and east and by mountains to the west. These were augmented by a string of fortifications to the north that stretched some two li (two-thirds of a mile) out from the city proper and had recently been reinforced. He hoped that concentrated fire from his heavy guns could reduce the city gates and create gaps for exploitation. Li had Korean generals Yi Il and Kim Ungso station their forces, which totaled about 3,000 men, to attack the east wall as he arrayed a variety of cannon around the other walls and directed his men to launch flaming arrows and smoke bombs into the city. Wu Weizhong was stationed on the Koreans' flank, poised to attack the southeast corner. Zha Dashou was to attack Moranbong Hill with Korean monk-soldiers. Zhang Shijue and Yang Yuan were stationed at Seven Stars Gate. Zu Chengxun and Luo Shangzhi led a detachment of Ming troops to the southwest corner of the city disguised as Korean troops, whom the Japanese despised and belittled, and thus they paid them little attention. Li gave orders for one hundred "death-defying bravos" to be stationed at each major gate to key the advance once the defenses were destroyed.[15] Early on the morning of February 8, Li burned incense and readied his generals for the attack.

At dawn the drums within the city sounded and the Japanese attacked, their boulders, bullets, and arrows raining down on the besiegers. The ground shook and smoke filled the sky as the armies joined battle, and losses mounted quickly on both sides, the attackers running across the frozen ground and weaving a web of steel with their swords and spears. The initial assault by Kim Ungso and Yi on the east wall was repulsed by Sō and his men, armed with great spears and vats of boiling water. Li then had his forces feign a major assault on the southeast corner of the city as he and his brother led their troops against the west walls. As the front ranks began to break, Li personally killed a fleeing soldier to restore order and announced that the first man to scale the walls would receive 5,000 liang of silver (nearly 100 times an average soldier's annual pay). Fires broke out all over Pyong-yang, and noxious vapors filled the air. Luo Shangzhi managed to fight his way into the city with a great halberd, followed by a group of Zhejiang men, who were the first to scale the wall and plant the Ming flag, aided by Korean monk-soldiers.[16]

Li galloped back and forth, directing the battle from the thick of the fighting with some two hundred mobile cavalrymen; at one point his horse was shot out from under him. He gathered a group of stout-hearted men and scaled the walls with cloud ladders. He then directed Yang Yuan to proceed through the small west gate while his brother, Li Rubo, followed through the great west gate, setting fires so that the smoke and flames blinded and disoriented the enemy. Fire arrows streamed down "like silken threads," and winds fanned the flames inside the walls, reducing anything wooden to cinders. The Japanese continued to resist fiercely with great spears and swords, their defenses around the city walls "looking like the spines of a hedgehog."[17]

A few more cannonades allowed the attackers to blast their way through the walls. Yang Yuan ordered his houseman Yang Shilong to open the small west gate to admit the allied troops. Zhang Shijue and Qian Shizhen burst through the north gate, and Li Rubo and his men hacked through the west gate. Li lost his helm as he entered but forged on with just a cotton cap to protect his head. His cousin, Li Ruwu, was clipped in the left arm but fought on as well, heedless of his personal safety as a bloody street fight ensued. The Korean monk-soldiers also acquitted themselves well in the assault, prompting Li Rusong to comment: "These monk soldiers have no desire for fame or profit. Now everyone will know of their devotion to the Buddhist path." Indeed the monks played key roles in many of the major battles of the first two years of the war, sustaining very high casualty rates due to their propensity to situate themselves in the vanguard of any attacking forces.[18]

The allied troops took heads, clothing, and armor from the troops of the defending garrison in order to receive rewards for kills. Unfortunately, though, the men always claimed to have killed Japanese commanders because the rewards were higher. Intense competition flared among the men for glory, particularly between northern and southern Chinese troops. While this competition may have spurred the men on to greater actions, it also had the potential to lead to atrocities. Allegations soon after emerged that some of the troops had killed civilians in order to gain greater rewards, though both Korean and Ming investigations failed to yield any definitive proof.[19]

Song Yingchang led reinforcements against the north, south, and west sides of the city. Konishi boldly led his men out to break through the encirclement, but he was turned back by a hail of arrows and cannon fire. The Japanese then turned to cut their way through the troops stationed to the southwest, whom they believed to by Koreans. To their dismay, however, the men shed their disguises and revealed themselves to be Ming, a revelation said to have thrown the Japanese into a panic. Wu Weizhong later entered the city in triumph, blood streaming down his thigh from a hit by a Japanese bullet.[20]

Resistance remained stubborn, and even though badly defeated, Konishi was able to retreat to Pungwǒlru Pavilion outside the city. Li Rusong pursued him and set the structure ablaze with fire arrows, but the Japanese could not be dislodged. The defenders created a pile of Chinese corpses with their arquebus fire, so Li decided to pull back to regroup. This break allowed Konishi to cross the Taedong in the middle of the night and retreat south. Korean sources argue that Li made an arrangement with Konishi to minimize casualties for both sides, but Chinese and Japanese sources maintain that Konishi managed to effect his retreat under cover of darkness.[21] One source states that Li even curtailed a Korean ambush, then changed his mind, though a blunder by Yi Il allowed the enemy to escape. Sō Yoshitoshi and his men proved especially doughty in covering this retreat, killing dozens as they fell back.[22]

The Japanese were sorely shaken by this defeat, and they never recovered their momentum. The Battle of Pyongyang convinced them that they could not go head to head with the Ming when the latter could bring their big guns to bear. Accounts stated that the great cannons of the Ming "shook the earth for tens of *li* and even the mountains around the city trembled." The smoke from the artillery blotted out the sky, and the whole city was ablaze from Ming fire arrows. The surrounding forest also caught fire. For the rest of the war, the Japanese preferred to use ambushes and hit-and-run tactics against the Chinese. The estimate of Japanese dead was approximately 1,300–1,700 troops, with another

5,000 dying in the smoke and flames and perhaps as many as 6,000 more drowning in the Taedong as Konishi tried to escape.[23] The Japanese continued their retreat pell-mell, some hiding in commoners' homes, others seeking refuge in temples, as the Koreans sought to exact a measure of revenge. Many wounded and starving soldiers straggled around the city, falling prey to the allied patrols. An ambush led by Zha Dashou and Li Ning claimed another 362 Japanese, three commanders being captured alive in the process. The allies also captured 2,985 horses, recovered 452 pieces of Japanese military equipment, and rescued 1,225 Korean prisoners. By contrast, according to Song Yingchang, Ming dead numbered just 796, with an additional 1,492 wounded.[24]

Konishi and his commanders hastily convened a council of war. They were rattled, and some advocated retreating all the way to Pusan to await fresh troops and supplies. Ōtomo Yoshimune, who had been stationed at P'ungsan south of Pyongyang and was responsible for supporting Konishi, had already pulled back, a decision that would cost his clan their honor and their fief. For the time being the council decided to retreat only as far as Seoul. The Chinese and Koreans followed in hot pursuit. As Konishi and his men reached the city of Yongchonsŏng, they reportedly sighed with relief as they saw the white banner of the Kuroda still flying above the city walls.[25] Still, the allies were close behind them, and the forces there were already short on supplies. Konishi asked that Kuroda Nagamasa rush in more food from his station at Paechŏn.

In light of the defeat at Pyongyang and subsequent reverses, Kuroda Yoshitaka sent a memorial to Hideyoshi, calling for Konishi's removal on the grounds that he did not get along with his fellow commanders and was a poor leader. Some argue that after Pyongyang, Konishi became the primary advocate for peace on the Japanese side, while Katō Kiyomasa continued to champion war. Expressing concerns felt by many, Kuroda Nagamasa exclaimed, "We thought Korea was defeated but then the Great Ming army came to the rescue." The Koreans supported this: "After this the Japanese did not dare advance west due to the might of the celestial empire."[26]

Recognizing the profound effect his artillery had on the Japanese, Song Yingchang requested that more guns of all sizes be sent by sea with all due haste. In addition, he requested rakes, polearms, carts, fuses, bows, arrows, caltrops, gunpowder, and iron whips. Sŏnjo also requested firearms for his own divisions. Liu Huangshang memorialized the king regarding the manufacture and deployment of cannon, saying they would be best utilized in conjunction with mixed units of archers, spear-men, and swordsmen. Song promised that the leading Ming firearms experts could assist the Koreans in firearms training and proper deploy-ment in a variety of battlefield contexts and scenarios. Finally, he asked that silk and other goods be sent from China to trade with the Koreans for local supplies.[27]

Song invited Sŏnjo to return to Pyongyang on March 6, noting, "We were able to retake Pyongyang in less than a day because our sagacious Son of Heaven manifested his martiality and burned with Heavenly awe and indignation." He added that because Pyongyang was a key city that could be used for coordinating activities and governing the realm, the king should hasten there and urge those who had fled to return to reclaim their city and their honor. The Ming also wanted him to assemble "heroes" and select generals to train troops, amass stores, repair walls, and fashion weapons. In response, Sŏnjo said that Wanli had sent help in recognition of Korea's generations of loyal service and thanked the emperor for taking pity on his kingdom's plight.[28] Kim Myŏngwŏn would garrison Pyongyang with 8,000 troops and await Ming reinforcements.

With the speedy recapture of Pyongyang, the allies became more con-cerned about supplies and logistics. Yun Tusu and Yu Sŏngnyong were named supply and liaison officers. According to Ming official Zhang Sanwei, 45,550 piculs (3,037 tons) of rice could sustain an army of 40,000 for about fifty days. Likewise, 35,560 piculs of yellow beans and 88,090 bales of hay could feed 30,000 mounts for about a month. The Koreans at this point could come up with about a month's worth of additional sup-plies from various provinces. Because Chŏlla and Ch'ungch'ŏng provinces were less ravaged by war, they might provide more. But production was difficult to estimate because so many peasants had fled the pre-vious year. Therefore the Ming requested detailed information from their hosts as to the state of roads, waterways, and ocean currents to facilitate the quickest delivery of needed supplies by land and sea. Song asked for another seventy supply boats to bolster naval transport as well as more oxen, donkeys, and mules from China to move food and supplies overland because of shortages of draft animals in Korea. He did ask the Koreans to provide animal-husbandry services. The Ming also asked them to supply porters, estimating that 200 additional porters would be needed every ten li (3.45 miles) for an army of 10,000 troops. They suggested that the Koreans could raise a total of 10,000 men for duty from those deemed unfit for other military service. Monks also served in such roles, being especially desirable because they were competent and efficient and did not expect to be paid.[29]

Supply problems notwithstanding, the allies decided to continue their pursuit of the Japanese, believing that they needed to retake Seoul fast before the enemy could get reinforcements there. They also hoped to establish contact with fifth columnists within the capital. The army set forth along semi-frozen muddy roads littered with Japanese corpses, the state of the roads helping them move their heavy cannon at a fairly quick pace. The Ming were initially concerned about being flanked by the enemy coming from the northeast, but a captured soldier said that there were now less than 10,000 Japanese in Hamgyŏng, and most of the crack troops had already retreated to Seoul. Li Rusong told him: "I am currently leading 150,000 troops with another 100,000 on the way. So how do you think you can resist me?" At this the captive kowtowed and replied: "Honored sir, this news will shake the capital. When the troops in Hamgyŏng hear this, they will certainly flee, for how can we stand against so many men and horses?"[30]

Despite concerns about the weather, the allies decided that retaining the initiative was key, so Li Rubo, Zhang Shijue, and Yang Yuan marched out at the head of 8,000 elite troops, with others joining later. As the allied forces reached the city of Kaesŏng, they saw the Japanese arrayed in three divisions: the left under a green banner; the right under a white banner; and the center under a yellow banner. Each Japanese general shouted exhortations to his men while brandishing a two-handed sword on horseback. But the Japanese will to fight had obviously been sapped, and the ground was soon littered with the severed heads of their soldiers. The invaders left behind many weapons and copious provisions as they retreated. Li Rubo liberated Kaesŏng on February 19, killing 165 more Japanese, and restoring the four provinces of Pyŏngan, Hwanghae, Kyŏnggi, and Kangwŏn to the kingdom.[31] (Meanwhile, Korean general Ko Ŏnbaek led recovery operations across the north, though Hamgyŏng would remain in Japanese hands.) The victorious allied forces distributed food and money to the ravaged residents of Kaesŏng and crossed the Imjin on floating bridges.

The king was able to return to Pyongyang as a result of these victories. In a letter to Song Yingchang, Wanli said, "Pyongyang has already been recovered and now the Korean king will be able to occupy and defend it like before and when he returns he needs to ride the tide of victory and rouse the populace to brave deeds so when the troops are united and advance to smash the enemy, they will be crushed and the matter will be settled in no time." Li Rusong was in favor of maintaining the momentum and wanted to press his advantage, but others urged caution, due to both supply issues and the relatively small size of the allied army. This last was a valid concern, for even though estimates showed as many as 172,400 Korean soldiers on paper, the actual numbers in the field were much less. By contrast, Song reported to Shi Xing that the Japanese still had some 200,000 troops in Korea with a military potential of 660,000 men. But despite the concerns over numbers, others argued that if Seoul could be secured, then allied supply routes by land and sea probably could be stabilized, greatly lessening their logistical strains and further securing their position.[32]

The Koreans were duly impressed with Chinese firepower and military prowess. Sŏnjo exclaimed: "Their army is said to number 30,000. This is not a lot, but they know how to use them. This is military ability!" When the king asked his advisers about Chinese and Japanese firearms, his ministers said: "When the Japanese fire their arquebuses, you can still hear, even if they fire from all sides. But when the Chinese fire their cannon, the sky and earth vibrate and the mountains and plains tremble and you can't even speak." The king replied, "With weapons such as this how can we not fight and win?"[33]

Still, the Ming faced a conundrum. Advancing fast was essential to maintaining momentum and shocking the invaders into retreat. But commanders worried about overextension and isolation as well as being outnumbered and undersupplied. Li Rusong decided to take the aggressive approach. He first ordered a vanguard to reconnoiter the environs of Seoul and look for places suitable for ambush and battle. A couple of days later, Yang Yuan, Li Rubo, and Zhang Shijue were detailed to lead 2,000 crack troops to Masangwan, ninety li (31 miles) north of Seoul.[34]

This set the stage for the Battle of Pyŏkchegwan, one of the most controversial engagements of the entire war. Li Rusong had heard that the enemy was already pulling out of Seoul, and he galloped ahead with his vanguard, leaving his artillery train behind. He sent Li Ning and Zu Chengxun ahead, against the protests of other officials, including Song Yingchang. The muddy roads made the going difficult, but Li was determined to see the enemy defeated as quickly as possible, allegedly saying: "The spirit of the Japanese army was obliterated at Pyongyang.

So now a weakened army has withdrawn to Seoul and I'm not afraid of the likes of them!"[35]

The advance force, led by Zha Dashou, Zu Chengxun, and Korean general Ko Ŏnbaek, encountered and routed a Japanese force, killing more than a hundred. They pushed onward but fell into an enemy trap, as the Japanese had occupied the hills around the valley near the postal station of Pyŏkchegwan, some seventy li (24 miles) north of Seoul. Li Rusong rushed to the aid of his commanders with barely 1,000 cavalry and no artillery right into the ambush, which involved anywhere from 3,000–50,000 Japanese, depending on the source. The attackers fired from the high ground with their muskets and then closed in on the Ming cavalry with their katana.[36] Li rallied his men and tried to effect a fighting retreat.

The battle raged from late morning until dusk. Li Rusong found himself completely surrounded by the enemy, whose forces were spearheaded by Kobayakawa Takakage, a commander who had opposed the retreat from Kaesŏng. As a Japanese officer in shining armor approached the Ming commander, Li's brothers and bodyguards formed a cordon around him, firing arrows valiantly. His horse was again shot, and Li himself may well have been killed or captured had it not been for the valiant efforts of his subordinate Li Yousheng, who used his own body as a shield to save the general. This action bought Rusong some time, for a relief force led by Yang Yuan and Zheng Wenbin arrived and caught the Japanese forces in a pincer attack. Li's assailant was just about to cut him down when his brother, Li Rumei, shot the officer's horse.[37]

Although some Japanese sources claim that as many as 38,000 allied troops were killed in this battle, more-plausible accounts indicate that both sides suffered about equal losses. Regardless, the Japanese withdrew to Seoul, the Chinese again being hampered in their pursuit by heavy rains that slowed their weapon trains and horses.[38] The allies were also stymied by Japanese snipers with muskets stationed in the forested hills along the Han River. In the face of these difficulties, they decided to retreat to Kaesŏng for the time being. Wanli authorized the release of another 200,000 liang of silver to meet expenses and more troops from China, lest the Japanese counterattack. Li Rusong stationed Li Ning and Zu Chengxun in Kaesŏng with 10,000 troops and ordered Yang Yuan to guard Pyongyang and the Taedong River. The Japanese burned the grass around Seoul to deny the fodder for Ming horses.[39]

Some sources erroneously refer to the Battle of Pyŏkchegwan as the largest or most important conflict of the entire Korean campaign.[40] Yoshi Kuno, for example, says that after Pyŏkchegwan, Li Rusong "lost all hope and no longer had either military spirit or energy. He realized that the Ming army of China could not cope with the fighting power and military spirit of the Japanese, and was convinced that China had no fighting chance against Japan." Likewise, many Chinese sources argue that the defeat seriously undermined Ming morale and forced them to consider peace talks. They add that Song Yingchang acted quickly so he could secure terms most beneficial to the Ming. Indeed, the *Ming shilu* reveals that Song felt that too much troop strength had already been expended, and he was wary of overextending his lines the way the Japanese had theirs.[41]

Other contemporary sources maintain that both sides were eager to open peace talks because they realized the tenuousness of their respective positions. Even Qian Shizhen, who was an officer under Song, asserts that only 160 Chinese died at Pyŏkchegwan. Sin Kyŏng argued that the Japanese withdrew from Seoul even after Pyŏkchegwan because they feared the might of the Ming army.[42] Thus, while the battle was important, temporarily slowing the allied advance and disheartening Li Rusong, in the end the Japanese were still forced to abandon Seoul and retreat all the way to the southeast coast of Korea. The main significance of the battle was that it rendered the Ming less aggressive for the remainder of the conflict.

Weather played a major factor in both the Ming defeat and the decision to pull back. Horses and carts had trouble negotiating the muddy terrain and the mountain roads, meaning that supplies could sometimes travel only ten li (3.5 miles) in an entire day. There was no grass for grazing, and many horses, some of which contracted diseases, died. Some of the diseased horses were then eaten by hungry soldiers, which led to the spread of illness among the men. Additionally, bows often did not function at maximum effectiveness in the cold, damp climate. Li Rusong pointed to all these problems when discussing his reluctance to press the offensive after Pyŏkchegwan. He also feared that Katō Kiyomasa, who was still in Hamgyŏng, might take advantage of the opportunity to attack Pyongyang. For all these reasons he ordered a general withdrawal to Pyongyang, leaving Wang Bidi at Kaesŏng. Li also suggested that the Koreans might wish to temporarily pull back north of the Imjin River, but they refused, imploring the general to remain in Kaesŏng. But Song Yingchang echoed Li's concerns in his own communications to Shi Xing, stressing that it might be best to delay the advance to Seoul until the proper men and supplies could be mustered. Others suggested having Koreans lead Ming forces through the difficult terrain to facilitate quicker movement.[43]

Pyŏkchegwan also impressed upon both sides the importance of firearms and superior military technology. The Japanese were able to prevail on the peninsula at first because they had longer, sharper swords and more guns, but when the Ming main force arrived with additional cannon, the Japanese were forced to withdraw south. Northern cavalry units were at a serious disadvantage in mountainous Korea. There was not enough grassland to pasture their horses, especially in the winter, and their mobility was severely curtailed in the rugged terrain. The weapons these horsemen typically carried, namely bows and short swords, were ineffective against Japanese arquebuses fired from cover and katana wielded in hand-to-hand combat. Some Ming commanders complained that Japanese guns fired too fast for their men to counter. Others said the arquebuses had range but lacked accuracy, maintaining that their troops should just close on the Japanese and take advantage of this weakness. If the men did this, however, they would have to contend with the longer swords of the Japanese. Therefore, as the war dragged on, the Chinese rotated in more southern troops, infantry-based units trained in the tactics of Qi Jiguang.[44]

Moreover, the rivalry between northern and southern Chinese troops became one of the central features of the war. The Koreans generally appeared to have regarded southern troops as better fighters against the Japanese, though the northern troops did not lack in bravery. Part of this bias also comes through in the primary sources, many of which were written by southerners. They relate, for example, that in the Battle of Pyongyang, southern troops scaled the walls on foot, using the bodies of their slain comrades as steps, while northern troops simply pranced through the gates on horseback (though such charges were countered by northern soldiers and their commanders). But Li Rusong himself acknowledged the superiority of southern tactics in fighting the Japanese, telling Sŏnjo: "I am a general who hails from the north and I have much experience in the fighting tactics used by the nomads but here they are of no use. Now that I've come here, I am using the tactics of battling the Japanese discussed in General Qi [Jiguang's] *Jixiao xinshu* and I am able to attain total victory."[45]

The Koreans reportedly were greatly impressed with the training and discipline of southern troops and believed that Li Rusong should unleash them against the Japanese. They listened eagerly when Wu Weizhong, a southern Chinese general, said, "If I had another 20,000 southern troops along with your country's forces to support me, then your king's problems would be over." Some Korean sources asserted that Song and the southern troops itched to fight the Japanese in Seoul, but Li sought to slander them and prevent them from attaining their rightful glory. They charged that Li's wistful promises to crush the Japanese were no more than empty talk and complained that he owed his high rank and status solely to his family connections. As one Korean official argued: "The very survival of our country is at stake. How can one have thoughts of making peace?" Li replied by stating: "This has been the way of dealing with barbarians and protecting the state since ancient times. But you Koreans don't understand this." Song agreed: "The Japanese are no different from other barbarians, nor can they be trusted. But because they have been overawed by the might of the Celestial Empire, they dare not act again. Therefore, we will talk peace with them. The enemy is certainly duplicitous. And no doubt this [invasion] was a great insult and humiliation. But our little neighbor should not think of this as a hollow victory, but leave thoughts of these lofty matters to your superior." Unmoved by such arguments, some in the Korean camp even argued that Li should be replaced by Luo Shangzhi. They also believed rumors that Li's men had killed civilians in Pyongyang to get higher rewards. When the general asked them where they heard such lies, they simply responded, "It's public knowledge."[46]

Li also came under fire from his own subordinates. Wang Bidi charged: "Our leader is not insightful, trustworthy, or benevolent. How can it be said that he knows how to use troops properly?" Li asked him angrily how he could say such things, to which Wang responded that Li denied his men adequate food and drink, directed the battles from the rear, and refused to give the money or titles he promised to the first to ascend the walls of Pyongyang. Then afterward he proceeded to rush ahead of the whole army, get himself surrounded, lose heart, and retreat. "How can it not be said you don't know what you're doing?" concluded Wang. In his defense Li retorted that Korea had too many rice paddies and was ill suited to cavalry warfare. In addition, he was running short on supplies and food, and an epidemic was decimating his horses. Li also took shots at Song Yingchang, saying that Song, as a civil official, should leave military decisions to those who best understood them. Chastising his subordinate commanders, Li continued: "When we went together to put down the rebellion in the west [Pubei's] you went for days without food and none of you dared utter a word about it. Upon our return all my followers were amply rewarded. Now when we go a few days without proper rations in Korea, you dare to talk like this! If you want to leave, then leave. We have not yet exterminated the Japanese and I will not turn my horse around and return [to China] until I have attained my goal."[47] With this, the assembled commanders bowed and left in search of food around the city. Li dispatched Zhang Shijue to spy on the Japanese in Seoul.

Urging the Koreans not to rely so much on Chinese assistance, the Ming Ministry of War nevertheless sent another 3,000 liang of silver to reward them for their valiant resistance. Wanli also ordered the Ministries of War and Revenue to procure and send the needed men and supplies. Specifically, Liu Ting was expected soon with as many as 10,000 troops and 300,000 piculs (nearly 20,000 tons) of supplies by sea. The Ming reassured the Koreans that Hideyoshi now had to deal with not only Korea but also the vast resources of China, so they should not be too hasty in pushing for action. They also reminded that the very survival of Korea was due solely to Ming aid. After all, the Chinese could have simply defended the Yalu and left the peninsula to Japan. But instead they had spent huge amounts of silver and dispatched troops hundreds of miles to Korea.[48]

Castigating the Koreans, Song Yingchang said:

Now in eight to nine months you Koreans did not recover even an inch of territory, yet in the space of just a couple of months and in one decisive action two capitals have been recovered and the Japanese have fled the northern provinces; this requires no great investigation [as to why it happened]. Our great celestial empire has nine frontiers, all crawling with barbarians. Now if they enter and raid, we punish them; but if they beg for tribute trade tomorrow, we allow it. This case is no different. To love life and hate killing is the Way of Heaven. . . . Now if the Japanese ask for negotiations to open trade relations, we may temporarily allow it, perhaps along the lines of Ningbo like before, but even if we withdraw our troops, we'll leave anywhere from 4,000–5,000 to 10,000 troops behind to guard key points, and over the next ten to twenty years, your officials and troops can recover and select generals to train the soldiers while your country gradually rebuilds itself. Only after your preparations are complete and you are strong enough to defend yourselves will we completely withdraw.[49]

Song went on to emphasize to his hosts that the allowance of tribute trade was merely an expedient to buy time. Their forces were not quite ready to assail what could be a very stoutly defended Seoul, but they had no intention of allowing the Japanese to stay there for long. The king replied that since ancient times China had always sought victory first, then talked peace. But now the Ming contended that supply woes were slowing the advance even as the Japanese were overawed. The Koreans also argued that the Japanese were negotiating for exactly the same reason as the Chinese. Attempting to mollify the monarch, Song said that he would send the Koreans skilled armorers and craftsmen to oversee the expanded production of weapons so that the kingdom could rely on its own strength in the future. He also recommended the wider implementation of military farms. Other Ming officials told Korean commoners that they would be rewarded and gain official rank with the submission of Japanese heads.[50]

Allied commanders looked to Korean civilians to take an active part in wearing down the invaders. They hoped that the 40,000 or so Koreans still in Seoul could serve as spies and possibly help in the event of an assault upon the city. The southern populace was instructed to make efforts to sink Japanese boats coming from Tsushima while at sea or even with shore batteries, if available. On land, because they were excellent archers, the Koreans could be used in point positions to decimate the Japanese from the flanks while the Ming brought their heavy guns to bear in the center. Chŏlla was still seen as essential to the whole country in terms of both supplies and manpower reserves. If its grain stores could be kept out of enemy hands, then soldiers could keep the pressure on the Japanese from the south. The key, from the government's perspective, was ensuring that national interests trumped local interests in effecting a restoration of royal power. A memorial from the Korean Ministry of War estimated that they could provision the Ming forces for another six months under current conditions.[51]

The Ming had also sent envoys to meet with Katō Kiyomasa, apparently just prior to the Battle of Pyŏkchegwan. At that time he indicated that the minimum he would accept in exchange for the captured Korean princes was the cession of half of Korea to Japan. They dismissed this out of hand. Referring to Hideyoshi as "*taikō*, minister to the king of the petty state of Japan," the Ming informed Katō that lesser countries had been blessed with investiture from the Chinese court for a hundred generations. But now they were forced to assemble an army to punish the Japanese for their insolence, and 400,000 more troops were mustering in Liaodong. Katō responded that the Japanese could wipe out an army of 400,000 in a mere forty days, adding that even a mountain of jade (as a bribe) would not be enough to stop the Japanese now. He vowed to march to Beijing, burn down its palaces, and take the emperor prisoner alongside the Korean princes he already held, thereby securing for himself China's four hundred prefectures.[52]

Katō's boasts and the success at Pyŏkchegwan notwithstanding, Japanese armies were in dire straits. Troop strength had declined in every unit. Konishi Yukinaga's division was down 60–65 percent, and Kobayakawa Takakage's divisional strength was off by 44 percent. Of the more than 160,000 troops that had first landed in Korea, by the spring of 1593, perhaps 100,000 or so were still fit for combat. The winter had been hard on the occupiers, losing large numbers of men to frostbite, starvation, and diseases. Japanese troops hoping to find refuge in Seoul were faced with severe food shortages, a problem that would soon worsen.[53] Korean guerrilla attacks also took their toll. Some Japanese even fell prey to hungry tigers as they retreated from the northeast south toward Seoul.

The allies were enthused about these reports and started leaning toward attacking Seoul. Zha Dashou led a small group of troops to the city, where they burned 100,000 piculs (6,666 tons) of grain stores, shot three Japanese, and captured another, thereby learning just how precarious the invaders' situation had become. There were now perhaps 30,000–40,000 troops in city, and they wanted to withdraw but had to wait for Hideyoshi's order. Although 200,000 more Japanese were anticipated, the defenders had no clue as to when these troops would arrive. In any case, Song felt that within ten days the ground would be dry enough for the Ming to transport their cannon to the city walls and blast their way in as they had done at Pyongyang.[54]

The allies now hoped to establish firmer ties with the Korean resistance south of Seoul, in large part because they needed access to provisions. But they were hampered by many people's lack of faith in the central government's ability to restore and maintain order in the long run.[55] Some guerrilla leaders like Kwak Chaeu resented being shackled by the central authorities. Others were eager to forward heads to the court to collect their rewards. Still others demanded compensation from the government even if they had done very little for the cause. Furthermore, many commoners were upset that allied victories in the north often resulted in more vicious Japanese reprisals in the south.

Just before the Japanese abandoned Seoul, they tried to take the nearby fortress of Haengju. Katō Kiyomasa and Nabeshima Naoshige had joined their comrades at Seoul, and they hoped that another quick victory could throw water on the surging spirits of the Koreans. Haengju was a mere fourteen kilometers southwest of Seoul on a hill along the Han River. It was defended by Kwŏn Yul, who had a total of perhaps 10,000 men under his command, including 1,000 warrior-monks. He also had a number of ingenious hwacha, or fire carts, which consisted of a wooden cart on two wheels topped with a honeycomb-like structure holding either one hundred steel-tipped arrows affixed with small gunpowder charges or two hundred smaller arrows.[56] Although unwieldy, they could be devastating against massed formations. As Haengju was situated atop a steep hill, it was the ideal setting for the deployment of such a weapon.

The Japanese launched their attack on March 14. Because they had a significant numerical advantage, they rotated their units in assaults on the stronghold. Kwŏn ordered his archers to rain arrows down upon the attackers while soldiers and commoners hurled rocks. Women even carried rocks in their aprons to the men on the walls. Hwacha were used to great effect. Corpses piled up outside the walls, reportedly hampering the attackers still more. At one point the defenders ran out of arrows but were resupplied in the nick of time. Nine successive assaults were turned back, the defenders putting out numerous fires within the fortress as well. The warrior-monks were especially valiant in defending the northwest corner of the fort. The Koreans took 110 heads and recovered 727 weapons in repulsing the Japanese. Ukita Hideie, the Japanese commander of Seoul, was wounded in the engagement. Knowing the Ming were approaching and seeing a Korean relief force coming up the Han, the Japanese broke off the attack and returned to Seoul.[57]

Hailed as one of the three great Korean land victories of the war, Haengju coupled with the daring raid on the Japanese grain stores and the increasing pressure from guerrilla forces in Ch'ungch'ŏng and Kyŏnggi provinces, rendered the Japanese position tenuous indeed. Jubilant Koreans hung Japanese heads from the gates of Kaesŏng, prompting a Ming officer to exclaim, "The people of Korea now chop off enemy heads as if they were splitting balls." Li Rusong dispatched Zha Dashou to meet with Kwŏn Yul; upon meeting him Zha remarked, "Foreign lands do have formidable generals, after all!"[58] Kwŏn then went to Paju as the Japanese attempted to reinforce Seoul in anticipation of an allied assault. Some Japanese commanders apparently advocated attacking Kwŏn in revenge, but his position was deemed too strong to seriously threaten.

Song Yingchang again called upon Shen Weijing's services, dispatching him to Seoul to negotiate with Konishi Yukinaga. But because the court did not completely trust Shen, they assigned another official of equal rank to accompany him to the Japanese camp to present their demands, which included total withdrawal from Korea, the return of the princes, and leaving grain in Seoul. The meeting took place at Yŏngsan, ten li (3.5 miles) south of the city's great south gate. As he was out of supplies and his forces had suffered a series of defeats, Konishi was of a mind to retreat and agreed to abandon the city so formal talks could begin. According to some sources, the Japanese "felt repentant for the disaster" they had inflicted upon Korea and now just wanted to resume tribute-trade relations.[59] This suggestion is belied, however, by the fact that the Japanese looted and plundered Seoul as they retreated, desecrating tombs and creating all manner of havoc.

Regardless, after consulting with Ukita Hideie and Ishida Mitsunari, Konishi and Katō met with Shen again. The Japanese tentatively agreed to return the princes and effect a gradual withdrawal to Pusan and its environs, where further negotiations would take place, as long as the Ming agreed to pull back to Kaesŏng and send a delegation to Japan. Katō apparently was furious that because of Konishi's defeat in a single battle, the Japanese were going to cast aside everything they had gained. He was also perturbed that if recalled to Japan, he would be unable to influence events in Korea, even maintaining that he could still take Beijing with only 20,000–30,000 men.[60]

As could be expected, the Koreans were displeased with these talks. One Korean official had seen the two princes and determined that they were unharmed and so therefore suggested that the Japanese might really be interested in peace. But others were not so sure. Vigorous debates ensued as virtually no one trusted the Japanese and the Koreans were eager for revenge. Some suggested that the Korean princes and their ministers be returned in front of the whole allied army as a gesture of good faith, but the Japanese refused to do so just yet. Li Rusong dispatched men to the Korean camps for talks, but the allies were soon bickering over the best approach, even getting into squabbles over the Koreans' refusal to bow before the Ming imperial banner at one point. The Chinese finally told the Koreans that they would allow the Japanese to withdraw after turning over the princes and their ministers, but then they would pursue them. The Koreans were still angry, but Qian Shizhen taunted them by bringing up the king's flight the previous year.[61]

Shen Weijing met the Japanese commanders again on a boat in the Han River on May 9. He told them that they must withdraw or face total annihilation, but that if the princes and ministers were returned, the Ming would allow Hideyoshi to be enfeoffed as a Ming vassal king. But if the taikō did not change his ways, the Son of Heaven would amass troops from all over the Ming empire as well as the vassal states to gather and assemble secret weapons to punish the Japanese. In their own discussions the Japanese commanders complained about supply woes, the difficulty of receiving timely orders from Hideyoshi, and the problems of moving reinforcements from Japan to Korea and then across the peninsula. They understood too the very real possibility of much larger Ming armies coming via land and sea. According to the *Chōsen seibatsuki*, Hideyoshi "cried many tears and complained how utterly frustrating it was to have been born in a small country and be unable to conquer China because of lack of troops. . . . He gnashed his teeth and those who heard him were all impressed by his ambitions and wetted their sleeves."[62] As things stood, only Katō opposed releasing the princes. Song Yingchang named Xie Yongzi and Xu Yiguan as his envoys. They arrived in Seoul on May 17, just in time to accompany the Japanese south. The envoys were instructed to go to Nagoya, discern Hideyoshi's true intentions, and return with a recommendation of a course of action.

The Japanese abandoned Seoul on May 18, 1593. Li Rusong and Song Yingchang entered the city together and were shocked at the pitiful sights that greeted them. The general populace had been systematically brutalized ever since the Japanese loss of Pyongyang. The people were starving and "looked like ghosts." The stench of decaying men and horses was so powerful that the troops had to cover their noses. Zha Dashou saw a starving child sucking on the nipple of its dead mother. Deeply moved, he took the baby back to the Ming camp to be raised by the Chinese. The liberators distributed some 1,000 piculs (67 tons) of food to the populace, and Yu Sŏngnyong appointed a starvation-relief commissioner, telling him to find creative ways to feed the people, even using pine needles if necessary. The Ming distributed more food, but it was insufficient, and Yu imagined the spirits of the dead wailing through the night, keeping him awake.[63]

The rebuilding process started immediately, aided greatly by contingents of monks. Korean officials went to the state ancestral altars and wept. Li Rusong moved into the Palace of the Little Princess, a residence formerly occupied by Ukita Hideie and one of the few palaces still standing. Asked about pursuing the Japanese, he said that he could not cross the river due to the lack of boats. When Yu offered to procure some, Li replied, "That would be great!"[64] Korean officers gathered some eighty boats and sent word to the Ming commander.

His bluff called, Li ordered some of his men to go after the Japanese, with Li Rubo actually taking 10,000 men across the river in pursuit of the enemy. But the Japanese were able to make their escape. Li Rubo in explaining himself complained that it got dark as they tried to cross and that he had developed a foot ailment. Song Yingchang reported allied forces killed 149 Japanese and captured 1 alive as they took the capital. Kwŏn Yul arrived soon after Rubo's abandoned chase and urged the Ming to pursue the enemy, saying that he would lead the troops himself. Li Rusong praised Kwŏn's valor but cautioned against ruining the peace talks. Li was eventually overridden by Song, who ordered Ming forces to follow the Japanese. But because the Japanese had retained the two princes and had them in the rear of their column, the Ming only shadowed them and did not attack.[65]

Song told the allied forces to stay about one or two days behind the Japanese, close enough to check them, but far enough away to not provoke them. The Koreans asked the Ming to station contingents of troops in key cities and at strategic passes around the southeast to check possible Japanese aggression. These Chinese troops were also expected to help train Korean units. Li Rusong crossed the Han River on May 31 at the head of 30,000 troops, and Liu Ting moved to Ch'ŏngju four days later with his 5,000 men. But they then had to wait for supplies from the southeast and suggested building floating bridges to expedite grain shipments. The Koreans were not pleased with this strategy, wanting faster and more aggressive action. Even in the countryside, Ŏ Hŭimun lamented that the Chinese had "turned their backs on manifesting the awe of Heaven."[66]

The Ming forces proceeded rather slowly, Li Rusong evincing concern about running into ambushes. Rumors circulated about possible further Japanese attacks, including strikes upon the coast of China itself. Nevertheless, because the allies were still outnumbered, commanders deemed it prudent not to rush into anything. As more troops were already coming from China, the Ming still believed they could fight later if necessary. At the very least a formidable interlocking defense system could be created. For example, 8,000 troops were detailed to Choryŏng Pass, where Sin Ip had fallen the previous year. Song Yingchang also recommended that the Koreans adopt the same kinds of coastal-defense measures implemented in China. Many Koreans burned with anger upon hearing that Ming soldiers had been instructed not to kill Japanese.[67]

Despite the horrors that had greeted them in Seoul, Song sent a congratulatory letter to Sŏnjo, saying: "Now the Japanese villains have been trampled underfoot and the three capitals of the kingdom of Korea as well as all of the prefectures and districts have all been recovered. Gazing out there is no one who can match the bravery of these heroes alongside their righteous armies. The difficult task of recovering your country is nearly accomplished." For his part, at least according to Korean accounts, Li Rusong was now eager to go home, believing his mission accomplished. He sent a letter to Song telling him that he would pull out as soon as the Japanese withdrew.[68]

Katō Kiyomasa had retreated with his royal bargaining chips in tow alongside the other Japanese commanders. He was told that if any harm came to either of the princes, the Ming army would annihilate the entire invasion force. Although Hideyoshi had already issued orders for the dispatch of reinforcements and supplies, he had altered his directives to allow for a strategic retreat pending the stabilization of the situation. Many troops stayed in Korea, reinforcing strongholds that became known as wajō, or Japanese castles.[69] Essentially, the Japanese expanded existing Korean mountain fortresses by erecting additional defensive works of earth and stone in circles radiating out from a fortified inner bastion. In both form and function, they closely resembled the castles then found in Japan. As the inner bailey was situated on high ground, it exposed attackers to sniper fire from Japanese arquebuses and cannon and often made it difficult for the Ming to get their heavier artillery into place.

These castles were located both along the coast and on nearby islands. This allowed commanders to support one another if threatened and also receive supplies from Tsushima and Japan proper. Katō Kiyomasa established himself outside Ungchŏn proper with 6,790 men; Konishi Yukinaga, Sō Yoshitoshi, and Nabeshima Naoshige were stationed in three castles around Sŏsaengpo with more than 15,000 men between them; Mōri Hidemoto commanded just over 17,000 in the environs of Pusan; and Kobayakawa Takakage had 6,600 men in Ungchŏn. The total number of Japanese in these castles as of mid-1593 was around 78,000. The larger garrisons were expected to house 5,000–7,000 troops; the smaller ones about one-third this number. All were outfitted with at least a few large-caliber guns and greater numbers of smaller firearms in addition to bows, arrows, swords, spears, helmets, armor, gunpowder, lead, sulfur, and saltpeter.[70] Hideyoshi dispatched physicians for all divisions, and both Buddhist and Catholic chaplains arrived to minister to the spiritual needs of the troops. The fortresses themselves were usually built by Korean slave labor or common Japanese brought along by the troops to perform menial tasks. Korean cooks and entertainers, including women, were also brought in for the enjoyment of the men.

But even though the Sino-Korean allies had some reason to believe they held the upper hand in the impending peace talks by virtue of their recapture of Korea's three ancient capitals, the Japanese were not quite ready to surrender all the initiative. The city-fortress of Chinju, which the Japanese had failed to take the previous autumn due to the exploits of the martyred Kim Simin, lay within easy reach of their strongholds along the coast. Taking this city could serve the purposes of revenge and restore some of Japan's lost military mystique, thereby perhaps putting them in a stronger negotiating position. Since Hideyoshi had issued multiple orders to attack the city dating back to March 1593, Ukita Hideie, Katō Kiyomasa, Konishi Yukinaga, Mōri Terumoto, and Kobayakawa Takakage led some 90,000 troops against the city, their forces bolstered by reinforcements from Japan that had arrived too late to garrison Seoul. Prior to this renewed assault, the Koreans under Kwŏn Yul and Kim Myŏngwŏn closed in on the Japanese positions, hoping to take advantage of the enemy's weakened state. The Koreans advanced to the city of Haman, which they found abandoned. They were unsure as to what to do next, but Ming and Korean units occupied a number of fortresses in Kyŏngsang and Chŏlla provinces to forestall any Japanese thrusts at the capital. Li Rusong promised help from Namwŏn, believing that city could hold out for awhile if attacked.[71]

Liu Ting sent a letter to Katō saying that Wanli remained red with anger over the invasion and that even now a million troops were on their way to obliterate the Japanese should the peace talks fail. Katō rightly believed that Liu was bluffing and led his men on to Chinju.

Kim Myŏngwŏn realized that city was in danger and hoped to mobilize help, but none was forthcoming. Yi Chong'in was forced to hold his position alone at Chinju as his co-commander Kim fled, prompting Yi to say: "Even now the righteous armies and their generals are coming to our rescue. Those who are so faithless as to want to abandon the city deserve to be executed!" Kwak Chaeu recommended abandoning the city, arguing that it was isolated and indefensible. Still, Chinju was strongly protected by its walls, the Nam River to the south, and a large moat to the north. Nevertheless, the Japanese assembled a force of some 60,000 east of the city for their attack. The city's permanent garrison was about 4,000 men. Yi dispatched a man to get help from Liu Ting, but Liu did not arrive in time. Korean official Kim Ch'ŏnil arrived to aid in its defense as did a small contingent of Chinese troops on July 17, promising that more help was on the way.[72]

The Japanese detailed several thousand troops to the mountains northeast of the city as their main body surrounded Chinju. Rather than engaging them, the Koreans fell back into defensive positions. The Japanese erected tall bamboo shields to protect their advance. A Japanese spy reported that there were virtually no soldiers in the city, only civilians, prompting one commander to suggest withdrawing altogether. But Sō Yoshitoshi and Matsura Shigenobu pointed out that Korean soldiers could sneak into the city and set up an ambush. This led Katō to order a massive assault. The Japanese hit the city in force on July 21, with their troops on the surrounding hills raining bullets, stones, and arrows down on the hapless Koreans. The defenders had filled their moat, but the attackers broke it and diverted the water toward the river. They then used stones, sticks, and earth to fill in the empty ditch. Remembering how they had been bested the previous year, this time the Japanese erected massive siege towers and devised ingenious *kikkōsha,* or turtle carts, that consisted of frames with reinforced covers that allowed the attackers to get close to the city walls for sapping operations. The Koreans countered by dropping burning pine torches atop them, incinerating the carts and roasting the soldiers within. Katō then ordered new kikkōsha built with specially treated ox hides for fire prevention.[73]

Kim Ch'ŏnil continued to lead the defense, despite the fact that he was barely able to walk and often had to be carried on a palanquin, supposedly even making rice gruel for the soldiers with his own hands. Through the next several days, the Koreans resisted stubbornly, with some escaping by scaling the walls and moving through the forested hills in hopes of finding the Ming forces. Most of these men were rounded up and killed by the Japanese. Korean officer Hwang Chin was killed by a bullet. His command was assumed by So Yewŏn, who led mobile defense efforts around the city. On July 24, relief troops approached from the east, but they could not break the siege. That night the attackers breached the east gate, which fell with an earthshaking crash. Fierce fighting ensued, but the Japanese were forced to retreat. Four more assaults were turned back on July 25, the Koreans inflicting heavy losses with their black mark cannon.[74]

The Japanese attacked the north and west sides of the city the next day, erecting great wooden stockades outside the east gate after the Koreans set up cannon there. Katō's men countered with battering rams and tried to set fires in the city. These efforts were initially successful, with fires breaking out all over, but they were doused by heavy rains. Asked to surrender, Kim replied, "I'll give my life in battle for the country and that is all." Still, the Japanese would not be denied, and they finally breached the walls on July 27, as Katō and Kuroda clashed with Yi Chong'in and his personal retinue. The rains that had doused the city's fires also undermined the walls, which started to collapse. The people fought back with sticks, stones, and thorns, but their fate was obvious and many fled. The Japanese advanced in stout armor with large shields and forced their way in, but they were turned back by a doughty Korean official from Kimhae, who slew five men by himself, and by commoners hurling vats of boiling oil. According to Korean accounts, at least 1,000 Japanese were killed.[75]

Japanese corpses piled up outside the fortress as Korean spears and arrows took their toll. It seemed that Katō was actually going to pull back and wait to finish the attack the next day. At this juncture, however, the soldiers defending the north gate, feeling that all was lost, started abandoning their positions. The Japanese quickly took advantage and swarmed in. Kim Ch'ŏnil and his son saw this from a pavilion overlooking the fortress, and they committed suicide by jumping into the river below. So Yewŏn was decapitated by the Japanese upon their entry into the city; his one of 20,000 heads taken that day.[76]

When the Japanese finally entered the city, they systematically slaughtered virtually everyone within, allowing just one person to live to report the tragedy to his countrymen, according to some sources. An area for some five li (1.75 miles) around the city, plus the river, was allegedly filled with Korean corpses. One survivor warned the Japanese that the Ming were on their way, but they shrugged him off, saying, "The Ming have already withdrawn." Even cows, horses, and chickens reportedly did not escape the carnage. This massacre of some 60,000 Koreans was the single greatest atrocity of the entire war. It was widely believed at the time that Katō had orchestrated the slaughter to curry favor with Hideyoshi and overshadow his rival, Konishi Yukinaga. Hideyoshi is said to have been delighted with the results of the siege, and he bestowed Katō with the greatest honors for being the first commander into the city.[77]

Chinju also provided one of the most romanticized episodes of the war. The legend is that as the victorious Japanese generals celebrated in Chinju Castle, one of them was enticed to a balcony by a beautiful Korean courtesan named Nongae, who then pulled him with her off the edge of the parapet to their deaths among the rocks below. A memorial shrine to Nongae was later erected at the site. She is even honored in contemporary Korea as a symbol of female patriotism and sacrifice by virtue of "Miss Nongae" contests.[78]

In the wake of this defeat, Li Rusong ordered his generals to move to cut off all key routes to the capital. Some Korean units skirmished with the enemy, supposedly even driving them back after an ambush. Liu Ting did not join them, though, claiming he had no authority to act. Liu did, however, send a letter to Katō, warning him: "The fighting is not over. When our emperor hears of this, he will be furious and send a tigerish official with the aim of completely wiping you out and extending the battle across the Eastern Sea. . . . You have no idea of the resources of the Celestial Empire." The Chinese also warned that the massacre might abrogate any existing arrangement, adding that if all the Japanese withdrew from Korea, then it might not be necessary for the Ming to send more troops. Katō and his forces soon pulled back to their wajō, some strengthening their defenses, others heading home.[79] Chinju was eventually reoccupied by Luo Shangzhi and Yi Pin.

It is somewhat startling that the massacre at Chinju did not derail peace talks entirely. The Koreans were certainly outraged and wanted discussions stopped. But the Ming envoys were already in Japan, having left Pusan for Nagoya on June 13. In addition, the Japanese returned the captive princes, supposedly at the behest of Konishi Yukinaga, though sources differ as to whether they were returned before or after the attack on Chinju. Some suggest that they were released after the attack in

order to prevent the negotiations from failing, while others indicate
that the princes were released before the sack, possibly to lull the allies
into complacency.[80] Deflecting the blame, Konishi would later claim
that it was at the express orders of Hideyoshi that the castle was sacked
and that he himself had nothing to do with it. Furthermore, Shen Weijing
had allegedly heard of the impending assault while in Katō's camp and
attempted to warn the Chinese and Korean commanders, as well as dissuade Katō from attacking, but failed. Song Yingchang and Li Rusong
did not believe his explanation. When asked how Shen could have let
this happen, Song replied: "At the time he was still in Japan and the
Korean princes were in Japanese hands. This was simply done to vent
Hideyoshi's wrath." Konishi said that if the city had simply been abandoned, the Japanese would have just returned east, adding: "This stops
at Chinju. There will be no more incidents." He then dispatched his
houseman, Konishi Joan, with Shen to go to China to continue negotiations. Konishi Joan reached Seoul in mid-August 1593.[81]

Almost as galling to some Koreans were reports that Ming troops
were indiscriminately commandeering food and supplies from commoners' homes, including valuables and livestock. Such activities
were curtailed by Chinese officers. Adding to the confusion, Korean
commoners took to dressing themselves as Japanese and raiding towns
and villages themselves. These problems were exacerbated by food
shortages all over the country.[82]

In a letter to the king, Song Yingchang requested that 20,000 troops
be left behind. These would be arrayed in two major camps: one at
Taegu, to guard Kyǒngsang and the approach to Seoul, and the other in
the vicinity of Chinju, perhaps Namwǒn. Chinese troops stationed in
Korea received 1.5 liang of pay per month but were eligible for additional
hardship pay, including money for rations, bringing total pay to 3.6 liang
per month. At this rate it would cost 1 million liang of silver to leave a
force that size in Korea for one year. Ming officials were worried about
the Koreans' ability to sustain such a force, noting that while China's
resources were plentiful, Korea was deficient in mineral wealth. The
Chinese therefore pledged to provide 30 percent of the upkeep for their
soldiers.[83] Extra funds were authorized for winter uniforms as well. Most
of the troops left behind would be southerners and would provide assistance with training and repairing defenses.

Acting on requests from Song and Li Rusong, Wanli issued an order
for a general withdrawal. Li had already detailed some 12,000 troops to

stay behind, and Song was looking for 8,000 more to reach his goal. Of these 12,000 men, 1,000 were specifically noted as being firearms specialists and would be deployed in key spots in Chŏlla and Kyŏngsang. They were to be augmented by Korean forces trained and outfitted like southern Chinese. But the aforementioned supply woes soon forced the Ming to revise their total figure down to 16,000 troops, provided the reports from their envoys to Japan were positive.[84]

Li Rusong's services were also apparently needed to help quell another troop mutiny in the northeast. Before leaving, he had sent a letter to the king concerning the reinforcement of walls and improvement of defenses all over Korea. He also addressed high Korean officials about how the Ming had rescued a weak and imperiled Korea and that they should never forget.[85] Nevertheless, even though he himself had repeatedly asked to be recalled, the general expressed regret that the mission had not been fully accomplished. Upon his departure, Li wrote a poem to one of his Korean hosts:

> I have heard it said that all us generals will take off our armor
>   and return home
> Certainly your dynasty now lies between survival and ruin
> If the [Ming] court gives the command to withdraw
> Then not only will the lips die, the teeth will freeze.[86]

The majority of the Ming troops headed for Liaodong on September 16. The Chinese even set about creating a twenty-year defense plan for Korea, arguing that even if only able-bodied men from the ages of twenty to forty were raised, the Koreans should be able to come up with 10,000 soldiers per province, totaling 80,000 for the whole kingdom. Ming officials circulated memorials concerning the exact dimensions of various town walls and their suggested improvements for each, detailing the types of materials to be used in construction and the best weapons for defending certain structures and areas. Commanders were given specific training responsibilities; Song Dabin, for example, was entrusted with helping the Koreans cast and deploy cannon, while Liu Ting was to help in regular drilling exercises.[87] Ming officers emphasized the value of using Korea's rugged terrain to best advantage. They even offered to assist their hosts in locating and exploiting mineral resources so that the troops could be paid.

Song Yingchang and King Sŏnjo engaged in many discussions concerning the improvement of Korea's military. The Ming also told their hosts that, as noted by Qi Jiguang, ferocity was not enough, training and drilling must come first. They stressed that Korea's entire military culture needed to be overhauled, recommending that first the king should appoint one general in overall command with total authority to make and enforce regulations. They said that if the king himself acted sternly, all others would fall in line. Sŏnjo finally returned to Seoul on October 27, taking responsibility for the calamity and performing a series of ceremonies at the ancestral altars. Although pleased, Wanli warned him that the Ming were not inclined to make a habit out of saving Korea.[88]

The Koreans followed these recommendations. Yi Sunsin was promoted to be the naval commander of the three southern provinces. Troop-recruitment efforts were stepped up all over the south. Special military examinations were held, and men were given military rank if they submitted one severed Japanese head, though this allegedly led to the decapitations of hapless commoners. In the twelfth month of 1593 alone, the king appointed 11 new civil and some 1,600 new military officials. Kwŏn Yul selected another 900 military officials for service at Hapchŏn. On the defensive front, many sansŏng (mountain fortresses) were rebuilt and firearms sent to key garrisons. The court also ordered the disbanding of the ŭibyŏng forces, fearing that they would now start causing chaos themselves. But many ŭibyŏng leaders refused, saying they would not now take orders from officials who had earlier fled their posts or took no part in resisting the initial invasion.[89]

Song Yingchang's misgivings were confirmed by skirmishes between allied and Japanese forces throughout the fall. Liu Ting, for example, had to be saved by Korean general Ko Ŏnbaek after the Japanese encircled his position. The Chinese sent more investigators to ascertain the state of affairs along the coast. While Konishi repeatedly denied that Japanese looting had anything to do with him, rumors that another offensive was planned for the spring permeated the Korean countryside. These tales were given added veracity by the fact that they often came from those who had escaped Japanese captivity or others freed by the allies after battles. While admitting that the improved security of Kangwŏn and Chŏlla was due largely to the presence of Chinese troops, the Koreans remained upset that the Japanese occupiers were allowed too much freedom to act in the southeast, thereby affording them the opportunity to reinforce their castles and prepare for renewed hostilities.[90]

In late August, Kobayakawa Takakage and Mōri Terumoto received permission to return to Japan with their troops. They would soon be joined by many others. By early fall there were only about 43,000 Japanese remaining in Korea. Of the major commanders left, Katō Kiyomasa was stationed at Sŏsaengpo; Konishi Yukinaga, Sō Yoshitoshi, and Matsura Shigenobu were around Ungch'ŏn in three separate wajō; Shimazu Yoshihiro was at Yŏngdŭngpo on Kŏje Island; and Shimazu Yoshihisa held a fort on Cheju Island. Shimazu's wajō at Cheju, for example, had a garrison of 2,000 men. The fortress mounted 105 artillery pieces, including one heavy gun, a number of medium-caliber weapons, and seventy-two light (two *monme*) short guns. Ammunition and supplies for these weapons consisted of 400 jin (532 pounds) of saltpeter, 400 jin of gunpowder, 450 jin of lead, 40 jin of sulfur, and 4,000 bullets. The garrison also had 100 bows, 2,000 arrows, 400 swords, fifteen suits of armor, seven helmets, and 100 spears.[91] Supplies such as these suggest that the Japanese were not planning on pulling out soon but do not necessarily indicate a particularly long occupation. But the arrival of Catholic missionaries in the camps of Christian daimyo such as Konishi and Sō the following year suggest the expectation of a longer stay.

Indeed, Jesuit Father Gregorio de Cespedes would be Korea's first European visitor. He had originally arrived in Japan in 1577 and interacted with a number of that nation's most prominent Christian converts, including Konishi Yukinaga, whose daughter married Sō Yoshitoshi, convincing him to convert too. In late 1593 Konishi invited Father de Cespedes to come to Korea to console the Christians there, which especially pleased Konishi's daughter, who had apparently accompanied her husband to Korea.[92] In fact, of all the daimyo serving under Konishi, only the Matsura were not Christians. Unfortunately the Jesuits encountered virtually no Koreans in amiable settings, and their accounts are generally testaments to Japanese brutality. When not receiving spiritual solace, the Japanese diverted themselves with sports, dancing, singing, theatrical productions, and tiger hunting, the latter being a particular favorite of Katō Kiyomasa, who forbade his men from engaging in frivolous pursuits like drama despite the fact that it was a favorite pastime of Hideyoshi himself.

The castles also served as transit points for Korean products, including pottery, and of course, slaves. Women and children were sent back to Japan in large numbers, and traitorous Korean officials and commoners were apparently the major suppliers of slaves. Some of these hapless individuals would remain in Japan for years or even settle there permanently. Nonetheless, there were some positive ramifications from these activities. Some Korean officials developed friendships with their Japanese captors and helped introduce Neo-Confucian teachings to Japan in a way previously unknown. And for the historian, the diaries of captives such as Kang Hang provide a great deal of information about social and intellectual life in Japan at the turn of the seventeenth century.[93] But these positive aspects should not obscure the inexcusable actions that led to their development. Even today descendants of Korean captives are often treated as second-class citizens in Japan.

But as the Japanese strengthened their position in and exploitation of Korea, peace negotiations continued. Song Yingchang was angry that the invaders had still not pulled out of Korea entirely, and his letters from late 1593 include frequent references to Japanese raids and unrest in the countryside. He continued to doubt the wisdom of Ming withdrawal but felt that his hands were tied. Song gave Liu Ting instructions for offering military safe havens for the common folk and told him that those who no longer wished to be soldiers could now return to their previous occupations.[94] The Ming even discussed measures for reintegrating those who had been impressed into Japanese service into Korean society, though these individuals often came under suspicion from their countrymen. Interestingly enough, the Ming troops left behind were forced to assume many of the duties and functions expected of international peacekeeping forces in the modern era, albeit with absolutely no real training or clearly defined spheres of responsibility.

Song finally asked to resign on account of illness, blaming Korea's climate and lack of proper doctors for his deteriorating health. In actuality, he was clearly fed up with the factional wrangling that undermined his war efforts and tired of coming under fire from officials in China who had little understanding of the military situation in Korea. Some sources indicate that Song was actually impeached and dismissed, though the many honors he received upon his return to China argue against this. A modern Chinese historian has also suggested that Song was perturbed that Li Rusong received undue credit for what the Ming had managed to achieve. Korean sources report that it was Song who strongly advised leaving at least a token Ming force in Korea as a deterrent because of his distrust of the Japanese, urging the court not to throw away what had already been achieved. He believed that Korea's interests were also China's and that defending Korea should remain the top Ming priority. Wanli accepted Song's resignation and replaced him with Gu Yangqian. Gu was instructed to proceed directly to Ningyuan and confer with the generals there about logistical matters. Yi Hangbok and Yun Tusu immediately asked Gu to reconsider the Ming position on continuing peace talks.[95]

The emperor thanked Song Yingchang and received four sets of red python robes, 100 liang of silver, and a hereditary official post for one son. He was also promoted to the post of censor in chief of the right. Other Ming officers and military heroes received promotions and awards as well. In order to ameliorate the plight of starving Koreans, the emperor ordered the dispatch of another 100,000 piculs (6,666 tons) of grain from Shandong. Diaries from the time indicate that starvation was widespread, and many ordinary Koreans resented the armies for consuming so much food.[96] But when the troops were not fed, they often preyed upon commoners, despite explicit prohibitions against such actions.

Meanwhile, as Li Rusong returned to Liaoyang, the Ming court was still divided over how to handle the Japanese. Many argued that investing Hideyoshi as a king even without allowing trade was bad enough, but entering into a marriage alliance, as some rumored, was utterly beneath the dignity of the Celestial Empire. Moreover, the Ming needed to consider the views of Korea and China's other tributary states. Some officials continued to advocate the use of force, even if just to improve their negotiating position. Others favored a more conciliatory stance. Shi Xing finally recommended investing Hideyoshi as a tributary prince without the privilege of tribute trade (xu feng bu xu gong). Many were unhappy with this decision. Xiao Ruxun, who had earned rewards for valor in the suppression of the Ningxia mutiny the previous year, said: "the Japanese will always be vicious pirates. How can the Ming show favor to the rapacious kampaku with his reckless disregard for life?"[97]

The Koreans agreed with Xiao's assessment, calling the decision "an error of state" and questioning the motives of Shi and Shen Weijing. They also criticized Ming planning and gullibility, asking how many deals with the Japanese they were prepared to make, adding that empty titles of investiture would not satisfy the Japanese. Comparing the Japanese to the Mongol ruler Altan Khan, the Koreans felt that they were "caught between the wolf and the tiger." They argued that cutting off all ties with Japan and driving the invaders from the peninsula entirely was the only real way to attain peace—doing anything less would damage China's prestige as the Middle Kingdom. Additionally, the Koreans noted that they were militarily weak and if the Japanese were not totally driven out, a larger and more expensive Ming force would be needed to keep the peace on the peninsula. The king also complained that two hundred years of loyal service by Korea was going unrecognized, and the duplicity of the Japanese was going unpunished.[98]

The Ming Ministry of War acknowledged receipt of the Korean memorial but did not respond directly at this time on the particulars, though they did chasten the Koreans, telling them to put their house in order and not rely solely on Chinese assistance. Gu Yangqian tried to mollify Sŏnjo by pointing to China's coastal-defense preparations and the presence of Liu Ting and his cohorts in Korea. If the Japanese attacked again, the Chinese would be ready to act fast. Liu and other officials there could certainly buy enough time for Ming reinforcements to arrive by sea. Yu Sŏngnyong and the other high Korean ministers continued to meet with one another and with Ming officials in Seoul. Qi Jin, a Ming mobile corps commander, showed the articles of peace to Yu, who rejected them outright. Undeterred, Qi and Shen Weijing pointed out that the Japanese were in fact withdrawing from Pusan. But widespread reports of Japanese looting and pillaging still set Korean officials on edge. In response to such concerns, Ming officials cited the likes of Sunzi, suggesting that the Koreans simply did not understand long-range military strategy.[99]

Nevertheless, Sŏnjo and his ministers remained suspicious of the Japanese and continued with their defensive and training efforts. They also kept asking the Ming to send more troops and supplies. The Chinese responded by encouraging them to expand their own military farms, though nearly 9,000 piculs (600 tons) of supplies were sent by boat from various coastal prefectures early in 1594. They also authorized the delivery of significant numbers of firearms. As before, a major concern was facilitating faster delivery of needed items. The Chinese remained concerned about the possibility of supplies being intercepted by the Japanese at sea, even though it seemed that Yi Sunsin and his fellow commanders had matters well in hand. Captured Japanese reported that additional troops were en route, so Yi Sunsin and Wŏn Kyun were ordered to step up their patrols.[100]

The Japanese military threat was exacerbated by famine and unrest in the countryside. The king was eager to improve the distribution of famine relief because he had little political capital after the disasters of the previous year. Therefore, he pressed both his own officials and Ming representatives for additional food, hoping to curtail the widespread banditry and looting. Chinese officials pointed to these difficulties as justification for their rather limited troop presence. As one explained, stationing more Chinese troops in Korea would only increase the subsistence burdens on the populace. But Sŏnjo argued that his kingdom was impoverished in large part because it had been forced to provision the Ming armies. The Chinese responded by agreeing to send another 100,000 piculs of food.[101]

The twists and turns of the negotiations and threats leading up to the war itself and the subsequent Korean pleas for help illuminate much about the workings of the Chinese tributary system in early modern East Asia. Status and legitimation went hand in hand, but both could only be conferred by the Chinese, who remained at the apex of the system. Even Hideyoshi apparently recognized this fact and therefore resolved to earn his status by conquest, which was perfectly acceptable within the Chinese political tradition. If he had managed to defeat Korea and China, then he would have had legitimate claim to the "Mandate of Heaven." The fact that Hideyoshi aspired to even greater things should not obscure this realization.

The Ming relief effort also highlights the importance of logistics. The Chinese were faced with the considerable challenge of transporting massive amounts of weapons, supplies, fodder, and other equipment across rugged terrain in the winter. That they managed to do even as well as they did is a testament to the organizational capacity of the late Ming state and its military apparatus. Contemporary European states experienced serious difficulties supplying forces one-quarter as large over much shorter distances. European rulers eventually surmounted their logistical difficulties with contractors—the Ming Chinese and Chosŏn Koreans relied on their sophisticated bureaucracies to move men and materials over vast distances.[102]

This does not even take into account the planning and effort required to get the men and materials from the distant corners of the empire (a subject worthy of study in its own right). The very fact that Beijing's calls for assistance were answered suggests that Wanli's state was still functioning at a reasonable level of effectiveness. While there was some effort on the part of the Ming to portray the war as the selfless defense of its loyal vassal, they did not really try to "sell" the war except by offering monetary inducements to mercenaries. It seems that the government still had enough clout to force its subjects to act, though there were scattered mutinies and some desertion in the ranks. But again this was a characteristic of all early modern militaries. Wastage rates in contemporary Europe were at least 2 percent a month during hostilities and could be much higher, in some instances approaching 90 percent of a force on campaign.[103] The Ming's ability to hold most of their forces together and maintain some semblance of discipline and order, Korean reports of malfeasance notwithstanding, is a testament to the ability of the Ming bureaucracy to account for, outfit, and supply its armies even in a foreign land, albeit with significant Korean aid.

Factionalism was another emerging problem that would become even worse during the ongoing peace talks and Japan's subsequent invasion. Ming officials were split into pro- and antiwar factions that tended to work to the detriment of positive action in favor of any policy. The result was confusion that continually undermined the military effort. There were also tensions in the field, as indicated by the rivalries between civil and military leaders and northerners and southerners. The Ming was by no means a homogeneous empire, and problems between various ethnic and regional groups often developed. Such petty rivalries frequently created dissent in the ranks and canceled out the advantages that might have been gained by a better integration of regional units.

With respect to Wanli himself, the campaign illuminates both his assets and his faults as a ruler. The emperor overruled many of his officials in making the decision to go to the defense of Korea. While his decision was undoubtedly motivated in part by the selfish desire to protect his own state, he also sincerely desired to help his loyal vassal. His leadership would be praised by Song Yingchang, who hoped to prosecute the war his monarch entrusted to him. Wanli certainly felt constrained by the various factions at court and around the empire. But a strong military had long been his dream, and military affairs continued to be one area in which he could flex his power. The emperor did what he could to make the expedition a success by appointing men whom he thought were the best for the job, whether or not they were well liked by the bulk of officialdom. The emperor also acted unselfishly when it came to approving funds for the expedition. He was especially generous when it came to authorizing money for special rewards within the military, not to mention his authorization of extra funds to purchase winter uniforms.[104]

Moreover, Wanli solicited advice from officials throughout the empire. He corresponded regularly with his representatives in the field and did his best to ascertain what was transpiring in Korea. He also exchanged a number of letters with King Sŏnjo, acting the role of the benevolent ruler-father toward the Koreans and asserting the kind of authority he apparently lacked at home. Wanli's directives to Sŏnjo and Hideyoshi demonstrate how seriously he took his status as the legitimate Son of Heaven—Sŏnjo was expected to conform to his directives, and Hideyoshi was expected to tremble before his commands.

On the negative side, Wanli still placed too much trust in some officials and often issued vague and contradictory directives. He asked for advice but punished those who criticized his handling of affairs. Like a spouse who really does not want to know whether their partner is cheating on them, Wanli was often content to accept things at face value or believe very implausible explanations when it came to negotiations with the Japanese. Some of this blame may be laid at the feet of Shi Xing, Shen Weijing, and others, but Wanli himself cannot be completely absolved. These problems would become increasingly evident during the ensuing peace talks.

5

CAUGHT BETWEEN THE DRAGON AND THE RISING SUN

Peace Talks and Occupation, 1593–96

The Japanese are deceitful by nature.
I do not think we can consider this matter finished.
—Emperor Wanli

In retrospect it is obvious why peace talks between the Chinese and the Japanese were doomed to failure. Both sides were far apart on the fundamental issues and neither was willing to budge. The Ming dealt with Hideyoshi much the same way they dealt with other "barbarian" annoyances. But the major difference between the Japanese and Yang Yinglong or Pubei was the status and sophistication of the opponent. The Chinese were not dealing with a tribal chieftain or disgruntled general. They were dealing with an enemy with years of practice in the arts of diplomacy and war, one who would not be so easily bought off or crushed.

Although they failed utterly, we can learn much from the peace talks concerning the rhetoric and operation of the Chinese tributary system and the nature of international relations in early modern East Asia. The framework of the tributary system encompassed all manner of international relations, including war, trade, and diplomacy. In this case the Chinese fulfilled their obligations to their vassal state both militarily and diplomatically. The Koreans had good reason to be unhappy about the way discussions were handled, but the very existence of their kingdom was preserved by virtue of the Ming intervention, and the Koreans never forgot this. At the same time, Hideyoshi's own presumptions about his power and authority were couched in the same language as those of the Chinese. He wanted to be regarded as the superior of the Ming emperor, with an empire that combined aspects of Japanese federalism and Chinese-style universal despotism.

In the wake of the Japanese evacuation of Seoul, Shen Weijing initially met with Li Rusong, emphasizing Shi Xing's desire for peace.[1] Shen left a representative with Konishi Yukinaga and returned to Beijing to discuss the terms of a possible peace agreement with Shi. When Shen returned to Korea, he held several conferences with Konishi and Katō Kiyomasa to discuss the terms under which a peace agreement could be reached.

According to Konishi, the Japanese had seven conditions for peace:

1. Marriage relations (heqin), which would involve Wanli sending one of his daughters to marry the emperor of Japan. An alternate version has Hideyoshi being made king of the Ming (Ming guo guowang).
2. Japan would be allowed to keep the four provinces south and east of Seoul, with the Han River as a boundary.
3. The two countries would once again engage in tribute-trade relations.
4. The ministers of China and Japan were to exchange oaths of eternal peace.
5. Korea was to present a prince and several ministers as hostages to demonstrate their good will, as was the custom in Japan.
6. The two captured Korean princes and their retinues would be turned over to Shen Weijing.
7. Korea must swear to never break the peace.[2]

These demands show that Hideyoshi regarded himself as the victor in the conflict. He also stipulated that a certain number of troops must be allowed to remain in Korea until all talks were finished. Still, it is unclear how much the taikō knew about the military situation in Korea, and it is possible that he had already inwardly conceded that conquering China, not to mention India, was out of the question. A major factor in his perception of these matters was the continued rivalry between Katō Kiyomasa and Konishi Yukinaga. Katō either remained faithful to his lord's vision or was impelled by an overwhelming desire to glorify himself at the expense of his rival. At the time the demands were presented, Kim Ungso reportedly asked Konishi, "How could Japan, a small country, dare to ask the Ming for the hand of a princess, and what would they do when the Ming refused?"[3] Kim was sure that these ridiculous demands were put forth at the urging of Katō, who wanted to see the peace talks fail. But one must be wary of attributing too much to Katō, for it is possible that Hideyoshi dictated these terms on his own.

Li Guangtao argues that Konishi's statements are indicative of Hideyoshi's will because he was the primary Japanese negotiator. While this may be the case, the fact that Konishi continually misrepresented things to both his overlord and the Chinese calls his credibility into question. If he really did have the full confidence and understanding of the Japanese ruler, then Hideyoshi would have been aware of what was at stake when he received his patent of investiture from Wanli in 1596. It is possible, however, that Konishi simply misread Hideyoshi and believed that his desire for lucrative trade would supersede all other concerns. But if this was the case, then he should have pushed harder for regular trade relations instead of the rather empty title of king of Japan sans trade privileges that he eventually secured. Konishi and Hideyoshi may have considered getting this title as a way to save face and improve Hideyoshi's status at home vis-à-vis the daimyo.[4]

The terms listed above were countered by the Chinese, who regarded themselves as the victors. Shen informed Konishi that should negotiations fail, Ming forces would isolate and annihilate the Japanese in Korea, a threat Konishi took seriously: "[T]he Celestial Empire has already mobilized a great army which is crossing the western sea to Ch'ungch'ŏng province to cut your lines so you will not be able to retreat. . . . If you return the princes and their ministers and withdraw your troops to the south, then the Celestial Empire will allow investiture and tribute trade and our two countries will no longer be at war."[5] The Chinese conditions for peace were:

1. The Japanese must immediately withdraw all troops from Korean soil.
2. They must acknowledge Ming authority over both Korea and Japan.

3. The captured Korean princes must be returned.
4. Hideyoshi must apologize for his transgression, and if the Ming
   deemed that he was truly sorry, then he might be invested as
   king of Japan and perhaps granted trading privileges.
5. The Japanese must pledge to never invade Korea again.[6]

These terms were negotiated between Konishi and Shen, as Konishi
had agreed to the return of the captured princes in exchange for Shen's
promise to grant the Japanese marriage relations with the Ming, which
would enable them to engage in tribute trade (gong) like other neighboring states. There was a misunderstanding, though, for what Konishi
portrayed as marriage ties (heqin) to the Japanese was described as the
mere investiture of Hideyoshi as a vassal (feng) by Shen to his superiors
in China. Such an arrangement would put Hideyoshi in an inferior
position vis-à-vis Wanli. Konishi apparently felt that he could pull the
wool over his master's eyes because the lure of trade was so great, or
perhaps he figured that he could obscure the true significance of the
title. Regardless, Japanese sources relate that Konishi told the taikō
that he was going to be invested by the Chinese as the emperor of the
Ming, an assurance that seems utterly ridiculous but was apparently
accepted with delight by Hideyoshi.[7]

On the Chinese side, Grand Secretaries Zhang Wei and Shen Yiguan
both favored war, as did a majority of the Chinese court, though many
chose not to speak up at this time for fear of being executed. Many
believed that the negotiations were nothing more than a stalling tactic
to allow the Ming to bring more troops and supplies to the front. Those
in the peace party were led by Shi Xing, who reasoned that the Japanese
had already been driven from Seoul and would most likely abandon the
peninsula altogether, especially if Hideyoshi was invested as king of Japan.
Since Korea had been saved, its two capitals recovered, and the righteous
indignation of the Ming manifested, Shi argued, why expose Ming troops
to further hardships there.[8]

The issue of tribute trade was also important. Many officials argued
that Hideyoshi should be made a ruler without the right to participate
in tribute trade (yi feng, bu yi gong). Some advocated allowing Japanese
tribute trade at Ningbo at a level lower than that allowed the Mongols
and also opening free markets along the coast where taxes could be
levied to pay for defenses. Others voiced concerns about the continued
cost of defending Korea in terms of both men and supplies. Hawkish

officials maintained there was no reason and no historical precedent for leaving the peninsula. Accusing Li Rusong of timidity, they said more supplies for the troops was all that was needed.[9]

Still other officials argued that Korea should bear the burden for its own defense, though Chinese forces could help train their recruits and assist them in establishing military farms. This was contested by Shi, who advocated a complete withdrawal of all troops during the peace talks as a demonstration of sincerity. Even Shen opposed going that far, saying, "Our [civil] officials can leave but our troops must certainly not be recalled."[10] Most agreed that leaving even just a token force in Korea would give the Ming greater leverage in negotiations. There was widespread concern among the court that Hideyoshi still had designs on China, thus they must not abandon Korea, the "lips" to China's "teeth."

Despite the misgivings on both sides, Konishi escorted Shen to Pusan in early June. Xie Yongzi and Xu Yiguan were China's official representatives as designated by Song Yingchang. In Japanese sources they are often referred to as little more than spies, though given Shen's relationship with Song and Li Rusong, their duties may have involved keeping tabs on him more than the Japanese. Shen was given gifts and clothes to present to Konishi and other Japanese leaders. Upon seeing this, Li laughed and said: "The Japanese are poor and in awe of us. Yet now we give them gifts like this! This is what can be called rewarding robbers and honoring bandits!" Song was also concerned that the Japanese were still entrenched around Pusan, for they could easily strike at other cities such as Taegu and Namwŏn. Nonetheless, offensive actions by allied troops were discouraged so they would not undermine the peace talks.[11]

Konishi and the Chinese envoys left Pusan for Nagoya on June 13. They were met by Hideyoshi himself and enjoyed a banquet with the taikō on June 21. Shen Weijing was treated quite well as his hosts showered him with gifts, Japanese chronicles mentioning how the Chinese seemed enamored of beautiful things. But there continued to be issues of protocol as the envoys squabbled over where different people should sit. Talks were also strained by Keitetsu Genso's accusation that the Koreans had actually helped the Japanese attack the Ming by opening roads for the invaders. He wanted the Koreans punished, but the Ming brushed these requests aside, saying that if the Japanese did not believe the Chinese version of events, they were free to kill the messengers.[12]

The negotiations were carried out via written Chinese notes, the content of which were supposedly kept secret from the taikō. The Ming envoys noted that Wanli did not tolerate equals on his borders, so Hideyoshi must accept a lesser tributary status. Genso helped the Chinese write up the terms of the peace agreement, wherein the Japanese clearly stated they believed that Hideyoshi was entering into a marriage relationship with Wanli. The Koreans were blamed for everything, and Hideyoshi assumed he was going to get to keep the four provinces south and east of the Han River to go with his Ming princess.[13]

It may be that Genso misunderstood or deliberately misrepresented the implications of *heqin* and tributary status to Hideyoshi. For the Japanese leader this relationship implied equality; for the Ming it implied subordination. Hideyoshi probably felt that he was being magnanimous to a bested foe and savvy in allying with a formidable rival. After all, this was the way business was conducted between rivals in Japan. The Ming perspective was quite different. They regarded Hideyoshi as a penitent barbarian, eager to partake in superior Chinese culture and desperate for acceptance in the international community that revolved around the Middle Kingdom.

Hideyoshi did agree to turn over the Korean princes and sent the order to Ukita Hideie. The envoys were sent off in grand fashion with many lords in attendance.[14] The talks in Japan lasted over a month, and it was during this time (July 27) that Katō's army sacked Chinju. This act was of course regarded with outrage by the Koreans and confirmed fears among the hawks in China that the Japanese could not be trusted and did not deserve the benefits of trade, even if they did submit to the Ming and withdraw from the peninsula. Nevertheless, arguments for peace prevailed, and preparations were made for the recall of the Ming troops.

Nevertheless, Li Rusong continued to prepare for further conflict. Liu Ting and his 5,000 men were stationed at Sangju, in order to hold Choryŏng Pass, and Zha Dashou and Zu Chengxun were sent to chase the Japanese back toward Pusan, which they did. Liu eventually encamped at Taegu and Zu at Ch'ungju as the Japanese withdrew to Pusan. Li also had Yi Sunsin and his vessels patrol the waters around the southeastern coast. Li's actions ran counter to the charges leveled by some at the time and repeated later that he sought to get out of Korea as soon as Seoul was recovered.[15]

Although Kwŏn Yul ordered Buddhist monks to rebuild the walls of Sachŏn, finding manpower to participate in other rebuilding efforts was still problematic. In some districts nine out of ten homes lay empty. And training revisions had not yet taken hold. As Cho Kyŏngnam complained, there were no fear-inspiring generals or brave soldiers—most continued to run away at the sight of the enemy. The difficulty of moving supplies through rugged and war-torn terrain did little to help matters. Recognizing these problems in the wake of Chinju, the Japanese launched a few probing strikes. Over the next several years, they would send out small forces to test the Koreans, not unlike a chess player tests his opponent's defenses early in a match.[16] These challenges would be answered by transfers of Chinese and Korean forces followed by rounds of negotiations and drinking.

Actions such as these prompted Zhang Fuzhi, supervising secretary of the Ministry of War, to memorialize Wanli, saying: "The Japanese massed at Pusan, pretending to retreat, and tried to deceive us into demobilizing our troops with the aim of dissipating our strength. Then they falsely requested tributary relations in violation of our benevolence. Now they have quickly struck Chinju and made their true intentions evident. Therefore we should organize an expedition to crush them." His suggestion was overruled by Shi Xing. Song Yingchang agreed with Zhang, saying the Japanese were "outwardly obedient but inwardly traitorous" [yang shun, yin ni], he agitated for a remobilization of Ming forces. But from the perspective of many at court, peace talks were preferable to expending more resources militarily. They also considered the possibility that the Koreans might be better ready soon to defend against another Japanese offensive with diminished Ming help.[17]

Shen returned to Pusan with Konishi Joan, named the primary Japanese envoy, in midsummer. Negotiations were understandably hampered by news of the massacre at Chinju and the fact that the Japanese were still on the offensive throughout southern Korea. Wanli was furious when he received word of the massacre, and his initial response was to call for the complete sundering of negotiations. Rumors circulated concerning what had transpired at Chinju, including the story that the Japanese attacked the city because the invaders were starving. Commanders were still under the impression that a border would be set at the Han River, so they felt it was within their rights to consolidate what remained of their holdings in Korea. Hideyoshi maintained that before the envoys arrived to meet with him personally, the peace talks could not begin. Countering Chinese and Korean concerns with those of his own, Konishi Yukinaga asked, "If the Ming want peace, why do they keep sending more troops into Korea?"[18]

The Korean military had taken advantage of the arrival of the Ming and were now creating serious problems for the Japanese both on land

and at sea. Military commanders were in no mood to negotiate with the invaders and sought to press their attacks whenever and wherever possible. Yi Sunsin said, "I pledged with the army commanders to launch an amphibious attack by joint action on land and sea, but there is no way to request the participation of the Ming Chinese reinforcements in our planned operation, to our annoyance."[19] The Ming never placed their men under the command of Korean generals, though Koreans were often placed under Chinese leadership. The Chinese always had superiority in the chain of command when it came to tactical decisions and rarely even bothered to inform the Koreans of their activities unless they needed their support.

Li Rusong had a series of discussions with Sŏnjo during which he explained that, while the Ming could no longer afford to keep so many troops in southern Korea, if the Japanese were granted trading privileges, in his opinion they would leave and there would be no need for the troops. He added that if the Japanese had the temerity to invade again, the Ming would assemble an even mightier host and crush them once more. Gu Yangqian figured just 21,000 men would be enough to garrison Korea. Yet even a force of this size would be costly to maintain, requiring 50,000 liang of supplies a month. The Koreans were upset by this because they wanted to continue offensive operations. Yi Sunsin complained that "the Ming army stands idle without sending me a single line to inform me of its intention to attack the common enemy, who now moves freely in a more threatening attitude than ever without the least sign of escaping home."[20]

These allegations are challenged by a number of other sources that note that Liu Ting was charged with training Korean troops in the use of firearms and the construction of defense works. During the course of the war, the Korean military adopted the use of firearms, fire carts, cannons, and poison gunpowder bombs in their tactics. Sŏnjo created a Military Training Agency and ordered his commanders to distribute Qi Jiguang's *Jixiao xinshu* and put its teachings into practice, creating units of arquebusiers and improving training in all areas. Yu Sŏngnyong advocated reviving old systems of defense and the creation of new militia units as auxiliaries. Men formerly exempt from military service were now enrolled in the ranks, and new companies were created. Platoons were organized into three squads consisting of foot soldiers armed with swords, pikes, or spears; archers; and arquebusiers. The Koreans focused on creating smaller, better-trained units since they lacked the organizational capacity to create and direct a massive army.[21] They also made efforts to rebuild fortifications and improve communications. As in China, Korean military commanders agitated for more power and jurisdiction.

This is not to say the Koreans effected a complete military transformation. Their ranks were still plagued by cowardice and a lack of discipline. As Yi Sunsin observed, "Among our Korean people, out of every ten there are eight or nine faint-hearted persons as against one or two lion-hearts." Yi compared Korean soldiers to the Ming troops, whom he noted came from 10,000 li (nearly 3,500 miles) away "but are on alert to fight the enemy to the death with a glad heart."[22]

Korean forces were also hampered by a lack of adequate provisions, owing in large part to the devastation wreaked on agriculture by the Japanese. Their generals remarked on having to traverse corpse-filled roads, with their starving troops barely able to march. Yi Sunsin complained that his forces "are so hungry and weak that they can hardly draw bowstrings or pull the oars at this time when we are facing the enemy for a decisive battle." Yu Sŏngnyong observed, "Not only are soldiers eating the flesh of corpses, but the living are killing and eating one another." Yi Tŏkhyŏng concurred, lamenting, "Fathers and sons, elder and younger brothers alike, are all eating one another." Korean officials continued to press the Chinese to send more grain, troops, and supplies, arguing that the empire was wealthy enough to spare these things.[23] While Liu Ting acknowledged that China did have troops and silver aplenty, he noted the great difficulty of transporting them to the peninsula; Yu suggested using boat transport from Shandong.

These woes were exacerbated at times by the behavior of Korea's Ming allies, as Yi Sunsin noted: "the arrival of the Ming Chinese army has brought worse evils than those in the war-devastated areas, because the Ming soldiers in southern Korea robbed the people of their treasures at home and damaged their crops in the fields as they entered the Korean farm villages and pillaged everywhere they passed through, so the innocent local inhabitants ran away at their sight and moved to the out of the way places." Commanders such as Liu Ting did their best to keep their men under control. Liu proved to be quite the diplomat during his tenure, earning the respect of Korean soldiers for his bravery and assistance in their training and that of the king for his opposition to Shen Weijing.[24]

The talks dragged on through the summer of 1593 as the Chinese waited for word that the Japanese had withdrawn completely from the peninsula and were prepared to show their repentance and accept investiture, if not tribute privileges. The Ming court finally received word that the Japanese had abandoned Pusan on August 28 and that only a small force remained with Konishi Yukinaga at Sŏsaengpo. But this account was actually based on some Japanese generals and their troops having returned to Osaka to congratulate Hideyoshi on the birth of his first son, Toyotomi Hideyori.[25]

The report of a full-scale Japanese withdrawal was disputed by some, but Shi Xing reassured Wanli, who completely trusted Shi and approved the plan for investiture, having been convinced that this was Hideyoshi's wish. The emperor felt that the taikō feared the might of the Ming and wished to atone for his transgressions, so how could he not accept their submission in good faith? Moreover, the Japanese had returned the two captive Korean princes as a demonstration of their sincerity. Shen reportedly bore with him a letter from Hideyoshi himself that requested a resumption of tribute-trade relations. Some question the veracity of this letter, but the simple, straightforward language it employs and the emphasis on substance over style attest to its legitimacy. But such a letter, if it did in fact exist, was probably penned by Konishi Yukinaga.[26]

Regardless, Ming officials were satisfied enough to let the Japanese mission continue. Konishi Joan proceeded to travel to Pyongyang with thirty retainers and escorted by two Korean officials, reaching the city on October 6, 1593. Konishi and his entourage would not be sent to China until the Ming withdrew all of their troops. He eventually went as far as Liaodong but had to wait there for word from Shen, who went ahead to Beijing. Shen knew that Shi Xing strongly favored peace, but he also knew many at the Ming court favored keeping at least some forces in Korea as a safeguard. It was at this point that the Ming ordered a withdrawal of all but 16,000 of their troops.[27]

As Li Rusong departed the peninsula, he was chided by Liu Ting, who composed a poem:

The general led myriad troops and cavalry [into Korea]
Emerald streamers shining, brocade robes of red trailing behind
But the six unorthodox commanders could not effect a stratagem
    for peace
And the five successes led only to the hard-bought peace of
    crimson weapons

Now my head is bald and ugly
And the people tremble in fear along coastal frontiers
Afraid to rely on heroes
A lord was sent with the plan of demonstrating ferocity to all
    under heaven
But now we have come to this ridiculous investiture
So surely you cannot call this an achievement?[28]

The rest of the Chinese forces crossed the Yalu on September 27 and reached Shanhaiguan on October 25. Gu Yangqian was named military commissioner of Korea and assumed the powers previously held by both Li Rusong and Song. Gu was a member of Shi's camp and favored the resumption of tribute trade with the Japanese as the means to obtain a lasting peace.[29] Wanli, though, was still angry about Chinju and opposed trading privileges at Ningbo, fearing for the safety of the local inhabitants.

Meanwhile, the emperor addressed Sŏnjo directly in a letter. Wanli lambasted the king for his overindulgence in trivial pleasures, his improper leadership of the people, and his lack of sympathy for the lives of his subjects. He added that Sŏnjo's refusal to shore up his defenses invited the Japanese to attack and now his ministers had lost all faith in him. Wanli asked, "If the cart in the lead has overturned, how can those behind it not follow it?" He also instructed the king to return to Seoul, strengthen his defenses, and make sure his navy patrolled the coasts, warning him that after these steps were taken, the Ming would withdraw all their forces from Korea. He concluded by stating that he would not be able to save Sŏnjo should the Japanese attack again. Wanli included presents of congratulations on the "victory" over the Japanese, including red python robes.[30] The king responded by pledging to listen to Wanli's counsel and thanking him for his advice and assistance. Sŏnjo finally returned to Seoul in November 1593.

Still concerned about the situation, Song Yingchang memorialized the throne: "If the Japanese see our troops withdrawing, then certainly they will attack again immediately. The Koreans will be unable to protect themselves and all we have gained will be thrown away. Although Korea is the target, in reality Hideyoshi is after China. A strong Korea protects our eastern defense line of Ji[zhen] and Liao[dong] and thereby protects the capital like Mount Tai. Now mobilizing troops to defend Korea is the number one plan. Thus we should wait for the Japanese to completely withdraw before we do. Even afterwards we should leave 3,000 crack southern troops in Korea." Song added that because the number of troops greatly favored the Japanese, there could be no equal negotiations until the invaders withdrew completely. While Wanli remained confident about the progress of the talks, he also favored continued vigilance. Song's advice to leave a token force was heeded, and even when he ordered all troops withdrawn from Korea in the twelfth lunar month of 1593, Wanli warned: "The Japanese are deceitful by nature. I do not think we can consider this matter finished."[31]

In the tenth lunar month of 1593, the emperor convened a meeting of his nine ranking ministers and supervising secretaries and censors to debate the merits of restoring tributary relations. A heated debate occurred over what should be done, with a number of officials, including He Qiaoyuan (1558–1632) of the Ministry of Rites, staunchly opposed resuming trade. Another official pointed out that ever since the Japanese were granted trading privileges by Hongwu, they have continually broken agreements and raided and plundered deep into Ming territory. Now China had a chance to cut the Japanese off forever and should seize it so as to demonstrate their superior position. These sentiments were shared by another official, who said, "The Japanese are not satiated; therefore I recommend we [continue to] cut off tribute trade relations." Shi Xing was furious at these opinions and continued to press for peace. Even Shi, however, assumed a firm position with regard to the Koreans, telling Sŏnjo that China would not be able to rush to their aid every time they got themselves into trouble. While acknowledging their debt to China, the Koreans continued to naturally look at the crisis from their own perspective. It was their survival at stake. Moreover, they continued to find sympathetic ears among the hawks in Beijing.[32]

Liu Ting was promoted to vice commander in charge of resisting the Japanese and acting military commissioner in chief, with orders to remain in Korea along with Luo Shangzhi and Wu Weizhong. Nevertheless, a supervising secretary from the Ministry of War lamented: "Although Liu Ting is valorous, what can a few thousand do against 100,000? If we could not achieve our aims before with Li Rusong and Song Yingchang, how can we do so now with so few?" A letter from Sŏnjo pointed out that Korea's position was still precarious and asked how the Ming could even think of abandoning his kingdom when the issue was still undecided (though in their defense, the Ming court had received news of a rebellion in Sichuan, discussed below).[33]

The Japanese generals were also testy. They did not want to spend another winter in Korea subjected to endless harassment by the populace. Some commanders allegedly even hatched a scheme to assassinate Hideyoshi if he came to the peninsula. Troops under Katō skirmished with Ming troops under Liu Ting in December 1593, though neither side was ready to engage in full-scale hostilities. Hideyoshi told his commanders to strengthen their defenses and to be prepared to launch another major assault if peace talks failed. Some assumed the Japanese would take up the offensive again the next year, while others were annoyed at the indecisiveness of the policy and wanted to either go home or get back to fighting. A few even advocated striking at China directly. When not worrying about combat, the Japanese entertained themselves with games and plays and sometimes struck off into the mountains to hunt tigers. Commanders held tea ceremonies and poetry contests, danced, gave sake parties, and played kick ball. They also rounded up slaves for service in their camps and for shipment back home.[34]

In early 1594 Sŏnjo dispatched Kim Su to Beijing at the head of a delegation to thank the Ming for their assistance. The envoys also related the full story of Chinju, prompting officials such as Censor Huang Yilong to voice the opinion that Shen Weijing was in league with the Japanese. Huang added that in the grand scale of things, Song Yingchang's transgressions were minor, but to grant Japan's wishes would be a major blunder. Kim agreed and said the invaders did not desire peaceful relations but demanded submission from the Ming, adding that negotiations were just a delaying tactic designed to lull them into complacency while Hideyoshi readied his forces for a renewed attack. He suggested dispatching another official to keep an eye on Shen, who was widely believed to be the chief culprit in a chain of lies extending to Shi Xing.[35]

Wanli replied that any agreement should be withheld until the Japanese completely evacuated Pusan. He instructed Gu Yangqian to go to the city and force the Japanese withdrawal, telling him to demonstrate courage and resourcefulness and not simply rely on literary talents to resolve the situation, for they would be of no use against the crafty and unsophisticated Japanese. Thereafter the emperor warned that anyone who did not fully speak their mind would be punished for shirking their responsibilities.[36]

Shi convened a meeting of the high Ming officials in which he described the discussion as a matter of granting tributary status and nothing more. The officials responded that if this was indeed the case, then Shi needed to cut off talks if the Japanese remained in Pusan. Others continued to be in favor of a military solution, calling for more troops to be rushed to Korea. They also questioned Shi in detail about the communications between Shen and Konishi Yukinaga. Seeing these documents, they learned that the Japanese wanted much more than tributary status. Wanli reiterated his orders to Gu and voiced his opposition to troop demobilization.. In June Gu sent Assistant Commander Hu Ze to Korea to meet with Yu Sŏngnyong. Yu told Hu how the Japanese continued to rampage even after negotiations began. After much debate, the Ming prepared to resume hostilities.[37]

Grand Secretary Zhang Wei was among those pushing for a renewal of military action. He said the Japanese were stupid, aggressive, and cut off from the ways of heaven, therefore they needed to be pushed out of Korea. Zhang submitted a memorial identifying positions the allies should garrison and attack routes they should take. He also advocated, like many other officials, the establishment of military farms in Korea and the wholesale training of Korean soldiers in Chinese tactics. He estimated that the kingdom could be completely self-sufficient within a year if its subjects studied under the Chinese. Promoting the use of Ming firepower, Zhang emphasized the importance of severing Japanese supply lines.[38]

The confusion in the court at this time illustrates the shortcomings of the Ming system and Wanli's style of leadership. There was no official who commanded the respect of all the others. Thus it was up to the emperor to break the impasse among the equals, but he was reluctant to do so. Instead Wanli put the burden of the decision on Shi, who, though he did have a clearly articulated position, was in the minority. That Shi's decision to pursue peace was supported by Wanli is somewhat odd in itself. After all, the emperor still distrusted the Japanese and seemed to favor war. It is possible that he realized the Ming would have a difficult time continuing the campaign through the harsh Korean winter and figured the Japanese would be satisfied with becoming tributaries. Yet given his contentious relationship with his civil officials, Wanli may have simply acted capriciously, knowing this decision would anger and frustrate many of his ministers. When some officials questioned his decision to pursue peace, the emperor reportedly became enraged. This was an especially tense time in Ming government, for Wanli was becoming involved in the personnel controversies that would cripple the bureaucracy and governmental action during the second half of his reign.[39]

In October Wanli sent a directive to the Ministry of War demanding to know the state of the negotiations. He was frustrated at the lack of progress and was angry with the more hawkish officials who continued to obfuscate the peace process. Shi said that while he agreed sending troops to oust the Japanese from Pusan was the preferred plan, the difficulty in sending them 1,000 li (345 miles) from Liaodong to Pusan suggested the best option still might be to allow the Japanese some type of trade. He thought the Ming could appoint a vice commander with 10,000 troops to deter the enemy and also train and ready troops along the coast. Meanwhile, northern-frontier commanders could assemble 30,000 more men to act as possible support in case of military action. It was now up to Li Hualong and Sun Kuang to select generals, train troops, gather supplies, make weapon, and prepare for all eventualities. They established military farms in Liaodong to help provide additional food for both the Chinese and the Koreans.[40]

Simultaneously, Gu Yangqian memorialized the throne asking that Hideyoshi be invested as king of Japan and the Japanese granted trading privileges at Ningbo once all of their forces withdrew from Korea. He immediately came under heavy criticism from other officials and asked to be replaced by Sun Kuang, which was granted. The court was still vacillating when Sŏnjo himself asked the Ming to grant Hideyoshi these privileges in order to save Korea from further depredations. Shi continued to argue for peace on the grounds that mobilizing another punitive expedition would be far too costly.[41] He argued that if some sort of peace settlement were reached, Korea would have at least three to five years to prepare itself in case of another invasion, but if no treaty was signed, then Chŏlla province at the least would probably be lost and the Chinese would again be forced to expend valuable resources on the peninsula. He also said investiture and tribute trade were minor issues, but bringing the Ming troops back to China was a major issue.

Wanli finally acceded to these requests, but he ordered Konishi Joan to come to Beijing and meet with the high ministers of the Ming to explain the actions of Japan and demonstrate his sincerity. If the Chinese were not convinced of this, talks would be sundered and another punitive expedition would be mounted. Wanli gave three conditions: first, total withdrawal of all troops from Korean soil; second,

Hideyoshi would be invested as king of Japan without tribute trade privileges; and third, the Japanese had to pledge never to trouble Korea again.[42] Konishi Joan readily agreed to all terms.

This decision met instant criticism from Ming officials. One hundred of them protested the terms, to which Wanli issued an order for their dismissal from office. Their stance was based on the fact that they still had not received credible evidence of a total Japanese withdrawal from the peninsula. In addition, the wording of the negotiated documents, as they understood them, was ambiguous. Therefore they suggested that Ming envoys return to Japan and meet with Hideyoshi to ensure that all of his forces withdrew. Assuring the Koreans that his sincerest desire was their security, Wanli noted that changes to any agreement could still be made if the Japanese did not observe his conditions. Some in the Ming court apparently knew exactly what Hideyoshi's real demands were, but because those who spoke up were censured or even beaten, they feared to speak out.[43]

Although the Koreans had been largely cut out of the negotiating process, they did not desist from continuing military operations against the Japanese. As Konishi Joan was en route to Beijing, Korean naval forces skirmished with the Japanese among the islands off the southeast coast. While turned back by Shimazu Yoshihiro in their initial assault, the Koreans came back in force and managed to kill Yoshihiro's son in fighting off the coast of Tangdo Island. (Actions such as this prompted some Japanese commanders to request transfers back home.) Liu Ting wanted to continue fighting the Japanese on land, but he was prevented by the orders of Shi.[44] Other sources maintain that Liu was fed false information by Katō, who led him to believe that the war was going to start again soon.

Korea was also at the mercy of native bandits who roamed about the countryside, looting isolated towns, stealing grain, and burning slave records. Food costs were high and cloth was in short supply. Popular rebels in the countryside protested government factionalism and inefficiency, sometimes having to be quelled by government forces that ostensibly should have been used against the Japanese. In one battle 3,000 bandits were rounded up and beheaded by 300 government troops. Starving refugees lined the sides of roads, and women and children did not travel alone for fear of being waylaid and possibly even cannibalized. Liu eventually distributed food to the starving populace. Disease was rampant, and many people became covered with ulcers and boils.[45] Rains, earthquakes, and floods were reported by Korean officials as well.

Unsure of what was taking place at the Ming court, in May 1594 Kwŏn Yul sent the monk Yujŏng to meet with Katō at Sŏsaengpo, adopting the Japanese practice of using monks as envoys. At this time Liu was camped nearby to check any aggressive movements by Katō and Shen was still with Konishi Yukinaga. Liu had met with Katō himself, and it seemed that Chinese commanders strongly favored the talks. When asked by Yujŏng about Japanese terms, Katō replied, "Cede the three southern provinces to Japan and then our troops will go home." The monk was taken aback, for this differed greatly from the demands Konishi Yukinaga had given the allies. True to form, Katō provided the Korean and Ming representatives Hideyoshi's "real" conditions, which included the cession of territory, the hand of a Ming princess, and a formal apology from and exchange of hostages with the Koreans. Given how many times Katō reiterated these conditions, it is quite surprising that he was not taken more seriously, but his obvious dislike for Konishi Yukinaga might have rendered his opinions suspect in the minds of allied negotiators. He maintained that Konishi's plan would never succeed, to which Yujŏng agreed, though unlike Katō, the monk did not actively work against peace.[46]

Among themselves, the Koreans were skeptical that Shen and Konishi's plan would succeed. They also added that there was no way they would send a prince to Japan as a hostage given the invaders' despoliation of ancestral altars and the countless Korean lives already lost. To emphasize their superior negotiating position, their envoys threatened the Japanese again with huge Ming armies, stressing that their unbroken supply lines gave them a huge advantage over the Japanese. Stretching the truth more than a little bit, the Koreans told Katō that the Ming had 300,000 troops ready to go in Pyŏngan province and had reserves offshore ready to land in the event of Japanese aggression.[47]

Yujŏng also visited the camp of Liu Ting. Liu informed him that the Chinese would never give in to Japan's territorial or marriage demands, so the Koreans need not fear. He also reiterated China's respect for its longstanding close ties with Korea. But Liu admitted that the Ming did not mobilize troops lightly and expressed his own misgivings about the peace talks. These concerns were passed along to Katō, who sought to meet with Liu himself, feeling that since both distrusted Shen and Konishi Yukinaga, they might find common ground for negotiations. Katō revisited the issue of Hideyoshi's status as kampaku and noted that the conditions left out of the letter carried by Konishi Joan to the Ming were in fact the most critical from Hideyoshi's perspective. He also boasted that had he been present at Pyongyang, the results would have been different, and the Chinese would not be negotiating at all but would be begging for peace. Katō also said that Konishi was using the bogus talks as a way to cover up his own role in the defeat at Pyongyang. Unimpressed, the Koreans responded that the Japanese were no match for the combined might of the Sino-Korean forces, so they should just submit. Katō countered by saying that he might consider partitioning Korea with the Ming.[48]

The Koreans emphasized the superiority of the Ming emperor in the tributary relationship but admitted privately that Katō's words seemed more in line with what Hideyoshi would wish. They were concerned that the peace talks as represented to the Ming were predicated on the words of Konishi Yukinaga. In response to Katō's claims, Yujŏng issued a directive to monks and commoners to rally together and form militias to garrison key points and attempt to drive the Japanese out, hopefully with Ming assistance.[49]

Meanwhile, a censor from Fujian named Liu Fangyu sent forth a scathing memorial regarding the invasion. He noted how the Japanese first invaded and desecrated Korea, inflicting countless casualties but, when their supplies ran out, fled without having conquered any territory. They then concocted a duplicitous scheme to attain victory by means of false peace talks even as Hideyoshi ordered the construction of more boats to effect a second invasion. Liu went on to say that the Japanese had always threatened China's southeast coast to the extent that they were cut off from official trade ties, yet now the court was sending Hideyoshi fine silks, wood, gold, and jade. Liu asked, "Has the court not heard that the Japanese are secretly building *folangji* cannon so as to invade Guangdong?" He added that the Japanese were just buying time, and if the Ming were not vigilant, then the people of Zhejiang, Fujian, and Guangdong would soon suffer the same fate as the hapless folk of Korea: "Therefore your majesty should manifest your awesome might and dismiss this talk of tribute trade and investiture. For the Japanese warlord Hideyoshi has committed a crime against the world and he certainly should not go unpunished." In fact, anyone suggesting investiture should be impeached, added Liu, and Hideyoshi and his ministers should be executed because "the court does not invest tiger-like bandits!"[50]

In arguing against those who favored investiture for economic reasons, Liu said that it was much easier for the Ming to get supplies to Korea than the Japanese. He suggested that Wanli release 1 million cash from the inner treasury and appoint two or three high officials to distribute the funds to all provinces for the construction of some 2,000 warships and the selection and training of 200,000 crack troops. Although the costs might seem high, if properly done the task at hand could be completed in only about one year. The emperor acknowledged receiving the memorial, but Liu's plan was not implemented.[51]

Neither the Koreans nor the Japanese were idle while the Ming delayed Konishi Joan in Liaodong. A Japanese spy named Yōzira was apparently making the rounds in Korean circles, spreading all manner of rumors concerning future actions and acting in the role of a double agent. Genso also participated in discussions with the Koreans, warning them that the Ming were going to allow the resumption of tribute trade. The Japanese seemed inclined to belittle and intimidate the Koreans in these discussions, deliberately provoking them with talk of Hideyoshi being invested as king of Japan. When Kim Ungnam asked Konishi Yukinaga where he received such information, Konishi replied, "[f]rom the old Ming master Shi [Xing] himself" via an official in Liaodong. Konishi told the Koreans not to fret because soon all three countries would be at peace and the hardships of the past could be forgotten. The Koreans refused to believe his words and were enraged to hear the explanation that Japan had attacked them because Hideyoshi desired the resumption of tribute trade. Blaming Katō for all the misunderstandings, Konishi explained: "Kiyomasa and I really don't get along. Surely you've heard people say this? When I heard that Kiyomasa told the monk-soldier Yujŏng about requesting marriage ties and taking land, I was really worried."[52] Konishi then accused Katō of making up Hideyoshi's demands for his own purposes.

In the eighth lunar month of 1594, Liu Ting moved back to Seoul, stationing smaller divisions in key areas. Lookout posts were established at intervals of thirty li (ten miles), with five men assigned to each. At sea the Chinese assigned a naval officer to patrol the shipping lanes between China and Korea. On the Korean side, Yi Sunsin continued to skirmish with the Japanese at sea while Kwŏn Yul and Kwak Chaeu mounted land expeditions with varying degrees of success.[53]

As the Ming court debated the pros and cons of granting the Japanese legitimate status as a tributary state, they also had to address the military threat posed by Yang Yinglong in Sichuan. In May 1594 Yang's forces laid an ambush and decimated the army of Ming commander Wang Jiguang with crossbow fire at Baishi Pass. In November Xing Jie, the minister of war of the right in Nanjing, was made supreme commander of Sichuan and Guizhou in charge of suppressing Yang's rebellion. Shortly after Xing's appointment, a Ming force sent to crush Yang was also ambushed and annihilated at Loushan Pass. The court wanted Liu Ting and Li Rubo to hasten to Bozhou to assist in crushing the revolt. Liu, a native of Sichuan, knew Yang and had quite a reputation among the southwestern tribal peoples. He was recalled from Korea in the winter of 1595. At the behest of Xing, Yang was allowed to redeem himself by paying a 40,000-tael fine, so Liu was not needed in Sichuan for the time being.[54] Xing would later be transferred to Korea when the Japanese invaded again in 1597.

Konishi Joan finally proceeded to Beijing in January 1595, after more than a year of delays. He spent more than a month there being wined and dined by Ming officials and was allowed to ride his horse freely all over the Ming capital. On January 20 they all attended festivities at Honglu Temple, and three days later the treaty documents were presented at a lavish audience. The Chinese conditions for peace, which Konishi Joan accepted once again, were that the Japanese would be invested as a tributary state without trading privileges (xu feng bu xu gong) as long as they withdrew all troops from Korean soil and pledged never to attack Korea again. Hideyoshi was going to be made king of Japan and invested with the official title of Shun hua wang (king who has become obedient).[55] If all of these terms were not met to the satisfaction of the Ming, then there would be no treaty at all and the Japanese would be "punished" once again. The envoy was likewise told that the Ming would wait until they received word from King Sŏnjo that the Japanese were all gone before proceeding with investiture ceremonies.

As Konishi Joan was being feted in Beijing, Sŏnjo was addressing his officials concerning the Japanese situation. The double agent Yōzira had let slip that a fleet of 300 Japanese ships was readying for another attack. This was allegedly done at the order of Hideyoshi, who was supposedly angry upon hearing that the Koreans continued to block his efforts at resuming tribute trade with China. Chŏlla province was supposedly going to bear the brunt of this renewed Japanese assault. Sŏnjo, however, was not quick to believe these allegations, reminding his officials

that the Japanese were crafty and duplicitous by nature, but wanted
the rumors reported to the Chinese so that they could be on alert to
act if needed. The Ming told their allies to increase sea patrols and lay
in provisions.[56]

The allies also held discussions concerning Koreans who had been
captured and sent to Japan. By Chinese estimates some 10,000–20,000
Koreans from the vicinity of Pusan alone had been shipped overseas,
and the Japanese had shown little inclination to repatriate them. Just as
bad for these hapless captives, the Koreans were of a mind to execute
many of them upon their return as suspected traitors. Ming officials
implored them not to kill any escaped or repatriated captives, but
rather to allow them to return to their former occupations. They should
even be allowed to drill as soldiers and train as militia, because if the
government were to lose the hearts and minds of the people, its restoration would be all the more difficult. While acknowledging the Ming
position on these matters, the Korean court was particularly suspicious
of former officials who had spent time with the Japanese, believing that
they had turned their backs on the beneficence of the state. Thus any
such men who surrendered were to be thoroughly investigated before
having their former ranks restored.[57]

In Beijing, Konishi Joan was subjected to a series of interrogations
before Wanli and his officials. When pressed about why the Japanese
acted as they did, he replied, "Japan invaded Korea because the Koreans
had been deceiving them for three years so they had to be punished."
Konishi also said that his people wanted to establish and extend the
teachings of the Buddha to Korea but were forced to attack the Koreans
because of repeated deceptions. He added that Japan never wanted to
invade China at all but simply sought the restoration of tribute-trade
relations, a position that he said they clearly articulated after taking
Pyongyang in 1593 (repeating what his master had told Kim Ungso the
previous year). Konishi maintained that the Japanese had actually not
even tried to engage the Chinese in battle after the Ming entered Korea
but had simply embarked upon a series of fighting retreats. When pressed
about Chinju, he replied that the Koreans were slaughtered because they
tried to hinder Japan's orderly retreat.[58]

Finally the Ming officials asked: "If Hideyoshi has already pacified
Japan's sixty-six provinces then he should declare himself king. Why
does he need investiture from us?" Konishi replied that Hideyoshi did
not want to be tainted by association with Akechi Mitsuhide, and

"Japan, like Korea, receives its ruler's title from the Celestial King-dom. This puts the hearts of the people at peace and as everyone rec-ognizes the value of such peace, he [Hideyoshi] is therefore requesting investiture." The court then queried: "Your country already has an emperor who is also called king. We do not know, is the emperor not also the king?" The envoy responded, "The emperor is king, but he was already killed by Oda Nobunaga."[59]

In the end the Ming agreed to graciously allow Hideyoshi some of the benefits of being a vassal. But Konishi Joan was told that trade was not going to be allowed because the Japanese had continued to behave in an untrustworthy fashion as evidenced by the massacre at Chinju. Konishi readily agreed to all terms. He was told to return to Korea and await further instructions from the Ming. Although having decided to make Hideyoshi a vassal, the court still had doubts. They discussed the precedent of investing the Ashikaga shoguns and compared Hideyoshi to Altan Khan.[60] When the Ministry of Rites investigated the matter, they discovered that Hideyoshi was neither king of Japan nor even the shogun, which raised concerns as to how he could be granted such a title if he was not even a legitimate ruler by the standards of his own country. The Ming reiterated to Konishi Joan that not a single Japanese soldier could remain in Korea, or even in Tsushima, though it is not clear how they would have enforced this last part of the prohibition.

King Sŏnjo continued to pressure the Chinese to ensure that all Japanese troops withdrew before granting any kind of investiture. The Ming assured him that investiture would happen only after that condition had been met. Sŏnjo countered that the very existence of Chosŏn was still threatened and that the Ming had done a poor job of investigating the real situation. Back in China, in a meeting of the nine ranking ministers and supervising secretaries, He Qiaoyuan again argued against granting either tributary status or trade privileges. A secretary from the Ministry of Rev-enue also submitted an opposing memorial reminding the emperor that he had authorized punishing the Japanese; how could the fighting spirit of the troops dissipate after just one setback at Pyŏkchegwan? He continued: "Now the Japanese are hiding behind these insincere pledges as they loot and pillage the Korean masses. Song Yingchang has been replaced by Gu Yangqian, but if the armies are all withdrawn, how will the peoples' hearts be at peace?" He went on to argue that the court had not really considered the long-term ramifications of such an action for either Korea or China, including the costs of coastal defenses.[61]

The cost of maintaining Ming troops in Korea remained a major topic of discussion between the allies. The cost for each regular soldier was estimated at 17.52 liang per two seasons of campaigning. There were also costs associated with transporting supplies and even funds allocated for items such as candles and incense for ceremonial uses. The Ming complained about the difficulty of getting supplies to Korea; Sŏnjo countered by offering porters and saying that even at reduced levels of productivity, the southern provinces of Korea could sustain 3,000 troops for eight months. The king added that Chosŏn was now implementing *tuntian,* and these military farms could help too in the long run, despite the fact that Korean soil was deemed "loose and unproductive." He was also placing commanders and troops with firearms in positions designed to deter Japanese advances, acting in accordance with Chinese recommendations. The Ming estimated that some 1,300 firearms experts would be needed to train these Koreans.[62]

With Chinese help, the peninsula's defenses were reorganized under the overall command of Kwŏn Yul on land and Yi Sunsin at sea. But perhaps because of the demobilization of the ŭibyŏng the previous year or the government's persistent fears of independent military power, the actual military strength of the country remained rather low. One account, which includes regular and so-called mobile ŭibyŏng (despite their disbandment), gives a total estimated strength of just 12,577 men. Indeed, Nam-lin Hur estimates the total strength of the Chosŏn military during the war to have hardly exceeded 25,000 due to a number of "structural impediments" embedded in Chosŏn society, most notably the persistence of various exemptions from military service inhibiting the government's ability to raise troops. Korean manpower concerns were allayed somewhat by the news that 3,700 more Zhejiang troops were en route, though there were questions about how these new units would be paid and fed.[63]

Konishi Yukinaga maintained that the Japanese would withdraw from Pusan soon, but Sŏnjo said that at least 15,000 troops were still encamped in the southeast. In addition, there were more reports about Japanese boats sighted off the coast, some of which may have fired upon Korean positions. Konishi said that these were transport boats coming to ferry Japanese soldiers home. But the Koreans were unconvinced, pointing to Konishi's long record of deception since his first meeting with Shen Weijing.[64]

Despite this opposition, the court went forward with its preparations for investiture, telling the Koreans to put aside past quarrels and dispatching an official to justify and explain the court's decision. After receiving this communication, Sŏnjo's court became divided into two major camps. One group, which included Yu Sŏngnyong, believed that Korea had no choice but to accept the decision. As Yu put it: "Our country is weak and we must rely on the help of the Celestial Dynasty. If the Celestial Dynasty does not send help, then there's no way we can stand up for ourselves." The other group took a tougher stance, proclaiming that the Japanese should not be granted anything at all. Sŏnjo expressed his disappointment at the Ming not living up to their filial obligations as the tributary parent.[65]

Wanli soon censured some officials for their bad advice, even as others made recommendations for the renewal of military operations. Wang Dewan, for example, maintained that Gu Yangqian had deceived the court and that the Japanese were in fact digging in and looting the Korean countryside. Many of the wajō still held more than 1,000 troops apiece, a fact sufficient to invalidate any investiture agreement. In addition, Wang reminded the court about the two hundred plus Ming soldiers who had perished at Chinju. He continued to appeal to Wanli's vanity, saying that Hideyoshi saw himself as superior to China and that any Ming concessions would practically constitute an invitation to invade Korea again. But the die had been cast at this point, and the court was resolved to play out the negotiations and place its trust in Shen Weijing and Konishi Yukinaga. They did, however, threaten Konishi Joan with decapitation if there was any evidence of Japanese duplicity.[66]

The Ming sent a number of documents to Hideyoshi and his underlings and invested his court and commanders with flowery titles, as was standard practice. These communications were laden with classical allusions to the sage kings, the way of Confucius and Mencius, and the art of war of Sunzi and Sun Wu, among other things. They recounted how since ancient times those from the surrounding lands had come to offer tribute in acknowledgement of the superiority of the Chinese, who always placed peace first and rejected war unless absolutely necessary.[67] Wanli's imperial edict making Hideyoshi king of Japan, drafted on March 1, 1595, was typical of such documents. First, he chastised Hideyoshi for his behavior, then continued:

Now that you have realized with regret how serious was your error, you have withdrawn your troops and have returned the royal capital of Korea to that country. You have permitted the royal princes of Korea and their attendants to return to their homes. You have now reverently prepared in written form your former petition and have presented it to our court. . . . [Y]our troops in Korea have been causing much bloodshed in the district of Chinju. This untrustworthiness and duplicity has finally caused us to cease proceedings in your case. However Yi Yŏn, King of Korea, has appealed to our throne on your behalf and you have finally presented your petition to our throne stating that Japanese troops have remained at Pusan for more than a year in a most quiet and orderly manner, solely for the purpose of awaiting the arrival of the imperial envoy charged with investiture. . . . The facts of the whole matter have been discussed and are now understood to our satisfaction. We have at last discovered sincerity and loyalty in you. We no longer have any suspicion of your motives in our heart. We commend your doing good and practicing virtue. We have instructed Shen Weijing to proceed to Pusan and to have all your men in that place to return to their homes in Japan immediately. We have especially selected two men, appointing Li Zongcheng as senior envoy and Yang Fangheng as junior envoy. These envoys have been provided with the imperial letter of sanction. They are therefore qualified to hand you the imperial edict and to invest you as King of Japan, conferring upon you the imperial gift of the golden seal as well as the official crown and robes. Our official titles and ranks shall likewise be conferred upon a number of your subjects in recognition of their individual abilities and merits. Our imperial grace shall thus be more widely extended.

We hereby instruct all the people in your country to respect and obey your commands and to adhere strictly to your regulations in order that both yourself and your descendants may maintain a prosperous existence in your country, generation after generation, and may rule the country well. In the past our Chengzu Emperor conferred the investiture upon your country. Now, in our reign, your country has again been honored by the imperial investiture. Your country's having thus been twice so invested by us is a most glorious event that rarely takes place in this wide world.

Now that our investiture has been conferred upon you, henceforth you shall faithfully adhere to our three term agreement. You are instructed always to concentrate your mind upon and to manifest your loyalty and sincerity to our throne. You should always be faithful and just, thereby maintaining friendly and harmonious relations with neighboring nations. As to the pirate bands who maintain their existence near your country, you must deal with them strictly and severely. You shall not allow them to approach our coastal districts and the surrounding waters. . . .

By carrying out all these instructions, you will comply with our desires and at the same time you will fulfill the heavenly command. Concerning the sending of tribute to the throne, we fully realize your loyalty and sincerity in so cheerfully and promptly meeting this obligation incumbent upon a tributary state. However, our military officers who guard the coast district are always zealous in performing the work entrusted to them. Their sole attention is always turned towards warfare, as they know nothing else save to fight and to defend. On days of wind and storm, when the coast districts are swept by destructive gales, our coast guards may fail to differentiate between a jewel and a stone and may mistake tribute bearing ships for pirate vessels. You have already strongly impressed us with your loyalty and sincerity. We hereby exempt you from this duty to the throne. This step is also taken to prevent possible misunderstandings and unfortunate happenings. You shall not deviate from our instructions, but you shall reverently obey and adhere to our imperial command. Heaven looks down on the earth below and the will and laws of Heaven are strict and severe. Our imperial words and codes are brilliant and effective. Always revere Heaven and the throne.[68]

The wording of the document laid out the status relationship between the two states and put Hideyoshi in his place. But the Koreans argued that the Japanese did not understand the ways of words and would not honor the terms of the agreement. They were certain the Japanese were going to attack again and urged the Chinese to ready naval defenses. Japanese records indicate that Konishi Joan was not at all pleased with the wording of the documents presented by the Ming, but there was nothing he could do. In the meantime the Koreans had continued to hold discussions with Katō Kiyomasa, but because these were not sanctioned by the Ming court, they carried no weight.[69]

On February 8, 1595, Wanli appointed as chief envoy Li Zongcheng, the hereditary earl of Linhuai and assistant central military commissioner, with Yang Fangheng, a regional military commissioner, as his deputy. The envoys were laden with gifts, including ceremonial robes, a crown, and seals of authority.[70] Shen Weijing also selected nearly three hundred horses to present to Hideyoshi, which the Chinese felt the Japanese would greatly appreciate, having no fine horses of their own. Once again there were personality clashes, as Li did not respect Shen, and Shen regarded Li as nothing more than an incompetent court dandy. New seals of investiture had to be created because the old ones had been lost. Gifts were also sent for Konishi Yukinaga, Mōri Terumoto, Tokugawa Ieyasu, Keitetsu Genso, and other Japanese notables, angering the Koreans, who protested that their own people were starving and yet the Ming were giving fancy gifts to the perpetrators of the war. Li and Yang crossed the Yalu and reached Ŭiju on May 15. Shen was sent ahead to make sure everything ran smoothly on both sides.[71] Actually, after talking with Konishi Yukinaga, Li Hualong and Sun Kuang realized that there was little chance Hideyoshi would accept the terms, but as all the regalia, seals, and the like were finished and the envoys had been dispatched, they figured that nothing could be done. Li Hualong and Sun made plans to assemble more troops. Shi Xing still put his faith in Shen, who maintained that all Hideyoshi wanted was investiture.

A memorial submitted in June stated that the envoys had reached Namwŏn and the Japanese were leaving Pusan. Shen soon arrived in Pusan, assisted by the Korean official Hwang Sin, a descendant of Koryŏ royalty. Upon their arrival in Pusan, protocol disputes broke out over who should sit where, a sinister harbinger of things to come. Under continuing pressure from Shen and Hwang, the Japanese finally pulled out of Ungchŏn, Cheju, and Sŏsaengpo as a gesture of good faith, Katō being among the first to depart. But when Li Zongcheng and Yang reached Pusan, they discovered that troops were still there, albeit in reduced numbers, and refused to proceed to Japan. In August Shen reported to Wanli that the Japanese were finally burning their fortifications and breaking camp. The Koreans, still fearing another invasion,

asked the Ming to grant the Japanese trading rights at Ningbo, but they
were refused.[72]

Both Li Zongcheng and Sun Kuang reported that Konishi Yukinaga
was stalling. Although several Japanese divisions had already withdrawn, many others remained and the threat of a new offensive loomed,
though some rumors of military actions turned out to be no more than
tiger-hunting expeditions. Konishi continued to protest his sincerity
and blamed Katō for the continued delays. He added that Katō was still
using poisonous words to undermine the restoration of peace and was
behind the request for a Ming princess. Besides, argued Konishi, "[t]he
Great Ming is the mightiest country under heaven and Japan is only a
small island state. How could they dare presume to ask China to
engage in marital relations? Moreover, what can I do if the Ming refuses
to send a princess?"[73]

It was becoming increasingly obvious that Konishi and Shen had
misrepresented Hideyoshi's real demands. The envoys realized that with
all the troops and weapons still in Korea, the Japanese had no real time-
table for withdrawal. Konishi maintained that he had to meet with
Hideyoshi again. He went to Japan in the fall of 1595 and returned in
early 1596 with no real news. Shen said he would go back to Japan with
him to see what was happening and instructed Yang and Li to stay in
Pusan. They had no idea what was going on as Shen boarded the ship in
a fine silk suit, setting up a huge banner in the prow of the vessel that
read "let there be peace between our two countries." There was no news
for a long time after this, though eventually Shen gained an audience
with Hideyoshi, giving him python robes, a jade belt, a swan feather cap,
a map of the Ming empire, and a copy of the *Seven Military Classics*,
somehow managing to avoid conveying the true nature of his visit.[74]

In fact, in communications to his commanders since the previous
year, Hideyoshi had made it abundantly clear that he regarded himself as
the victor in the war and that hostilities would be renewed as soon as
the situation was right. An order dispatched to his commanders in early
1594 emphasized the need for maintaining adequate supplies and good
lines of communication. In this directive he questioned the sincerity
of the Ming and stated: "We shall therefore prepare for a permanent
military occupation of Korea by strengthening all the military castles
and strongholds to the fullest degree. We regard Korea as a part of our
domain, the same as Kyushu."[75]

But life was by no means easy for the troops left behind in Korea. Most were not of high-enough status to enjoy servants, dancing girls, and tiger hunts like Katō Kiyomasa. Like their Korean counterparts, they were often forced to engage in grueling labor such as digging wells and planting fields. As Jesuit priest Gregorio de Cespedes observed: "The cold in Korea is very severe and without comparison to that of Japan. All day long my limbs are half benumbed, and in the morning I can hardly move my hands to say Mass, but I keep myself in good health thanks to God and the fruit that our Lord is giving. I am cheerful and don't mind my work and the cold. . . . All these Christians are very poor, and suffer from hunger, cold, illness, and other inconveniences very different from other places. Although Hideyoshi sends food, so little reaches here that it is impossible to sustain all with them, and moreover the help that comes from Japan is insufficient and comes late."[76]

Many Japanese fled as a result of these harsh conditions and surrendered. Some even became a permanent part of the Korean military and remained after the war, assimilating into Korean society to an extent never achieved by their counterparts who were dragged to Japan. Koreans hired surrendered Japanese as swordsmanship instructors. Other deserters joined the Ming armies and later served with distinction in campaigns in distant corners of the empire. The method of recruitment was essentially impressment into service. When offered the chance to escape and start a new life on their own terms, it is unsurprising that many Japanese soldiers might have chosen to stay in Korea. After all, Japan had been at war for over a century, and commoners were most likely tired of the constant threats to life and property. Additionally, Korea was in many respects more advanced than Japan, which might have appealed to some, though it is impossible to estimate the allure of high culture for the likes of foot soldiers and porters. Still, conditions were not much better than rural Japan in the Korean countryside. Bandits ran amok and corpses lined the roadsides.[77] Chinese soldiers often requisitioned supplies and demanded that locals billet them in their homes. But some deserters must have felt their chances of survival were better among the Koreans than going hungry while huddled in their castles along the coast.

As he waited in Pusan for word from Shen, Li Zongcheng was reportedly miserable and wanted to return to China. Shi Xing accused Sun Kuang of trying to undermine the talks yet again, while Sun retorted that the Japanese were using them to ridicule China. Some in Korea even

feared that the envoys were being held prisoner in the Japanese camp
while they rushed new troops to Korea. Matters improved somewhat
when Hideyoshi recalled Shimazu Yoshihiro and Nabeshima Naoshige
and Sŏnjo sent a letter to the Japanese ruler thanking him for his fine
treatment of the captured Korean princes. Konishi Yukinaga related that
Hideyoshi's mindset was that troops would be recalled once the envoys
crossed the sea. The Japanese also maintained that the primary reason
they had not yet returned home was because the winds were unfavorable.
This prompted one Chinese official to quip, "In all this time there was
not one day of favorable winds?"[78]

As a result of these lingering doubts, the Ministry of War dispatched
yet more officials to Korea. Sŏnjo expressed his doubts too, saying, "If
you permit investiture, there's no estimating the scale of disaster, but
if you cut it off, you'll still be in a position to send troops quickly if the
situation calls for it." He added that letting even one Japanese soldier
stay in Korea would be a disaster for the country—they were just spying
out Korea's weaknesses and preparing to overrun it like insects once
more. If the Chinese wanted to be benevolent, he argued again, they
should open Ningbo to Japanese trade.[79]

Nevertheless, a report from the Korean Ministry of War indicated
that eleven of the sixteen Japanese camps had been abandoned and more
than 5,200 Japanese homes were now empty. Finally, in February 1596
the Ming learned that Japanese ships were reportedly on their way from
Nagoya to convey the Ming envoys to Japan. Li Zongcheng remained
skeptical and again asked to be dismissed from his post. This request
was denied, but the next month Li's request for more funds to support
his retinue was honored. There was also continued unrest in the Korean
countryside and at court. Officials were impeached, beaten, or even
executed for failure to control popular dissent. Uprisings plagued the
Hŏnam region. Fed up with the factionalism in his court, Sŏnjo retired
to the East Palace of the royal compound, ignoring the entreaties of his
officials for several days in protest. By this time Hideyoshi was also
becoming suspicious. The continued delays only served to irritate him.
In addition, he was becoming mentally unbalanced as a result of the
stress in securing the country for his beloved infant son.[80]

Meanwhile, back in Beijing Shi answered his critics, saying that
although there had been no progress in the negotiations, there had also
been no further plundering by the Japanese. He told his colleagues to rest
assured, for the mission would no doubt succeed. Wanli was mollified

somewhat, but Sun Kuang stirred things up by calling for an end to the mission and a buildup of Ming forces for another offensive. Li Zongcheng was viewed as a counter to Shen, whom most believed was firmly in Shi's camp and therefore less likely to be completely forthright regarding the progress of the negotiations. In May 1596 Li Hualong confirmed that only five out of sixteen Japanese camps remained in Korea, and the rest seemed on the verge of withdrawing. Still, Xu Chengchu, a secretary in the Ministry of Justice, said: "Japanese people have already occupied Pusan for over a century. Their property and families are completely established there. How can we expect their myriads to leave altogether, based on one word from Shen Weijing?"[81]

Yet even as this welcome news was received in Beijing, one of the more bizarre events of the entire war occurred. Li Zongcheng abandoned his mission in the middle of the night, disappearing just days before he was to go to Japan. There are conflicting stories as to the exact circumstances of Li's flight. According to Li himself, he learned that the Japanese were not going to submit at all but were in fact going to launch another surprise invasion. Knowing the mission was doomed to fail and fearing for his own life, he fled into the forests around Pusan and eluded the Japanese, only to reappear in Kyŏngju days later, bedraggled and hungry, with the news of Japan's duplicity. Li said that Hideyoshi actually had seven demands, which did not stop at mere investiture. He remarked that the taikō was "as fierce as a wolf or tiger and as sneaky as a snake."[82] The Japanese had gone in search of Li but had turned back at a stone bridge near Yangsan without luck. Yang Fangheng placated them and sent a letter to the Koreans telling them not to mobilize their forces, assuring them all was well.

Another version of the story relates that Li was a noble fop who spent most of his free time dallying with beautiful women. While engaging in his favorite pastime in Pusan, Li apparently became infatuated with the favorite consort of one of the Japanese generals.[83] Never one to deny himself, he asked if he could have her. This elicited an angry response from the commander, who rounded up some of his retainers to arrest Li. The envoy therefore fled for his life in the middle of the night, abandoning not only his mission but also the entire country to the possibility of another onslaught. Li escaped by hiding in a tree in the forest and reached Kyŏngju several days later. Still another version of the story has Shen sending Li a letter informing him that the talks were going to fail. Li was reportedly very angry and fled alone in the middle of the night. According to Li Sixiao, a censor from Shandong, the envoy heard that Shen had been taken prisoner by the Japanese and fled in the middle of the night, casting away the seals of investiture. He then wandered through the Korean wilderness for six days without food before reaching Kyŏngju on June 3.[84]

The Ming court feared the incident would ruin peace talks. Xu Chengchu declared: "Shen Weijing fell into Hideyoshi's trap and Shi Xing fell prey to Shen Weijing's duplicity. And now there is no way we can extricate ourselves from this mess and set things right!" An official named Zhou Kongjiao remarked: "If the Celestial Empire is all powerful, why do we dread the Japanese as if they have the strength of tigers? We certainly don't need to receive them as tributaries. Now the best plan is to defend Korea. If Korea falls, then Liaoyang is imperiled. If Liaoyang falls, then Beijing is next, so you see we can't just abandon Korea and as the investigations have proven, this so-called investiture is groundless."[85]

Wanli was livid and ordered his officials to begin preparations for war. Li Zongcheng's father, Li Yangong, a commander in the capital garrisons, was blamed for his son's action and removed from his post. He requisitioned 300,000 liang of silver from the Ministry of Revenue, with another 100,000 for special rewards to be raised by the Court of the Imperial Stud. Local areas were to send supplies and begin mustering troops. Finally, an arrest warrant was issued for Li Zongcheng.[86]

Yang Fangheng, who had misgivings before Li's flight, was even more nervous now. Shen Weijing consoled him: "It is the duty of ministers to take on the hardships of state. It is proper that we should exert ourselves to the utmost or even die for our state. What reason do you have for weeping?" Yang complained that his mother was old and his son was young and he just wanted to go home. Shen replied that if he wanted to go home, that would not be a problem. Yang trusted him and later sent a letter to Shi Xing, saying Shen could handle the job and there was no cause for alarm. In addition, Konishi Yukinaga had ordered the withdrawal of Japanese forces from Sŏsaengpo and Cheju Island, meaning just four smaller camps remained at Pusan. The Ming decided to listen to Shen and promoted Yang to chief envoy, with Shen as his deputy. While many officials clamored for war, Shi offered to go to Korea himself to finish negotiations, but Wanli refused to allow this. Meanwhile, Shen sent a gift to Shi's house, which infuriated him because it clearly looked like a bribe. Now even Shi came to suspect Shen, and he asked several trusted men to spy on him in Pusan. When they reported nothing was amiss, Shi was assuaged.[87]

At about the same time, Yue Yuansheng, director in the Ministry of Works, impeached Shi in a scathing memorial. Shi's mistakes included errors of judgment and tactics ranging from the dispatch of Zu Chengxun in the summer of 1592 with a token force, to the granting of an audience to Konishi Joan, to poor supply and stationing of Ming forces in Korea.[88] Yue also requested that Wanli convene a council of war. But instead of having the desired effect, Yue only managed to anger the emperor, who demoted the hapless director to the status of a commoner and deprived him of office. But this did not dissuade other officials from submitting their own memorials criticizing Shi and others. One censor, Cao Xuecheng, was especially vociferous in his critique of Shi's peace policy, believing Li Zongcheng's story and that Shen was a pawn of the Japanese. Cao's outspoken criticisms eventually got him arrested by the Embroidered Uniform Guard and sentenced to death. Although several officials tried to intercede on his behalf, their pleas fell on deaf ears until Cao's son wrote a letter with his own blood asking to be killed in place of his father, who had already been beaten severely by his jailers. Others appealed to Wanli's well-known filial piety. Because Cao's mother was already over ninety years old, they argued that his execution would hasten her death as well. Eventually the emperor was moved, and Cao's sentence was commuted to ten years in prison.[89]

Shi reiterated his preconditions for peace, but Wanli, despite his continued backing of his envoy, also ordered preparations for war. The three camps in Ming officialdom divided between those favoring investiture, those favoring only defensive measures, and those favoring another offensive campaign. As was the case originally, the Ming were most concerned with logistics. This time, however, the allies at least had most of Korea under their sway and were better prepared to supply their forces by sea, for many of the naval stations were on alert and the ships were already constructed. Ming officials busied themselves preparing lists of key defensive points in Korea and studying possible routes of advance. Sŏnjo was told to marshal his forces, secure essential points, and wait for the Ming army to come to his rescue in the event of attack. The Ministry of Revenue reported that they were having difficulty raising the required funds and only 120,000 liang would be immediately forthcoming, though they estimated more cash could be raised from local and provincial sources.[90]

Amid the swirling rumors and tension, Yang, Shen, and four hundred followers set sail for Japan on July 10, 1596, to invest Hideyoshi as a Ming vassal. They had to request new ceremonial clothes and documents at the eleventh hour because the outfits originally sent with them had become soiled during their lengthy stay in Pusan. Shi figured this signaled a successful conclusion to the affair, but Wanli demanded a report on the ceremony as soon as the envoys returned to Korea. The envoys went first to Tsushima, where they were briefly delayed, landing at Sakai on July 20. They were followed shortly thereafter by a Korean delegation, which had been requested by Shen. Sŏnjo and his ministers were reluctant to send anyone because they had no desire to legitimize Hideyoshi, so they finally sent a military official named Yi Pongch'un as their chief delegate. But because Yi lacked diplomatic skills, he was replaced with Hwang Sin at the last moment.[91] Hwang had already visited the Japanese, so he was well regarded by them. He was assisted by Pak Hongchang.

Upon landing in Sakai, the envoys were greeted by a number of dignitaries, including a daimyo named Masashige, but Hideyoshi was not among them, having urgent matters of state to which to attend. He was also upset that no Korean or Chinese royalty had deigned to come and give him proper respect. The investiture ceremony was originally scheduled to take place at Fushimi Castle, but an earthquake had severely damaged the area—reportedly more than four hundred women were crushed to death and Hideyoshi himself barely escaped—and it was moved to Osaka. The Chinese delegation finally reached Osaka on October 22. Knowing there might be problems when Hideyoshi realized exactly what was happening, Konishi Yukinaga and Shen did what they could to maintain the fiction that the taikō's demands were being met and tried to enlist others in their conspiracy. Shen also had to allay the misgivings of the Koreans.[92] The envoys were understandably nervous when conducted into the presence of the overlord of Japan, surrounded by a phalanx of warriors in their splendid armor. Yang was in the front of the delegation and Shen carried the seals of office.

As Kawaguchi Choju described the scene: "The yellow flaps of the tent parted and Hideyoshi entered, attended by a pair of sword-bearing samurai. The samurai in attendance heralded his entrance with reverence and Weijing was filled with dread as he lay prostrate clutching the seals." Hideyoshi was initially delighted at the robes and crown, as the envoys bowed five times and kowtowed three times while shouting "Long live Hideyoshi!" Shen handed over the seals and ceremonial garb, politely, with two hands. In addressing the delegation, Hideyoshi reiterated the claim that the Koreans had instigated the whole affair by preventing Japan from gaining access to trade with China. Then after he had been kind enough to return the princes, the Koreans had not even offered thanks.[93]

Shen and a Korean translator met with several monks to discuss the terms outlined in the Ming documents. Hwang heard rumors that the Japanese were going to invade the peninsula again because the Koreans had not shown Hideyoshi proper respect. Hwang stood his ground, saying that full relations could only be restored after all Japanese troops were recalled.[94]

The delegates then spent the next three days in Hideyoshi's palatial castle being feasted and entertained. The Chinese guests even gave the Japanese gifts for the relief of victims of the great earthquake. In these gatherings Hideyoshi always sat in an elevated position, resplendent in the Ming regalia. The leading Japanese delegates also proudly wore their Ming clothing. The Chinese soon asked to be allowed to return home because the weather would soon be unsuitable for traveling. Finally, Hideyoshi retreated to the mountains and asked the monk Saishō Shotai to read the letter of investiture from Wanli. Konishi Yukinaga secretly told the monk the true contents of the letter and begged him to alter it to avoid Hideyoshi's fury. Saishō refused to entertain Konishi's request, and he translated the letter accurately, ending with the fateful words, "We hereby invest you king of Japan."[95]

Hideyoshi was livid when he heard the letter and its demeaning language. He is alleged to have exclaimed: "Why would I want to be king of Japan? Yukinaga said the Ming emperor was going to make me ruler of the Ming. I want to mobilize troops immediately. Yukinaga is not my loyal follower, but is secretly in league with the Ming. His transgressions are not small and I won't be happy until I have his head!" According to Nihon gaishi, when Hideyoshi heard the edict of investiture read to him, he lost color and stood up, casting off his crown and robes, grabbing the letter and tearing it up, and cursing the envoys: "I've already taken Japan in my grasp. If I wanted to be king then I would be king. What is this investing me like a bearded caitiff? Moreover, if I am king, then what does that make the Celestial Dynasty?"[96]

The monk tried to mollify the taikō, telling him this was the way China had conducted its foreign affairs since ancient times. Hideyoshi had Konishi Yukinaga brought before him and scolded him. Konishi blamed another retainer and even claimed to have letters to prove his charges. Katō Kiyomasa was summoned, and he said, "The Ming did not meet our demands." Therefore Hideyoshi decided the peace was nullified and issued the order to mount another expedition to exterminate Korea once and for all.[97] Again Katō and Konishi were called upon to lead the vanguard of the invasion forces. But this time Hideyoshi had no illusions about his ability to overrun all of China. His motive seems to have been simple revenge for the great indignity he had suffered at the hands of the Koreans and the Chinese.

Hideyoshi was still of a mind to execute the envoys as an example, but another monk intervened and remonstrated with the irate warlord. Shen still hoped that he could salvage matters and asked to see Hideyoshi again. Konishi replied: "Now that we plan on attacking Korea again, do not ask me for help. I can no longer treat with the enemy." He added that he was saddened by the unfortunate turn of events and thought the second invasion was a big mistake. At the same time, Konishi blamed the Koreans for undermining the peace talks.[98]

The sources vary as to when Hideyoshi actually realized what had been done. According to some Japanese sources, it was the day after the audience that Saishō read the document aloud and Hideyoshi realized he had been made a vassal of the Ming. Other sources relate that Hideyoshi was angry but had been suspicious from the start. He was irritated that the Koreans and Chinese had dispatched what he perceived (rightly) to be inferior envoys, expecting Korean princes at the very least to be in attendance to acknowledge his overlordship. After all, he had already returned the captive princes, ministers, and provinces to the Koreans. The taikō allegedly chided their delegates, declaring, "You should be coming here to thank me but instead you envoys come here to ridicule me!" He demanded an apology and a Korean prince as a hostage. The Koreans refused, at which Hideyoshi exploded in rage. He then dismissed Yang Fangheng and Shen "without a word of thanks for the propriety of the celestial empire."[99]

In hindsight, it is astonishing that Hideyoshi could really have been unaware of what was transpiring, and if so, this was truly one of the great diplomatic blunders of history. Yet it is also possible that the Japanese were confused about the true meaning of investiture in the Ming world order. Mary Elizabeth Berry has suggested that what Hideyoshi desired more than anything was homage and recognition of his status as the ruler of Japan. She posits that he allowed the inconclusive talks to drag on because he preferred ambiguity to an acknowledgement of defeat or inferiority.[100] The edict of investiture not only confirmed that the Chinese and the Koreans regarded him as their inferior but also rubbed salt in the wounds of his military defeat. Hideyoshi might have accepted the edict if it had been presented by Korean royalty or been couched in more conciliatory language. As it was, he had effectively painted himself into a diplomatic corner and had no choice but to back up his boasts with action.

Li Guangtao believed that the sending of inferior envoys to invest Hideyoshi was the most serious blunder made by the allies in the negotiations, for it caused him a huge loss of face. From this point on, he no longer trusted Konishi Yukinaga and instead listened to the counsels of Katō, whose maxim was "words are no use, actions are what matter." This opinion is born out by none other than King Sǒnjo, who told Wanli in a letter that the Japanese were attacking again because Korea had refused to dispatch a prince to pay his respects to Hideyoshi. Had the Chinese possessed a more sophisticated understanding of Japan's political situation, they might have acted differently.[101]

Others have argued that trade relations were paramount to Hideyoshi because he felt he needed control of foreign trade to maintain his authority. Zheng Liangsheng has asserted that Konishi and Katō incorrectly surmised that what their leader wanted was a noble title, so they caved on the tribute-trade issue and were content to accept investiture without trade. Hideyoshi might well have accepted the title from Wanli if it had included provisions for trading, but because it did not, he was forced to invade again in the vain hope of establishing these coveted ties. Zhu Yafei has claimed that the fact the Japanese acquiesced on all other issues but still wanted tribute trade attests to its primacy. But he also suggested that Konishi may have misrepresented the importance of trade due to his own interests. While the Ming were explicitly clear about not allowing trade, this was not conveyed to Hideyoshi. While this argument has its merits, it was Hideyoshi's wounded pride that was the primary factor in provoking the second invasion. His own statements say little about trade, but several contemporary observers, including Jesuit Louis Frois, commented on his overweening desire for recognition by his peers. Hideyoshi's repeated statements concerning the Korean refusal to pay respects to him bear this out.[102] This is not to say that trade was unimportant, however, for most Asian rulers were becoming increasingly sensitive to the political and military benefits of greater participation in international trade at the turn of the seventeenth century.

When Yang and Shen returned to Korea, they immediately sent a letter to the Ming court telling them the Japanese accepted the terms of investiture. As if this lie was not bad enough, they then procured a number of items from southern China and the islands of Southeast Asia, including gold, pearls, swan feathers, and an orangutan, and sent them to the court as "tribute" submitted by Hideyoshi. Apparently Shen and Yang hoped to talk the Koreans into sending a prince to recognize Hideyoshi as king of Japan and thereby smooth over the crisis without having to divulge the truth to the Ming.[103] They even rejected a proposal by one Korean official to launch a quick strike on Japanese positions around Pusan before reinforcements could arrive.

The court was not fooled by the lies, as they had their own spies in Korea and had been in touch with the Korean envoys. The court inquired why Hideyoshi would send items known to come from Guangdong as tribute, one wag remarking, "If small matters were handled like this, we can only speculate how the important issues were handled." All involved tried to pass the buck, with Yang blaming Shen who blamed Shi Xing. Shen and Shi were disgraced, with arrest orders issued for both of them. Shi implored Wanli to let him go to Korea and negotiate in person, but the request was denied. Xing Jie was made minister of war and concurrently supreme commander of Jiliao and Baoding and military commissioner in charge of resisting the Japanese. He suggested attacking the Japanese on the high seas before they even got to Korea, but his plan was not implemented.[104]

Although Shen tried to pretend nothing was wrong, a letter from Hideyoshi soon arrived announcing his intention to invade Korea again and articulating the reasons for this, principally: first, sending Ming envoys with a private agenda; second, accepting the return of the Korean princes without offering proper thanks and recognition, instead sending low-ranking Ming officials as ambassadors; and third, going against the agreements that had been hammered out over several years by the Ming on behalf of Korea. The Japanese were most upset that Sŏnjo himself or at least one of his sons had not come to pay their respects in person. Konishi Yukinaga also dispatched another servant,

Takenouchi Hajime, to deliver a message to the Ming: "The forces we have in Korea now are but a tenth of our strength. There are many more camped around Nagoya under our great generals. By contrast your Ming troops are so weak as to hardly constitute a threat. If you go up against us, your losses will be high."[105]

After receiving such news, the Ming hawks went back on the offensive. Zhou Kongjiao said that it was high time that the errors of Shi Xing were rectified. He then blamed Wanli for errors in judgment, identifying eight ways in which the emperor had been deceived and four errors committed by the monarch himself: trusting Shen's assurances; pulling out Zhejiang and Sichuanese troops, whom the Koreans trusted; not mobilizing troops after Li Zongcheng fled; and blissfully listening to happy words of peace and demobilizing troops even as the Japanese rebuilt their fortifications and sent more and more soldiers to Korea. But Zhou acknowledged that "[i]f your majesty selects loyal and courageous civil and military officials and entrusts them with managing this affair, repairing and maintaining defenses, . . . then certainly this disaster can still be managed."[106]

As the Ming began preparations for yet another costly campaign, the Koreans tried to forestall the Japanese by sending gifts. But Hideyoshi reiterated his demand for a prince to come and apologize, which the Koreans refused. Rumors put the gathering invasion force at more than 200,000 men. This time Korean pleas for help were answered quickly as the Ming moved to bolster naval defenses and get troops into position. Wanli again issued a call for plans and soldiers, especially southern troops. The Koreans for their part now had far more battle-tested generals and soldiers, some of whom had been training with Ming drill instructors for years. Unfortunately, however, Yi Sunsin had run afoul of political enemies and lost his naval command.[107] Had Yi been in charge of the Korean navy at this time, subsequent events might have been far different. The Ming wanted to appoint another military commissioner to administer affairs on the peninsula, but the Koreans were afraid the Chinese were now considering making Korea a colony. For the time being, Ma Gui was made supreme commander of Korea and Yang Hao was invested with the post of military commissioner.

Despite his bravado, the evidence suggests that Hideyoshi was not overly enamored of the prospect of invading Korea again. Many of his commanders, most notably Tokugawa Ieyasu and Konishi Yukinaga, opposed the action. Another message was sent to Sŏnjo, telling him the invasion could still be curtailed if he simply came to Japan, apologized, and paid his respects. Sŏnjo stubbornly refused, saying this was not within Korea's ancestral traditions. Katō acidly replied: "If a prince crosses the sea [to pay his respects] then your ancestral traditions will be preserved. Otherwise our troops will destroy your ancestral traditions and then what will you do?" The Koreans remained unmoved, and Katō stated simply, "If we capture the king, we will kill him."[108]

In the final assessment, the peace talks were probably doomed from the start. The two sides were too far apart in their initial demands, and the negotiators lacked the power necessary to enforce their side's wishes. Moreover, both the Japanese and the Chinese were ignorant of the other's political situation and refused to adapt to the realities of the situation. The attempt to conceal the truth of Ming terms from Hideyoshi by Konishi and Shen was ill conceived and poorly executed. The Ming tributary system may have been anachronistic in some respects, but it was how trade was conducted in East Asia at the time. There was quite a degree of flexibility built into it, and Hideyoshi in all likelihood could have exacted trade concessions had he played the game according to Ming rules. But what he really wanted was another set of rules entirely, or at least a game that put him at the top of the East Asian world order. The real losers in this great game were the Koreans, who barely had a voice in determining their own fate. Not including them from the beginning contributed to the profound misunderstandings between the negotiators.[109] All Hideyoshi would end up doing after the talks collapsed and he committed to a second invasion of Korea would be to create a fount of ill will that persists into the twenty-first century.

6

BACK INTO THE GATES OF HELL

The Final Japanese Offensive, 1597–98

The only thing I've managed to do is make tens of thousands
of men ghosts overseas. Alas, what is to become of me?
—Toyotomi Hideyoshi

L earning from the experience of the earlier invasion, the Chinese
and Korean bureaucracies sought to coordinate their defense activities. King Sŏnjo instructed his ministers to "[a]ssemble your generals
and muster your strength, for we will not relive the hardships of Ŭiju."
Yi Wŏn'ik went about repairing defenses at a number of key positions.
Fortresses received more food and weapons in anticipation of evacuating
the populace to them. The Chosŏn government this time hoped to clear
the countryside and deny resources to the invaders in a more systematic
fashion. As for the Chinese, Yang Hao was appointed commissioner for
Korean affairs. The Ming Ministry of War earmarked nearly 140,000
liang of silver from its coffers for the initial war effort and ordered
provinces to begin sending in additional funds. Feeding the troops
would be the joint responsibility of the Ministries of Revenue and War
in China, augmented by their hosts in Korea. The Ministry of War also
issued orders for the mobilization of troops from the far corners of the
empire.[1] The Ming intended that the arrival of units from all over China
by land and sea, with their varied weaponry, uniforms, and fighting styles,
would overawe the Japanese.

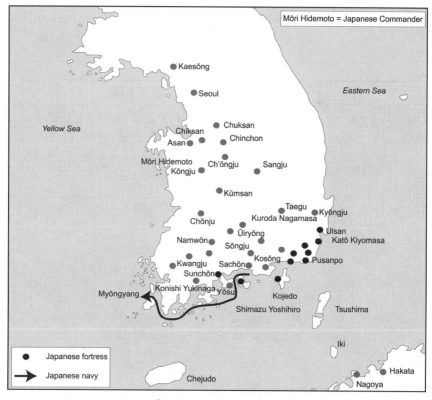

Second Japanese Invasion, 1597–98

Sino-Korean discussions focused on Korea's geography and how it affected supply and transportation from China and defensive operations against the Japanese. The Ming emphasized the importance of keeping sea lanes open and the need for capable local logistics officers. Sŏnjo gave Chinese commander Ma Gui his full appraisal of the situation, drawing on intelligence reports from the southeast. His officials started issuing calls to arms all over the south, and all men from the ages of fifteen to sixty were pressed into service repairing sansŏng walls. Those who avoided their duty were to be punished, but when Kwŏn Yul mustered all his troops at Taegu, the force numbered only 23,600 men.[2]

The first wave of the invasion force reached the Korean coast on March 1, 1597, supply boats landing at Pusan and Sŏsaengpo, as Korean troops pulled back to various mountain fortresses. Kobayakawa Hideaki seized Pusan and Tachibana Munetora garrisoned Angolpo. The first reports received in China said that there were about two hundred small boats capable of holding no more than 100 men each, giving a maximum number of 20,000 men. Spies reported that Konishi Yukinaga and the others planned a thrust toward Seoul through Kyŏngsang, though Hideyoshi himself apparently had planned on sending the troops north from the coast this time rather than west across the peninsula from Pusan.[3]

The Chinese reckoned that they could deal with such a force. They probably could have, but there were far more Japanese just behind this first wave, and massive amounts of supplies were being shipped over as well. Yi Ŏkki and Wŏn Kyun engaged some of the Japanese ships and killed forty sailors in a fierce clash at sea, then another fifty-two near Cheju Island. But the Koreans were unable to thwart the main landing force, which linked up with units still on the peninsula and began bulking up existing defense works.[4]

Because the allies decided not to attack these remaining forces earlier, the new arrivals were able to establish themselves quite securely. Yangsan was the first city attacked, and the next day Konishi and his men started fanning out and seizing beachheads. Sŏsaengpo fell two days later. The hapless commoners of Kyŏngsang were forced to flee their homes once again. Konishi hunkered down in Pusan and prepared for an extended campaign. Meanwhile, Yu Sŏngnyong was entrusted with getting grain and fodder to other imperiled cities, such as Sangju.

The monk Yujŏng resumed his diplomatic duties, hustling to the camp of Katō Kiyomasa to try and find a peaceful solution to the renewed crisis in early May. Katō told him that Korea was again being punished for "refusing to lend a road to Japan" for the invasion of China and that should they choose to do so this time, no harm would come to Korea. Moreover, he argued that Japan had acted properly and in good faith earlier in returning the Korean princes, but Korea had been disrespectful in return. Hideyoshi was very angry that the king had not formally thanked him or even deigned to send his sons back to Japan to thank him personally for their good treatment. If they had simply done this, then there would have been no need to send another large invasion force, Katō maintained—the Koreans were merely "bringing ruin upon themselves." Katō also told Yujŏng that the Japanese still planned on invading China through Shanhaiguan and that the various divisions were going to link up and advance together. Yujŏng noted that Katō's words were fierce and his evil intentions were obvious.[5]

In reply Sŏnjo sent a letter to Hideyoshi, berating him for his insolence in causing trouble once again after the Middle Kingdom had sent a
special envoy to Japan to invest him as king. He charged that because of a
desire to have his fierce name spread throughout the Japanese islands and
beyond, Hideyoshi was turning his back on the benevolence extended by
the Ming emperor. And since Japanese troops had already launched a
new invasion of Korea, Sŏnjo mentioned that he had likewise dispatched
a messenger to China with this news, which enraged the emperor and
provoked him to send more high officials to deal with the renewed threat.
Sŏnjo added that the earthquake Japan had experienced the previous
year was but one manifestation of heaven's displeasure: "How could
Hideyoshi expect to stop the combined might of the Ming empire and
its vassals when he could not even quell domestic unrest? And given
his advanced age of over sixty and the fact that his child was less than ten
years old, what did he really think he could achieve?" Korea remained
under China's protection, he declared, and myriad troops were coming
to settle this matter.[6]

The substance of these exchanges raises the issue of this second
invasion's objective. Some argue that assuaging Hideyoshi's wounded
pride and wreaking havoc were the only real goals. Others contend that
the aim of the 1597 invasion was to secure Korea's southern provinces,
which Hideyoshi had expected to receive by virtue of the agreement he
had hoped to conclude with the Ming.[7]

It is also possible that the goals of Hideyoshi and his commanders
differed. Samuel Hawley has noted that some of Hideyoshi's daimyo,
most notably Katō Kiyomasa, wanted to conquer the southern three
provinces and turn them into Japanese provinces to glorify their lord's
name and attain larger, richer fiefs for themselves, but that Hideyoshi
himself merely wanted his forces to rampage for a few months to restore
his damaged honor and impress the Ming with his military might.[8] The
conversations between Yujŏng and Katō indicate that the latter at least
evinced a desire to "finish the job" of conquering the Ming, but it is
impossible to ascertain whether he was being serious. Given Hideyoshi's
mental state at the time of the second offensive, it appears that he wanted
revenge first and foremost, with hopes to get whatever he could from the
endeavor but otherwise no clear long-term goal.

Ming official Sun Kuang, who had replaced Gu Yangqian, memorialized Sŏnjo concerning supplies for the armies, especially saltpeter.
He also recognized that Korea could not feed the troops by itself but

told the king that his country had to supply some provisions. He also requested more funds from the Ming Court of the Imperial Stud and suggested opening markets along the army's travel routes to facilitate trade, a request that presaged policies adopted later during the Qing dynasty and also paralleled developments in contemporary Europe. Sun then submitted a comprehensive plan for victory that entailed making extensive use of defensive points and integrating Chinese and Korean units to block possible lines of advance. He also proposed creating mobile corps that could be quickly dispatched to trouble spots, a practice used in China. Sŏnjo instructed his ministers to act in accordance with Sun's suggestions, though he was reluctant to alter the existing administrative hierarchy. The allies also generated lists of sansŏng relative to Korea's major cities and identified areas that were suitable for the establishment of *tuntian*.[9]

Wu Weizhong, who commanded 3,785 southern troops, and Yang Yuan, who was being dispatched from Liaodong at the head of 3,000 additional men, were to be the first line of defense, holding key positions until more troops arrived. Sŏnjo made arrangements for these forces to be deployed throughout southern Korea in mixed formations with Korean units, many of which were newly created.[10] The Koreans requested 500 more Chinese guns, presumably cannon, and 1,700 arquebuses as well as training in their use and manufacture.

As during the earlier crisis in Korea, Wanli actively solicited advice and convened a meeting of the nine ranking Ming ministers and supervising secretaries early in the third month of 1597. The emperor was told that the Koreans had withheld information on the failure of the peace talks but now professed that they were in danger of annihilation. Brushing aside these spurious claims, Wanli asked why the officials he had dispatched to Pusan had not been forthright in their own reports, then ordered their arrests. The court decided that 3,000–4,000 Liaodong troops should go at once to guard Choryŏng Pass and the approach to Seoul. They noted that southern troops were more desirable due to their prowess at fighting the Japanese, but getting them north quickly might be a problem unless more boats were constructed fast. The port city of Lushun was designated the major staging ground for landing Ming men and supplies.[11]

Some officials, citing the danger of Yang Yinglong in the southwest, were not keen on opening up another military front. But Xu Chengchu, a supervising secretary in the Ministry of War, sent a memorial warning his superiors that the Japanese were already penetrating deep into Korean territory. Xu argued that Korea's very existence was threatened once again and a relief force was required with all due haste. He lamented that rampant factionalism in the Ming government had allowed this to happen, for if it had taken a firm stance the first time and simply driven the Japanese out of Korea, the affair would have been settled years earlier. This time there could be no wavering, declared Xu. Other officials agreed, reiterating Korea's importance as China's loyal neighbor and contending that not helping now would just be throwing away earlier achievements. As before, the strategic importance of Korea for China's defense was also highlighted, one official stating, "This cannot be said to be solely a Korean affair."[12] Historical precedents were invoked too, this time China's involvement on the peninsula during the Han era (202 B.C.–220 A.D.) in addition to the Tang actions discussed during the first invasion.

This conference also revealed the ongoing factional strife within Wanli's administration. Those who had favored a more aggressive approach earlier spared no effort in pointing fingers at those who foolishly put their trust in Shen Weijing and Konishi Yukinaga. They said that all those who perpetrated "errors of state" must be punished and issued an arrest warrant for Shen. Yang Fangheng was also ordered arrested and interrogated. Sun Kuang was implicated as well because he was responsible for overseeing what was transpiring in Korea during the talks. Shi Xing lost his post as minister of war and was replaced by Tian Le. Xing Jie replaced Sun and would aid Yang Hao in coordinating military operations in Korea. Gen. Ma Gui, a veteran of the campaign in Ningxia, assumed the post of military superintendent.[13]

Some officials also took the opportunity to criticize Wanli's practice of sending out eunuch mining intendents to extract revenue from the countryside, but it was agreed that Korea took precedence. These operations and the war in Korea may have actually been more intimately connected than has generally been acknowledged. Harry Miller has suggested that Wanli's use of eunuch mining officials was actually a "luxury tax" of sorts on the wealthy that he implemented in order to get the revenue needed to fund the war, among other things. Those who supported sending troops argued that if China did not help its neighbors, then the Ming would be no better than the Song, who had allowed the barbarians to overrun everything: "China has managed barbarians for hundreds of years, how can they let the Japanese assail Korea now?"[14]

Time was now of the essence since Katō Kiyomasa had greater authority in 1597, and his aggressiveness was well established. Katō's appointment possibly accounted for the extreme brutality of the second invasion, which far exceeded that of the first. Hideyoshi's anger was transferred to his men, who were clearly not pleased with the prospect of becoming embroiled in another lengthy standoff. Many Koreans lucky enough to escape death were pressed into service and slavery. Another sign of Hideyoshi's desire to demonstrate his total mastery over Korea was his lust for local items such as tiger skins and ginseng, the latter of which he hoped could restore his flagging health.[15]

One of the most chillingly frank accounts of the second invasion comes from the Buddhist priest Keinen, who kept a diary of his time in Korea later published as *Chōsen nichinichiki* [Korea day by day]. Forgotten for centuries in Anyōji Temple in Bungo province until rediscovered during the Meiji period, the diary provides a basic narrative chronicle with some 330 poems and religious reflections interspersed throughout. Seventy poems deal with religious themes, but others deal with homesickness or human suffering and battlefield conditions. The greatest number, more than ninety, deal with human emotions and the destruction wrought by the Japanese armies.[16] Certainly the most memorable descriptions are those of slavers and the tales of Koreans taken forcibly to Japan.

Although difficult reading, Keinen's diary offers a rare human perspective from the Japanese side, serving as a counter to many of the vainglorious daimyo house chronicles compiled well after the fact. As the personal physician to Ōta Kazuyoshi, Keinen was appalled by the atrocities he witnessed: "Among the many kinds of merchants who have come over from Japan are traders in human beings, who follow in the train of the troops and buy up men and women, young and old alike. Having tied these people together with ropes about the neck, they drive them along before them; those who can no longer walk are made to run with prods or blows of the stick from behind. The sight of the fiends and man-devouring demons who torment sinners in hell must be like this, I thought." Those too young or too old to be of use were simply killed. As many as 60,000 Koreans were sent back to Japan, many of them artisans. Their contributions to Japanese art and culture would be one of the few positive legacies of the second invasion.[17]

The offensive of 1597–98 is also infamous for the practice of severing Korean noses, which were packed in brine and presented for rewards.

Huge numbers of noses were shipped back to Japan for inspection, sometimes tens of thousands at a time. In the space of six weeks in 1597, Nabeshima Naoshige sent 5,444 noses, while Kikkawa Hiroie's unit sent 18,350 noses in the space of a month. The largest figure allegedly exceeded 30,000 noses, a shipment presented by Shimazu Yoshihiro after the Battle of Sachŏn in 1598. All were reportedly interred in the Mimizuka. The main purpose of this practice seems to have been to utterly humiliate the Koreans for wounding Hideyoshi's pride, a supposition born out by captured letters allegedly from Hideyoshi ordering wholesale destruction and kidnapping.[18]

Learning from the first invasion, the Japanese significantly bolstered their naval strength, at least in terms of numbers, and though they made few technological improvements on their warships, they were reportedly better armed.[19] In accordance with Hideyoshi's instructions, Katō directed his men to secure key points all along the south and east coasts and make sure the supply lines were kept open and flowing. He was again going to make a thrust for Seoul, but this time he resolved to attack from the south, hoping to outflank Chinese and Korean positions along the original invasion route. Katō also wanted all the men under his command to reinforce existing defenses and hastily erect new ones. The plan was to take key cities before Ming relief columns could arrive. Katō was wary of Korean guerrillas and believed there might be more-spirited resistance this time around from Korean regulars.

Although forewarned, many Korean generals and their men abandoned their posts immediately. A message sent to China begging for help claimed that more than a million Japanese in thirteen divisions were already swarming through Korea, though a more plausible estimate from Kwŏn Yul put the invaders' strength at about 130,000 men. Regardless, the Ming had already resolved to send significant forces to Korea, so this report merely hastened the process.[20]

There was concern on the Ming side over how quickly they could assemble and mobilize an initial force of 40,000 to 50,000 troops. They therefore decided to send a token force to secure the most important defense points and guard the approaches to Seoul. The Koreans asked for a faster, more interventionist response. The Ming tried to allay their concerns by recognizing Korean ferocity in defensive warfare. They also told them that the northern troops were to undergo training in southern tactics, making them more adept at fighting the Japanese. At the same time, Wanli chided Sŏnjo for not improving Korea's readiness and making it clear that the Ming were not about to make a habit of saving his kingdom.[21]

Allied commanders continued to fret about supply issues and worried that Korea's lack of arable land would hamper efforts to establish military farms. The Ming also wanted more horses from the Koreans to serve as draft animals, but Sŏnjo said he had few to spare. But the Ming were helped somewhat because the Japanese were wary of overextending their own lines and acted much more deliberately than in the first invasion. Indeed, some accounts seem to indicate that during the early months of 1597, the Japanese did not really want to fight at all and were rather relieved that the Chinese had not yet arrived in force. A supply strategy of living off the land could not work this time because Korea was still ravaged after so many years of fighting.[22] The Japanese remained dependent on supplies from overseas.

Despite his negative portrayal in Korean sources, Wŏn Kyun, who had recently replaced Yi Sunsin as the overall commander of the Korean navy, did manage to harass Japanese naval forces somewhat and delayed the full-scale invasion as land-based guerrillas struck at Japanese strongholds. The circumstances behind Yi's dismissal are somewhat murky and clouded by the factional bias pervading the era and the posthumous glorification of Yi for his various exploits. The most common version of the tale is that officials had received word from the double agent Yōzira that Katō was en route from Japan with a large naval force that could be easily intercepted and destroyed en route. Not believing the rumors and suspecting a trap, Yi refused to advance. Yōzira then told Kim Ungso that Katō had already landed, meaning that Yi had missed his opportunity to seize the initiative. Therefore Yi was impeached and arrested, his command given to Wŏn. Hearing the news supposedly killed Yi's aged mother. There was talk of executing the admiral, but on account of his previous meritorious service, he was eventually reassigned to service as a low-ranking soldier under Kwŏn Yul.[23] Yet despite the fact that Yi had been accused of cowardice and laxity before the enemy, further calls for joint land-sea operations were either ignored or not implemented fast enough.

It was not until April 1597 that sufficient supplies arrived to allow the Japanese to engage in serious offensive operations; even then the full capacity of Japan to supply and outfit its armies was equal only to a large Chinese province. The invaders had two months' of supplies, but Katō figured his men could campaign for up to a year if they just kept advancing, never retreated, and maintained their supply lines.[24] Even he was not overly optimistic about the chances of success, though rumors of a massive Japanese offensive struck fear in the hearts of Koreans all over the countryside, many of whose lives were finally starting to return to normal.

But the allies were more decisive this time and confident in their ability to move troops and provisions where needed, in part by investing local officials with more-sweeping authority to facilitate logistical matters. The Ming hoped to streamline matters even further by having their own commanders appointed as temporary commanders in chief in all eight of Chosŏn's provinces. The Koreans contested this arrangement on the grounds that their regulations dictated that no single official should have jurisdiction over more than one province. They also feared that such a move would lead to annexation by China. Sŏnjo petitioned Wanli against making such appointments on the grounds that Korea lacked the resources to support Ming officials in the proper style. Nevertheless, there is no evidence whatsoever to suggest the Chinese ever considered incorporating Korea into their empire. There is, however, a passage in the Ming shilu where the Chinese acknowledge Korean misgivings about having one official coordinate civil and military affairs for the entire kingdom.[25]

The first positive actions taken by the Ming were to detail 3,000 naval troops to patrol the waters around Tianjin to guard against a possible Japanese naval invasion of the Chinese mainland and to send another 3,000 troops across the Yalu. They assured the Koreans that more soldiers were being raised, and Chinese commanders were told to "rush day and night without stopping" to Korea. Xing Jie sent a mobilization order to Sŏnjo, promising him 13,900 land troops. The Ming also urged their allies to continue drilling recruits and establishing military farms for provisioning troops. Yang Hao even accused the Koreans of hoarding grain so that the Ming had to supply Korean armies, a charge that riled his allies. Ming plans also called for commanders already in Korea to teach the locals "Chinese style fighting" and instill some spirit into the Sŏnjo's army.[26] Their strategy was to blunt the enemy advance at Choryŏng Pass and keep the Japanese pinned down in the south until reinforcements arrived. The Chinese feared it might take as long as a year to return all their troops and supplies to the peninsula.

Ma Gui was placed in overall charge of military affairs. Xing Jie warned the Koreans that initial deployment would be delayed somewhat by summer rains, which greatly reduced travel. Xing's first order was to send Yang Yuan and Wu Weizhong from Seoul to garrison the areas around Namwŏn, Taegu, and Kyŏngju. They did very little actual fighting in the first six months of 1597, being content to threaten the Japanese from Ch'ungju. Ma did not reach Liaoyang until June 23, and when he crossed the Yalu nine days later, he was at the head of a mere 17,000 troops. The general was concerned about his lack of manpower and memorialized the Ministry of War asking that mercenaries be recruited from around the empire. He also asked for naval units from Fujian and Wusong because the Koreans were undermanned.[27] Meanwhile, the Koreans assumed defensive positions as they drilled and waited for additional Ming relief forces to arrive.

Help was on the way in the form of Liu Ting at the head of 6,700 mixed Han and aboriginal troops from Sichuan. Liu, probably because of his earlier experiences in Korea and his rapport with the men, received an enhanced role this time. As he waited for Liu's arrival, Ma sent a secret memorial calling for a quick strike to drive a wedge between Katō and Konishi in the southeast. Ma reached the vicinity of Pyŏkchegwan just as the summer rains began to fall. Yang was camped at Namwŏn; Mao Guoqi at Songju; Chen Youyuan at Chŏnju; and Wu at Taegu. The allies hoped to take advantage of Korean geography and exploit their advantages in naval warfare. They deemed denying the Japanese access to the west coast as crucial.[28]

But as the allies prepared to begin their offensive, the Japanese finally started their own advance and quickly isolated allied units. Before long half of Kyŏngsang province was in Japanese hands. They laid ambushes all along the routes to their heavily reinforced strongholds. The area around Yangsan was especially fortified. The invaders hugged the coastline as they transported supplies from the east to the south coast of Korea and were not eager to engage allied forces in naval combat. Meanwhile, the China and Korea hoped to stall the enemy long enough to surround them with land and naval forces and crush them in a series of quick engagements.[29]

Ming leaders hoped to make use of Koreans in more offensive operations, but officials feared time was insufficient to whip everyone into fighting shape. In terms of numbers, the Koreans claimed they had around 17,000 troops in Kyŏngsang, including naval units. The Chinese repeated their plan to standardize training by assigning the same Ming officer—in this case Wu—to train all Korean units. They suggested that the Koreans establish training grounds in all prefectures and districts and raise both mercenaries and militia. Sŏnjo protested that such measures were impractical in Pyŏngan, Hamgyŏng, and Kangwŏn, because they were distant and impoverished, and unfeasible in Kyŏngsang, due to the presence of the Japanese, but he pledged to do so elsewhere.[30]

Intelligence reports coming in from the south gave information on troop landings at Pusan and Kadŏk Island. Word was that the Japanese were planning a three-pronged offensive up the center of the peninsula toward Seoul. Japanese spies had reportedly canvassed the countryside. There were about 12,000 Ming troops currently deployed in the south to act as some deterrent, but even Sŏnjo admitted that his Korean troops were still unreliable. The allies had to delay joint land-sea operations while waiting for more food from China.[31]

The Japanese offensive began in earnest in July, striking toward Seoul by way of Sachŏn and Namwŏn. Some were still uneasy about the invasion because they knew the Chinese were coming in force. Hideyoshi was disgusted, pointing out that Japan also had a mighty army whose positions this time were not isolated. He issued orders for the systematic razing of the entire country, telling his commanders that noses should be severed in lieu of heads due to their portability. The first battles took place on the islets off the southeast coast. Korean commander An Hongkuk was forced to retreat to Chuk Island and was later killed in battle. Many of his troops scattered and fled. At this time Shen Weijing was still at large but led a sizable personal retinue to Pusan, hoping to curry favor with the Japanese. Nothing came of the meeting, and he eventually went to Hoeryŏng, where he was finally arrested by the Ming (though one source maintains that Shen was actually seized by a Japanese officer and handed over to Yang Yuan). The Ming ordered Shen interrogated by the dreaded Embroidered Uniform Guard, noting that his earlier crimes were compounded by his perceived attempt to flee to the enemy—at the very least he would be subjected to caning.[32]

In the meantime, Wŏn Kyun abandoned Hansan and Kŏje islands, leaving all of Korea's southern coast unprotected and giving the Japanese the opening they needed. Reportedly, when Wŏn took control of the navy, he abandoned Yi Sunsin's strategies, removed the latter's trusted subordinates, and dissipated himself in liquor. He applied punishments indiscriminately, resulting in the men becoming indignant and refusing to serve under him. As the Japanese approached Hansan, Kwŏn Yul ordered Wŏn to go forth and join battle. Wŏn found himself cornered and had to obey because he was among those who had seen to the removal of Yi for allegedly retreating before the enemy.

Wŏn finally met the Japanese navy under Tōdō Takatora in mid-August 1597 off Hansan Island. The channels were narrow, and the Japanese launched a combined land-sea assault, with cannons blazing from their small ships and bullets raining down from arquebusiers under Shimazu Yoshihiro on the shore. The fighting was fierce, and Wŏn directed his forces to advance to the vicinity of Choryŏng Island. But the night was dark and winds were high, and with the Korean fleet was in danger of drifting apart, Wŏn was forced to retreat to Kadŏk Island. As he directed his men to land on the island, they were ambushed by the Japanese, and many sailors and officers were killed.[33]

Shimazu detailed 2,000 men to cut down the Koreans who managed to swim to shore. Subsequent victories by Tōdō resulted in the capture or destruction of sixty more Korean ships and the deaths of thousands among their crews, most of whom drowned. Much of Korea's navy, which had been the bane of the Japanese during the first invasion, was destroyed in these engagements. Wŏn, however, was still in a predicament, as he was censured by Kwŏn, who told him the whole country was relying on him. Fearing that he was going to be deprived of his post for cowardice, Wŏn had no choice but to continue to fight.[34]

At dawn on August 28, Wŏn led his fleet in retreat to Kŏje Island, where he was caught in a pincer attack by Tōdō and Katō Yoshiaki. Katō was especially valiant, boarding a Korean vessel and slaying several men himself. The Koreans closed in on him, and he fell into the sea as he tried to escape to another boat. Undaunted, Katō managed to clamber back aboard and even captured another vessel. Sixteen Korean warships were captured and several sailors died. Wŏn's own boat was wind-tossed into the enemy's midst, but he somehow managed to escape with the rest of his fleet and retreated to Yŏngdung Island. Seeing the Japanese in hot pursuit, he directed his men to land on Kadŏk Island and flee, but they ran into another Japanese ambush. Wŏn then fled to Onna Island, where he once again found himself surrounded. Instead of fighting his way out this time, the commander climbed a hill and proceeded to get drunk. Addressing his men, he told them there was no chance for escape. Some advocated flight, but Wŏn angrily retorted: "We have death before us and that is all. There's no need for more talk!" Red from drinking and unable to rouse himself for action, Wŏn simply sat under a pine tree at the top of a hill, cane and sword by his side until he passed out. When a subordinate rushed to his side to ask for orders, he could not tell whether the admiral was dead or alive. When morning came, Wŏn awoke terrified and ordered an attack, but his men were overwhelmed by the enemy. Yi Ŏkki killed himself by jumping into the sea, provincial commander An Hongkuk was shot and killed, and naval commander Pae Sol fled to Hansan Island, where he torched the barracks and evacuated the local populace but did manage to salvage a dozen warships. This victory not only led to the Japanese capture of Namhae and Sunchŏn but also resulted in the reinstatement of their nemesis, Yi Sunsin, on September 13, 1597.[35]

Recognizing the strategic significance of the area, Ma Gui detailed a naval force of 3,000 to patrol the waters around Hansan Island, but they were unable to prevent the invaders from massing troops for an assault on Namwŏn. Japanese units looted and burned their way toward Namwŏn, converging on the city on September 22. Tōdō, Shimazu, Sō Yoshitoshi, and Konishi were all present with the advancing force, which allegedly numbered more than 60,000 troops. Meanwhile, other Japanese armies were striking through Ch'ungch'ŏng province. Yang Yuan and his Korean allies had barely 4,000 troops under their own banner. Ma recognized their plight but was reluctant to commit many more troops to Namwŏn because he did not want to leave Seoul vulnerable.[36]

Yang was not completely unprepared. Against the advice of his Korean allies, who had recommended retreating to the nearby sansŏng of Kyoryŏng, he had detailed 1,200 men to reinforce the existing defenses of the city, adding walls and mounting three cannons. Another 1,000 troops were placed on mobile duty, coordinating their efforts with those of the Koreans.[37] Yang also had a network of fences built around the surrounding fields and excavated the moats. But when the inhabitants saw the Japanese advancing, most of them panicked and fled, leaving Yang and his sturdy Liaodong troops to protect Namwŏn alone. Yang requested help from Yi Pongnam, who arrived with a few hundred more troops, but the Japanese prevented further reinforcement. Escaped Koreans spread the news.

Circumventing well-defended cities and fortresses in the interest of taking their major objectives, the Japanese advance was rapid. Konishi Yukinaga and Matsura Shigenobu were in the vanguard of the attacking force, and they initially camped some forty-five li (fifteen miles) southeast of Namwŏn. As the Japanese assembled, their torches and campfires blazing through the night, the people of the city grew restless. Bolstered by even more reinforcements, the army launched its initial attack on September 23. The assault began with an arquebus volley by around one hundred men. Using newly erected livestock fences for cover, the Japanese rotated around the castle, attacking in small groups of three to five and making it hard for the large victory mark cannon to hit them.[38] The Japanese then withdrew, rather than closing within range of the cannon mounted on the walls, in hopes of goading the defenders, whom they knew they outnumbered, into sallying forth to do battle.

Yang was concerned that his inability to repulse the continual assaults would reveal the weakness of his defenses. But he thought that if he attacked aggressively, then he might at least shock and frighten the besiegers into thinking help was on the way and pulling back. His Korean allies argued that if a stout defense was maintained, then help might still come, but that launching an attack was suicidal. Eschewing their advice once more, Yang selected 1,000 volunteers and sent them out, where they were lured into an ambush by the Japanese at a stone bridge on the outskirts of the city. Suffering heavy casualties, the Chinese beat a hasty retreat.[39]

The next day the attackers closed in on the city from three sides, unveiling great siege ladders. They also started cutting logs from the forests around the city to construct makeshift bridges to cross the moat. That night, using the burned-out shells of houses just outside the walls for cover, they launched a probing attack on the south gate, resulting in heavy allied losses. The following day they started cutting down wild rice stalks and grass to bundle into sheaves and using covered wagons to shelter their approach to the walls, particularly the west gate, near which the forces of the Matsura were stationed. That night witnessed another concerted attack on the defenders with arrows and gunfire. The Japanese were able to maintain this pressure because of their great numerical superiority. The allies could never pause to catch their breath as fresh Japanese units, competing for glory in this first major land battle of the second offensive, rotated into firing positions and kept a steady barrage on the hapless defenders. Even the elements conspired against the allies, with the moonlight rendered the evening "as bright as day" when it reflected off the green rice growing in the surrounding fields.[40]

At one point Konishi dispatched an emissary to ask Yang to abandon the city. The Ming went to meet the Japanese at the east gate, but before they could talk, Koreans opened fire and killed three. Nonplussed, Konishi sent another delegate, to whom Yang responded: "I have been a general since I was fifteen and I have traveled all over the empire. Never have I not known victory in battle. Now the Son of Heaven has ordered me to defend this city, and I have not yet received an order to withdraw." Upon hearing this Konishi laughed and replied: "One thousand odd troops certainly cannot resist one million fierce soldiers. Korea accepts your sacrifice but will they have sympathy for your efforts later?"[41]

The overmatched defenders somehow managed to hold out against incredible odds for four days. They continued to rain cannon fire and rocks down on their besiegers. Yang sent men out at night to litter the ground with nails and caltrops. The Japanese kept their fires burning all night and created smokescreens to cover their advance. Civilians noticed that the Ming troops appeared to be preparing to flee. That night a great roar burst from the Japanese ranks and they attacked, raining bullets, arrows, and cannon shot down into the city. The defenders hid deep inside, and the noise stopped after a couple of hours. Finally, the Japanese managed to move in close enough to secure the moat. Moving up against one of the highest and most lightly defended portions of the wall, they then piled up their massed bundles of green-rice stalks, using them as natural ramps. By the time the defenders realized what was happening, the Japanese were scaling the walls with ladders. Although initially driven back, some managed to enter the city and start fires. The first allied heads were taken by the Matsura and their retainers on the west wall, where they became to first to plant their battle standard.[42]

The besieged finally opened the livestock pens within the city and let the animals out, hoping to create holes in the ranks of the attackers. Another barrage ensued during a heavy rainstorm, the city shaking with the reverberations of cannon fired by both sides. When the city gates were finally forced open by defenders seeking to escape, they were confronted with Japanese troops several ranks deep. Many Chinese troops tried to flee but were prevented by the spooked horses "running around as if their legs were bound" in the muddy ground. Some men simply bowed their heads and allowed themselves to be decapitated. Yang Yuan, seeing the situation was hopeless, escaped on foot with eighteen followers. All of the other commanders died. Tōdō Takatora was the first to scale the walls and enter the city proper, for which he was honored by Hideyoshi.[43]

All told, some 3,900 allied troops were killed and nearly 2,000 were captured, though some Japanese sources give figures as high as 10,000. A Chinese source stated that barely 100 men made it out of the city alive. The monk Keinen claimed that men and women, young and old alike, were slaughtered indiscriminately. He saw this as shallow and pointless, his sentiment reflecting his Buddhist sensibility about the illusory nature of earthly rewards. Indeed, family chronicles, such as those of the Matsura and the Shimazu, contain careful lists of the number of heads, ears, or noses taken by the notables and their retainers. Confronted with such gruesome realties, Keinen persistently sought solace in his faith.[44]

Despite the overwhelming odds, this defeat was a reification of northern soldiers' inability to fight the Japanese in the eyes of some Koreans. They argued that Zhejiang tactics may have prevailed against the Japanese, but Yang, a northerner, was unfamiliar with these methods. At this time Chen Youyuan was stationed at Chŏnju and Wu Weizhong was still at Ch'ungju. When Namwŏn fell, the people of Chŏnju began to panic. In fact, Chen had been called upon by Yang to help defend Namwŏn, but even though Chen was but 100 li (35 miles) away, he timorously avoided mobilizing his troops. Even now he wanted to abandon his position, but there was an important storehouse nearby that the Koreans did not want to fall into Japanese hands. With both the local peasants and the Korean military evacuating, however, Chen decided to withdraw from Chŏnju on September 30.[45] Ma Gui was now very worried about the defense of Seoul and knew the allies had to hold Ch'ungch'ŏng province. Therefore he sent mobile-corps commander Niu Boying to assist Chen Youyuan in the defense of Kŏngju, north of Chŏnju. The Japanese continued to advance through Chŏlla province with the aim of taking Seoul. They proceeded cautiously, requisitioning rice and taking great care to maintain their supply lines. Katō's forces met up with those advancing from the south at Chŏnju, where they turned north toward Seoul, civilians fleeing before them.

Sŏnjo said: "Everyone is always saying depend on the Chinese troops. But now the Japanese have mobilized their forces and are advancing. How can a few thousand Chinese troops defend us?" Ma reported that the Chinese navy was on the way with significant reinforcements and some of the Ming empire's most decorated commanders. This pleased the king, who informed him that the Koreans were already rebuilding their own shattered navy.[46] Ma also asked Sŏnjo to detail more men to defend Hansan Island, which he saw as the linchpin of Korea's southern defenses.

The weakened allied forces made a fighting retreat toward the capital, as major strongholds fell due to the overwhelming numerical strength of

the invaders. Yang Hao, who had been stationed in Pyongyang, hastened to the capital. Ma even considered retreating toward Pyongyang
or even as far as Ŭiju before resolving to establish a line of defense at
the Han River. He ordered his men to work day and night constructing
rafts so they could get their troops and supplies across the river. Ma also
dispatched units to Chiksan, directly south of Seoul. Korean commander
Yi Wŏn'ik advanced from Choryŏng to Ch'ungch'ŏng province, harrying
the right wing of the Japanese army. This action proved to be quite
important, for it served to restore tottering allied morale. When asked
what his master plan was, Xing Jie replied: "Overtly fight, covertly seek
peace; overtly crush the enemy, covertly soothe and pacify them. These
eight words are secret and must not be revealed." Ma then presented a
plan for an allied counteroffensive.[47]

Tensions continued to run high in Seoul as the Japanese fanned out
through Chŏlla province, seizing supplies and erecting defense works.
The king issued a directive to local officials to steel the resolve of the
people. Ripping the Koreans for casting away generations of achievement and for even having the temerity to speak of things such as loyalty
and righteousness, Xing Jie told Sŏnjo that the first order of business
was to boost morale, then the newly appointed Korean commanders
needed to assume defensive positions. Chŏlla was most vital, and its
autumn harvest had to be secured for the allied forces. Xing suggested
sending Prince Kwanghae on a tour of the south to shore up civilian
morale. Advocating the adoption of Chinese disciplinary measures,
Xing added that anyone fleeing their post should be subjected to summary decapitation.[48]

In the meantime, the Koreans brought in vital supplies from the
northeast for the Ming armies. Although these were not sufficient for
extended campaigning, they did provide a cushion until further shipments arrived overseas from Tianjin. Still more provisions were being
rushed south from Ŭiju. The soldiers in Seoul also received word that
troops were being raised in southern China, in addition to which some
Jurchen tribespeople and Ryukyu islanders had offered to join the allied
armies. This delighted the Chinese, who figured that they could now
use the time-honored strategy of using barbarians to fight barbarians. It
also appears that Ming training methods were finally paying dividends,
for the Koreans were surprising the Japanese and severing supply lines
both on land and at sea. The allies knew that they did not necessarily
have to defeat the Japanese in the field, just sever their supply lines and

keep them cut. Once the Japanese abandoned the field and evacuated the peninsula, the allies still might be able to smash them at sea as they sailed back to Japan.

When news of the allied defeats reached China, officials in the Ming court became quite concerned. Zhang Wei sent an urgent memorial to Xing Jie enumerating methods for combating the Japanese. He emphasized the importance of recruiting more troops from areas all over north China and added that they should be concentrated around Tianjin under the control of one man to guard the approach to Beijing. Zhang also called for the construction of more warships, the training of additional aboriginal units, more widespread use of firearms, and the establishment of military farms. He also suggested offering great rewards for the heads of Katō and Konishi. Zhang argued that Japanese swords and arquebuses were no match for the superior firepower of the Chinese and that training in and deployment of more firearms should be paramount.[49]

Like any good bureaucrat, Zhang was acutely aware of the importance of obtaining the necessary funds for his proposals. He believed that southern boats were the best the Chinese had and figured it would cost 60,000 strings of cash to build one hundred seaworthy vessels for use against the Japanese. Five liang could support the family of one sailor, so it would cost about 1,000 cash to staff a full ship. To crew one hundred warships would require 10,000 men, preferably from Fujian, costing 150,000–160,000 liang to recruit and deploy. Wanli was of a like mind and issued an order for officials stationed along the northeast coast to establish training offices in order to prepare for a naval war. Most significantly, Chen Lin, a veteran naval officer and firearms expert, was appointed head of the Ming navy.[50]

Zhang also called for raising aboriginal troops in the southwest. These soldiers would be given their clothes, armor, and weapons beforehand and offered special rewards as additional inducement to fight. Aboriginal chieftains who already possessed hereditary ranks were promised promotions if they excelled at recruitment. Many scholars have interpreted this as an indication of Ming military weakness. Yet modern scholars should not be so quick to judge the Ming, for those outside the mainstream of society have been recruited even into modern armies for their perceived proclivities toward violence and toughness.[51] Moreover, even if the use of such troops was prompted in part by the disintegration of the hereditary military system, it is also a testament to the logistical capabilities of the Ming state, for these men were recruited in the far corners of the empire and transported all the way to Korea, where they acquitted themselves well.

They were typically led by local commanders who often volunteered their troops because they were eager to gain fame and riches for their exploits.

Zhang concluded his missive on a positive note, saying that even though the Japanese had invaded again with a force of some 350,000 men, already their supplies were dwindling and they were hesitant about advancing from their bases around Pusan. He stressed making sure the Koreans pulled their weight, then finished by acknowledging the generosity of Wanli, saying, "The Son of Heaven is not selfish and once again he has committed his strength to Korea's cause." In accordance with Zhang's suggestions, Xing Jie continued to recruit Han and aboriginal forces from Huguang, Sichuan, and other southern provinces. The Court of the Imperial Stud chipped in with 257,000 liang of silver for food, pay, and special rewards for the next three months. This was especially welcome, as Xing was distressed that the Koreans continued to abandon or burn food stores. He was worried that even if he got the troops he requested, he would not be able to feed them. Additionally, he recognized that Korea's terrain was more suited to foot soldiers than mounted troops, thus requesting more southern troops and even wanting all northern troops to be trained by southern generals, who had more experience fighting in such terrain. Wanli approved these recommendations.[52]

Nevertheless, in July 1597 Xing complained that he had but 38,000 troops under his banner, whereas Song Yingchang had had 70,000 (actually around 40,000) in 1593. This was in part because provincial officials said they needed troops to protect their localities. While their function was ostensibly to prevent banditry and aboriginal strife, many administrators refused to part with their private work gangs, whose "real business was war," according to Xing. Still, there were many positive responses to this call for troops, especially from coastal officials, who feared their districts were threatened. Among his other directives, Xing elevated Li Rumei, Li Rusong's younger brother, to the post of vice commander of Korea and acting military commissioner in chief. Xing chastised the Koreans as well: "This time your king should not lightly abandon his capital but should die defending it and await the arrival of the celestial troops." It is interesting to speculate on what might have happened had Sŏnjo abandoned Seoul again, but luckily for the Koreans, events never came to that.[53]

Supplies and manpower continued to be issues. As one Korean minister lamented, "How can we resist the Japanese with our bare hands?" When asked how many troops and horses the Koreans possessed, the same minister replied: "Our small country has been ravaged and the soldiers and people have all been killed. Where would we get men and horses? We're barely able to round up the remnants to defend key points. Now all the generals of Kyŏngsang could muster was about 10,000 and those of Chŏlla barely 10,000, but even these will be weak and trembling. I fear that if the Japanese come in force we will not be able to withstand them on our own."[54] The official added that the fate of his country and all its people rested on the speedy arrival of Ming troops. The Chinese agreed to sell the Koreans saltpeter, bows, and other equipment to hold them over until more forces arrived.

Ma Gui also tried to rally the spirits of the men in Seoul and prepare them for a decisive engagement. He dispatched Yi Wŏn'ik was sent to Ch'ungch'ŏng to intercept the enemy vanguard, then personally led Niu Boying and Jie Sheng to Chiksan, where they set an ambush for the Japanese near the river's mouth outside town. The ambush, sprung on October 17, 1597, and its subsequent fighting became known as the Battle of Chiksan, the decisive land engagement of the second invasion.

While the allies made their preparations to defend the capital, the Japanese continued their push north after capturing Namwŏn. Katō, Naneshima Naoshige, and Kuroda Nagamasa all participated in the capture of the Hwangsŏk mountain fortress on September 26. Some 27,000 Japanese surrounded the sansŏng, which had been abandoned by the former district magistrate of Kimhae, Paek Sarim, who had been dispatched by Yi Wŏn'ik to defend that city. The defense was then left in the hands of the elderly Cho Chongdo and Kwak Chun, the local county magistrate. They fought valiantly but died defending the fortress, as did Kwak's son-in-law and Cho's family; hearing that her husband had died, Kwak's daughter committed suicide by hanging herself. Some 350 heads were taken and thousands more died in the valley below the fortress.[55]

The Japanese decided that Mōri Hidemoto, Kuroda, and Katō would take about 64,000 men to secure Chŏlla and Ch'ungch'ŏng provinces while perhaps also threatening Seoul. Kuroda led the thrust toward the capital. In planning their advance the Japanese observed: "In the campaign of 1592 the Koreans relied on the strength of the two Chŏlla provinces and on keeping the sea lanes open. But now we can prevent their land and sea forces from linking up and prevent help from arriving with this plan of taking the western route [to Seoul]." They also decided to attempt to place Seoul in a vise with forces approaching from the east and west while Konishi protected the rear. The rural populations scattered before the enemy advance but proved unable to give accurate figures of Japanese troop numbers. Hearing this news, the king readied himself for a possible retreat to Kaesŏng. Konishi's men looted briefly but then pulled back to Sunchon in early October. Others went to Waegyŏ and started erecting fortifications. Both groups also took food and supplies from the locals, erecting signs demanding rice. Eyewitnesses reported that the general violence perpetrated by the invaders this time was much worse than in 1592; young or old, no one was spared.[56]

When Yang Yuan reached Seoul, he immediately met with Ma Gui and Xing Jie to determine a course of action to blunt the Japanese advance.[57] Together they devised a plan and sent Jie Sheng forth at the head of a group of hand-picked troops. The soldiers used floating bridges to cross the Han River and headed south. Near Chiksan they laid their ambush in a narrow pass near a river. During the subsequent action, as in so many of the battles of the Korean war, artillery and terrain were the two primary determining factors. The area around Chiksan was very mountainous, perfect terrain in which to lay an artillery-based ambush. Meanwhile, Chen Youyuan had fallen back from Chŏnju and was being pursued by the invaders. The main body of the Japanese force entered Jie's position around 3:00 P.M. The allies opened fire and feigned retreat, leading the Japanese further into the trap. As the invaders tried to flee, they ran into another ambush farther up the road; alarms sounded, cannons roared, banners waved, and spears flew, inflicting further losses on the Japanese.[58] After repeated skirmishes the Japanese withdrew, but then Katō decided to order a dicey night assault on the Ming camp. Jie ensconced his men to resist them, and the Japanese decided to wait for morning.

Both sides hoped to gain high ground near the river, so the Japanese attacked early in the morning, their blades flashing in the sunlight. The Ming responded with cannon blasts and a charge by their stoutly mailed cavalry. Neither side gained a definitive edge, but the Japanese were forced to pull back at the end of the day. Ma Gui decided not to pursue, fearing that he might be flanked by other Japanese units reportedly heading for the capital. It soon became evident that this relatively minor battle was one of the turning points of the war. According to the chronicles of the Kuroda family, when the Japanese force came over the mountains, they saw an allied army of perhaps 5,000–6,000 on the plain below crossing a bridge. Despite being heavily outnumbered, Kuroda decided to engage the enemy, his retainer Gōtō Mototsugu saying that for every ten who died, one man might still live to tell the tale of their glory.[59] But while the fighting was intense, the Japanese could not take the bridge and were driven back.

The allied victory was made possible largely by their cannon, but these heavy weapons apparently hampered them when they considered pursuing the Japanese into the mountains. More Japanese were cut down on a foggy plain near the river, sealing the victory. The reference to superior Ming armor in this engagement is also noteworthy, for the Chinese had developed a stronger design that was at least partially bulletproof. Mōri and Kuroda admitted that when they engaged Jie in battle, they were defeated because their bullets could not penetrate the iron shields used by the Ming. Japanese losses were estimated at nearly 600 men, though only thirty heads were taken; Jie took two heads himself. Subsequent engagements resulted in more allied victories as the belligerents clashed in the mountains and bamboo forests around Chiksan, though reports of nearly 10,000 Japanese being killed are almost certainly exaggerated.[60]

Ma soon afterward ordered some reinforcing units to remain in rear positions near the Chinese border and issued a proclamation for a whopping 700,000-man naval force to be assembled to crush the Japanese at sea. While there is no way the Ming could ever have assembled a fleet of anywhere near that size, the order was leaked to the enemy, reportedly discouraging them from advancing farther for fear of being cut off by the allied navy.[61] Japanese commanders scattered and eventually retreated to their respective wajō along the eastern and southern coasts. They never again mounted an offensive but simply withstood numerous allied sieges until finally evacuating the peninsula the following year.

Indeed, Japanese accounts suggest that the invaders retreated because they feared the arrival of the Ming navy. Some of these sources even report higher Chinese casualties than those of the Japanese and contend that it was the Ming who withdrew. In addition, Kawaguchi Choju states that the Ming actually sued the Japanese for peace, saying they did not really want to fight for Korea.[62]

Some Ming officials questioned the veracity of Ma's victory reports, also contending that the threat of a naval assault was what had forced the Japanese to withdraw, not their defeat at Chiksan.[63] In accordance with standard Ming practice, the Chinese armies were accompanied by censorial officials, whose duty was to report on events and determine who deserved rewards and punishments. In theory the system was designed to check partisanship and wrongdoing, but in practice it often led to the very abuses it was designed to prevent. But sometimes these censors did indeed prevent officials in the field from lying or distorting the truth to their own advantage. The situation was perhaps not unlike that which exists in internal-affairs divisions in modern U.S. police departments.

In any case, after Chiksan several censorial officials found allied victory reports very dubious. In the words of one, "The army did not even fire one arrow at Chiksan; how can it be called a victory?" He further contended, like the Japanese, that the reason for the withdrawal was a letter supposedly written by Shen Weijing threatening the invaders with a massive naval counterattack. True to form, Wanli ignored these charges and supported the men he had placed in the field. Korean scholar Park Yune-hee asserts that the Japanese withdrew on account of the reappointment of Yi Sunsin to command of the navy.[64]

Whatever the truth of the matter, the Battle of Chiksan's significance is obvious when looking at the course of the second invasion, marking as it did the closest the Japanese got to Seoul. The first phase, lasting from middle to late 1597, covered Japan's penetration into Korea and offensive operations against allied forces. The second phase, lasting from the end of 1597 until the autumn of 1598, was a period of allied counterattacks and sieges. The last phase, which lasted from late 1598 through the second month of 1599, marked Japan's final and full defeat and withdrawal. Viewed this way, Chiksan was indeed a turning point, transforming the fear in Seoul into resolution and bolstering the hearts of the defenders. It also demonstrated the bravery and loyalty of the Ming troops toward their Korean allies. Subsequent skirmishes resulted in more Japanese deaths and even elicited a poem from one giddy Korean official who commemorated the "glorious success of the eastern expedition and the Japanese dread of the myriad horsemen tramping over the grass." One Korean commander allegedly killed another 500–600 Japanese with a massive crossbow assault as they retreated south. A battle south of Kwangsan resulted in an estimated 9,600 more Japanese dead.[65] The Koreans were also heartened by reports of 700,000 Ming reinforcements supposedly already on the way.

Additionally, Yi Sunsin was reinstated in mid-September. The admiral had difficulty rounding up both ships and men to sail them, though he did immediately set about dispatching spies to ascertain the locations and situations of the various Japanese commanders in his vicinity. Yi was allegedly so distraught at the plight of the common people reported back to him that he contracted an eye disease from constant weeping. Still, he finally managed to put a force of a mere dozen ships on the seas, though he did apparently manage to raise sufficient provisions and even build or acquire a few cannon for use on his vessels. The Koreans asked the Ming to supply another 130 warships, even specifying the types they needed. But even with his tiny force, Yi was back to his old tricks, darting in and out among Japanese vessels and creating havoc with his turtleboats. He killed one Japanese naval commander and nearly finished off another. It is said that the enemy "lost all color and wept in fear" when they saw Yi once again at the head of a Korean fleet.[66]

The turning point at sea was an engagement off Chin Island on November 2, 1597. The Koreans, knowing the Japanese had no respect for them, feigned a retreat, then took advantage of the wind to close in on the pursuing vessels from all sides and hammer away with smoke bombs, cannon, and smaller firearms. Hundreds of Japanese sailors perished as nearly their entire fleet of 133 ships was destroyed in what has become known as the "Miracle at Myŏngyang." The Japanese also lost their admiral, Kurushima Michifusa, whose body was allegedly fished from the water and decapitated, the severed head then mounted on the top of a mast to strike terror into the hearts of the enemy. Eleven more vessels were sent to the bottom in a follow-up action. Yi earlier had had his men stretch an iron chain through the water across the anticipated Japanese escape route. When the enemy retreated, Yi had his men lift the chain to capsize the fleeing warships.[67] He stationed some 8,000 troops on land to kill or capture any survivors who made it to shore. As a result of this victory, Yi not only cut the western Japanese supply lines but also captured grain, supplies, and ships that were added to his fleet. It is said that after this battle, the Japanese did not dare traverse the western seas for fear of the allied navy, especially after the arrival of Chinese forces under Chen Lin in December 1597.

As Yi was enjoying renewed success at sea, Chinese commanders began discussing plans for a joint land-sea offensive to commence toward the end of the year. Ma Gui told Sŏnjo that Wanli had already ordered the mobilization of 300,000 troops from the southern coastal provinces to attack Tsushima from China and Korea simultaneously. Other units would set out from Seoul in a three-pronged offensive. Captured and surrendered Japanese could be expected to provide intelligence on conditions in the Japanese fortresses. Sŏnjo noted that the victory at Chiksan had blunted the enemy advance and was very supportive of a quick offensive to turn the tables. The allies once again commenced extensive discussions concerning the delivery of needed supplies and firearms.[68]

It was at this point that Yang Hao entered the story. Yang has come down in history as a tragic figure, blamed for his failure to defeat the Manchus in 1619. He was also embroiled in controversy twenty years earlier during his tenure in Korea. Yet Korean sources indicate that he played a critical role in turning the tide of the Japanese advance, one stating that he "combined civil and military talents, was keen and active, and possessed great fortitude." In taking charge in Korea, Yang declared: "If the heart is secure, then morale is unwavering. If the heart is disturbed, then the will to fight is lost." Significantly, Japanese sources also credit Yang with turning things around for the allies by disciplining generals and advocating a strategy of attacking, then retreating, to wear down Japanese forces and further tax their already overextended supply lines.[69]

Yang addressed Sŏnjo and his high officials on the state of war operations and on restoring the spirit of the people. He began by reminding the court of the disasters of 1592, then continued: "Regarding Korea as a parent cares for his children, the sagacious Son of Heaven dispatched an army to come to the rescue. And [the Ming's] heavenly awe was manifested from the smashing of Pyongyang to the recovery of Seoul as the bandits fled for the border." He added that this allowed Korea to recover what was lost and allowed the people to return to their homes. But now the Japanese had once again assembled a mighty host and invaded, so Korea's civil and military officials needed to act in concert and gather up those who had already fled. Yang then recounted more abominable actions perpetrated by the Japanese as well as the sacrifices of men like Chŏng Pal and Song Sanghyŏn.[70]

Overall command of the combined operation was entrusted to Xing Jie, who had been invested with the double-edged sword of authority by Wanli. As was the case in the first Ming campaign in Korea, Xing stressed strict military discipline, ordering the death penalty for anyone who molested the locals. Stealing food or supplies was punishable by beating, and rape also brought a death sentence. Military censors were assigned to all units to investigate charges of misconduct. Sŏnjo ordered that placards clearly displaying these rules were to be posted in all the cities and asked that all Chinese soldiers be properly notified so that there would be no repeat of problems that had occurred in previous years. Unfortunately, the measures were not totally effective, and diaries from the time report Ming troops looting the homes of commoners and the necessity of burying valuables in strongboxes or hiding them somewhere outside one's home.[71]

Further discussions centered on training the Korean divisions and obtaining accurate information about the locations and dispositions of Japanese forces. Xing suggested using those who had escaped Japanese imprisonment as potentially useful informants. The wajō were strung out in a line some 700–800 li (250–275 miles) long stretching from Ulsan southwest toward Sunchŏn, with the Pusan area being the most fortified. The enemy was finding ingress more difficult as the allies moved into defensive positions and started winning skirmishes on land to complement Yi Sunsin's stunning victories at sea. But the countryside remained ravaged and depopulated—supposedly one could travel more than 100 li (34 miles) in some areas and encounter nary a dog or chicken.[72]

The invaders were more than fulfilling Hideyoshi's instructions concerning the brutalization of the Korean populace. Their interactions with Koreans took many forms, but few were pleasant. Many women were forced into prostitution; others were simply enslaved. Still other Koreans took to collaborating to save their own lives. Many were rounded up to assist in building fortifications along the coast, supposedly working day and night to complete these structures in advance of the anticipated allied assaults. Keinen described the horrors he witnessed as reminiscent of hell itself. It was rumored that the double agent Yōzira was deeply involved in human trafficking.[73] Japanese units were frequently dispatched to the countryside to loot and pillage, stealing livestock and driving the locals into the mountains.

Upon hearing of the defeat at Namwŏn, Wanli ordered the execution of Yang Yuan, who was then in Seoul. He also approved of Xing's plan of attack and ordered supplies be rushed to the front before the Japanese had a change to wriggle free. Ma Gui was placed in overall command and ordered to lead the troops through Choryŏng Pass toward Kyŏngju to attack Katō. Xing also ordered the allied navy to close in on the enemy in order to cut off any chance of a naval escape. Sŏnjo allegedly asked to accompany the army, but Yang Hao forbade it.[74] Yang led the army from Kwangju early in the twelfth lunar month. Thereafter the allies moved steadily toward Katō while feigning an attack on Sunchon in order to distract Konishi. Katō sent his men out to guard the approaches to Ulsan and dispatched messengers to ask for reinforcements. The Ming figured they would once again have more success once winter set in because they could use their cavalry more effectively and the Japanese could no longer rely on riverine transport.

Yang Hao discussed joint naval operations with Sŏnjo. Recognizing that Korea's coast was full of shoals and fast-changing currents that could pose serious problems, Yang asked for Korean guides. He also suggested that the allies participate in joint naval maneuvers with gunboats. The Ming would sail first to Kanghwa Island, then proceed south. Yi Sunsin had some 2,000 men under his command by the tenth month of 1597 and had added a few ships to his fleet, though they still needed Ming help to cover the entire coast.[75] Ma chimed in as well, stressing the need for improved coastal defenses, secure supply lines, and allied cooperation. Kwŏn Yul was placed in charge of training and mobilization efforts on land.

Japanese commanders in the field harbored few illusions about their ability to sustain the campaign. They knew their supplies were dwindling and the Chinese were coming in greater numbers than earlier. They also continued to fear the power of Chinese weaponry, as born out in their defeat at Chiksan. As one commander wrote back to his father: "When troops come from the province of Kai, have them bring as many guns as possible, for no other equipment is needed. Give strict orders that all men, even the samurai, carry guns."[76]

The invaders hunkered down for the winter, entrenching themselves in heavily fortified strongholds often located at the end of narrow mountain passes, where it was harder for the Ming to bring their big guns to bear. Yang and Ma led their army from Seoul to engage Katō's forces. When Li Rumei led a force toward Sangju, the Japanese retreated farther, skirmishing with the advancing Chinese and Korean columns. Some commanders chafed at the orders to retreat, arguing that the Koreans were wont to flee at stiff breezes, let alone determined attackers. But given the harsh weather and the size of the allied force, they pulled back.

By late December 1597, Chinese commanders were ready to embark upon their tripartite assault. One prong was to attack Katō at Ulsan, another was to strike at Konishi in the south, and the third was to head for Pusan. Korean troops served in these divisions too, though Li Fangchun emphasized that they were to adopt Chinese regulations and patterns of military organization. The allies hoped their numbers would be enough to sever Japanese lines and keep enemy commanders from rushing to one another's aid. Allied naval forces would assist the army.

The left wing of 13,000 troops was led by Li Rumei. Gao Ce led the central army of 11,690 mounted and foot soldiers. Li Fangchun and Jie Sheng had joint command of the right wing of 11,630 troops. Ma and Yang were the grand coordinators of the left and right wings, going after Katō, while the central army was to attack Konishi at Sunchŏn. These Chinese units were augmented considerably by Korean forces, most notably Chŏng Chaenyŏng's 1,000 troops from Hwanghae and Ko Ŏnbaek's 2,300 men from the environs of the capital. Supplies, including more than 1,000 cannon, 118,000 fire arrows, 69.745 jin (93 pounds) of gunpowder, and 1,796,967 jin (1,195 tons) of bullets and shot (large and small) were transported to Korea from Liaoyang. The main problem confronting the allies was that they had barely one month's worth of food, though it was determined that some supplies could be requisitioned locally. The king also estimated that two to three months' more could be raised in Korea. Xing reported that more food was on the way from China, but rough seas could delay its arrival.[77]

Xing lectured the Koreans on the importance of courage and resolve in ousting the enemy from the peninsula. Small detachments fanned out all over southern Korea, wiping out isolated Japanese units. A pincer attack launched by Yi Sunsin and Chinese forces dislodged the Japanese from some coastal islets. These regular forces were joined by bands of Korean guerrillas, whose presence continued to have a profound psychological effect on the Japanese. Sŏnjo again thanked the Chinese for sending troops, silver, and supplies, noting that "the Ming have made their righteousness paramount by taking the punishment of Japan as their root."[78]

As the allied armies prepared to march, Xing sacrificed to the spirits of heaven and earth to bestow their grace upon his men. Ma and Yang accompanied the troops, while Xing remained behind to direct operations from Seoul. The allied force reached Kyŏngju on January 26, 1598. Ma knew that the mountainous terrain around Ulsan provided the Japanese with additional defenses, and fearing that they would send reinforcements from Pusan, he sent Gao Ce and Wu Weizhong to block them and dispatched others to guard against any possible water landing by relief forces. Yang and an old eunuch officer were the first Ming commanders to reach the vicinity of Ulsan, and they sent word to Kwŏn Yul and Yi Tŏkhyŏng to join them.[79] In the middle of the night, Ma reached the outer defenses, some sixty li (twenty miles) distant from the fortress proper. Bai Sai, Yang Dengshan, and Po Gui were sent out as vanguard commanders and met with a hail of fire arrows.

The siege of Ulsan began on January 28 after allied forces had pushed the Japanese back into the mountains, smashing through the city's outlying defenses. When the attack began in earnest, the sky became filled with arrows and cannons thundered. Winds spread fires that ignited from explosions and sparks, throwing the Japanese into a panic, many perishing in the flames. The initial onslaught was so surprising that, when he first heard the gunfire, the Japanese commander erroneously believed that his men were hunting the swans that frequented a nearby pond. The next day Li Rumei and Yang Dengshan led their crack troops in an attack on Ulsan proper. Their cavalry retreated before the defenders' onslaught, enticing them into a deadly ambush that claimed at least 400 Japanese. Yi Tŏkhyŏng thanked Ming commanders, saying, "this can certainly be called a minor victory. But when we exterminate the bandits at Sŏsaengpo and Pusan, then I will really be excited."[80] After the Japanese retreated again, Li Fangchun and Jie Sheng crept up to Ulsan and tried to create confusion within by starting more fires, but they were discovered by the defenders and only narrowly escaped. There was also considerable confusion among the attackers as to whether or not Katō was actually there in command. An official was nevertheless dispatched to the Japanese camp to present him with articles of surrender.

Japanese commanders debated vigorously as to what course of action they should take, for they were sorely outnumbered and their supplies were almost gone. Claims that the allied forces numbered 800,000 were vastly overblown, their actual numbers being somewhere in the vicinity of 55,000. But the defenders had perhaps 20,000 men. And their supply situation was desperate. The Japanese were already out of water and were forced to collect snow to melt and drink. Food supplies were so scarce that the soldiers took to sneaking out of the fortress at night to search the bodies of the dead for scraps of food; many of these scavengers were captured by Chinese forces, who mercilessly interrogated them for information. The Japanese later resorted to eating paper and even mud, desperately attempting to keep their bellies full. Keinen's diary offers dramatic images of the suffering experienced by the garrison, evincing his own belief that he would soon "go to bliss in paradise."[81]

On January 30 Ma Gui and Mao Guoqi attacked one of the reinforced outposts, burning the stockade around it. Five hundred more Japanese perished in the conflagration while the rest retreated. Allied losses were also heavy. The next day they attacked the heavily fortified Tōsan fortress as the Japanese rained bullets down upon them, inflicting grievous losses once again. In the end, though, the besiegers, led by Mao's Zhejiang men, took the outer fortress, killing 661 more Japanese in the process. The Ming attacked the inner sanctum the following day, only to be surprised by the arrival of Katō himself at the head of a relief column of 500 troops, having marched from his post at Sŏsaengpo. His boat "flew through the sea as if transported by a dragon god," according to one chronicler. Ōta Kazuyoshi and the other Japanese commanders were jubilant upon seeing the reinforcements. A detachment of 150 Japanese sallied forth and opened a passage in the besiegers' ranks to allow Katō and his men to enter the fortress. Although shocked and dismayed, the allies still held the outlying areas.[82]

The Japanese then shut the gates and waited for additional reinforcements, hoping too that the weather might impel the allies to lift the siege. The Chinese continued their assault, as Chen Yin personally braved a hail of arrows to set up scaling ladders. Inside the walls Katō galloped about in white robes urging on his men. Young samurai Asano Nagayoshi whirled his spear in an arc of death atop the walls, drawing the admiration of his peers inside Ulsan. Li Rumei arrived on the scene late, and the allies were turned back again by the high, stout walls of the fortress. The assembled generals held a meeting in which they decided to cut off the water supply completely and tighten their hold on the areas around the city, thereby starving them out. Fearing the Japanese would send a rescue force from Pusan, Ma sent Gao Ce and Wu Weizhong to Yangsan and Dong Zhengyi to Namwŏn, while another commander was detailed to guard the water approach from Sŏsaengpo. For ten days and nights, they continued their siege under heavy fire from those within. Again the Ming had trouble getting their heavy cannon up the narrow roads, as their men were exposed to concentrated fire every time they tried to advance. Spent artillery shells reportedly piled up high within the fortress while the Japanese kept up their dogged resistance, the Ming troops apparently making good targets with their red armor and white helms.[83] Still, Ma figured the Japanese would soon be unable to resist for lack of food and water.

The allies stepped up their assaults, pummeling the walls with heavy cannon, though to no great effect. The defenders continued to riddle their ranks with bullets from their arquebuses and shot from larger-caliber weapons. One Ming commander managed to ascend the wall briefly, only to be clipped by an enemy bullet. On the evening of January 31, the skies clouded over and freezing rain fell, turning the ground around the fortress into a quagmire. Allied forces continued to attack, and despite losing 700 Chinese and 200 Korean troops in the process, an equal number of Japanese were killed. Yang received a tip that Katō was planning to escape on his own. Further allied assaults claimed many more Japanese lives and even breached the wall for a short time before being turned back. Forty Japanese ships were spotted approaching on the Taehe River, so 2,000 infantry and 1,000 cavalry were dispatched to guard the riverbank. Captured Japanese reported that Katō had fled two nights before but a messenger could be sent to talk with him and negotiate a ceasefire. Yang demanded to see Katō personally. Wu suggested laying a trap for Katō in order to kill him, but Yang favored capturing him if possible. Katō was eventually talked out of personally attending any meeting by his fellow commanders. Yi Tŏkhyŏng and Kwŏn Yul were hopeful that the Japanese would soon capitulate as the freezing rains continued to fall, though there were rumors that Katō, if he had ever left, was returning.[84]

The battle raged again the following night, as lead from the besieged came down with the rain, inflicting heavy casualties on the allies. At one point Yang pulled the Chinese back to rest, telling Kwŏn to lead Korean troops in the attack. Kwŏn did so and suffered heavy losses in another hail of Japanese bullets. There was reason for hope, though, as captured Japanese reported the situation within the city as growing worse by the day. They also reaffirmed the fact that Katō himself was still inside.[85]

On February 5 the Japanese sent a letter to the besiegers: "We want to negotiate a peace agreement, but no one in the city is literate [in Chinese]. There is a Buddhist monk on a boat in the river. If you dispatch an envoy [to meet him] then we can negotiate." Considering the Japanese situation, the allies decided not to negotiate further. Western winds augured that the time might be right to launch one last great incendiary attack. The Japanese still held out some hope, both because they received word that help was on the way and because spies reported there were no cooking fires in the Ming camp, suggesting that they were also running low on food.[86]

Finally, on February 8, just as Japanese resolve was crumbling and they were on the verge of capitulating, Konishi arrived by sea with a large relief column. Konishi was initially reluctant to advance, seeing the numbers arrayed against him. Instead he sent a force of 3,000 crack troops upriver to see if there might be a weakness somewhere in the allied lines. Yi Tŏkhyŏng saw this and sent word to Yang, who then asked him what he felt they should do. Yi replied that allied forces should be able to hold off the relief columns until the city fell, but Yang was less sure, pointing out that thus far they had attacked the city for several days to no avail. In addition, the freezing rain and sleet that had been falling for days continued, seriously hindering assaults, and the cold and lack of adequate fodder conspired to kill many horses. Yang also believed his casualties had been too high and that it was best to order a temporary retreat.[87]

Subsequently, however, Yang fled the field, apparently believing that he was about to be flanked, causing the entire allied army to break ranks. The Japanese emerged from Ulsan to attack the Chinese and Koreans as they fled, killing more than 60,000 according to some Japanese accounts.[88] Countless weapons and suits of armor were reportedly abandoned as soldiers fled for their lives. The allied troops might have suffered heavier losses had it not been for the valiant efforts of Mao and another Ming commander, generally identified as Wu, who turned back the Japanese onslaught with heavy losses. Yet according to Li Rumei, while 3,000–4,000 Chinese and Korean troops were killed, they also inflicted significant casualties on the Japanese, forcing them to return to Ulsan. Yang returned to Seoul, sending Ma to Andong, Li Fangchun and Niu Boying to Namwŏn, and Zu Chengxun, Mao, and Lu Degong to Sangju.[89]

A slightly different version of the story maintains that when Konishi's forces arrived, they were immediately attacked by allied troops stationed along the river. The fighting raged inconclusively for hours, at which point Yang turned to Kwŏn and said, "The only way we can win is if your troops burn them out." He added that if they feigned negotiating, they might be able to catch the Japanese off guard. The Japanese response was short and to the point: "If you want to fight, then let's fight. If you want peace, then open a way for us to leave the fortress and dispatch a general so we can begin peace talks." A more colorful version of the tale has Katō laughing at the request, saying, "Master Ma wants to fight but he doesn't want to meet me face to face and Master Yang prefers to observe from the middle of his forces, so tomorrow afternoon I'll come and pay my respects." Kawaguchi Choju's account relates that Katō knew Yang was trying to trick him, for in his feigned retreat, Yang forgot to detail a rear guard. His ploy having failed,

Yang continued to urge the Koreans to join him in burning out the Japanese, citing strong winds blowing into the city. As they were preparing to execute this stratagem, another twenty-six ships with reinforcements arrived to the cheers of those within the city. The allied forces drove them back at first but found themselves under enemy fire from behind. Ma and Yang decided to pull back and try to starve out the defenders. Soon thereafter, however, the Chinese decided to withdraw for fear that Japanese reinforcements were coming in much greater force, and their own forces were already depleted by the elements.[90]

Despite the fact that Ulsan had clearly been a debacle, Xing Jie reported it as a qualified victory, saying the allies killed 120 Japanese officers and more than 1,200 soldiers but were forced to withdraw because they had been assailed by relief columns on all four sides. This was understandably received with great joy back in China since it indicated the Japanese were on the verge of defeat. All the commanders were showered with rewards and honors. It would not be long, however, before conflicting reports began to arrive.[91]

The controversy started as soon as allied forces returned to Seoul. The Koreans knew, despite Chinese claims to the contrary, that the battle had not been a great victory. They asked Ma about conflicting reports of the siege, and he responded angrily: "This is how you earn merit in your country? By taking it away from those who have earned it? What kind of deceitful anger and trickery lead to this?" Unsatisfied with this response, Sŏnjo then put the question to Yang, who said he was forced to withdraw because supplies were low and no reinforcements were coming, whereas the Japanese were aided by the arrival of a large relief force. The king suggested that the general should have been better prepared. When asked why he fled, Yang said to be able to fight another day. He added that he was expecting naval reinforcements from China that could boost his fighting power. Yang then requested horses, saying the Japanese feared Chinese cavalry. The king asked, "Where would we get 10,000 horses?" When Yang responded that the supply of horses had formerly been part of Korea's tributary obligations, the king noted that livestock had been decimated by the war.[92]

Meanwhile, allegations of conspiracy and corruption emerged that pointed all the way to Grand Secretary Zhao Zhigao, who asked to resign. Military censors were dispatched from Beijing. One, Ding Yingtai, a vociferous critic of the war policy adopted by the Ming in 1597, was soon on the scene looking for evidence to impeach Yang. The supreme commander offered to resign on account of illness, but Wanli reviewed his case and ordered him to remain in office.[93]

Yang tried to save himself by writing letters to Ming grand secretaries Zhang Wei and Shen Yiguan, asking them to intercede on his behalf. But he was dismissed and replaced by Wan Shide. Sŏnjo memorialized on Yang's behalf and asked that he be allowed to stay until the war was over, remembering what he did for Korea at Chiksan. Wanli refused the request, and Ding Yingtai issued a scathing denunciation of Yang and his cronies, listing some twenty-eight crimes committed by Yang. Most serious among the charges were the allegations that he deliberately made tactical mistakes and falsified reports so as to benefit Li Rumei, to whom he was very close.[94]

Fearing Ding's charges might undermine Ming support for the war effort entirely, officials of all ranks and even commoners protested in favor of Yang and even tried to prevent his carriage from leaving Seoul after he was recalled. While some of these efforts were orchestrated by Korean officials, at least some of the protests appear to have been spontaneous outpourings of genuine affection for Yang and appreciation for his efforts on behalf of Korea. Most people were unaware of the intricacies of Ming court politics and patronage networks. All they knew was that when Yang arrived, the tide of war turned in favor of the allies. This was enough for them. Demonstrations in his favor continued throughout the next year, both in Korea and in Chinese towns along the border.[95]

Wanli refused to be moved by Ding's allegations. He addressed a letter to Sŏnjo, saying: "For years we have used troops and expended resources in order to repay your country's loyalty and obedience. I won't doubt you on the words of one person." Nevertheless, Yang was ordered stripped of his posts and to return to his home in Henan.[96]

Yang remained upbeat, reassuring Koreans that the Japanese would be defeated within a year as China's most-talented generals, including Liu Ting, would soon arrive. Privately, however, Yang was less sure of both his and Korea's fate, though he continued to profess his dedication to the cause. While drinking with subordinates one night, he declared, "If the Japanese are quelled, I'll die in Korea; if they aren't quelled, I'll die in Korea." He then told one of his servants, "Buy me a seven foot coffin and when I die, bury me in Korean soil." Ding's charges were presented to Wanli on July 6, 1598, after the censor returned from Korea. He listed twenty-eight crimes committed by Yang, ranging from losing battles with which he was not involved, to consorting with prostitutes, to bribing

Zhang Wei. On top of these specific offenses, Ding listed ten others for which Yang should be ashamed.[97] Xing Jie and Yi Tŏkhyŏng both felt the charges were groundless and pointed out that some censors just liked to stir up trouble. They also noted that Ding had ties to the now-discredited peace party, which may be the reason for his attacks on Yang.

Yi consoled Yang, telling him that he had seen Ding's memorial, and it was full of holes and groundless statements. Yang agreed that the whole matter sprung from the lies of Shen Weijing: "Shen messed up everything. He messed up everybody!" Then, gazing up at the sky, he lamented: "On the outer frontier we have Japanese outlaws, on the inner frontier we have our own traitor-outlaws! So many outlaws! Who can tell what will happen in this world?" The Koreans also felt Konishi Yukinaga was involved, implicating him because he intervened to save his countrymen. As one official remarked: "Yukinaga certainly is talented, . . . more so than most people. He attacks Namwŏn and kills 3,000 Chinese troops . . . and yet they all still say Yukinaga is in favor of a peace treaty!"[98]

The Koreans convened a court conference to discuss the matter. Yi Tŏkhyŏng maintained that the misunderstanding concerning Yang's actions at Ulsan was due to the omnipresent struggles for glory between northern and southern troops. While this may have been the case, the Koreans knew they had to come up with a stronger defense lest Ding's charges destroy all support for the war in China. As Sŏnjo put it: "Everything is up to Heaven, everything has its number. Hideyoshi was born in Japan, Shen Weijing was born in China. Such things were not caused to happen, but they happened. . . . It's a pity such a petty person can ruin the affairs of the world. How in the world did we get this Ding guy?" The king warned that Yang's departure would have a deleterious effect on Korean morale and that his people's unity with China was due largely to Yang Hao.[99] He then asked why Li Rumei's defense had not carried more weight. The officials replied that Chen Yin's voice carried more weight, but did not go into specifics. Since the Li family was not overly popular in Beijing, Yang's association with them was probably a black mark against him.

Li Rumei was also indicted by Ding, who charged him with conspiring with Yang, Shen Yiguan, and Zhang Wei to cover up the truth about Ulsan. He also said Liaodong soldiers refused to talk because they were intimidated by the Li family. Li was accused of six punishable crimes and ten lesser counts, which included having unusually close relations with Katō Kiyomasa and engaging in unauthorized peace talks with the Japanese commander. Li and Yang were also accused of neglecting their duties by getting drunk at night and allowing enemy soldiers to sneak in and out of Ulsan. Ding added that Li sent his subordinates out to buy food and wine so he could feast while their troops were starving and freezing. Li also allegedly allowed his men to loot Korean homes and violate their women.[100] Zhang, Shen, Li, and Ma were branded a cabal seeking to undermine the war effort and discredit southern soldiers. Ding's charges lost some of their sting, however, when letters between Zhang and Yang revealed no evidence of a conspiracy.

As the debate in Korea continued, more sordid stories emerged. One official reported that Chen Yin nurtured a grudge against Yang because he had punished him in the past. Another alleged that a low-ranking official opposed to the general got the men drunk and encouraged them to speak against Yang, then reported their comments to Ding. The Koreans realized there was no way to get at the whole truth, but they were predisposed to accept the report of Yi, who was on the scene with Yang. In the end, though they did not find Yang completely blameless, the Koreans decided to draft a memorial in his support and send it to Beijing. Ding was dispatched to Korea again. In the border town of Liaoyang he crossed paths with the Korean ambassador, who sent a report back to Seoul warning the Chinese and Koreans of Ding's impending arrival and telling them his net was being cast ever wider.[101]

The news reached Seoul on September 9, 1598, as the war was drawing to a close. This time Ding was followed by Xu Guanlan, a much more stoic and unbiased military censor. While Xu took great pains to ascertain the precise details of events in Korea, most importantly body counts, Ding continued to attack Yang's supporters, including Sŏnjo himself. Ding attacked the king for having the temerity to champion Yang's cause and question the decisions of the Chinese. Ding also perpetrated all manner of outrages during his investigation, including the arrest and torture of Korean officials and the ransacking of houses and offices in a desperate search for incriminating evidence.[102]

Ding's impeachment hearings had finally gone too far. Instead of gaining the result he sought, namely a full and thorough investigation of Yang and all his associates, Ding incurred the enmity of virtually every official in Korea and most of those at the Ming court. Sŏnjo, deeply hurt by the charges and feeling he had no recourse, withdrew from government altogether for several days and even vowed to die for the sake of Yang. Finally, a report from Xing Jie, informing the king that Xu was presenting a report of exoneration for all involved, moved Sŏnjo into returning to his duties, though he refrained from entertaining Chinese guests for a time.[103]

The Koreans continued to press for full and complete exoneration and drafted an official memorial of protest in which they answered in detail all the charges leveled by Ding. The Chinese for their part considered the matter more or less settled, for they had much more pressing matters by that time. The issue was vitally important to the Koreans, however, and on November 19, 1598, Yi Hangbok set forth from Seoul at the head of a mission to Beijing to formally protest and refute Ding's charges against the court and their monarch. Ding and Xu continued to serve in Korea as army inspecting censors, following their usual modes of operation: Xu sober and reserved, Ding outrageous and unrestrained. When the war was over, Sŏnjo snubbed Ding but met with Xu as the two Ming officers returned to Seoul. In this meeting Xu confided to the king that he agreed Ding's charges were unfounded and assured him he would secure an exoneration for all concerned as soon as he returned to Beijing.[104] Wanli's Edict of Exoneration was finally issued on March 31, 1599.

Yet even as the controversy was mounting around Yang Hao following the defeat at Ulsan, the allies nonetheless knew they still had the upper hand in the war. A large Chinese navy was assembling at Lushun, ready to sail with more men and supplies. Allied forces on land were stronger than ever in early 1598, exceeding 140,000 men. Boat production in southern China was stepped up to meet military demands. Ming officials went about searching for ways to raise more money to pay and supply the armies, as costs were estimated at 800,000 liang per year. New taxes were levied, most significant among them being additional taxes on merchants and shipping. Yang Hao had commenced planning for another three-pronged offensive in the fall of 1598. Sŏnjo questioned Chinese officials vigorously about their plans for future offensives and ordered his men to continue training and establishing military farms. Allied forces were reorganized under the command of Ma Gui, Liu Ting, Chen Lin, and Li Rumei, though the latter was replaced by Dong Yiyuan when a brother, Li Rusong, was killed in an ambush by Mongols in the spring of 1598. Xing Jie also made new arrangements for the transportation and delivery of supplies, placing greater emphasis on sea routes and cutting out some of the middlemen who siphoned off precious provisions and other goods along the way.[105]

The massive expansion of Ming naval power was an important factor in the final defeat of the Japanese. This allowed the allies to dominate the sea lines and transport men and supplies much faster than their adversaries. Chen Lin was placed in charge of the Ming navy, though Korean sources maintain that he was not much of a factor but rather was given recognition by the magnanimous Yi Sunsin, who was careful to treat his ally with the utmost respect and deference. Some sources even assert that Chen, "realizing his inability to fight off the enemy even though he had more ships [than Yi], rode on one of our board roofed warships whenever a battle commenced in order to receive instructions from [Yi] and to leave command of the fleet with him." Given Chen's reputation in China and his previous experience in battling pirates in Guangdong, it seems highly unlikely that he would have ceded control of his navy to Yi. In fact other sources indicate that the basis of Chen's friction with Yi was due to Chen's well-earned reputation as a strict disciplinarian. He was irritated by the lack of training and order among the Koreans, and they resented him for trying to improve their esprit de corps.[106] Chen was assisted by his longtime comrade in arms, Wu Guang, and by Deng Zilong, who had served with Chen in the southwest and was still a strapping warrior at seventy years of age.

Despite their victory at Ulsan, the Japanese did not engage in any significant offensive operations but spent their time reinforcing their defenses and waiting for the next allied strike. Many commanders suggested that they should begin a retreat, for the situation was clearly hopeless. Katō Yoshiaki scoffed at such suggestions, saying, "Who retreats when they have not even seen the enemy's flags?" His sentiments were outwardly shared by many, but even Hideyoshi came to doubt the rationale for remaining in Korea, especially as his own health declined and he began to fear what might happen to his son and his empire after he died, allegedly remarked, "How could I have sent 100,000 soldiers overseas to become ghosts?"[107]

When he questioned his generals about the situation in Korea, they said: "Korea is a big country. If we move east, then we have to defend the west; if we attack to our left, then we are assailed on the right. Even if we had another ten years the matter still might not be resolved." They also estimated that far more men would be needed for any hope of recommencing offensive operations. The taikō then lamented: "We are a small country and our resources are insufficient. Now I cannot fulfill my eight military goals. What is to be done?" He also complained of his advanced age and the fact that there appeared to be no way out of the quagmire, asking them, "If we were to stop the troops and sue for peace, what then?" At this the generals answered, "That would be best."[108]

Thus the decision to withdraw from Korea was actually made by Hideyoshi himself and not by the regents after his death. This evidence contradicts the popular notion that the Chinese and Koreans were at a loss as to what to do and were only saved by the timely death of Hideyoshi.[109] There were many practical reasons for a withdrawal. Despite their success at Ulsan, the invaders were in a precarious position with respect to food and supplies. Other battles and the harsh Korean winter also took their toll on Japanese fighting strength. As Korean scholar Yi Chin-hui notes, "It was not true that the Japanese invaders withdrew from the peninsula because of the death of Hideyoshi, but the fact was that the Japanese force in Korea dwindled to 75,000 men from the original strength of 147,000 by May 1598, or three months before his death, losing the capability of continuing the fight." Stressing that he wanted all Japanese troops to return home, Hideyoshi told Asano Nagayoshi and Ishida Mitsunari to hasten to Kyushu with the withdrawal order as well as word of his grave illness. But apparently when Hideyoshi actually died, his senior advisers decided to keep his instructions secret so they could effect a truce and perhaps save themselves some trouble by disclaiming responsibility for the war and taking the credit for negotiating peace. Thus a later directive emanating from the elders in Japan told those commanders still in Korea to break off talks and pull out immediately if tribute-trade privileges could not be extracted from the Ming.[110] This apparently became the basis for the common misconception that Hideyoshi himself never ordered withdrawal from Korea (a myth akin to those surrounding German militarists like Ludendorff with respect to the end of World War I in Europe).

Whatever his mental state at the time, it remains that Hideyoshi was a brilliant military commander and recognized a hopeless situation when he saw one. Supplying their troops was the greatest difficulty faced by the commanders in Korea. From the start of the first invasion, Hideyoshi decided upon the strategy of a multipronged advance in part to make the best use of his talented commanders. This strategy was flawed, though, as it meant the Japanese had to keep supply lines open along a number of fronts simultaneously, a difficult prospect in the best of circumstances. Yet despite the fact that his troops were constantly under attack from all sides, Hideyoshi refused to change this principle.

These inherent weaknesses were compounded by the fact that the commanders were more or less equal in power and authority. Such an operation required a single commander, and that commander was the taikō himself. Giuliana Stramigioli concurs with this assessment, saying, "The main reasons for [Japan's] failure were Hideyoshi's mistake in not assuming personal command of the invasion and the lack of a navy to back up and keep supplies flowing to the continent."[111]

In describing Hideyoshi, his contemporaries and biographers alike note that his greatest asset was his indomitable will and charisma. Hideyoshi could inspire and compel people to do things by virtue of his personality alone. This could not be delegated to another, nor even passed on to his own son. Of course it is still likely that even had he gone to Korea personally as originally planned, the invasion would have failed, but there is no doubt the war would have taken a different course. Still, this does not support Yoshi Kuno's assertion that had Hideyoshi lived but a few years longer, the national existence of both Korea and China "would have come to an end one way or another."[112]

In the late summer of 1598, Jin Xueceng, an official in Fujian, reported that Hideyoshi had died on August 10.[113] Japanese troops had been withdrawing since the spring, and as early as the fifth month of 1598, twenty of the top thirty Japanese commanders were already recalled, and most of the others were in the process of retreating. In fact it appears that Japanese raiding and looting activities increased through the summer in part to cover their retreat, though they were prevented from doing too much by the presence of Ming troops. Additionally, the lack of supplies made the troops restless, and many units were on the verge of mutiny. Others defected to the allies. Still, many commoners grew fearful when hearing reports of more Japanese boats landing on the southeast coast, unaware that most of these were troop transports sent to ferry the Japanese home. Many commanders received their withdrawal orders from Hideyoshi in mid-July. In fact Konishi Yukinaga even tried to parley with the Ming, though to no avail. Yōzira's efforts met with a similar rebuff, and he was eventually arrested in Seoul and sent to Beijing for punishment.[114]

News of Hideyoshi's death was greeted with great joy in both Korea and China, and Sŏnjo urged the Ming to attack the Japanese in force before they had a chance to escape. Wanli and his court decided to press the attack. By this time the remaining Japanese forces, totaling about 65,000 men, were entrenched in four major strongholds. Katō

Kiyomasa, with about 10,000 men, was still at Ulsan. Sachŏn, another heavily reinforced fortress, was held by Shimazu Yoshihiro. Konishi Yukinaga garrisoned Sunchŏn at the head of 13,700 men. The Japanese fleet, which still possessed as many as 500 ships manned by more than 12,000 sailors, was stationed at Pusan.[115]

Throughout the summer the allies had put limited pressure on the Japanese while also endeavoring to establish and maintain their own supply lines. Military requisitions and corvee requirements often caused hardships for the locals, particularly once the agricultural season commenced. There were still scattered reports of Chinese troops beating up Koreans and taking their goods. When the main Ming force of more than 28,000 reached Seoul in midsummer, the king instructed all local officials to solicit or make their own contributions of food to help feed the army. But because of the sufferings of the previous several years, not much was forwarded, and the roads were reportedly lined with starving peasants. Tigers took advantage of the situation to sneak into villages and attack livestock and weak, helpless refugees. The food shortage was finally alleviated by the delivery of some 1 million piculs (66,665 tons) of rice from Shandong, grain designated for both feeding the army and helping the famished populace.[116]

The allied advance was initially planned for June, but a military revolt in Liaodong postponed the action until September. They would again use a multipronged attack strategy, this time joined by the naval forces of Admirals Chen and Yi. As was the case before, Korean officials were attached to Ming units. Wu Guang and Cao Xibin led 6,000 infantry to Namwŏn, another 5,000 headed toward Sunchŏn, and Liu Ting led 10,000 men from Chŏnju, with more troops and supplies following behind him. Korean warrior-monks also participated in these actions. It was hoped that the offensive could be concluded before winter set in and hindered transportation. Xing Jie also peppered his superiors in Beijing with requests for more warhorses and draft animals, eventually obtaining both funds to purchase them, presumably from the Koreans, and a few hundred mounts themselves.[117]

The main allied force, numbering more than 30,000 soldiers, was under the command of Ma Gui and advanced toward Ulsan. Ma still believed that defeating Katō Kiyomasa was critical to ousting the Japanese from Korea. The allied advance was effective, as Ma made good use of his numerical superiority and learned from his experiences earlier in the year. In a series of engagements, his forces managed to kill more than 2,200 Japanese and burn their provisions as the enemy retreated to the coast. A clean victory was denied him, though, and his men were eventually lured into a trap and forced to pull back, though the Chinese remained vigilant against any Japanese attempts to go on the offensive once more. Katō's men boarded ships for Japan in the dead of night on December 14, just as their naval comrades were sailing to their doom in the straits of Noryang.[118]

Dong Yiyuan, with more than 15,000 allied troops under his banner, was charged with attacking Shimazu Yoshihiro and his son, Tadatsune, at Sachŏn. This was another exciting and controversial battle, immortalized in Japanese art and called a defeat snatched from the jaws of victory by Li Guangtao. Sachŏn actually comprised two major fortresses and a number of outlying structures. The original structure was built by the Koreans and occupied by the Shimazu after the sack of Namwŏn in 1597. The newer castle was built by the Japanese between 1597 and 1598 on a hill overlooking the sea to the rear of the original fortress.[119] The route leading to the newer castle was narrow and easily defended, as was the preference of the Japanese. Both fortresses were defended by stone walls and wooden stockades. The perimeter defenses extended some forty li (fourteen miles) around the main works.

In examining the Japanese defenses from afar, Mao Guoqi remarked that they looked like a snake stretching to the sea, so all the allies had to do was cut off the snake's head (Shimazu Yoshihiro). After breaking camp at Chinju and crossing to the south bank of the Nam River, the allies moved forward steadily under cover of darkness. Advance scouts killed twelve Japanese in a skirmish near Kŭmyang. The initial assault was very successful, capturing a number of smaller fortresses en route to Sachŏn. Dong urged caution, waiting for news from the other allied columns. His Korean counterpart, Chŏng Chaenyŏng, wanted more aggressive action, and they finally pushed forward with 7,000 troops on November 6. While meeting stiffer resistance on the outskirts of Sachŏn, the allies still managed to kill 130 Japanese and a commander in fancy armor, who was reportedly felled by a single arrow.[120]

With information and possibly assistance from inside, the Chinese managed to burn the provisions of the Japanese camped along a river outside the city proper. They also learned that the defenders had but one well within the walls, so they surely could not hold out for long.

Dong's forces then captured a large number of outer buildings and two more stockades as the Japanese retreated to the fortress closer to the sea, harassing the attackers to cover themselves. Shimazu Tadatsune itched to sally forth and go down fighting but was restrained by his father, though he did shoot some enemies from the walls with his bow.[121]

Allied commanders also debated their course of action. Some wished to wait for more reinforcements. Citing the lack of wells in the city, Chŏng suggested letting nature run its course and just waiting for morale to decline within the city. Eventually the desperate defenders would have to come out to fight or die of thirst inside. Mao agreed, noting that there were still lots of Japanese within the fortress, and victory was by no means assured. In contrast to his earlier cautiousness, Dong advocated a quick and powerful attack, asking, as he stroked his beard, "When the thunder claps, who has time to cover his ears?"[122]

The full-scale assault began on November 9, as the allies hit the walls repeatedly with cannon fire and battering rams. The Japanese responded in kind. Although one of the outlying forts remained in Japanese hands, Dong decided to concentrate on the main prize. Mao, Peng Xingu, and Ye Bangrong led the frontal assault. Cavalry units were deployed along the flanks in supporting positions. Chŏng was alongside Peng in the vanguard, which smashed the gate with a huge battering ram. The Japanese knew they were in a tough spot. Shimazu Yoshihiro remarked to one of his subordinates, "If reinforcements don't come soon, this will be my grave."[123]

Finally, on November 11 the allies managed to breach the walls. Just as the Chinese and Koreans were streaming in to finish off the enemy, a gunpowder magazine exploded, though it is still unclear whether the blast was touched off accidentally by the attackers or intentionally by the defenders. Most Chinese accounts charge that Peng, who was said to be unfamiliar with gunpowder despite his previous service in the Capital Guards, accidentally ignited the Japanese stores as he forced the gates open with cannon and battering rams. Other sources maintain that the Japanese actually set a trap for the attackers. Realizing that he was badly outnumbered, Shimazu Yoshihiro dispatched some close retainers to sneak outside the walls at night and plant gunpowder-filled jars in the ground by the main gate. Although they tried to hold the gate, when it was clear it would be breached, the defenders ignited the jars themselves. It is also possible that the Chinese battering rams

THE FINAL JAPANESE OFFENSIVE

themselves contained explosive charges that went off by accident or by design at the crucial moment.[124]

At any rate, the explosion created chaos in the allied ranks as smoke and flames filled the breach they were trying to scramble through. The defenders took advantage of the situation to counterattack and reap a grim harvest, though allegations of taking more than 30,000 heads are almost certainly greatly exaggerated. Still, reports state that only 50–60 of Peng's contingent of 3,000 men survived the attack, and Mao lost 600–700 more. Even worse from a military standpoint, the Japanese recovered valuable supplies and provisions. Dong then called for a general retreat to Sangju to await reinforcements. The Japanese did not pursue because they lacked the necessary numbers and adequate provisions. Subsequent censorial investigations called for the execution of the soldiers deemed responsible for the blunder, though Dong was given the chance to redeem himself by meritorious service.[125] Peng blamed his Korean allies.

In order to buy some time, Dong sent Mao to negotiate with Shimazu Yoshihiro. Upon seeing his Chinese counterpart, Shimazu gloated: "Today was a great victory for me. First I'll seize Seoul, then I'll head west and soon you'll see me in Liaodong!" Dong was concerned when he heard this and dispatched a messenger west to warn Xing. Xing, however, was livid: "Don't resume peace talks. I'll kill you before I authorize doing that!" He also declared that he was raising more troops to send against the Shimazu. These warnings convinced the Japanese commander to evacuate Sachŏn, and his men were forced to fight as they embarked on their ships and set sail for Sunchŏn, losing fifty men to Chŏng. When Dong entered the abandoned complex, he found a great deal of treasure, including gold, silks, decorative fans, and fancy carriages, stolen from the Koreans.[126]

Liu Ting, who commanded about 24,000 allied troops, was ordered to attack Konishi Yukinaga at Sunchŏn. His army was supported by a naval force of more than 20,000 led by Chen Lin and Yi Sunsin, fresh from their victory off Kŏjedo, where they sunk fifty Japanese ships and killed hundreds. The joint offensive against Sunchŏn commenced in late October. Because Konishi's fortress of Waegyŏ was well fortified and additionally protected by mountains and the sea, Liu first tried to trick the Japanese commander into surrendering by dispatching a subordinate to invite him and fifty followers to meet with Liu and discuss an arrangement whereby the Japanese would be allowed to withdraw.

Unsuspecting, Konishi agreed, and brought fifty retainers with him for the meeting. In the meantime, Liu stationed men all around his tent and told them to wait for a signal to emerge from hiding and slaughter the guards and capture Konishi. When the Japanese commander arrived, Liu broke out the wine and they started talking. Unfortunately, the signal was not properly sounded and fighting broke out between the two sides. Liu found himself in dire straits until a contingent of aboriginal warriors came to his rescue. Konishi jumped on his horse and galloped away to safety. Japanese sources credit Matsura Shigenobu with ferreting out the ambush and making sure his men were alert. Although Matsura was wounded, his valor enabled Konishi to escape.[127]

Despite this deceit, the next day Konishi remained very obsequious toward Liu, even sending him a female companion. This behavior was the basis for allegations that Liu was bribed by Konishi. This ploy failed, though, as Liu led his men in attacking Waegyŏ. Allied forces killed ninety-two defenders and took the bridges leading up to the fortress. Liu erected siege equipment around the perimeter, but heavy Japanese musket fire made it difficult to get too close. After an initial assault failed, he then offered a sixty-liang bounty to the first man to scale the walls. Li Fangchun galloped around the outside of the fortress, daring the Japanese to come out and fight. His taunting was greeted by bullets, logs, and stones from within.[128]

The Ming hit the northwest corner of the fortress with their siege engines once again, blasting away through the night. As dawn broke, the defenders charged out, inflicting heavy casualties and burning carts, the smoke blotting out the sky. That day alone an estimated 800 Ming troops died, but they still rallied sufficient to drive the Japanese back into the safety of the fortress. Liu was beside himself over his inability to take the city and began discussing alternative measures with his Korean allies.[129] One option was sending in more troops with heavy armor and shields in an effort to get the defenders to exhaust their ammunition supplies. Ultimately, Liu asked Chen to launch a simultaneous attack by sea. Once landed and in position, Chen's men were to enter the fortress from behind upon hearing a trumpet signal from Liu.

Chen's initial assault off Sachŏn was successful, as his squadron wiped out a large supply convoy. He and Yi also managed to free more than 1,000 Korean prisoners of war. Seeking to press his advantage, Chen sailed up the narrow islets in an attempt to land behind enemy lines. Undaunted, Japanese troops rallied and drove their assailants back when the tide ebbed and stranded much of Chen's fleet; the admiral himself narrowly escaped alive. That night an angry Chen went ashore and met with Liu, but the latter could not console him. The Japanese took advantage of the lull to repair their defenses. Further skirmishes followed the next day as allied troops assaulted the fortress via the narrow mountain approaches; they too were driven back. The Japanese tried to fight their way out through the northeast corner of Waegyŏ but were forced to retreat, though a few managed to escape in search of help. Konishi lit signal beacons in hopes of attracting help by sea. Korean sources record that there was much friction between allied commanders regarding coordination of their attacks, as Liu ordered a brief withdrawal against the wishes of Kwŏn Yul and Yi Tŏkhyŏng. This gave the Japanese another respite as well as some food left behind by the retreating units.[130]

Liu's army returned just a couple of days later. Another assault by his forces was turned back by sword-wielding Japanese just as the attackers reached the top of the walls. Night assaults by the Japanese burned more siege equipment. Although he managed to prevail temporarily, Konishi's time in Korea was just about up. Shimazu Yoshihiro, fresh from his so-called victory at Sachŏn, was on the way, and by now Japanese commanders in Korea had all received news of Hideyoshi's death. Konishi tried to buy time by parleying with both Liu and Chen, with Japanese envoys bringing Chen gifts of swords, wine, and food and Konishi visiting with him several times.[131] Unresponsive to these overtures, the allies arrayed their fleet in the straits of Noryang, a narrow passage between Namhae Island and the mainland, the only route of approach for the Japanese warships coming from Pusan. The defenders of Sunchŏn managed to hold off Chinese and Korean ground troops long enough to start embarking soldiers on vessels still moored there. This set the stage for the most famous military engagement in Korean history, the Battle of Noryang Straits.

The Japanese navy under Shimazu Yoshihiro entered the straits on December 14, and the two sides fought the following day, though sources differ as to exactly when the battle commenced. Deng Zilong, salty dog that he was, was the first to engage, sailing into combat with 200 Chinese sailors on a borrowed Korean warship. In the confusion of the battle, Deng's ship was hit by friendly fire and began to list, giving the Japanese a chance to close and board it. Although he fought valiantly and took many Japanese with him, Deng eventually went down with his burning ship, though his corpse was recovered for a proper burial.[132]

Yi Sunsin sank ten boats quickly, including one carrying a Japanese commander in shiny armor. Realizing what the enemy was attempting to do, Yi hoped to cut off Konishi's escape. But now it was Chen's turn to act recklessly. Seeing what happened to Deng, Chen sailed ahead of the majority of his fleet, only to be surrounded by Japanese vessels. Yi rushed to his aid and managed to smash through the encirclement and rescue the admiral. In the process, however, Yi was struck by a bullet near the left armpit and killed, possibly by friendly fire. Fearing a loss of morale, his dying words were allegedly, "This is the key moment of the battle, so you must not say anything about my death." His nephew directed the rest of the battle from the flagship. Yi Sunsin would later be canonized as "Lord of Loyalty and Martiality" (ch'ungmugong), and shrines to his memory were erected all over Korea.[133]

Meanwhile, Chen's heavy guns sank several Japanese vessels, and the admiral himself killed numerous Japanese in hand-to-hand combat as they tried to board his vessel; Chen's son Jiujing was killed defending his father. By this time Chen Can arrived with the rest of the Ming navy, and the rout was on. Allied forces opened fire on the Japanese with their fearsome crouching tiger cannon and wreaked great havoc on their fleet. More than 200 Japanese vessels were sunk and thousands of Japanese were killed; the sea reportedly turned red with the blood of the Japanese. Shimazu's vessel sprouted so many arrows that it looked like a hedgehog on the water. Survivors who swam to shore were hunted down or blown away by the allies' heavy guns as they hid in caves. Chen Lin later estimated that as many as 20,000 Japanese were killed in the battles at Sunchŏn and Noryang.[134]

The diversion of the battle was enough for Konishi and Shimazu to effect a narrow escape. Some Japanese units even captured heads and war trophies as they fled. This outcome provided additional fodder for critics of Liu, who charged that he was hesitant in his final assault on the fortress for fear of his own safety as well as that of his men. The allies did capture a good amount of weapons, armor, rice, livestock, and other provisions, though Kwŏn was upset that Liu had not advanced faster, his delay allowing the Japanese to burn 3,000 piculs (200 tons) of rice. (Liu responded that he feared a trap such as that sprung at Sachŏn.) Liu's report that he killed 160 in occupying the fortress was disputed by some Koreans, who said that by the time he arrived, there were only a handful of Koreans and a few horses left, prompting Sŏnjo to retort, "Even a small child could have taken that city." And there were still rumors of bribery in the air—even Chen was reputedly angry at Liu for letting Konishi escape—but nothing was ever proven.[135]

Mopping-up operations continued for months, as Chinese and Korean forces hunted for stragglers in the mountains around Sunchŏn. The next few years were punctuated by occasional Japanese scares, with the Ming even dispatching a small force to Taiwan to wipe out stragglers hiding out there after the war. The reality of the Japanese withdrawal contradicts Yoshi Kuno's assertion that "[b]ecause they had been victorious, the Japanese withdrew successfully without any serious difficulties, although Chinese and Korean military forces made desperate attempts to attack the Japanese on their way home and thus avenge themselves for the seven years of suffering that they had gone through."[136]

The Koreans were understandably overjoyed at the news of the great victory, even as they were saddened by the death of Yi Sunsin. As soon as the triumph was confirmed, Chen Lin was feasted by the Korean king and rewarded for his exploits. Deng Zilong was also honored, being conferred with the posthumous designation *zhong wu* (loyal and martial). Chen would later be rewarded with the highest honors of any Ming field commander in Korea, followed by Liu Ting and Ma Gui. Recognizing the hardships experienced by the generals and the men alike, Wanli released an additional 100,000 liang of silver for special rewards, against the protestations of Ding Yingtai, who charged most of the commanders with having accepted Japanese bribes.[137] The emperor in response proceeded to angrily dismiss several censors who brought charges against the military commanders,. clearly fed up with such chicanery. Xing Jie was made grand guardian of the heir apparent and received a hereditary title for one son. Ma was made military commissioner in chief of the right. Dong Yiyuan was restored to his former rank. Mao Guoqi, Chen Yin, and Peng Youde all received monetary rewards, and Yang Hao's official rank was restored, though he remained in retirement for a decade.

The Battle of Noryang Straits put a fitting exclamation point on the war in Korea, for once again the allies' heavy guns prevailed over the Japanese arquebuses. As one Japanese chronicler observed, "With respect to warships, those of China are the best, followed by those of the Ryukyus, and then Korea."[138] It remains rather puzzling why the Japanese never adopted heavy guns for their warships. They must certainly have seen the great vessels of the Europeans, ringed with cannon. Hideyoshi even tried to buy several of these warships for his invasion but was politely refused. There was some attempt by the Japanese to expand their navy for the second invasion, but this seemed confined to increasing the numbers of men and ships, rather than improving technology and tactics. One problem was the fact that Japanese naval commanders were most familiar with land warfare. They never really adapted to fighting at sea and preferred to close and board enemy vessels and skirmish with their superior swords. At first glance this might seem odd because of the success the wokou had enjoyed earlier in the sixteenth century. But it needs to be remembered that many of these "Japanese pirates" were actually Chinese. In addition, even they preferred to engage in what are best described as amphibious operations, landing and looting locations along the coast.

In contrast to Japanese commanders, both Yi Sunsin and Chen Lin were experienced naval commanders with a thorough understanding of the strategy and tactics needed to win. Ironically enough, the very success of Japanese pirates earlier in the sixteenth century directly contributed to Japan's undoing during the invasion of Korea. The repeated depredations of pirates forced both the Chinese and the Koreans to bulk up their naval forces and construct new ships equipped with the latest technology to protect both their coastal citizens and their commercial interests. It is probably no coincidence that improvements in Chinese naval technology took place in the latter part of the sixteenth century, for this was precisely the time when overseas trade was once again officially sanctioned by the Ming and international trade exploded in East Asian waters.[139] If there was more cargo to be had by pirates, there was also more incentive to protect it on the part of merchants and governments.

In the immediate aftermath of the war, the Ming seemed quite pleased with their success. Wanli gave Wan Shide instructions to pass along to the Korean government. These emphasized how the Koreans needed to adopt Chinese-style training and military-farming methods. They also offered to provide trainers and encouraged all lower-ranking Korean civil and military officials to participate. Wan then condescendingly told the Koreans that if Chinese methods were adopted, problems such as this could be easily avoided in the future. In a subsequent communication, Wanli emphasized the need for unity among all Korean officials in solving the kingdom's problems and warned them against the dangers of factional politics, a minefield with which he was well acquainted.[140] The Ming could now direct their full attentions to quelling Yang Yinglong's revolt in Bozhou. For Korea, it was time to embark upon the long and painful process of rebuilding.

Yi Sunsin in civilian garb. *Author's collection.*

Inspecting heads. From *Chōsen seibatsuki*.

Defense of Ulsan Castle. From *Chōsen seibatsuki.*

The Japanese at Sachŏn. From *Chōsen seibatsuki*.

Turtleboat replica. Author's collection.

東莞縣大頭船式

Ming warship. From *Chouhai tubian. Photograph courtesy Amy J. Hollaway.*

海滄船式

Ming warship. From *Chouhai tubian. Photograph courtesy Amy J. Hollaway.*

7

AFTERMATH AND LEGACIES

The First Great East Asian War in Context

After the Japanese evacuation, the Ming were interested in extracting themselves from Korea as quickly as possible in order to deal with the growing threat posed by Yang Yinglong in Sichuan. Li Hualong was appointed supreme commander of military affairs for Sichuan, Huguang, and Guizhou provinces. The high military officials of the empire, including Chen Lin, Liu Ting, and Ma Gui, were ordered to hasten directly from the Korean front to the distant territory of Bozhou. Their armies included significant numbers of surrendered Japanese soldiers, who, according to modern scholars, contributed significantly to the dissemination of small firearms in seventeenth-century China, their arquebuses being particularly effective in close-quarter terrain such as the forested mountains of southwest China, where Yang's rebellion was raging. Liu in particular is said to have made extensive use of Japanese arquebusier corps in battling Yang.[1]

The Koreans asked the Ming to leave 7,000 land and 3,000 naval troops behind, along with sufficient firearms and gunpowder reserves. Their requests were honored, and the Ming decided to leave one general and a supervising censor from Shandong as well. Wanli then authorized the distribution of some 100,000 liang of cash for special rewards. In discussing the dispensation of these awards, the court stressed how the emperor's majesty extended even to distant seas, affirming that Wanli had indeed asserted his superiority over Hideyoshi within the East Asian world order and restored the "proper" balance.[2]

The Koreans thanked the Ming profusely, sending a delegation led by Yi Hangbok to Beijing the following year, where they performed the ritual bows and kowtows and were entertained in the Hall of Martial Glory in the Forbidden City. Several Koreans, including Yi Sunsin and Yi Hangbok, were honored by the Ming for their efforts during the war. Sŏnjo himself sent Wanli a letter of gratitude in which he noted that the Son of Heaven regarded his neighbor as part of himself and treated the people of Korea like family. The king then officially proclaimed that the state had been restored, and Kwanghaegun was formally installed as heir apparent.[3]

Living shrines were erected all over Korea to the Chinese generals involved in the victory. A statue to Li Rusong was placed in Pyongyang. Wanli was made part of an annual ceremony of thanks, with an altar to him built in Seoul in 1704. Symbols of gratitude toward the Ming were so prevalent in Korea that great care had to be taken when entertaining Chinese visitors in the succeeding Qing dynasty, lest these monuments offend their new tributary overlords. Unsurprisingly, most were defaced or destroyed during the Japanese colonial period in the twentieth century. Korea's gratitude toward China was well deserved, for as Gari Ledyard observes, "one is forced to conclude that for all the heroics and turtle-boats, it was the Chinese alliance that was the most crucial military element in Korea's survival." Koreans were well aware of this, and they never forgot it, even sending troops to aid Yang Hao, Li Rubo, and Liu Ting in their campaign against the Manchus in 1619. As recently as 1991, Chong Haesung, a Korean scholar, remarked, "If we did not have aid from the Ming, we might have been a Japanese colony since 1592!" He continued, "If only some parts of the historical writings about the Imjin War are selected and facts are taken out of context, and if we underestimate and ignore the Ming's military aid, this does not cultivate a sense of our independence and it drives our people to become beasts who don't know appreciation."[4]

Early in 1599, Shen Yiguan suggested to Wanli that he should announce the victory over the Japanese to the empire as a manifestation of his martial spirit, just as he had done after Ningxia. The emperor heartily agreed and ordered the Ministry of Rites to select an auspicious day for the event. The victory over the Japanese was finally announced in Beijing on May 3, 1599, as sixty-one Japanese prisoners were dismembered before Wanli, their body parts later scattered along the frontier. Shen Weijing was decapitated in the western market of the capital that same day.[5]

Wanli talked of Japanese duplicity and how they were bested by the multipronged advance of the allies, who acted with one mind. Sending so many troops so far to aid an ally had not been achieved since ancient times. The Ming claimed that China and Korea had sacrificed 100,000 men and 10 million liang of cash (or more than one-quarter of the Ming Empire's annual revenue), but they had suffered together, two centuries of friendship prevailing in the end. Nowhere in all the four seas were two states so close. He also told the Koreans that their sacrifices, though pitiable, built character. But Wanli warned Sŏnjo not to forget the lessons he had learned and to take great care to rebuild his state and strengthen his armies. Soon thereafter, the additional taxes levied in China to underwrite the war effort were canceled.[6]

The Ming then issued directives on where to station the troops left behind and how to feed them, reiterating that such troops would not only help deter the Japanese but also assist in training and building defensive works. The proclamation also emphasized the importance of maintaining a capable navy. It was initially stated that 34,000 troops and 3,000 mounts were to remain in Korea at an estimated yearly cost of 918,000 liang. But because of the high costs of keeping so many troops on the peninsula and urgent military needs elsewhere, the Ministries of Revenue and War suggested that the number be reduced to 10,000 men. There was also the matter of feeding the soldiers, given the economic devastation of Korea. Wanli agreed with his ministers and told the Koreans to embark upon a program of self-strengthening so as not to rely so heavily on China for defense. His court also stated that they would not be leaving a coordinator of Korean affairs (jinglue) behind, a pronouncement that must have come as a relief to Korean officials fearing annexation by the Ming. In large part because of difficulties in feeding the troops, withdrawals began as early as May 1600, with a general withdrawal of all Ming forces issued in the tenth lunar month of that year.[7]

Late in the second lunar month of 1599, Wanli convened a meeting and ordered Ding Yingtai deprived of his rank and reduced to commoner status for his mean-spirited and petty actions and investigations in Korea. Xu Guanlan was also impeached and went back to Beijing to plead his case. Yi Hangbok and other Korean officials in China were ecstatic at this news. Sŏnjo again expressed his profound thanks to the Ming and sent gifts to Wanli, including robes, silks, and leopard skins. He also held a public ceremony of thanks outside Seoul's great south gate.[8] Chinese officials in attendance burned incense and bowed in appreciation.

Korea, meanwhile, was completely devastated. By some estimates, casualty and abduction figures were as high as two million people, constituting 20 percent of the population. Most of these people were illiterate commoners, but some, such as Kang Hang, Chong Huiduk, and No In, became minor celebrities in Japan by virtue of their education and left important chronicles of their time in captivity. One modern Korean scholar colorfully observes that the captives returned Japanese gunfire with "shots of cultural bullets." Perhaps the most important cultural transmission was bringing Chinese-style Neo-Confucianism to Japan, which would be among the most important intellectual developments of the Tokugawa era. Some even suggest that Japanese daimyo brought monks with them during the invasions for the express purpose of plundering Korean libraries. Shimazu Tadatsune returned with 48 volumes of classical Chinese texts, and one Japanese author estimates that the total number of volumes brought back to the islands approached 2,600.[9]

One such captive was Kang Hang, a native of Chinju who had passed the civil-service examinations in 1587 and had earned a post at the Sungkyunkwan. After later serving in the Ministries of Justice and Public Works, Kang became an assistant commander entrusted with defending Namwŏn in 1597. He initially escaped the fall of the city but was captured by Tōdō Takatora on November 2, 1597, as he and his family sought to escape by sea to the safety of Yi Sunsin's headquarters. He was first sent back to Tsushima and from thence onward to Tōdō's fief of Ozu on Shikoku. In June 1598 Kang was sent to Osaka Castle and later to Fushimi, where he made the acquaintance of one Fujiwara Seiki, a monk at Sogokuji Temple who had formerly known Korean envoy Kim Sŏngil. The two became friends and discussed Neo-Confucianism and poetry. In his diary, the Kanyang nok [Record of a Shepherd], Kang relates valuable information about Japanese climate, history, myths, language, and geography. Seeing himself as a potential Korean spy, he also included information on the backgrounds of prominent Japanese commanders and discusses politics in Japan, along with notes on the strengths and weaknesses of certain castles. Despite (or because of) its popularity in Korea, the work was often confiscated or burned by Japanese censors during their colonial rule in the twentieth century.[10]

Ordinary Korean prisoners also made significant contributions to Japanese society. Some introduced superior cultivation methods. New crops such as pumpkins, tobacco, red peppers, and much later potatoes were also brought to Japan. The Shimazu seized significant numbers of potters, and kilns were established in Satsuma that remained distinctive for centuries. Other daimyo did the same. Korean pottery soon commanded high prices and became synonymous with a sophisticated appreciation of the tea ceremony among Japanese elites. In the other direction Koreans repatriated from Japan were often in high demand for their martial skills and were expected to aid in constructing weapons and training troops, provided they were exonerated of retaining any possible connections to their former Japanese masters. Not all Korean prisoners stayed in Japan or returned to Korea, however. Some were bought by Italian traders and taken as far away as India or even Italy before they were freed, lending yet another international dimension to the conflict. In fact a family with the surname Corea still resides on Italy's southern tip and believes itself to be descended from one of these transplanted captives.[11]

In addition to the human costs, as much as 80 percent of Korea's arable land was ruined. For several years after the war, grain production was barely one-third of what it had been in years past; the hardest hit areas of Chŏlla were but one-sixth as productive. Many palaces were not rebuilt for decades or even centuries. Society was in shambles, banditry and dislocation were endemic, and tax collection was nigh impossible. In the immediate aftermath of the war, markets in Seoul were short on goods because all of the produce was being consumed by the Ming guest troops. Chinese soldiers were also accused of stealing from Korean commoners. But many of these troops actually settled and married local women, their descendants enjoying a fair degree of prestige for their fathers' roles in the war.[12]

On a broader level, the war was instrumental in inspiring institutional reforms in Korea. Many scholars wrote extensively about the many shortcomings and inequities in Korean society that were exposed by virtue of the invasions. Officials made efforts to improve finances, ameliorate the effects of widespread slavery, eliminate factionalism in government, streamline the bureaucratic process for career advancement and promotion, and more equitably distribute wealth in terms of land and property. Korean monks were granted the right to be certified once again, though such programs were more an attempt to control the Buddhist sects than to revive them. There were also attempts to revise the military-examination system and improve the status of the military as a whole.[13]

The main stumbling block for reform was that Korea did not have the resources to build its military forces or rebuild its infrastructure for some time. But Sino-Korean training exercises were conducted, eyewitnesses even reporting crowds gathering atop mountains to watch their impressive displays. The Chinese sold weapons to their allies and instructed them on techniques for constructing better ironclad vessels (which the Japanese lacked), for superior technology was deemed critical in facilitating their recent victory. Military reform efforts were lent added urgency by continuing rumors of a renewed Japanese threat as well as problems along the Chinese border, with Korean bandits looting back and forth between the two states. But the government's efforts were not entirely in vain, as reports from 1602 indicate the enrollment of some 17,000 new recruits, at least some of whom were equipped with new muskets. Unfortunately, before they could fully rehabilitate their military and government, Koreans soon found themselves the target of another ambitious man, this one destined to succeed in his aspirations and become the founder of imperial China's last dynasty, the Qing—Nurhaci. He began conducting raids along the Korean border as early as 1607, and before long Ming and Chosŏn officials were communicating about the rising threat his Jurchens posed to both of them.[14]

What is most surprising about the aftermath of the war is how quickly trade and diplomatic relations between Korea and Japan were restored. This was probably because Hideyoshi, the driving force behind the war, was already dead, and the Koreans needed the benefits of trade. Interestingly enough, the needs of the people of Tsushima were highlighted in such discussions by contemporaries, all involved recognizing the integral position of the island regardless of which government claimed sovereignty. The Koreans maintained their air of moral superiority and demanded the Japanese initiate all overtures. They also demanded the extradition of those who had desecrated the royal tombs as a face-saving gesture, even if those sent were mere scapegoats. The first Japanese envoy was summarily rebuffed.[15]

Unsurprisingly given their interests in the matter, it was the Sō family of Tsushima who took the lead in restoring diplomatic and trade relations between Korea and Japan. But even though ties were renewed rather quickly, the process was not completely smooth. The first Sō emissary, dispatched in 1598, never returned. In the summer of 1600, Sō Yoshitoshi repatriated some 300 Korean men and women as a gesture of goodwill. In exchange the Chosŏn government sent representatives from the Ministries of War and Rites to open talks, also dispatching envoys to reopen formal ties with the kingdom of Ryukyu. In his communication to the Ryukyuan ruler, Sŏnjo noted their respective positions within the Chinese tributary system and asked for their continued vigilance against the Japanese in the future: "The sins of the rebels increased and their wrongdoing accumulated, and a punishment was inflicted by Heaven. This is beneficial not only to our country, but indeed the whole world. The rest of the rebels have also been attacked by the Imperial army and driven away beyond the sea. We earnestly hope that at any sign of movements of the rebels in the future, you will immediately report it to the Celestial Court and have it relayed to our country."[16]

As he went about consolidating his hold over Japan, Tokugawa Ieyasu recognized the need for trade. In opening discussions with the Koreans, Ieyasu stressed that he played no part in the invasion and "did not send even one soldier" overseas. But many on the peninsula were understandably skeptical of his claims and argued that Japan could not be trusted after bringing a hundred generations of ruin upon Korea. They were also worried about the reaction of the Chinese, who had asked for bimonthly reports from the Koreans on the Japanese situation, and wondered if they could really expect military help from the Ming again if the Japanese were lying. Ieyasu subsequently authorized an exchange of POWs as a means to ease tensions between the two states. Keitetsu Genso and Sō Yoshitoshi went to Korea at Ieyasu's behest in 1603, and several hundred Koreans were repatriated shortly thereafter. In 1604, Tsushima residents were once again permitted to trade in Pusan. From 1601 to 1605, nearly 5,000 POWs and captives were repatriated to Korea. On the other side, the monk Yujŏng, drawing upon his prior relationship with Katō Kiyomasa, played a major role in repatriating additional Koreans, making several trips to Japan, including a visit to Kyoto in 1604–1605. Ieyasu met with Yujŏng and his entourage at Fushimi Castle in the third month of 1605. Saishō Shotai, Hideyoshi's former specialist in foreign affairs, was also present at these discussions. Yujŏng returned with 3,000 captives, and other Korean envoys brought another 1,240 home in late 1607 after more discussions at Edo.[17]

The Japanese sent another envoy to plead for the restoration of ties in 1607–1608, at the same time extraditing captured pirates for execution by the Koreans. The final Korean conditions for a return to normal relations were a request from the legitimate "King of Japan" for official recognition and the extradition of those who had desecrated the Korean ancestral graves. Because Yi Tŏkhyŏng and others remained wary of Japanese intentions, Tsushima again became the middle ground for negotiations. The Sō again resorted to forging letters from the "King of Japan" to Sŏnjo, using the Ming calendar and designating Ieyasu as the new king. Genso once again acted as the chief Japanese emissary, having gained the right to dispatch envoys and conduct trade from Japanese authorities. More Koreans were repatriated as a result of these efforts, but formal diplomatic ties were not yet restored. Interestingly enough, Genso and the others also apparently sent a letter of apology to the Ming and asked for a restoration of tribute trade, though without success.[18]

In all these communications, Ieyasu stressed that he had nothing to do with the invasion, and in 1615, after the death of Toyotomi Hideyori, Ieyasu even told the Koreans that he had avenged them. The two sides had finally signed the Treaty of Kiyu in 1609, which provided for limited trade under the supervision of the Sō at Tsushima and Pusan, with a new "Japan House" (waegwan) being established at Pusan. This permanent trading venue normally housed more than one hundred Japanese officials and served social and economic functions for the Japanese in Korea. Formal relations were not established until 1617. It is important to note that these agreements were negotiated between the Sō and the Chosŏn government, the bakufu having little to do with it. For their part the Koreans still regarded Tsushima as Korean territory occupied by foreigners. The Tokugawa shoguns still refused to be addressed as kings of Japan, as this implied they were of a lower status than China, but the matter was finally resolved in 1635 when they accepted the designation of "sovereign lord of Japan" in official communications with the king of Korea. Direct trade ties were never reestablished with China for this same reason. Thus Japan reentered the East Asian world order, "albeit in the same ambiguous position to the Chinese sphere it had always held." For example, the Japanese were confined to the environs of Pusan, and embassies were not permitted to go to Seoul. Korean missions to Edo, by contrast, were lavish affairs in which villagers were encouraged to come out and pay their respects along specially designated routes. In fact the Osako-Kyoto-Edo route along the Tokaido was popularly called the *Chōsenjin kaido* (Road of the Koreans). Once the Korean embassies reached the shogun capital, they were treated to lavish seven-course banquets.[19]

The Japanese invaded the Ryukyus in 1609 and compelled that tiny kingdom to render obeisance, though it also remained a nominal vassal of China and was considered a foreign state by the Tokugawa as well, judging from letters and diplomatic missions that aimed at creating a Japanese-centered international order.[20] Subsequent efforts to reestablish formal trade ties with Ming China failed because the two sides could not agree on the status of the shogun, and Ieyasu, despite his apparent willingness to turn a blind eye to the manipulations of the Sō on Tsushima, refused to accept vassal status. A 1619 letter from the provincial governor of Zhejiang addressed to the shogun and the magistrate of Nagasaki offered to open regular trade channels, but this was rejected by the Japanese.

In historian Ronald Toby's opinion, Japan's refusal to rejoin the Ming order had profound implications "for both the Japanese national consciousness and Japan's approach to international relations and diplomatic behavior."[21] Toby views the act as an assertion of Japanese independence, but it can also be viewed as a manifestation of the continued primacy of the Chinese international order, which would not be overturned until the nineteenth century. In the long term, however, it is possible that the creation of this Japan-centered order derived from the vision of Hideyoshi sowed the seeds from whence Pan-Asianism sprouted. Like Hideyoshi, Japanese imperialists in the twentieth century sought to create a new order that would afford them the resources and status to which they felt entitled. With a blueprint ready at hand, they would not be the first to draw upon and distort history for their own purposes.

Indeed, memories of the First Great East Asian War are in many ways as problematic as the war itself. In Korea it is remembered as an unmitigated disaster, another grim chapter in that nation's seemingly eternal struggle for freedom from foreign influence and domination. Some scholars opine that the psychological effects of the war exceeded even the pure physical destruction. Combined with the subsequent Manchu invasion of China that toppled the Ming, Koreans were forced to deal with the fact that the world as they knew it was coming to an end. Chosŏn stood alone as the last bastion of civilization in a barbaric world. The Koreans were doubly traumatized by the Manchu invasions because the military aid given them by the Ming deepened the sense of kinship between the two states.[22] Korea never lost its sense of disdain for the "barbarian" Manchus, and the Qing's inability to defend the peninsula against Japan in the 1890s could be easily contrasted with the Ming's success three centuries earlier.

In modern times Koreans remember the heroics of Yi Sunsin above all else, but they must also deal with the reality of having been occupied and pillaged for seven years by the Japanese, a memory that was revived during the period of Japan's colonial rule (1910–45). Indeed, as mentioned in the introduction, Japanese colonial rulers made a point of referencing Hideyoshi's earlier dreams of conquest, the so-called *Seikan ron* (chastise Korea) debate having raged in Japanese circles since the 1860s as expansionists sought an outlet for the energies of frustrated former samurai. Once annexation of the peninsula became a reality, the Japanese consciously studied and restored some of the old wajō for use as colonial headquarters, treating them as vital historical artifacts for the study of Japan's glorious past; commemorative stelae erected at sites such as Sachŏn in honor of the exploits of samurai clans like the Shimazu merely added insult to injury. Systematic studies of the castles' construction were also funded by the colonial government. As modern scholar Ōta Hideharu points out, some of these studies were unabashedly nationalistic, trying to prove that the Japanese were master castle builders and to demonstrate all the good they had done for Korea in the past.[23]

In studying the war of the 1590s, colonial leaders also searched for lessons in how the imperial army should occupy and discipline the peninsula. They hoped that honoring Japan's past triumphs could both boost Japanese morale and intimidate the Koreans. Late in the Second World War, a work on how the heavily outnumbered Shimazu forced a Ming retreat was published to inspire Japanese troops to prevail against overwhelming odds and material deprivation. This is noteworthy because Chinese and Korean authors were doing precisely the same thing to inspire their own anti-Japanese war efforts. Colonial Japanese work on Pyongyang glossed over the defeat in 1593 to focus on the more recent triumph over the Qing in 1894. Even more interesting, and somewhat surprising, were suggestions that Yi Sunsin's fame in Korea was due largely to the efforts of Japanese naval officers, who supposedly prayed to his spirit for success in battle on the eve of the Russo-Japanese War and then revived studies of his exploits as their nation assumed dominion over Korea.[24]

Nationalistic-minded Koreans are wont to excoriate the "feudal" Yi rulers for abandoning their people and then licking the boots of the Chinese who came to their aid.[25] Some see the Chinese intervention as nothing more than another plot to control Korea by a neighboring state, a charge that has little basis in the sources examined for this study.[26] The war is also a symbol of perseverance and the will to prevail against overwhelming odds. Koreans are rightfully proud of Yi Sunsin and the righteous armies, and their exploits are well chronicled and memorialized all over Korea. It is no accident that Yi's war dairy and memorials to court are among the few primary sources of Korean history that have been translated into English and that miniature statues of the admiral and his turtleboats are readily available in gift shops.

In China the war is most commonly interpreted as one of the key episodes leading to the fall of the Ming. This no doubt stems from early Qing historiography, when Ming loyalists and Qing collaborators alike were looking for the causes of the decline and fall of the dynasty. This perspective has been picked up by many contemporary writers. For example, George Elison, writing in the *Cambridge History of Japan*, calls the war a disaster for the Ming: "The drain on its public treasury and its military manpower seriously weakened a Chinese regime that was already burdened with an enormity of external and internal problems and made it sink deeper into the dynastic decline that was to overcome it a half century later." Donald Clark, writing in the *Cambridge History of China*, declares the war a disaster for all sides, saying the main beneficiaries of the conflict were Nurhaci and Tokugawa Ieyasu. Likewise, Nam-lin Hur opines that "[t]he expanding private trade networks and the newly established Japanese military super power gradually nullified the Chinese world order."[27]

Yet all of these interpretations ignore the fact that the Ming immediately mobilized a force of more than 200,000 troops to quell a domestic uprising across the empire. Some might contend that the very fact of Yang's rebellion was indicative of Ming neglect or governmental incompetence, but in fact it was in part a manifestation of the state's continued vitality. Far from contracting and ossifying, the Ming state was expanding its frontiers and opening up new lands for exploitation and taxation, albeit at the expense of local aboriginals, whose relationship with such state-building efforts was, of course, adversarial. And as to the military situation itself, the ability to face a wide variety of foes in diverse environments and to deal with these threats effectively is in itself a demonstration of the kind of bureaucratic and tactical sophistication that eluded most early modern militaries.[28] As we have seen, the Ming responded creatively to the challenges posed by their foes, even if they were sometimes constrained by the limits of either their resources or their political system. One must be careful of trying to judge seventeenth-century militaries by modern standards.

Wanli's leadership is another area worthy of consideration. He Baoshan and his colleagues, in their biography of the emperor, agree with the editors of the *Ming shi* by maintaining that the Ming government was corrupt and decayed and its officials were evil and selfish. They are also of the opinion that if Hideyoshi had not died, the war would have dragged on and the allies might have lost. Yet they also say that despite his many shortcomings, during the Japanese crisis, Wanli effected a stern and resolute attitude and carried himself with confidence. This was the high point of his life and his reign.[29] Wanli made the decision to go to war. He took a keen interest in the course of events and was always asking for suggestions and plans from his officials. He made appointments and backed those he put into positions of authority. When Ding Yingtai launched his investigations, Wanli made sure another official was sent along to check any abuse of power. He also saw through the petty factional rivalries of his officials and tried to seek truth from facts (to borrow Deng Xiaoping's famous line).

In fact it is hard to level charges of inattention at the monarch after reading the sources pertaining to the Three Great Campaigns. Inheriting a significant treasury reserve from Zhang Juzheng, Wanli adeptly made use of the resources at hand and sought imaginative ways to bring in more revenue to fund his wars and other activities. Even critic Ray Huang admits, "[t]hough Wanli's self-indulgence cannot be defended, there is little validity to the charge that he wrecked the fiscal foundations of empire single-handed."[30] Taking into account the evidence presented herein, even charges of personal self-indulgence need to be reconsidered. Although Wanli was notoriously tightfisted, with respect to the Korean campaign, he released funds almost without question and frequently authorized requests for additional money for use as special rewards. Many deliveries of food and cash were specifically designated to help alleviate the suffering of the Korean populace. The dispensation of extra funds to reward the Ming troops helped discourage them from abusing their hosts.

As for the charge that the war in Korea, along with the other campaigns, bankrupted the Ming, it is important to note that these military expenditures were dwarfed by those of contemporary empires. Even allowing for the fact that the Ming state provided far more in the way of services for its subjects than most of its contemporaries, the total combined cost of all three of Wanli's major military campaigns equaled about one-third of one year's revenue. By contrast England was spending about 90 percent of its annual revenues on military expenditures in the mid-seventeenth century.[31] Admittedly these figures come from the time when military expenses were increasing rapidly in Europe, but the same was true in China. In the case of the Ming, they could rely on increased revenue from the burgeoning international silver trade as well as a highly developed bureaucracy that was inherently fiscally conservative.

Turning to the emperor's personal character, one is struck by the sense that Wanli had the tools to be one of the better Ming rulers. He was by no means unintelligent, but he was easily hurt by criticism and lacked the strength of will that had enabled his ancestors to run roughshod over officials who opposed them. Instead, Wanli adopted a passive-aggressive approach that was simply insufficient to meet the problems of his reign, even if he was to achieve some concrete military successes. It appears that the constant wrangling with his civil officials over virtually every matter of state and ritual wore down the emperor and caused him to retreat in disgust from governing, seeking refuge deep within the Forbidden City. Later in his reign only truly dangerous military threats, such as that posed by the Manchus, could rouse him to action. The empire continued to function for awhile even without a strong central authority, but in the end rival factions of civil and military officials managed only to frustrate one another, to the great benefit of the state's enemies.

Returning to the Korean campaign, modern Chinese also view the war with a sense of pride, as their nation unselfishly helped out its weaker neighbor. Fan Shuzhi remarks that Wanli's benevolence in helping Korea is above reproach. The documents suggest that the emperor truly did empathize with the plight of Sŏnjo and resolved to do everything in his power to help the kingdom survive. This particular interpretation assumed greater prominence after the Korean War of the twentieth century, when it could be argued, as the Chinese themselves have done, that China was acting as much to protect its own interests as those of North Korea. But even if this was the case, it is hard to argue with the fact that the Ming sent a total of 167,000 troops on two different occasions to Korea's defense and spent millions of ounces of silver. All along there were those in the government who favored negotiating a truce, but in the end the conscience of Wanli prevailed and the Ming lived up to their tributary responsibilities, an interpretation favored by many Chinese scholars today. As Wanli declared: "The imperial court will not let losses get in the way and we won't rest until the bandits are extirpated and our vassal state is at peace."[32]

The memory of the war in Japan is much more problematic. Even though Japanese forces retreated without retaining a single inch of Korean territory, for over four hundred years some have praised the conflict as a Japanese victory, clinging to the myth that had it not been for the untimely death of Hideyoshi, all of Korea, and possibly China as well, would have fallen to Japanese hands. This interpretation has been echoed by modern writers in Japan and elsewhere.[33] They also directly attribute the weakening of the Ming to its eventual defeat at the hands of the Manchus nearly fifty years later. Yoshi Kuno goes so far as to say that Japan's demonstration of its military invincibility prevented anyone from invading the nation for the next 250 years, completely ignoring the wider international context.

Many of the Japanese commanders associated with the war became folk heroes or even deities. Katō Kiyomasa, for example, became a popular subject for woodblock prints in the late Tokugawa era and was frequently depicted on the stage, despite his own personal dislike for such frivolities. More importantly, the invasions assumed a special significance in the twentieth century and became a source of pride, encouragement, and inspiration for Japanese expansionists. Hideyoshi's blueprint for the conquest of China was later adopted by the Japanese invaders of the 1930s. Even now disputes between the Japanese and South Korean governments sometimes reference this conflict. There is also a tremendous body of secondary Japanese literature on the war and its participants that continues to perpetuate this national myth, though some of the more recent scholarship is certainly less politically charged. Likewise, where Japanese museums containing artifacts pertaining to the war once focused exclusively on the exploits of Japanese warriors, they are now including displays and discussions highlighting the suffering of Koreans.

To sum up, even if Hideyoshi's invasion of Korea was not the single greatest event in the history of East Asia, it was certainly one of the most complex and interesting. It was a curious affair, marred by military and diplomatic errors of the worst kind. The second invasion might have been avoided entirely had it not been for the pride of Hideyoshi and Sŏnjo, both of whom were too stubborn to yield to their rival.

Much more scholarship needs to be done on the war, especially considering the vast amount of primary-source material available. These documents offer the researcher the unique opportunity to get inside international relations in early modern East Asia, as materials survive from all three sides.

Finally, comparative military historians should find much of interest with respect to this war on the strategic, operational, and tactical levels. Whether or not one accepts the notion of a "Military Revolution" championed by Geoffrey Parker and his supporters, the First Great East Asian War provides a fascinating case study with respect to the dissemination and deployment of new military technologies. The Japanese initially prevailed by virtue of superior technology and better training and discipline. But when the Ming entered the war, the technological balance shifted, forcing the Japanese to alter their tactics. Recognizing their own well-developed abilities in siege warfare, the Japanese attempted to switch to a strategy that increased their chances for victory by minimizing the effectiveness of Ming heavy cannon. They also tried to improve their naval capabilities during the latter portion of the war but, probably due to a lack of time, were never able to close the technological gap between themselves and the allies. On the allied side, the Ming improved Korean training methods and gave them superior weapons. They also devised stronger armor to counter Japanese musket fire. Both sides also made use of foreign experts and technologies as they became available. Concurrent with the tactics developed during the repulse of the Spanish Armada, the allies used seaborne cannon to blast Japanese vessels from afar.[34]

The war also serves as an object lesson in the importance of logistics and the role of bureaucratic structures in enabling the persecution of foreign conflicts. As evidenced from the sheer number of surviving documents on such matters from the allied side, supply was considered at least as important as generalship, perhaps even more so. Allied records often contain meticulous calculations for the amount of food that might be lost en route to the front or for how much food was needed to support how many horses. By contrast, Japanese records speak far less about such matters and focus more on the exploits of individual commanders and their men, an interesting distinction. They seem to take for granted that the required amount of food and supplies can be wrung from the local populace. Where Chinese and Korean records stress obtaining proper intelligence and coordinating operations, Japanese records tend to highlight personal valor and feats of daring. Admittedly I have read far more from the Chinese and Korean sides, so these generalizations must be taken for what they are, but the differences are striking.

In describing the "modernization" of European armies, William McNeill discusses such factors as civilian control of supply lines, regular payment of the soldiers with tax money, the differentiation of military units, and the tactical coordination of cavalry, artillery, and infantry. Of course all of these characteristics can be found in the armies involved in the First Great East Asian War. Scholars also deem the role of repetitive drilling and standardization of training techniques crucial to creating modern military forces. The introduction of Ming general Qi Jiguang's training manuals to Korea was of much importance. Drawing upon Qi's model, the Koreans later created their own martial-arts treatise, the *Muye dobo tongji*, which includes a sword form attributed to Li Rusong. The allies also participated in sophisticated amphibious operations and in joint land-sea attacks. Even the use of maps and the creation of joint-planning operations by the allies predates such activity in Europe by some two centuries.[35]

The narrative of this study has only scratched the surface, and its primary purpose has been to fit the Korean campaign into the context of the Three Great Campaigns and of Wanli's reign as part of the First Great East Asian War. In leaving this story for now, it is useful to return to some of the various designations for the war discussed in the introduction. In Korea the invasions are known as the Disaster of 1592 and the Disaster of 1597. In China the war is referred to as the Rescue of Korea. But for capturing the essence and legacy of the war, it is perhaps most relevant to use one of the Japanese designations. In Japan the war is sometimes referred to as "A Dragon's Head followed by a Serpent's Tail," meaning something that has an impressive beginning but no real ending.[36] Given the nature of the conflict and its contemporary resonance in East Asia, this seems oddly appropriate.

DRAMATIS PERSONAE

Chen Lin: Ming admiral and firearms expert

Cho Hŏn: Korean official

Chŏng Pal: Korean commander killed in defense of Pusan

Chŏng T'ak: Korean official and chronicler of war

Deng Zilong: Ming general and naval commander

Ding Yingtai: Ming censor who impeached Yang Hao

Dong Yiyuan: Ming commander

Genso, Keitetsu: Japanese monk, ambassador, and negotiator

Gu Yangqian: Ming commissioner of Korean affairs (replacing Sang Yingchang in 1593)

Hwang Yungil: Korean diplomat and official

Katō Kiyomasa: Japanese commander who favored an aggressive prosecution of the invasions

Kim Chŏn'il: Korean official

Kim Myŏngwŏn: Korean minister and commander who lost Kaesŏng

Kim Sŏng'il: Korean diplomat and official

Kim Ŭngsŏ: Korean commander

Kobayakawa Takakage: Japanese commander and victor in the Battle of Pyŏkchegwan

Konishi Joan: Retainer of Konishi Yukinaga and Japanese emissary to the Ming

Konishi Yukinaga: Leading Japanese commander and negotiator

Kuroda Nagamasa: Japanese general

Kwak Chaeu: Korean guerrilla leader known as the "Red General"

Kwanghaegun (Yi Hon): Korean prince and heir apparent who rallied support in the countryside

Kwŏn Yul: Korean general who successfully defended Haengju

Li Chengliang: Ming commander in Liaodong; father of Li Rubo, Rumei, and Rusong

Li Hualong: Ming civil commander of Bozhou campaign

Li Rubo: Ming general, brother of Li Rumei and Li Rusong

Li Rumei: Ming general, brother of Li Rubo and Li Rusong

Li Rusong: Ming supreme commander of Korea; elder brother of Li Rubo and Li Rumei

Li Zongcheng: Ming ambassador to Japan who abandoned mission

Liu Ting: Ming general, also known as "Big Sword Liu"

Ma Gui: Ming general and chief commander in second Korean expedition, 1597–98

Mei Guozhen: Ming censor in charge of Ningxia campaign

Pubei: Mongol rebel and figurehead leader of Ningxia mutiny

Qi Jiguang: Ming general and tactician

Shen Shixing: Ming grand secretary, 1580s–1590s

Shen Weijing: Ming envoy to Japanese

Shi Xing: Ming minister of war, 1591–98

Shimazu Yoshihiro: Japanese commander at Sachŏn

Sin Ip: Korean general

Sō Yoshitoshi: Japanese daimyo of Tsushima

Song Sanghyŏn: Korean official and defender of Tongnae

Song Yingchang: Ming military commissioner of Korea, 1592–93

Sŏnjo (Yi Yŏn): King of Korea (r. 1567–1607)

Sun Kuang: Ming commander of Korean affairs, 1594–95

Tōdō Takatora: Japanese naval commander

Toyotomi Hideyoshi: Taikō; supreme ruler of Japan, 1582–98

Wanli (Zhu Yijun): Emperor of China (r. 1573–1620)

Wŏn Kyun: Korean admiral and rival of Yi Sunsin

Wu Guang: Ming commander and associate of Chen Lin

Yang Hao: Ming coordinator of Korean affairs, 1597–98

Yang Yinglong: Aboriginal rebel in southwest China

Yang Yuan: Ming commander and hero at Battle of Pyongyang

Yi Il: Korean general; defeated in several battles in 1592

Yi Ŏkki: Korean naval commander

Yi Sunsin: Korean admiral and inventor of the turtleboats
Yi Tŏkhyŏng: Korean ambassador to the Ming and high official
Yi Wŏn'ik: Korean minister
Yōzira: Alleged Japanese spy who betrayed Yi Sunsin
Yŏnggyu: Korean monk-soldier
Yu Sŏngnyŏng: Prime minister of Korea, ca. 1589–1607
Yun Tusu: Korean official and adviser to king
Yujŏng: Korean monk and guerrilla leader
Zha Dashou: Ming general
Zhang Juzheng: Ming grand secretary and tutor to Wanli
Zhang Wei: Ming grand secretary
Zhao Zhigao: Ming grand secretary
Zu Chengxun: Ming officer in charge of first relief column, defeated at
    Pyongyang

Selected Chinese
Character List

Akechi Mitsuhide	明智光秀
Altan Khan	俺答
Angŏlpo	安骨浦
Asano Nagayoshi	淺野長吉
Ashikaga Yoshimitsu	足利義滿
bao jian	寶劍
Beijing	北京
Bo Cheng'en	孛承恩
Bozhou	播州
Cao Xuecheng	曹學程
Chaoxian (Chosŏn)	朝鮮
Cheju Island	濟州島
Chen Lin	陳璘
Chen Yin	陳寅
Chiksan	稷山
Chin Island	珍島
Chingbirok	懲毖錄
Chinhae	鎮海
Chinju	晉州
Cho Hŏn	趙憲
Cho Kyŏngnam	趙慶男
Chŏlla	全羅

Chŏng Munbu	鄭文孚
Chŏng Pal	鄭撥
Chŏng Tak	鄭琢
Ch'ŏngju	清州
Chŏngmannok	征蠻錄
Chŏnju	全州
Choryŏng	鳥嶺
Ch'ungju	忠州
daimyo	大名
Deng Zilong	鄧子龍
Ding Yingtai	丁應泰
Dong Yiyuan	董一元
Donglin	東林
folangji (cannon)	佛郎機
Fujian	福建
Genso	玄蘇
Gu Yangqian	顧養謙
Gu Yingtai	谷應泰
Guangdong	廣東
Guangxi	廣西
Guizhou	貴州
Guoque	國榷
Haengju	幸州
Haman	咸安
Hamgyŏng	咸鏡
Han River	漢江
Hansan Island	閑山島
Hansŏng (Seoul)	漢城
Hapchŏn	陜川
He Qiaoyuan	何喬遠
Henan	河南
Hoeryŏng	會寧
Hŏnam	湖南
Hongwu	洪武
hucun pao	虎蹲砲
Huguang	湖廣
Hwang Sin	黃慎
Hwang Yungil	黃充吉
Hwanghae	黃海

Hyujŏng	休靜
Imhaegun	臨海君
Imjin River	臨津江
Imjin waeran	壬辰倭亂
Jiajing	嘉靖
Jiliao	薊遼
Jinglue fuguo yaobian	經略復國要編
Jixiao xinshu	紀效新書
jinshi	進士
Kadŏk Island	加德島
Kaesŏng	開城
kampaku	關白
Kang Hang	姜沆
Kangwŏn	江原
Katō Kiyomasa	加藤清正
Katō Yoshiaki	加藤嘉明
Keinen	慶念
Kim Ch'ŏnil	金千鎰
Kim Myŏngwŏn	金命元
Kim Sŏngil	金誠一
Kim Su	金晬
Kim Ŭngnam	金應南
Kim Ŭngsŏ	金應瑞
Kimhae	金海
Ko Ŏnbaek	高彥伯
Kobayakawa Takakage	小早川隆景
kobuksŏn (turtleboat)	龜船
Kŏje Island	巨濟島
Konishi Joan	小西如安
Konishi Yukinaga	小西行長
Kuroda Nagamasa	黑田長政
Kwak Chaeu	郭再祐
Kwanghaegun	光海君
Kwŏn Yul	權慄
Kyŏnggi	京畿
Kyŏngsang	慶尚
lang bing (Wolf troops)	狼兵
Li Chengliang	李成梁
Li Guangtao	李光濤

Li Hualong	李化龍
Li Rubo	李如柏
Li Rumei	李如梅
Li Rusong	李如松
Li Ruzhang	李如樟
Li Yousheng	李有昇
Li Zongcheng	李宗城
Liaodong	遼東
Liaohai	遼海
Liaoyang	遼陽
Liu Dongyang	劉動暘
Liu Ting	劉綎
Longqing	隆慶
Lu Kun	呂坤
Luo Shangzhi	駱尚志
Lushun	旅順
Ma Gui	麻貴
Mao Guoqi	茅國器
Mao Ruizheng	茅瑞徵
Mao Yuanyi	茅元儀
Mei Guozhen	梅國楨
Ming	明
Ming shi	明史
Ming shilu	明實錄
Mōri Hidemoto	毛利秀輝元
Myŏngnyang	鳴梁
Nagoya	名護屋
Nakpo	藥圃
Naktong River	洛東江
Namhae	南海
Namwŏn	南原
Nanjing	南京
Nanjung chamnok	亂中雜錄
Nanjung ilgi	亂中日記
Ningxia	寧夏
Noryang	露梁
Nurhaci	努爾哈赤
Ŏ Hŭimun	吳希文
Oda Nobunaga	織田信長

Okpo	玉蒲
Osaka	大阪
Ōta Kazuyoshi	太田一吉
Ōtomo Yoshimune	大友義統
Ping Bo quanshu	平播全書
Pubei	孛拜
Pusan	釜山
Pyŏkchegwan	碧蹄館
Pyongyang	平壤
Qi Jiguang	戚繼光
Qian Yiben	錢一本
Qu Jiusi	瞿九思
Ryukyu	琉球
Sachŏn	泗川
San da zheng	三大征
Sangju	尚州
Shaanxi	陝西
Shandong	山東
Shanhaiguan	山海關
Shanxi	山西
Shen Shixing	申時行
Shen Weijing	沈惟敬
Shen Yiguan	沈一貫
Shenzong (Wanli)	神宗
Shi Xing	石星
Shimazu Yoshihiro	島津義弘
shogun	將軍
Shuntian	順天
Sichuan	四川
Sin Ip	申砬
Sŏ Yewŏn	徐禮元
Sō Yoshitoshi	宗義智
Song Sanghyŏn	宗象賢
Song Yingchang	宋應昌
Songju	星州
Sŏnjo	宣祖
Sŏsaengpo	西生浦
Sun Kuang	孫礦
Sunchŏn	順川

Swaemirok	瑣尾錄
Taedong River	大同江
Taegu	大邱
taikō	太閣
Tan Lun	譚綸
Tan Qian	談遷
Tianjin	天津
tidu	提督
Tōdō Takatora	藤堂高虎
Tokugawa Ieyasu	德川家康
Tŏngnae	東萊
Tŏsan	突山
Toyotomi Hideyoshi	豐臣秀吉
Tsushima	對馬島
Tu Wenxiu	土文秀
tuntian (military farms)	屯田
ŭibyŏng	義兵
Ŭiju	義州
Ukita Hideie	宇喜多秀家
Ulsan	蔚山
Ungchŏn	熊川
Waegyŏ	曳橋
Wan Shide	萬世德
Wang Chonggu	王崇古
Wanli	萬曆
Wanli dichao	萬曆邸鈔
Wei Xueceng	魏學曾
wokou (wakō)	倭寇
Wŏn Kyun	元均
Wu Guang	吳廣
Wu Weizhong	吳惟忠
Wubei zhi	武備志
Xing Jie	邢玠
Xu Guanlan	徐觀瀾
Yalu River	鴨綠江
Yang Fangheng	楊方亨
Yang Hao	楊鎬
Yang Wen	楊文
Yang Yinglong	楊應龍

Yang Yuan	楊元
Yangsan	梁山
Ye Mengxiong	葉夢熊
Yi Dynasty	李朝
Yi Hangbok	李恆福
Yi Il	李鎰
Yi No	李魯
Yi Ŏkki	李億祺
Yi Sunsin	李舜臣
Yi T'akyŏng	李擢英
Yi Tŏkhyŏng	李德馨
Yi Wŏn'ik	李元翼
Yongsa ilgi	龍蛇日記
Yongsan	龍山
Yōzira	要時羅
Yu Sŏngnyong	柳成龍
Yujŏng	惟政
Yun Tusu	尹斗壽
Zha Dashou	查大受
Zhang Juzheng	張居正
Zhang Wei	張位
Zhang Weizhong	張維忠
Zhao Zhigao	趙志皋
Zhejiang	浙江
Zhu Yijun (Wanli)	朱翊鈞
Zhu Yuanzhang	朱元璋
Zhuge Yuansheng	著葛元聲
Zu Chengxun	祖承訓

NOTES

ABBREVIATIONS USED IN THE NOTES

BOC	B. Choi, *Book of Corrections*[*CBR* in translation]
CBR	Yu Sŏngnyong, *Chingbirok*
CHC 7	Mote and Twitchett, *Cambridge History of China, Volume 7*
CHC 8	Mote and Twitchett, *Cambridge History of China, Volume 8*
CHJ	J. Hall, *Cambridge History of Japan Volume 4*
CMN	Yi T., *Chŏngmannok*
CNE	Kuwata and Yamaoka, *Chōsen no eki*
CPC	Sin Kyŏng, *Zaizao fanbang zhi* [*Chaejo pŏnbang chi*]
CS	Hon Kyōan, *Chōsen seibatsuki*
CXSL	Li Guangtao, *Chaoxian "Renchen Wohuo" shi liao*
DMB	Goodrich and Fang, *Dictionary of Ming Biography*
ECCP	Hummel, *Eminent Chinese of the Ch'ing Period*
FGYB	Song Y., *Jinglue fuguo yaobian*
GQ	Tan Qian, *Guoque*
HMJSWB	Chen Z. et al., *Huang Ming jingshi wenbian*
IC	Lee Chong-young, *Imjin Changch'o*
IWSC	Han et al., *Imjin waeran saryŏ ch'ongso*
MHY	Long, *Ming huiyao*
MS	Zhang T. et al., *Ming shi*
MSG	Wang H., *Ming shigao*
MSJSBM	Gu, *Ming shi jishi benmo*
MSL	Yao et al., *Ming shilu*
MTJ	Xia, *Ming tongjian*
NC	Cho Kyŏngnam, *Nanjung chamnok*
NI	Sohn, *Nanjung Ilgi*

NYI   Chŏng T., *Nakp'o yongsa ilgi*
PBQS   Li H., *Ping Bo quan shu*
PRL   Zhuge, *Liang chao ping rang lu*
PXGJ   Zhi. *Ping xi guanjian*
SDZK   Mao R., *Wanli san da zheng kao*
SI   Kawaguchi, *Seikan iryaku*
SMR   Ŏ, *Swaemirok*
STS   Yujŏng, *Songun Taesa Punch'ung sŏnallok*
WBZ   Mao Y., *Wubei zhi*
WGL   Qu, *Zuben Wanli wu gong lu*
WKSL   Zheng L., *Ming dai Wokou shiliao*
WLDC   Qian Y., *Wanli dichao*
XZJ   Mei, *Xi zheng ji*
YI   Yi N., *Yŏngsa ilgi*
YM   Chŏng T., *Longwan wen jian lu* [*Yongman mun'gyŏnnok*]
ZDSJ   Qian S., *Zheng dong shiji*

PREFACE

1. Two English-language works on the war have recently appeared: Turnbull, *Samurai Invasion;* and Hawley, *Imjin War.* See my review of these works in Kenneth M. Swope, "Perspectives on the Imjin War," *Journal of Korean Studies* 12.1 (Fall 2007): 154–61.

2. For Huang's evaluation of the Three Great Campaigns, see *CHC 7,* 563.

3. Zhang H., *Zhang Juzheng,* 29–32. For biographies of Zhang Juzheng, see Crawford, "Chang Chü-cheng's Life and Thought"; R. Huang, *1587,* 1–41; and *DMB,* 53–61. For a more recent examination of Zhang, see Miller, "State Versus Society," 98–184. On silver and its role in the Ming economy, see Moloughney and Xia, "Silver and the Fall of the Ming," 51–78; Atwell, "International Bullion Flows," 68–90; and Atwell, "Notes on Silver," 1–33.

4. *MS,* 295. Chinese emperors were typically known by three designations: their personal names, reign titles used while they were alive as honorifics, and temple names used after their deaths for imperial sacrifices and other ceremonies. In the Ming and Qing periods, Chinese emperors generally had only one reign title, which are usually used to refer to the individual in question, even though this is not technically correct. Thus Wanli is the reign title for Zhi Yijun, whose temple name is Ming Shenzong. I discuss the traditional view of Wanli at length in my dissertation, "Three Great Campaigns," 1–39.

5. Harry S. Miller has also arrived at a revisionist interpretation of Wanli's reign that dovetails with my own at times but focuses more on Wanli's relationship with eunuch officials of the inner court. "State Versus Society," 185–343.

6. Lorge, *War, Politics, and Society,* 178; E. Park, *Between Dreams and Reality.*

INTRODUCTION. THE UNFORGOTTEN WAR

1. Turnbull, *Samurai Invasion,* 195; Kim Hong-kyu, *Hideyoshi mimizuka yonhyaku nen,* 66; McCormack, "Reflections on Modern Japanese History,"

276. The standard English-language biography of Hideyoshi is Berry, *Hideyoshi*. There are too many in Japanese to enumerate here, but for a solid foundation, see Kuwata, *Toyotomi Hideyoshi, Taikōki no kenkyū*, and *Toyotomi Hideyoshi kenkyū*. The title *kampaku* designates an imperial regent for an adult emperor and was bestowed upon Hideyoshi in 1585. He later assumed the mantle of taikō, or "retired imperial regent," after designating his nephew and successor, Hidetsugu, as regent in 1591. Berry, *Hideyoshi*, 178–81.

The general practice throughout premodern East Asia for proving one's battle prowess was collecting the severed left ears of opponents, though this practice often led to atrocities against innocent civilians. Commanders were expected to provide heads. On the presence of nose-less Koreans throughout the south for decades after the war, see *NC*, 8:137.

2. Kitajima, *Hideyoshi no Chōsen shinryaku*, 83–85; *CNE*, 305. For sample lists of noses, ears. and heads taken, see Kitajima, *Hideyoshi no Chōsen shinryaku*, 83; and Katō Noriaki's chapter in Kim Hŏng-kyu, *Hideyoshi mimizuka yonhyaku nen*, 69–73. These figures are taken from the chronicles of the various daimyo houses that participated in the invasion.

3. This conference, A Transnational History of the Imjin Waeran: The East Asian Dimension, was organized by Dr. Chung Doo-hee of Sogang University in Seoul. The conference volumes appeared in 2007.

4. Kim Hŏng-kyu, *Hideyoshi mimizuka yonhyaku nen*; Kristof, "Japan, Korea, and 1597" (accessed online). Samuel Hawley concurs, calling the memory of the war "a subtext to the resentment and at times animosity that Koreans still feel toward the Japanese for their occupation of the peninsula from 1910 to 1945." Hawley, *Imjin War*, 134.

5. Han, "Evaluation of the Activities of Ming Forces," 391; Neves, "Portuguese in the Im-Jim War," 20–24; Cory, "Father Gregorio des Cespedes"; Turnbull, *Samurai Invasion*, 172–74. Hideyoshi tried to purchase warships via Jesuit missionaries in Japan, and at least a few European priests accompanied his armies to Korea as spiritual advisers, providing some of the first direct information about the peninsula to European audiences.

6. *CXSL*, 1. Jahyun Kim Haboush has utilized a more qualified designation, referring to the war as Asia's first regional world war, which I believe connotes the same thing. See Haboush, "Dead Bodies in the Postwar Discourse," 415.

7. Kitajima, *Hideyoshi no Chōsen shinryaku*, 1. The imperial Japanese army conducted extensive studies of their old castles while in Korea. Ōta, "Gunbu ni yoru Bunroku-Keichō no eki no jōkaku kenkyū," 35–48.

8. *CXSL*, 1.

9. Wang's and Li's publications spanned some forty years, from the 1940s through the 1980s.

10. *CXSL*, 1.

11. Elleman, *Modern Chinese Warfare*, 233–309.

12. Bruce Batten calls these Sino-Korean conflicts, which lasted from 598–663, an "East Asian World War." *Gateway to Japan*, 18–23. Kenneth Robinson has vigorously argued the same position in a number of conversations with the author. On the Koguryŏ war and the fall of the Sui, see Graff, *Medieval Chinese Warfare*, 138–59.

13. Batten, *Gateway to Japan*, 22–23; Graff, *Medieval Chinese Warfare*, 198–200. Later Japanese militarists and expansionists often referred to Kaya as a Korean colony of Japan, but Bruce Batten suggests that it might be better considered as a trading outpost through which Japanese military services were exchanged for superior Korean goods. *Gateway to Japan*, 16–17.

14. Batten, *Gateway to Japan*, 24–31.

15. Many of these letters are translated in Kuno, *Japanese Expansion*, 1:300–326.

16. Ikeuchi, *Bunroku keichō no eki*, 1. For Meiji-era scholarship with nationalistic undertones, see, for example, Nakamura Tokugoro, "Ni-Min kōwa haretsu shi temmatsu," 957–83.

17. The Korean reforms are discussed at length in Palais, *Confucian State-craft and Korean Institutions*. Qi's most notable military manuals were *Jixiao xinshu* [A New Treatise on Training] and *Lianbing shiji* [An Account of Drilling Troops]. On Qi's influence in Korea, see Fan Zhongyi, *Qi Jiguang zhuan*, 579–52. On postwar Korean military reforms, see E. Park, *Between Dreams and Reality*, 50–60.

18. In addition to my own published works on the subject, see Kye, "Indirect Challenge," 423–29. For standard interpretations that stress the deleterious effects of the war for the Ming, see Han, "Evaluation of the Activities of Ming Forces," 391; and Hawley, *Imjin War*, 565–67.

1. WILD FRONTIERS

1. For a brief biography of Nurhaci, see *ECCP*, 594–99. For a discussion of the rise of the Latter Jin, see Wakeman, *Great Enterprise*, 49–66. For biographies of Li Chengliang, see *ECCP*, 450–52; and Swope, "A Few Good Men." On Nurhaci's relationship to Li, see Crossley, *Translucent Mirror*, 169–72. For more on Nurhaci's relationship with the Ming as a vassal and how it pertained to Korea, see Kye, "Indirect Challenge."

2. R. Huang, "Liao-tung Campaign," 30; *MS*, 6196. Note that Huang employs the older Wade-Giles system of Romanization of Chinese terms. For a detailed account of the campaign in English, see R. Huang, "Liao-tung Campaign." For a contemporary assessment, see Yu Y., *Chaonu yicuo*.

3. Waley-Cohen, "Civil-Military Relations in Imperial China," 4–7. For a general overview of the historiography of the Ming-Qing transition, see Struve, *Ming-Qing Conflict*.

4. Cao, *Wanli huangdi da zhuan*, 233. Late Ming factionalism has been addressed by a variety of recent authors. For more-standard explanations, see Dardess, *Blood and History*; and J. Zhao, "Decade of Considerable Significance." For a revisionist perspective, see Miller, "State Versus Society." For brief biographies of Yang Hao, see *ECCP*, 885–86; and Swope, "War and Remembrance." On Wanli's historiographical rehabilitation, in addition to the earlier mentioned works, see, for example, Cao, *Wanli huangdi da zhuan*; Fan S., *Wanli zhuan*; and Wang T. and Xu, *Ming chao shiliu di*, 310–44. Recently there was even a historical novel of his reign based on a dramatic television series: Hu, Tao, and Qian, *Wanli wangchao*.

5. Hucker, "Chu I-chün" [Wanli biography], in *DMB*, 324–38; *CHC* 7, 511–84; Mote, *Imperial China, 900–1800*, 1026n3; R. Huang, *1587*. Mote adds that Wanli "grew into a most perverse ruler, addicted to alcohol and sex, infinitely avaricious, and petulantly defiant toward his courtiers." *Imperial China*, 733–34. For another recent example of the continuing influence of such interpretations of Wanli, see J. Zhao, "Decade of Considerable Significance," 112–50.

6. Overviews of Wanli's running disputes with his officials can be found in *MS*, 261–92; *WLDC*; and *MSL*. The most concise traditional treatment of the major struggles is *MSJSBM*, 2386–2411. In English, see Dardess, *Blood and History*, 1–30.

7. Lorge, *War, Politics, and Society*, 2–3.

8. Lei and Lin, *Zhongguo wenhua yu Zhongguo di bing*, 94–103.

9. For characterizations of the Ming as defensive and insular, see Perdue, *China Marches West*, 56–72; and Waldron, *Great Wall*, 122–64. David Graff and Robin Higham contrast a "weak Ming China" with the more expansive part-foreign Tang dynasty in a recent survey work. *Military History of China*, 7. Also see Farmer, *Zhu Yuanzhang*, 17. Peter Lorge challenges such characterizations in *War, Politics, and Society*.

10. Gernet, *Chinese Civilization*, 431. Also see Chan, *Glory and Fall*, 187–210.

11. Fan Zhongyi, "Ming dai junshi sixiang jianlun," 38; Johnston, *Cultural Realism*, 27, 30. Sunzi's *Art of War* is one of these Chinese military classics.

12. Chase, *Firearms*, esp. 150–71. For a brief discussion of foreign firearms in late Ming China, see Li Y., "Mingmo dui hongyi pao de yinjin yu fazhan," 45–50.

13. Fan Zhongyi, "Ming dai junshi sixiang jianlun," 38–39; Sun Laichen, "Military Technology Transfers from Ming China," 495–517; Sun Laichen, "Ming–Southeast Asian Interactions," 31, 32, 35; Chase, *Firearms*, 166–71. For the classic discussion of the Military Revolution by the foremost proponent of its origins in the West, see Parker, *Military Revolution*. According to Parker, volley fire was not used until 1575 in Japan (by Hideyoshi's lord, Oda Nobunaga) and not until 1594 in Europe. *Military Revolution*, 19–20, 140–41. On the Qing integration of firearms into their armies, see Di Cosmo, "Did Guns Matter."

14. Needham et al., *Science and Civilisation*, vol. 5, pt. 6, 29.

15. Qi, *Jixiao xinshu*; Swope, "Cutting Dwarf Pirates"; Fan Zhongyi, "Ming dai junshi sixiang jianlun," 41. For more on the hereditary military system of the Ming, see *MS*, 2193–2234; Yu Z., *Ming dai junhu shi xi zhidu*; and Swope, "Three Great Campaigns," 43–54. For a discussion of later European efforts in this direction, see McNeill, *Pursuit of Power*, 125–40. For Qi's discussion of the use of different weapons, see *Jixiao xinshu*, 195–218. On the relationship between technology and tactics in Renaissance Europe, see B. Hall, *Weapons and Warfare in Renaissance Europe*, 210–16.

16. Qi, *Jixiao xinshu*, 219–81 (esp. illustrations); Fan Zhongyi, "Ming dai junshi sixiang jianlun," 42.

17. R. Huang, "Military Expenditures," 40; R. Huang, *Taxation and Finance*, 67. On the creation of the so-called *gou jun* system to replenish military strength, see Xu, "Ming dai de goujun." Desertion rates in contemporary

Europe, by comparison, ranged from one-seventh to one-half of recruits, who received enlistment bounties rather than simply being enrolled in the military registers. B. Hall, *Weapons and Warfare in Renaissance Europe*, 228.

18. Liew, *Treatises on Military Affairs*, 74–75, 364 (table); Swope, "Three Great Campaigns," 45–46; *MS*, 2204. Liew's work is an annotated translation of some of the military sections of the *Official History of the Ming Dynasty*.

19. Wang Yuquan, *Ming dai de juntian*; He Zhiqing and Wang, *Zhongguo bing zhi shi*, 253–58; *CHC 8*, 52–62; Liew, *Treatises on Military Affairs*, 48–76; *MS*, 2179; Tsai, *Eunuchs in the Ming Dynasty*, 59–97; D. Robinson, *Bandits, Eunuchs, and the Son of Heaven*, 99–120; *CHC 7*, 162–68; *MHY*, 1119–20.

20. R. Huang, *Taxation and Finance*, 67; *MS*, 2179. For a complete overview of the capital training divisions and garrisons, see Luo, "Ming dai jingying zhi xingcheng yu shuaibei."

21. *MS*, 2180; Liew, *Treatises on Military Affairs*, 81.

22. Lo W., "Self-Image of the Chinese Military," 1–6; Struve, *Southern Ming*, 6; Hucker, *Censorial System*, 34. Many of the commanders discussed herein were certainly literate, and several maintained close friendships with some of the leading artists and literati of their day.

23. *MS*, 2180, 2230. This was Machiavelli's assessment. See Mallett, "Mercenaries," 228.

24. *MS*, 2232; Chan, *Glory and Fall*, 201; Mallett, "Mercenaries," 228–29; He Zhiqing and Wang, *Zhongguo bing zhi shi*, 258–63; *MHY*, 1143. On the mercenary debate in Europe, see McNeill, *Pursuit of Power*, 73–77. Ming sources also mention the presence of the famed Shaolin Temple warrior monks, who allegedly were victorious in all their battles with Japanese pirates. *MS*, 2252. For more on local militia and minority troops, see Chen B., "Ming dai de minbing yu xiangbing."

25. See, for example, the discussion in *Tai Gong's Six Secret Teachings*, translated in Sawyer, *Seven Military Classics*, 33, 64–65.

26. R. Huang, *Taxation and Finance*, 25. On Wanli's alleged self-indulgence and greed, see Huai, *Shiliu shiji Zhongguo de zhengzhi fengyun*, 298–99.

27. Crawford, "Chang Chü-cheng's Confucian Legalism," 367, 370; Miller, "State Versus Society," 87 (Zhang quote), 109–15; *GQ*, 4252; Crawford, "Chang Chü-cheng's Life and Thought." There are many biographical studies of Zhang in Chinese and English. For a good introduction, see *DMB*, 53–61. On the relationship between the throne and officialdom in the late Ming, see R. Huang, *1587*; Miller, "State Versus Society"; Huai, *Shiliu shiji Zhongguo de zhengzhi fengyun*; Fan S., *Wan Ming shi*, 476–627; and J. Zhao, "Decade of Considerable Significance."

28. Zhang H., *Zhang Juzheng*, 29–60; R. Huang, *1587*, 16–26, 69–70; *GQ*, 4193. For more on Zhang's reforms during the first decade of Wanli's reign, see Fan S., *Wan Ming shi*, 204–310; and Huai, *Shiliu shiji Zhongguo de zhengzhi fengyun*, 237–55. . Zhang was angry that his contemporaries saw his reforms as solely designed to enrich the state and strengthen the army. Miller, "State Versus Society," 158.

29. Crawford, "Chang Chü-cheng's Confucian Legalism," 404. On the links between Zhang and factional strife, see J. Zhao, "Decade of Considerable

Significance"; and Huai, *Shiliu shiji Zhongguo de zhengzhi fengyun*, 244–62. Zhao blames Zhang's successor, Shen Shixing, more than Zhang himself. "Decade of Considerable Significance," 141.

30. *CHC* 7, 520; Miller, "State Versus Society," 88–90. For a full discussion of Ming military operations during the Wanli reign, see *WGL*.

31. Fan S., *Wanli zhuan*, 227; Wanli quoted in R. Huang, *1587*, 233.

32. Fan S., *Wanli zhuan*, 227. For a brief overview of Ming military actions along the frontiers in the 1580s and 1590s, see *MS*, 267–71; Swope, "Civil-Military Coordination," 49–70; Swope, "Deceit, Disguise, and Dependence," 757–82; and Swope, "All Men Are Not Brothers," 79–129.

33. Zhuan Z. et al., *Zhongguo junshi shi*, 397. On the peace settlement with Altan Khan, see Serruys, "Four Documents."

34. Fan S., *Wanli zhuan*, 228.

35. *SDZK*, 13; *GQ*, 4667; Cao, *Wanli huangdi da zhuan*, 233.

36. *PRL*, 116; Fan S., *Wanli zhuan*, 228; *MS*, 5977.

37. *HMJSWB*, 25:30; *WLDC*, 648; *MSL*, 4585; *PRL*, 124; *MTJ*, 2719. For details on the outbreak of the mutiny, see Swope, "All Men Are Not Brothers," 91–96.

38. *WGL*, 100a–100b; *SDZK*, 18. Ma's father had battled Altan Khan in the 1560s. *MS*, 6199–6203. Xuanda is a contraction of the combined military commands of Xuanfu and Datong.

39. *MS*, 5977. Details on Wei's career can be found in ibid., 5975–77. He was one of the few officials to speak out against Zhang Juzheng during the height of the latter's power and survive relatively unscathed.

40. *XZJ*, 1, 12a; *WLDC*, 660; *MS*, 5979.

41. *XZJ*, 1, 6b, 9b.

42. *MSL*, 4593; *XZJ*, 1, 3a; *HMJSWB*, 25:31–32.

43. *WLDC*, 660–62. Li Rusong and Li Rubo in particular had been accused of arrogance and high-handed behavior toward their civil counterparts, including slapping officials. Both had been censured on several occasions but had been cleared repeatedly by Wanli. *MS*, 6192.

44. *XZJ*, 1, 6b, 7b, 15a; *WLDC*, 661–62; *MSL*, 4602; Zhang Jincheng, *Qianlong Ningxia fuzhi*, 410; *MS*, 6192; *MTJ*, 2722.

45. *WGL*, 108a; *PXGJ*, 89–90.

46. *SDZK*, 23.

47. Fan S., *Wanli zhuan*, 232; *SDZK*, 24.

48. *WGL*, 112b; *SDZK*, 23; *MTJ*, 2726; *MSJSBM*, 2381; *WLDC*, 691.

49. Sawyer, *Fire and Water*, 284.

50. *PRL*, 155; *GQ*, 4676; *MS*, 275.

51. *SDZK*, 25.

52. Ibid., 26; *MTJ*, 2728.

53. *SDZK*, 27; *MTJ*, 2728; *XZJ*, 2, 17b; *PXGJ*, 22–23.

54. *SDZK*, 28; *PXGJ*, 27; *MTJ*, 2730.

55. *SDZK*, 29; *MTJ*, 2730.

56. The rebellion of Yang Yinglong is treated in much more detail in Swope, "Civil-Military Coordination"; and Swope, "Three Great Campaigns," chap. 7. A biography of Yang can be found in *DMB*, 1553–56. The earlier history

of the Yangs in Bozhou is recounted in *WGL*, 500a; and Huang Y., *Zunyi fuzhi*, 681–88.

57. Huang Y., *Zunyi fuzhi*, 689; Okano, "Yō Ōryō no ran ni tsuite," 63–66; *SDZK*, 65–66.

58. *MSJSBM*, 2383; *SDZK*, 66; *MSL*, 6631; Huang Y., *Zunyi fuzhi*, 900–901.

59. *MS*, 8045. For biographies of Li Hualong, see *DMB*, 822–26; and *MS*, 5982–87.

60. *PRL*, 419; Cao, *Wanli huangdi da zhuan*, 241.

61. See Li's letter of appointment in *PBQS*, 1. For a biography of Guo, see *DMB*, 775–77.

62. *WGL*, 522a; *MS*, 5985.

63. *PBQS*, 401, 413, 471–72, 650.

64. *WLDC*, 1177. The full text of Wanli's decree can be found in *PBQS*, 477–82.

65. *PBQS*, 96–97, 703; *MTJ*, 2801.

66. *MSJSBM*, 2384. For details of the speech, see Swope, "Three Great Campaigns," 423–24.

67. *PBQS*, 287; *MTJ*, 2811; *GQ*, 4866.

68. On Ming expansion in the southwest, see L. Shin, *Making of the Chinese State.*

69. Swope, "A Few Good Men"; *MS*, 6197.

2. DARK SAILS ON THE HORIZON

1. E. Kang, *Diplomacy and Ideology*, 13–14; Haboush and Deuchler, *Culture and the State in Late Chosŏn Korea*, 70–72; Elison, "Inseparable Trinity," 235–300. Ming-Korean families are the subject of a doctoral dissertation by Adam Bohnet at the University of Toronto, with an anticipated completion date of 2008. For an overview of evolving Ming perceptions of the Japanese, see the essays in Fogel, *Sagacious Monks and Bloodthirsty Warriors*, 1–62.

2. On these events from a Japanese perspective, see *CNE*, 55–57.

3. E. Kang, *Diplomacy and Ideology*, 2. For an overview of the Muromachi shogunate in Japan, see Grossberg, *Japan's Renaissance*. Grossberg also examines the foreign policy of Ashikaga Yoshimitsu (r. 1368–94). Ibid., 33–37. For a lively but dated account, see Sansom, *History of Japan*, 167–80. The history of Ming relations with Korea and Japan can be found in *MS*, 8279–8308, 8341–60 (respectively). The history of Sino-Japanese relations during the Ming is covered in Zheng L., *Ming dai Zhong-Ri guanxi.*

4. Haboush and Deuchler, *Culture and the State in Late Chosŏn Korea*, 68; *CPC*, 1. Other tributary states also were asked to supply eunuchs and women. See Tsai, *Eunuchs in the Ming Dynasty*, 14–17; and *CHC 8*, 291–93. For a more thorough discussion of the Chinese-Korean tributary relationship, see *CHC 8*, 272–300.

5. The Chinese sent the Koreans copies of the *Four Books* and the *Six Classics*, thereby stressing the Confucian virtues of their new empire as opposed to the Mongols. See *MS*, 8280. A biography of Yi Sŏnggye can be found in *DMB*, 1598–1603. Also see K. Lee, *New History of Korea*, 162–65. The disputes over

Yi's seizure of power form the backdrop of the Sino-Korean feature film *Musa* [The Warrior], released in 2001 (edited and released in the United States as *Musa: The Warrior*).

6. *MS*, 8283; *DMB*, 356. The name Chosŏn is usually translated as "Land of the Morning Calm," and as was the case for many Chinese dynasties, the name hearkened back to an ancient designation for Korea.

7. *CHC* 8, 280–93; *CPC*, 4–8; *MS*, 8284–85. For an overview of the tribute missions and their conduct, see K. Robinson, "Policies of Practicality," 29–40.

8. *CHC* 8, 281; *MS*, 8285. For essays on tributary relations throughout Chinese history, see Fairbank, *Chinese World Order*. For a discussion of how Korea and Japan fit into this order, see Nakamura H., *Nihon to Chōsen*, 1–4.

9. *CHC* 8, 282–83. Many Chinese ambassadors to Korea were eunuchs, some even of Korean descent. These envoys were sometimes charged with rounding up girls for the imperial harem. For more on eunuch-diplomats in Korea, see Tsai, *Eunuchs in the Ming Dynasty*, 135–40.

10. K. Robinson, "Policies of Practicality," vi, 20.

11. On Korean approaches to the Jurchen problem, see K. Robinson, "From Raiders to Traders."

12. *CHJ*, 239; Hazard, "Formative Years of the Wakô"; *MS*, 8342, 8346; K. Robinson, "Policies of Practicality," 104–105. After their unsuccessful raid the Koreans continued to regard Tsushima as occupied territory. See J. Lewis, *Frontier Contact*, esp. chap. 1.

13. *CHJ*, 242–45. For more on the roles played by the rulers of Tsushima in Korean-Japanese relations, see K. Robinson, "An Island's Place in History"; and "Tsushima Governor and Regulation of Contact."

14. Sansom, *History of Japan*, 170–71, 173, *CNE*, 57. Etsuko Hae-jin Kang concurs, stating that Yoshimitsu wanted to both strengthen the power of the shogun and by extension, the bakufu, and gain the profits of foreign trade. In 1863 samurai loyalists decapitated a statue of Yoshimitsu because they felt he had humiliated himself and Japan by accepting investiture from the Ming. *Diplomacy and Ideology*, 33–36.

15. *CHJ*, 245–48; K. Robinson, "Imposter Branch." For more on Korean maritime diplomacy, particularly the trade in Buddhist scriptures, see K. Robinson, "Centering the King of Chosŏn." One clash between Koreans and Japanese in the 1570s allegedly turned Seoul's Han River crimson. *CPC*, 9.

16. Wakeman, "China and the Seventeenth-Century Crisis," 3; Jansen, *China in the Tokugawa World*, 25; Wang Yong, "Images of 'Dwarf Pirates,'" 21. On the massive expansion of foreign trade, particularly the silver trade from the Americas to Asia in the late sixteenth century, see Flynn and Giraldez, "Born with a 'Silver Spoon'"; Atwell, "Notes on Silver"; and Moloughney and Xia, "Silver and the Fall of the Ming." For a broader discussion of the implications of the silver trade for East Asian economies in the sixteenth and seventeenth centuries, see Von Glahn, *Fountain of Fortune*, 96–138; and *CHC* 8, 376–416. For a full discussion of the *wokou* phenomenon, see So, *Japanese Piracy in Ming China*; and Fan Zhongyi and Tong, *Ming dai wokou shilue*.

17. On the use of monks as diplomats, see Osa, "Keitetsu Genso," 135–47; and K. Robinson, "Policies of Practicality," 485–90.

18. K. Robinson, "Centering the King of Chosŏn." Some have argued that this was the reason earlier Japanese states often eschewed formal involvement in the Chinese tributary order. See Jansen, *China in the Tokugawa World*, 2.

19. For a reexamination of Korea's tributary roles in northeast Asia, see Yun, "Rethinking the Tribute System."

20. There are far too many biographies of Hideyoshi in Japanese to enumerate here. For a traditional account by his personal physician, see Oze, *Taikō-ki*. Research on this source can be found in Kuwata, *Taikō-ki no kenkyū*. For a modern biography in Japanese, see Kuwata, *Toyotomi Hideyoshi*. In English, see Berry, *Hideyoshi*. On the phenomenon known as *gekokujō*, see the introduction to J. Hall et al., *Japan before Tokugawa*, 7–26. Osaka Castle, Hideyoshi's seat of power, was reconstructed in 1931 and now houses a fine museum of artifacts related to him and his age, including letters sent by samurai on campaign in Korea, many of which are reproduced in Watanabe T., *Hideyoshi to Momoyama bunka*.

21. Cao, *Wanli huangdi da zhuan*, 260; *CNE*, 59; Turnbull, *Samurai*, 186; Li Guangtao, *Ming-Qing dang'an*, 779; Wang Yong, "Images of 'Dwarf Pirates,'" 36. For the myth of Hideyoshi's birth, which is repeated by Hideyoshi himself often in letters to foreign rulers, see Berry, *Hideyoshi*, 8–9; and Kuno, *Japanese Expansion*, 1:302.

22. Yamazaki is discussed in Turnbull, *Samurai Sourcebook*, 275–79. For a discussion of Hideyoshi's domestic policies, see John Whitney Hall's essay in J. Hall et al., *Japan before Tokugawa*, 194–223. On Hideyoshi's relationship with the Japanese imperial family and his quest for legitimacy, see Berry, *Hideyoshi*, 176–205. For a discussion of his military campaigns between 1582 and 1590, see ibid., 66–98.

23. Fujiki and Kitajima, *Shokuhō seiken*, 277, 278. Part of the conversation with Frois appears in Berry, *Hideyoshi*, 207–208. For a discussion of the portrayal of the war in Korea in Frois's histories of Japan, see Matsuda, *Hideyoshi to Bunroku no eki*. Also see Yanigada, "Bunroku Keichō no Eki to kirisitan senkyōshi," 19. On the reasons for Hideyoshi's prohibition of Christianity, see *CNE*, 21–24.

24. *MS*, 8357. The *Ming shi* maintains that the Japanese acquired Ming cannon from Fujianese traders. *MS*, 8290–91. Also see Brown, "Impact of Firearms on Japanese Warfare," 236–53; and Parker, *Military Revolution*, 140–43. Most of Hideyoshi's information about China came from natives of Fujian and Zhejiang. Many Chinese did help the Japanese during the invasion, and several commanders had trusted Chinese advisers. Li Guangtao, *Ming-Qing dang'an*, 778–81.

25. *MS*, 8357; *CPC*, 9, 58–59; *CMN*, 430; E. Kang, *Diplomacy and Ideology*, 88–90; *BOC*, 21.

26. *CNE*, 60.

27. K. Robinson, "Policies of Practicality," 375–76. On Genso, see Osa, "Keitetsu Genso." Fujiki Hisashi and Kitajima Manji, citing the *Chōsen seibatsuki*, discuss this possibility. *Shokuhō seiken*, 286–87. Also see *CS*, 1, 1a–5a.

28. *CNE*, 60. Hideyoshi's instructions to the Sō can be found in Fujiki and Kitajima, *Shokuhō seiken*, 280–81. Yoshitoshi is also identified as Sō Yoshitomo in some sources. The complex negotiations between the Koreans and Japanese leading up to the invasion are discussed in Li Guangtao, "Chaoxian renchen Wohuo niangxin shishi," in *Ming-Qing dang'an*, 737–68.

29. *BOC*, 22–23; *CPC*, 22–23; *SI*, 474–75.

30. *BOC*, 23; *SI*, 478, 479; *NC*, 7:17; *CPC*, 46.

31. *BOC*, 25.

32. *SI*, 482; *CPC*, 24; *NC*, 7:21; Weems, *Hulbert's History of Korea*, 1:346; For Cho's quote and his assessment of the threat in a memorial from 1591, see Cho H., *Chungbŏng chip*, 299–303.

33. Choi S., "Factional Struggle," 60–70.

34. Ibid., 72–79, 80–81; *NC*, 7:21–22; Li Guangtao, *Ming-Qing dang'an*, 748.

35. *CPC*, 24.

36. E. Kang, *Diplomacy and Ideology*, 73; *BOC*, 28–29; *CXSL*, 1893–94.

37. *SI*, 485; Kuno, *Japanese Expansion*, 1:302. The full text of the letter is translated in ibid., 1:301–302.

38. Turnbull, *Samurai*, 187; Kitajima, *Hideyoshi no Chōsen shinryaku*, 8–9; *BOC*, 29–30; Li Guangtao, *Ming-Qing dang'an*, 749. On the siege of Odawara, see *CS*, 1, pp. 5a–6a.

39. *CPC*, 33.

40. The full text of the letter is translated in Kuno, *Japanese Expansion*, 1:302–303. I have modified Kuno's translation slightly. Another slightly different translation can be found in Berry, *Hideyoshi*, 208. Berry takes the three countries to mean China, Japan, and India, which was Hideyoshi's final destination. Also see Murdoch, *History of Japan Vol. II*, 308–10. For the original letter, see *NC*, 7:35–36.

41. Li Guangtao, *Ming-Qing dang'an*, 750–51; *CXSL*, 1893; *NC*, 7:36; *SI*, 489. On the role of deception and forgery in Japanese-Korean diplomatic relations, see Stramigioli, "Hideyoshi's Expansionist Policy," 75–78. For details on the mission, see *CXSL*, 1893–95. For more on the negotiations between Korea and Japan and the role of the Sō family in them, see Kim Hong-kyu, *Hideyoshi mimizuka yonhyaku nen*, 32–42.

42. *CXSL*, 1894.

43. This translation, slightly modified, is taken from Kuno, *Japanese Expansion*, 1:303–304.

44. *CPC*, 37–38, 48.

45. *NC*, 7:37; *CPC*, 40, 66–67. Provinces were designated left or right based on how they were viewed from the throne in Seoul.

46. *NC*, 7:41–42; *CMN*, 437. Privately, however, the Japanese did worry about such things as the range and strength of Korean bows, the difficulties of maintaining long overseas supply lines, and the contingencies of Ming aid.

47. Murdoch, *History of Japan Vol. II*, 311; *CNE*, 62–63; *CXSL*, 1902; *SI*, 492.

48. Li Guangtao, *Ming-Qing dang'an*, 756; *CPC*, 48–51; *CMN*, 429–30; *CXSL*, 1903–1904. On the relationship of the Ryukyus to China, Korea, and Japan at this time, see Suganuma, "Sino-Liuqiu and Japanese-Liuqiu Relations," esp. 47–53. On Hideyoshi's desire to enlist the Ryukyu islanders in his war, see Fairbank, *Chinese World Order*, 116–17; and *CMN*, 437.

49. *CXSL*, 10.

50. *SI*, 492–93, 495; *CPC*, 48; Kitajima, *Hideyoshi no Chōsen shinryaku*, 14. According to the *Chosŏn sillok*, some 300 Koreans submitted to the Japanese in 1591 and assisted them in building boats for the impending invasion. *CXSL*, 1.

51. It is unclear precisely which states these were since they are simply identified as the countries of the south seas (*nan yang*) in sources. This may be a reference to the islands around the Philippines or perhaps Hainan Island. Hideyoshi also sent a mission to Taiwan, called the "country of the tall mountains" (*gao shan*) in Chinese.

52. Li Guangtao, *Ming-Qing dang'an*, 757; Zheng L., *Ming dai Zhong-Ri guanxi*, 535–36.

53. Song M., *Jiuyue qianji*, 4b; *MS*, 8291, 8357; *CS*, 1, 13b–15a; *CXSL*, 1904–1905; Zheng L., *Ming dai Zhong-Ri guanxi*, 564–65; Li Guangtao, *Ming-Qing dang'an*, 760; He B. et al., *Ming Shenzong yu Ming Dingling*, 100; *WKSL*, 474.

54. *PRL*, 233; *SI*, 481; Sansom, *History of Japan*, 346. Hideyoshi's letters to the rulers of the Ryukyus, the Philippines, Taiwan, and India are translated in Kuno, *Japanese Expansion*, 1:305–14. Hideyoshi's ignorance of the outside world is revealed by his letter to the ruler of Taiwan, for at the time no such authority existed. Projected lists of the number of troops, supplies, mounts, and the like can be found in Li Guangtao, *Ming-Qing dang'an*, 757. For an examination of the expedition to Korea as seen through the eyes of Jesuits in Japan, see Yanigada, "Bunroku Keichō no Eki to kirisitan senkyōshi," 19–39. On the desire to unite East Asian traditions, see Zheng L., *Ming dai Zhong-Ri guanxi*, 538–39.

55. Fujiki and Kitajima, *Shokuhō seiken*, 301–303; Wolters, "Ayudhya," 167. Thus he continued to demand cession of part of Korea during peace talks to "save face." It is illuminating that Hideyoshi was dismayed when invested as a subject king of the Ming *without* gaining the right to participate in tribute trade, his pride grievously damaged by this dismissive gesture.

56. E. Kang, *Diplomacy and Ideology*, 84–85.

57. Berry, *Hideyoshi*, 213; Hur N., "International Context," 697–98. Park Yune-hee also suggests that the war was impelled in part by the territorial and trade ambitions of various powerful daimyo. *Admiral Yi*, 24.

58. Murdoch, *History of Japan Vol. II*, 306; Hawley, *Imjin War*, 22–24; *CHJ*, 268.

59. *CS*, 1, 7a–18b; Oze, *Taikō-ki*, 347–48; *CMN*, 437; Fogel, *Sagacious Monks and Bloodthirsty Warriors*, 57; *PRL*, 235–36. A summary of Japanese interpretations of war aims is found in Kitajima, *Chōsen nichinichiki*, 17–19. For an analysis of *Chōsen seibatsuki*, see Boot, "Chōsen Seibatsu." For a biography of Xu Guangqi, who was a famous Christian convert, see *ECCP*, 316–19. Also see C. Chang and S. Chang, *Crisis and Transformation*, 287–98.

60. Zheng L., *Ming dai Zhong-Ri guanxi*, 543, 544.

61 Hawley, *Imjin War*, 76; Fujiki and Kitajima, *Shokuhō seiken*, 289, 290; Nakura, "Hideyoshi no Chōsen," 33–34. On the relationship between the invasion of Korea and the development of Japan's military and agricultural systems, see Miki S., "Chōsen eki ni okeru."

62. Zhu, "Ming dai yuan Chao," 155; S. Takagi, "Hideyoshi's Peace," 56–62.

63. Zheng L., *Ming dai Zhong-Ri guanxi*, 549–50; S. D. Kim, "Korean Monk-Soldiers," 8–10.

64. Nakura, "Hideyoshi no Chōsen," 29–35; Ooms, *Tokugawa Ideology*, 44, 46, 49; S. Takagi, "Hideyoshi's Peace," 63. For a recent historiographic

essay about foreign affairs and frontiers in early modern Japan, see B. Walker, "Foreign Affairs and Frontiers."

65. Li Guangtao, *Chaoxian (Renchen Wohuo) Yanjiu*, 10–11. Other scholars have argued that had the Chinese allowed Japan to reestablish formal trade relations, the invasion would have been called off. See Stramigioli, "Hideyoshi's Expansionist Policy," 96–97.

66. Zheng L., *Ming dai Zhong-Ri guanxi*, 550–51; Kuno, *Japanese Expansion*, 1:314–17. These directives were sent to his heir, Hidetsugu, about one month after the start of the invasion.

67. Zheng L., *Ming dai Zhong-Ri guanxi*, 563. Hulbert states that the Japanese invasion force of 250,000 men (including reserves) had 50,000 mounts, 5,000 battle axes, 100,000 katana, 100,000 wakizashi, 500,000 daggers, and 300,000 firearms, mostly arquebuses. See Weems, *Hulbert's History of Korea*, 1:350.

68. *CNE*, 67; Lynn, *Tools of War*, 32.

69. Sansom, *History of Japan*, 353. Sansom's figures are taken from the archives of the Mōri family. Also see Zheng L., *Ming dai Zhong-Ri guanxi*, 559–62. Zheng gives these figures and also lists how many troops and supplies were levied from certain areas. Also see Kitajima, *Chōsen nichinichiki*, 36; Turnbull, *Samurai Invasion*, 240; and *SI*, 496–98.

70. A *koku* constituted the amount of rice needed to feed one person for a year. It became the system whereby daimyo wealth and power was calculated in Hideyoshi's Japan. For more on the so-called *kokudaka* system as it pertained to the invasion of Korea, see Miki Seiichirō, "Taikō kenchi to Chōsen shuppei," in *Iwanami kōza Nihon rekishi*, 9:81–87.

71. Oze, *Taikō-ki*, 356; Miki S., "Chōsen eki ni okeru," 141–45; Hawley, *Imjin War*, 95, 594; Murdoch, *History of Japan Vol. II*, 313 On people hiding from conscription, see Oze, *Taikō-ki*, 361.

72. *SI*, 499–500. Jesuit documents on the invasion should be used with care, for they tend to be biased in favor of Konishi Yukinaga and his perspective on the war. On Katō's Buddhism, see Turnbull, *Samurai and the Sacred*, 67, 107.

73. Murdoch, *History of Japan Vol. II*, 314; Turnbull, *Samurai*, 188; Underwood, 45. Also see Hawley, *Imjin War*, 103.

74. E. Park, *Between Dreams and Reality*, 11–13; Underwood, "Korean Boats and Ships," 50–51.

75. See, for example, *SDZK*, 32; and Palais, *Confucian Statecraft and Korean Institutions*, 76–77.

76. Ledyard, "Confucianism and War," 81–85.

77. *CPC*, 69; *BOC*, 42–43.

78. *CPC*, 69, 70.

79. Ibid., 70; Hawley, *Imjin War*, 113.

80. S. D. Kim, "Korean Monk-Soldiers," 16–17, 22–23. On slavery in Korea, see Palais, *Confucian Statecraft and Korean Institutions*, 208–73.

81. The preceding discussion is summarized from K. Lee, *New History of Korea*, 178–80.

82. *CNE*, 73; Palais, *Confucian Statecraft and Korean Institutions*, 75–78; E. Park, *Between Dreams and Reality*, 25–47. For a lengthier discussion of

Korean defense preparations in early 1592, see Kim Pong-hyon, *Hideyoshi no Chōsen shinryaku*, 79–82. Also see Palais, *Confucian Statecraft and Korean Institutions*, 80–81.

83. *SI*, 504; Hawley, *Imjin War*, 121.

84. Boots, "Korean Weapons and Armor," 15.

85. *CNE*, 225; Boots, "Korean Weapons and Armor," 4. Yi's archery range is part of the modern restoration of his naval base at Hansan Island.

86. *CNE*, 225; Yoshioka, "Bunroku-Keichō," 80–84, 95; Swope, "Crouching Tigers, Secret Weapons"; Hawley, *Imjin War*, 115. For photographs of Korean firearms accompanied by technical details, see Cho I., *Firearms of Ancient Korea*. The names for these weapons come from an ancient Chinese elementary reading primer.

87. *CNE*, 224; Underwood, "Korean Boats and Ships," 58–59. Also see Boots, "Korean Weapons and Armor."

88. *CNE*, 242; Underwood, "Korean Boats and Ships," 53, 55; Yoshioka, "Bunroku-Keichō," 86–87. There is much dispute as to what the turtleboats actually looked like as only later reconstructions survive. For a discussion of these issues, see Chang H., "Variation of the Turtleboat's Shape."

89. On the relationship between guns, military developments, and politics in Japan, see Brown, "Impact of Firearms on Japanese Warfare"; Morillo, "Guns and Government"; and Perrin, *Giving up the Gun*. For a revisionist take, see Chase, *Firearms*, 178–96.

90. Yoshioka, "Bunroku-Keichō," 72–73; Morillo, "Guns and Government," 96. On the artistic value of early Japanese guns, see Robert E. Kimbrough, "Japanese Firearms," *Gun Collector* 38 (1950): 445–65. For Nobunaga, see Lamers, *Japonius Tyrannus*. On volley fire, see Parker, *Military Revolution*, 140–44.

91. Miki S., "Chōsen eki ni okeru," 150; *CNE*, 68, 219; Yoshioka, "Bunroku-Keichō," 74.

92. *CNE*, 218.

93. See the illustration in Turnbull, *Samurai Warfare*, 110–11.

94. *CNE*, 241.

95. Ibid., 223; Yoshioka, "Bunroku-Keichō," 96–101; Swope, "Crouching Tigers, Secret Weapons," 27–28; Needham et al., *Science and Civilisation*, vol. 5, pt. 7, 408. For a discussion of siege warfare in Chinese history, see ibid., vol. 5, pt. 6. For gunpowder technologies, see ibid., vol. 5, pt. 7.

96. *WBZ*, 4760–69, 4775–76, 4780–89, 4797.

97. *CNE*, 221.

98. *CNE*, 221, 222, 223; Lorge, *War, Politics, and Society*, 111, 127.

99. For a comparison of Chinese, Japanese, and Korean firearms technologies, see Park J., "Study on the Fire Weapons."

3. A DRAGON'S HEAD

1. Sanbō honbu, *Nihon senshi*, doc. sec., 14–18; *CNE*, 76.

2. *CNE*, 250–52. This description is from Matsura, *Matsura Hōin seikan nikki*, 5. The book is a chronicle of the exploits of Matsura Shigenobu in Korea compiled by his descendants during the Meiji period. Also see Turnbull, *Samurai and the Sacred*, 7–8.

3. Oze, *Taikō-ki*, 364; J. Lewis, *Frontier Contact*, 32–33.

4. *SMR*, 1:4.

5. Huang K., "Mountain Fortress Defence," 227–30, 238–44; For more on mountain fortresses in Korean history, see Bacon, "Fortresses of Kyonggido"; and Yu J., "Mountain Fortresses." On popular disaffection with the Korean government on the eve of the war, see Choe Y., *Imjin waeran chung ui sahoe t'ongtae*, 3–14; and *SMR*, 1:4.

6. P. Lee, *Black Dragon Year*, 58–59.

7. *CPC*, 70–71. Some versions of the story maintain that Chŏng was out hunting when he first spotted the enemy boats. See *BOC*, 45; and Sanbō honbu, *Nihon senshi*, 153.

8. Matsura, *Matsura Hōin Seikan nikki*, 6. The lower figure is from Sanbō honbu, *Nihon senshi*, 154. For the higher number, see Oze, *Taikō-ki*, 365.

9. *CNE*, 253, 255; *SI*, 508–509; *CXSL*, 1. Chŏng allegedly vowed that the ghosts of those killed by the Japanese would haunt Pusan for eternity.

10. Park Y., *Admiral Yi*, 98; *CNE*, 254. For an overview of Konishi's actions in Korea, see Endō, *Tetsu no kubikase*, 119–40. On his role in the Battle of Pusan, see ibid., 132–33.

11. *CS*, 1, 21a–23a; *SI*, 510–11, 512; *NC*, 7:49; *CPC*, 71. *Chōsen seibatsuki* also adds a fictitious nighttime naval assault by Korean forces prior to the attack on Pusan.

12. *CNE*, 254.

13. *CXSL*, 2; *NC*, 7:50; *CPC*, 71–72; *CBR*, 289; Turnbull, *Samurai Sourcebook*, 242; Hawley, *Imjin War*, 139–40.

14. *SI*, 513; *NC*, 7:50; Matsura, *Matsura Hōin seikan nikki*, 6; *CPC*, 73, 74; *CMN*, 58–59.

15. *YI*, 216; *NC*, 7:51, 52; *BOC*, 48–49.

16. *BOC*, 48; *NC*, 7:52, 57; *CMN*, 35; *YI*, 224.

17. *BOC*, 48. See the original in *CBR*, 290. My translation differs slightly from Choi's.

18. *YI*, 221; *SMR*, 1:23.

19. *CPC*, 79–81.

20. Ibid., 86.

21. *CMN*, 245; *CBR*, 297–98; *SI*, 517.

22. *CPC*, 88–89; *SI*, 518; *CXSL*, 2. Yi Il was subsequently sentenced to death for his cowardice.

23. *CNE*, 118; *CBR*, 300; *CPC*, 89; *CXSL*, 2. Some local leaders did gather forces to aid the king, but they returned to their home districts when they heard the capital had already fallen. *CXSL*, 4. Wŏn Kyun is one of the more reviled figures in Korean history, partly because he serves as the foil for Yi Sunsin. In Korean sources he is described as a complete incompetent, a despicable sycophant, and an inveterate drunk.

24. *CPC*, 90, 91; *SMR*, 1:22. He had been selected over his elder brother, the Imhaegun, (Prince Imhae) because the latter was considered lazy, dissolute, and unfit as a role model for the people.

25. *CBR*, 285–87.

26. *CPC*, 93; *CNE*, 121–22; *NC*, 7:61, 64. It seems that this figure is greatly exaggerated.

27. *CXSL*, 2; Hawley, *Imjin War*, 155; *CPC*, 93. On putting armies into dangerous situations to instill them to fight better, see Sawyer, *Seven Military Classics*, 80–82, 168–73, 178–79.

28. *SI*, 520, 521; *CPC*, 95; Oze, *Taikō-ki*, 368. Sin reportedly killed seventeen Japanese himself before committing suicide. Murdoch, *History of Japan Vol. II*, 322–23. For more on the use of the "flaming ox attack," a classic technique in Chinese history, and an illustration of the fire ox in action, see Sawyer, *Fire and Water*, 117–18. On Sin's failed strategy, see *CXSL*, 2. This opinion of Ch'ungju was articulated by Yu Sŏngnyong at the time. *CBR*, 446.

29. *CS*, 1, 32b–34a; *SI*, 525.On the reaction to the news of Sin's defeat in the countryside, see *CMN*, 408–10. For communications between Hideyoshi and his commanders during the first month of the war, see Sanbō honbu, *Nihon senshi*, documents section, 22–45. On Japanese misgivings, see *SI*, 523–24. Despite the words of caution, Hideyoshi boasted in letters that he would take China by October. See Boscara, *101 Letters of Hideyoshi*, 45–46.

30. *NC*, 7:64; *CBR*, 301.

31. *CXSL*, 3; *DMB*, 1592; *CPC*, 96–97; *CNE*, 100.

32. *NC*, 7:65; *CBR*, 309 (an English translation is in *BOC*, 78–80); *SI*, 529.

33. *CPC*, 99, 101; *CNE*, 100.

34. Finch, "Civilian Life during the Japanese Invasions," 55.

35. *SMR*, 1:5–6. For a translation of Ŏ's remarks, see Finch, "Civilian Life during the Japanese Invasions," 58.

36. *SMR*, 1:10. Significantly, these Chinese kings managed to recover their states.

37. *SMR*, 1:7, 8. Studies of the *ŭibyŏng* are legion in Korea. On their initial emergence, see Choe Y., *Imjin waeran chung ui sahoe tongt'ae*, 25–37. On righteous-guerrilla activities in Chŏlla province, see Ch'o, *Hŏnam ŭibyŏng kangchang sa*.

38. *SMR*, 1:11.

39. Ibid., 13. This translation is modified slightly from Finch, "Civilian Life during the Japanese Invasions," 59–60.

40. *SMR*, 1:13.

41. *CMN*, 49–50, 54.

42. *SMR*, 1:14, 20; *YI*, 242–47; *NC*, 7:58.

43. This is evidenced from reading memorials contained in his collected works. See Kwak, *Mang'u sŏnsaeng munchip*, 25–30.

44. *YI*, 225, 241–42.

45. *SMR*, 1:18, 19.

46. Oze, *Taikō-ki*, 370–71; Hawley, *Imjin War*, 164–65; *NC*, 7:66; *CXSL*, 4. For more on the capture of Seoul by the Japanese, see Kitajima, *Chōsen nichinichiki*, 41–55.

47. *SI*, 542. Despite this nominal promotion, it does not appear that Kuroda ever had more jurisdiction over Korean affairs than Konishi or Katō. On the distribution of forces upon the occupation of Seoul, see Sanbō honbu, *Nihon senshi*, 162–69. On the allocation of provinces, see Turnbull, *Samurai Invasion*, 71; and *CNE*, 82–84.

48. *NC*, 7:85. The desecration of Seoul has never been forgotten, as evidenced by the number of prominent historical landmarks in the city today bearing the words "original destroyed during the Japanese invasion of 1592."

49. *CNE*, 81, 82; Kitajima, *Hideyoshi no Chōsen shinryaku*, 16, 17, 20.

50. Kitajima, *Hideyoshi no Chōsen shinryaku*, 21–22; *CNE*, 84; *Taiko-ki*, 400. For the letters concerning sea battles, see Sanbō honbu, *Nihon senshi*, doc. sec., 54–58.

51. *NC*, 7:75.

52. Ibid., 82–83, 84; *SI*, 538; *SMR*, 1:23. For more on the king's flight and pursuit by the Japanese, see Kim Pong-hyon, *Hideyoshi no Chōsen*, 113–38.

53. *CNE*, 101; *CPC*, 106.

54. *CPC*, 106–107, 108–109.

55. *SI*, 534.

56. *CPC*, 123–24; *SI*, 537; Matsura, *Matsura Hōin seikan nikki*, 8. The Battle of the Imjin River is described in more detail in Kitajima, *Chōsen nichinichiki*, 56–66.

57. Oze, *Taikō-ki*, 394–97, 398–99; *CMN*, 56.

58. S. D. Kim, "Korean Monk-Soldiers," 2–3, 50. On monk-soldier traditions and myths in Japan, see Adolphson, *Teeth and Claws*.

59. Translated from the *Hyujŏng taesa* in S. D. Kim, "Korean Monk-Soldiers," 28.

60. Ibid., 30, 76–78, 103–13.

61. Palais, *Confucian Statecraft and Korean Institutions*, 82; S. D. Kim, "Korean Monk-Soldiers," 60.

62. *SMR*, 1:30, 50–51.

63. Ibid., 31–33.

64. Ibid., 35, 36–37; *CMN*, 69.

65. *YI*, 236, 237–38; *CMN*, 83, 94.

66. *CXSL*, 6, 10–12.

67. *WKSL*, 478; Fan S., *Wanli zhuan*, 236.

68. *CXSL*, 13; Fan S., *Wanli zhuan*, 236; *WKSL*, 477, 478.

69. *WKSL*, 477.

70. *CXSL*, 14; *CPC*, 138, 139.

71. *CXSL*, 16; *CPC*, 141.

72. *CXSL*, 17; *CBR*, 340; *CPC*, 136.

73. *SI*, 544–45; *CPC*, 144–45; *CBR*, 340.

74. *CBR*, 326; *CXSL*, 19–20; *SI*, 545–46.

75. *CBR*, 329, 469.

76. *CPC*, 153, 155–56. On the state of Japanese knowledge about China's military situation in the summer of 1592, see Matsumoto, *Hō taikō seikan hiroku*, 44–46.

77. *NI*, xvii. On the comparisons with Drake, see Underwood, "Korean Boats and Ships," 82. On Yi as a national hero, see Austin, "Admiral Yi Sunsin." The classic biography of Yi, which was written by his nephew, Yi Pun, can be found in *IC*, 199–240. On Yi's rivalry with Wŏn Kyun, in particular, see Niderost, "Yi Sun Sin and Won Kyun."

78. *IC,* 23.
79. Ibid., 24.
80. Ibid., 26.
81. Ibid., 32. Other accounts give higher figures, but I follow Yi. For another reckoning, see *CPC,* 201.
82. *IC,* 37.
83. *CPC,* 202; *NI,* 5; *IC,* 212. According to Yi's biography he told his men: "During the time it takes to cut the head off a dead enemy you can shoot many living ones. Therefore concentrate on shooting the living enemy to death instead of cutting off the heads of the dead to offer for rewards." Ibid., 212. Regarding his shooting, Yi himself said the bullet went through his shoulder, and the wound was not serious. *NI,* 5.
84. Some sources state that the Koreans used turtleboats in the earlier engagement, but Yi himself does not mention them specifically until the Battle of Tangpo. *IC,* 40–41; *CPC,* 202–203; Turnbull, *Samurai Sourcebook,* 283–85. Park Yune-hee contends that Korean records mention turtleboats being used as early as 1413 and that Yi merely revived them for use against the Japanese. *Admiral Yi,* 70.
85. *IC,* 40–41. For descriptions of the types of cannon the Koreans and Japanese mounted on their ships, see Park Y., *Admiral Yi,* 74–78; and Swope, "Crouching Tigers, Secret Weapons."
86. *IC,* 48.
87. Underwood, "Korean Boats and Ships," 77–79. For variant conceptualizations of the turtleboat's appearance, see Bak, "Short Note"; and Chang H., "Variation of the Turtleboat's Shape."
88. Kuno, *Japanese Expansion,* 1:153.
89. Sadler, "Naval Campaign," 199; *IC,* 60–64, 65; Park Y., *Admiral Yi,* 167–69. A full description of the battle and a list of the exploits of various commanders can be found in *IC,* 56–60. Also see Park Y., *Admiral Yi,* 159–66.
90. *IC,* 72–73. The naval encounters of 1592 are also related in *CXSL,* 26–27; and *CBR,* 352–53. A Japanese version of the battles can be found in *SI,* 553–55.
91. *IC,* 85–86; Turnbull, *Samurai Sourcebook,* 82–283. On activity around Seoul, see *SI,* 553.
92. *SI,* 554; He B. et al., *Ming Shenzong yu Ming Dingling,* 101; Yang Hu, *Ming dai Liaodong dusi,* 205.
93. *MSJSBM,* 2375; *PRL,* 239; *SDZK,* 33; *SI,* 556.
94. *CXSL,* 28; *PRL,* 248; Zheng L., *Ming dai Zhong-Ri guanxi,* 586. On the Korean request for aid, see the letter in *FGYB,* 5–8.
95. *CXSL,* 23–24, 30; *CPC,* 219. The numbers given vary, but do not exceed 5,000 men, which is the figure given in Japanese sources. Chinese sources usually say the Ming sent 3,000 troops at this time, and Korean records give a figure of 1,000–2,000 initially, with reinforcements that brought the total to 2,864 men and 3,401 horses. *CXSL,* 22, 26.
96. *SI,* 556; *SDZK,* 33; *PRL,* 240; *SDZK,* 33; Matsura, *Matsura Hōin seikan nikki,* 11. Matsura Shigenobu commanded the defenders. *CNE,* 148. Shi Ru and his two lieutenants reportedly killed ten Japanese between them. As for Ming and Japanese losses, other sources put their casualties at about 300

each. Li Guangtao, *Chaoxian (Renchen Wohuo) Yanjiu*, 13–14. The Japanese allegedly had around 20,000 troops stationed in Pyongyang at the time. *SI*, 556–57. Yi Wŏn'ik, though, maintains that Japanese strength numbered only 7,000 men. *Yi Sanguk ilgi*, 648.

97. *CPC*, 220; *CBR*, 351; *CXSL*, 42, 44, 56. Zu Chengxun claimed that only one of the five Korean divisions he ordered to advance did so, the rest simply freezing or fleeing. Zu had one Korean commander flogged before his men to set an example. *CXSL*, 44.

98. *FGYB*, 10–11; *NC*, 7:253, 254. On the possible involvement of Siam, see *CPC*, 233. It appears that a Thai embassy had arrived in Beijing as the Ming were discussing anti-Japanese efforts and offered to help. Wolters, "Ayudhya," 167–69; Wade, "*Ming shi-lu* as a Source for Thai History"; and Lee H., "Military Aid."

99. Miller, "State Versus Society," 236. The Koreans were galled by such claims. *SMR*, 1:405.

100. *CPC*, 238–39. The Ming later refused offers from the king of Siam to launch a naval assault on Japan itself while the Japanese were preoccupied in Korea. Wolters, "Ayudhya," 168–73.

101. *CPC*, 239. Many later Korean accounts display a profound sense of gratitude toward Wanli. See, for example, ibid., 2.

102. *FGYB*, 15–18, 98. On the strategy of fighting the Japanese at sea, see Zheng R., *Chouhai tubian*, 12, 5a–5b. Mercenaries from Shanxi in the northwest were paid six liang of silver per month, with an additional allowance for food. *FGYB*, 77.

103. *FGYB*, 46–50, 59–60, 79–80.

104. Ibid., 93–95.

105. Ibid., 53–55.

106. *CXSL*, 44; *MSG*, 7:25; *GQ*, 4682; *FGYB*, 34.

107. *FGYB*, 28–30, 35–39; *WLDC*, 695–99.

108. *FGYB*, 37–38, 103–105. On the production requests, see Li Guangtao, *Chaoxian (Renchen Wohuo) Yanjiu*, 22; *FGYB*, 50–51.

109. For a comparison with contemporary England, see Fissell, *English Warfare*, 193–206.

110. *FGYB*, 111–12.

111. Ibid., 123–24, 134–35.

112. *WLDC*, 699. A slightly different translation of this edict can be found in Miller, "State Versus Society," 235.

113. *WLDC*, 694; Shen D., *Wanli yehuo bian*, 438; *MS*, 8292; *MSG*, 7:25; *SI*, 566.

114. *CXSL*, 57. On Chinese logistical concerns, see *WLDC*, 712.

115. *CPC*, 234–35, 236; Li Guangtao, *Wanli ershisan nian feng Riben*, 5. On Shen's initial meeting with the Japanese commanders and Konishi's conditions for peace, see Nakamura Tokugoro, "Ni-Min kōwa haretsu shi temmatsu," 960–61.

116. *CS*, 1, 38a–39b; Sanbō honbu, *Nihon senshi*, doc. sec., 180–81; *CBR*, 359. *Nihon senshi* contains Konishi's letter to Shen.

117. *CXSL*, 65, 74; *CS*, 1, 39b; *MSJSBM*, 2375. Konishi freely admitted that the Japanese were having supply problems and probably could not withstand a

concerted Ming offensive. See *SI*, 567; and *MS*, 8292. According to one Japanese source, a Korean informed Konishi that the truce was no more than a delaying tactic so that Li Rusong could arrive with his army, but Konishi did not believe him. *SI*, 568-69.

118. *CPC*, 125.

119. *CBR*, 322.

120. Ibid.; E. Park, *Between Dreams and Reality*, 119-21; *CNE*, 129. On the capture of the princes and Katō's desire to use them to exact a truce, see *SI*, 558-62. Also see Matsumoto, *Hō taikō seikan hiroku*, 40-43; and Oze, *Taikō-ki*, 372.

121. "Kiyomasa Korai jin oboegaki," 301.

122. *CNE*, 130. On administrative efforts by Hideyoshi's commanders, see Kitajima, *Hideyoshi no Chōsen shinryaku*, 29-34.

123. *CPC*, 169-70; *SMR*, 1:53.

124. *CNE*, 135; *CPC*, 196-97. For a complete examination of the Battle of Ich'i, see Choe Y. et al., *Imjin waeran kwa Ich'i taech'ŏp*; the original victory report can be found on 212-24. On some of the earlier defeats, see *CMN*, 263-66.

125. *CPC*, 171, 186-87; *NC*, 7:178-79. Ko would be posthumously honored. Ibid., 192. For the rumor that Kwŏn was moving to help retake the city, see *SMR*, 1:51.

126. *CMN*, 284, 298; *SMR*, 1:59-61.

127. Mōri cited in Park Y., *Admiral Yi*, 110; *CHJ*, 277; *CMN*, 270, 347. Concerning guerrilla activities, see Kim Hong-kyu, *Hideyoshi mimizuka yon-hyaku nen*, 12-29; and Kim Pong-hyon, *Hideyoshi no Chōsen*, 151-69. The Japanese tried to remove their dead from the battlefield so their heads (or ears) would not be taken.

128. K. Kim, "Resistance, Abduction, and Survival," 23; *CMN*, 112, 123.

129. *CXSL*, 70-71; *SMR*, 1:103-105. On Japan's strong position, see ibid., 102-103. For a contrary opinion, see Hawley, *Imjin War*, 292-303.

130. *SI*, 572.

131. *WKSL*, 479, 483, 484.

132. *PRL*, 247; Fan S., *Wanli zhuan*, 238. The directive and appointment order for Li can be found in *FGYB*, 136-37.

133. Sansom, *History of Japan*, 355.

134. *SMR*, 1:90. For more on occupation policies and the creation of tax rolls in Hamgyŏng province, see Kitajima, *Chōsen nichinichiki*, 97-107. Also see Park Y., *Admiral Yi*, 121-24. On collaborators, see Zheng L., *Ming dai Zhong-Ri guanxi*, 580.

135. *CNE*, 140-41; *CPC*, 208-209; Turnbull, *Samurai Invasion*, 124-25; *SMR*, 1:41-47, 48. Some rumors claimed that 50,000 Ming troops were coming overland and another 100,000 by sea. For short accounts of these battles, see Turnbull, *Samurai Sourcebook*, 245-46.

136. *NC*, 7:265.

137. *CPC*, 210; *NC*, 7:266. On Kim's tactics, see Kang S., "Strategy and Tactics." A statue of Kim stands by the approach to the Chinju National Museum.

138. *YI*, 259-60; *CNE*, 141-42.

139. *CNE*, 142; *SMR*, 1:107; *NC*, 7:268–69. On Japanese estimates of casualties, see Oze, *Taikō-ki*, 400–401. This source suggests that attackers lost 15,000 men.

140. *CNE*, 137, 138; Turnbull, *Samurai Invasion*, 131.

141. *NC*, 7:283–93.

142. Ibid., 278. In fact some scholars argue that Japanese strength was reduced by as much as a third by early 1593. See, for example, Sansom, *History of Japan*, 357.

143. *FGYB*, 160–62.

144. *CXSL*, 82; *CPC*, 242.

145. *NC*, 7:319; *SMR*, 1:139; *CXSL*, 85. This admiration of Li Rusong is also mentioned in Weems, *Hulbert's History of Korea*, 2:16.

146. *SMR*, 1:129; *FGYB*, 149–50.

147. *FGYB*, 142–45, 157, 160–61, 170.

148. Ibid., 171.

149. Ibid., 174, 180–81, 183–85. For images of Ming boats, see Wang Q., *Sancai tuhui*, 1145–53. On crew size for various boats, see *FGYB*, 183–84.

150. *FGYB*, 177.

151. Ibid., 179, 182, 185.

152. Ibid., 186–87; *SMR*, 1:134.

153. *FGYB*, 191–92, 193, 195; *SMR*, 1:135. For a discussion and illustrations of Qi's spear tactics, see Qi, *Jixiao xinshu*, 33–40. On the use of different types of cavalry as discussed in *The Art of War*, see Sawyer, *Seven Military Classics*, 342.

154. Li Guangtao, *Chaoxian (Renchen Wohuo) Yanjiu*, 40–41; *CXSL*, 67; Kye, "Indirect Challenge," 429–33. A Korean report put Ming strength at 48,000 men and 26,700 mounts. A force of this size consumed 720 piculs (48 tons) of rice and 810 piculs (54 tons) of fodder per day, according to contemporary sources. Therefore the Ming needed more than 90,000 piculs (6,000 tons) of provisions to supply a force of this size for just two months. *CXSL*, 73–74.

155. *FGYB*, 197, 202–204. For more on Song's preparations, see Li Guangtao, *Chaoxian (Renchen Wohuo) Yanjiu*, 42–45.

156. *FGYB*, 216. On resolving such transportation issues under the succeeding Qing dynasty, see Dai, "Qing State, Merchants, and the Military Labor."

157. *FGYB*, 209–10, 238. For all of Song's articles of war, see ibid., 232–39.

158. *CPC*, 250; *FGYB*, 249, 268–69. For an enumeration of the commanders and the number of troops under each, see *CPC*, 247–51. For the number of private retainers for each commander as well as the distribution of infantry and cavalry, see *FGYB*, 254–57. Also see ibid., 271–75.

159. For the equipment list, see *FGYB*, 256–62.

160. *MSJSBM*, 2375.

161. *CPC*, 257.

162. Ibid., 256; *SMR*, 1:131–32.

163. *BOC*, 156. For the original, see *CBR*, 374.

164. *NC*, 7:320–22; *FGYB*, 248, 276.

165. *CNE*, 86; Hawley, *Imjin War*, 302.

4. A SERPENT'S TAIL

1. *GQ*, 4690; *CXSL*, 60, 101. Some sources indicate that Wang Wen, leading another 2,000 men, also accompanied Wu. The *Chosŏn wangjo sillok* says Qian led 1,000 troops. *CXSL*, 86. Qian's own account splits the difference, stating that he and another officer were put in charge of 3,000 troops under Song Yingchang. *ZDSJ*, 896. Some sources, including Tan Qian's *Guoque*, maintain that the Ming did in fact reach their target figure. *GQ*, 4691. The Koreans give the figure of 70,000 men in their projections in late 1592, saying the Chinese relief force would comprise 60,000 western and 10,000 southern troops. *CXSL*, 66. The basic reward for a Japanese commander's head was 5,000 liang of silver and a hereditary commander post, though the monetary reward was doubled in the case of Hideyoshi himself. *WKSL*, 488; *CPC*, 261.

2. *PRL*, 245; *SI*, 573; Li Guangtao, *Chaoxian (Renchen Wohuo) Yanjiu*, 71.

3. *CXSL*, 88–89. Li had tea and wine with Sŏnjo and confided his dislike for Shen Weijing and the peace talks. *CXSL*, 96; Zhuan Q., *Zhongguo gu wai-jiao shiliao huibian*, 1415. Also see *MSJSBM*, 2375.

4. *IWSC*, 1:46–50. On the Ming intention of staying only six months, see *YM*, 2–5.

5. *CXSL*, 95; *MTJ*, 2731; *MS*, 6193. Nonetheless, this coarse image of Li can be tempered by the fact that he was a patron of the famous Ming artist Xu Wei (1521–93) and actually did a bit of painting himself. Swope, "A Few Good Men." On the distrust of Shen Weijing, see *FGYB*, 328–30.

6. *SI*, 574; *PRL*, 245.

7. *CPC*, 258; *SI*, 576. My translation differs slightly from that found in *BOC*, 157.

8. *CXSL*, 88, 91, 97. Also see *SI*, 575–76. On the amount of rations raised and needed to supply various levels of troops, see *FGYB*, 251–53.

9. *IWSC*, 1:5–6. Li's plans are expressed in a letter to his brothers Rubo and Rumei, which can be found in *FGYB*, 289–92. On directives to the men, see ibid., 368–69.

10. *CXSL*, 99, 100; *IWSC*, 1:5; Song's report to Shi Xing, Jan. 25, 1593, in *FGYB*, 293–94.

11. On the thinking behind this, see *NYI*, 318–19. Also see *FGYB*, 521.

12. *FGYB*, 421; *SDZK*, 34; *CPC*, 258; *MSJSBM*, 2375; *CXSL*, 101–02. The officers responsible were sentenced to death for their failure, but Li Rubo interceded on their behalf, and they each received lashes instead. *FGYB*, 522.

13. *ZDSJ*, 896; *SDZK*, 34; *SI*, 578; *CXSL*, 106; *MS*, 6193.

14. S. D. Kim, "Korean Monk-Soldiers," 92; *FGYB*, 523.

15. *CBR*, 374; *FGYB*, 312, 313; *PRL*, 248; *CXSL*, 106. For weaponry employed by the Ming, see *WBZ*, 4634–63.

16. Wang C., "Li Rusong zheng dong kao," 345; *CXSL*, 106–07. Qian Shizhen reports that Li promised 10,000 cash and a hereditary commander post to the first to scale the walls. *ZDSJ*, 897. For an image of the battle from a screen displayed in the Chinju National Museum, see Chinju National Museum, *Imjin Waeran*, 32–33. In this depiction Li Rusong directs the battle from the right, wearing red armor and holding a blue flag.

17. *CPC*, 264, 265; *MSJSBM*, 2375.
18. *FGYB*, 524–25; *CPC*, 271; S. D. Kim, "Korean Monk-Soldiers," 95.
19. *ZDSJ*, 897–98; Li Guangtao, *Chaoxian (Renchen Wohuo) Yanjiu*, 77; *CXSL*, 107.
20. *SI*, 579; *SDZK*, 35; *CPC*, 266.
21. *CPC*, 267; *CXSL*, 107. Some sources say Konishi retreated to Yŏnkwang Pavilion. See Wang C., "Li Rusong zheng dong kao," 346; and Li Guangtao, *Chaoxian (Renchen Wohuo) Yanjiu*, 77. According to one version of the story, the Korean troops stationed along the Taedong mistook a cannon blast to be a signal to attack and they cut down the Japanese as they retreated. See Wang C., "Li Rusong zheng dong kao," 346; Li Guangtao, *Chaoxian (Renchen Wohuo) Yanjiu*, 77; and Hawley, *Imjin War*, 313. Without reading any of the relevant primary documents from the Chinese side, Hawley feels confident that their sources are biased and inaccurate, so he uncritically accepts the Korean version of events. Li Rusong himself admitted that he did pull back but had every intention of finishing them off the next day. *IWSC*, 1:11. For a Japanese chronicle account from the records of Yoshino Jingozaemon, see *CNE*, 273–74. This is partially translated in Turnbull, *Samurai Invasion*, 141.
22. Yi W., *Yi Sanguk ilgi*, 649; *SI*, 581–82. On Yi Il's blunder, see *CPC*, 268.
23. *IWSC*, 1:78; *SI*, 579. On the Japanese dread of Ming firepower, see Li Guangtao, "Chaoxian renchen Wohuo yu Li Rusong," 270. On the number of Japanese killed, see *WLDC*, 729; *PRL*, 248; and *SDZK*, 35. Chinese scholar Yang Hu asserts that barely 10 percent of the Japanese in Pyongyang survived the battle, though this is probably an exaggeration. *Ming dai Liaodong dusi*, 206. Figures vary as to how many Japanese were actually in the city, but the number was probably between 15,000 and 20,000 as reported by Kawaguchi Choju. He reports the number of allied troops as being in the vicinity of 200,000, a figure that far exceeds that given in other sources. *SI*, 581–82. This is comparable to Zhuge Yuansheng for the other side, who states that Konishi may have had as many as 100,000 Japanese awaiting the Ming. *PRL*, 248. Reports of the victory and the battle can be found in *FGYB*, 345–52; and *IWSC*, 1:76–86.
24. *FGYB*, 268, 374, 528; *MSJSBM*, 2375; Wang C., "Li Rusong zheng dong kao," 343–74; *CPC*, 267. Japanese accounts differ again, asserting that the allies killed a mere sixty starving and badly wounded stragglers. See *SI*, 583. Slightly different figures were reported to Wanli by Sŏnjo. Li Guangtao, *Chaoxian (Renchen Wohuo) Yanjiu*, 78–79. For a list of battle rewards, see *FGYB*, 372–76.
25. *SI*, 586; Oze, *Taikō-ki*, 426; Turnbull, *Samurai Invasion*, 141–42. Kobayakawa Takakage supposedly wanted to check the allies at Kaesŏng but was overruled. *CNE*, 150.
26. *SI*, 584; Zheng L., *Ming dai Zhong-Ri guanxi*, 599; *CXSL*, 191.
27. *IWSC*, 1:22–24, 34–35, 111–12, 113; *FGYB*, 322–23. On currency issues in Chosŏn Korea, see Palais, *Confucian Statecraft and Korean Institutions*, 904–23.
28. *IWSC*, 1:52–53, 98–99; *FGYB*, 357–58.
29. *IWSC*, 1:32–33, 40, 62–64, 69–70; *FGYB*, 338, 366, 379–80; S. D. Kim, "Korean Monk-Soldiers," 95–102. On logistical concerns, see *NYI*, 361–62. For a comparative look at logistical capacity in the Western context, see Engels,

Alexander the Great, esp. 18–22. Also see Lynn, *Feeding Mars*. As time went by with the monks, however, many malingered, fled, or simply refused to work, and they were phased out of such duties.

30. *IWSC*, 1:124–25; *CXSL*, 113–14. According to a captive, the Japanese hoped to hold out in Seoul until Hideyoshi reinforced them or ordered their withdrawal. On the state of Korean intelligence, see *IWSC*, 1:108. As seen below in a report to Shi Xing, however, Song Yingchang estimated that some 200,000 Japanese remained in Korea. *FGYB*, 388–89. Other reports put the total figure at around 100,000, which was probably fairly accurate. Ibid., 397–98.

31. *ZDSJ*, 898; *SI*, 590; *MSJSBM*, 2375; *FGYB*, 529–30; *CPC*, 270–71. Zhuge Yuansheng reported the Japanese dead slightly higher at 178. *PRL*, 249.

32. *FGYB*, 352–57, 401–404, 443–45; *WKSL*, 490; *CXSL*, 108–109. Tan Qian states that Wanli actually commanded Sŏnjo to return to Pyongyang. *GQ*, 4694.

33. Zheng L., *Ming dai Zhong-Ri guanxi*, 597. On Korean observations about the utility of firearms, see *CXSL*, 256–57. The Koreans also arrived at the conclusion that "[b]ig cannons defeat small cannons and many cannon defeat few cannon." Ibid., 15.

34. *FGYB*, 532.

35. *CNE*, 151. In Li's defense, Zha Dashou, apparently after receiving reports from the Koreans, reported that the Japanese were in the process of strengthening the Seoul defenses.

36. *CPC*, 275; Wang C., "Li Rusong zheng dong kao," 348; Turnbull, *Samurai Sourcebook*, 247; Li Guangtao, *Chaoxian (Renchen Wohuo) Yanjiu*, 84–86; *CHJ*, 281. The figure of 50,000 comes from Zhang X. and Liu, *Zhongguo gudai zhanzheng tongjian*, 803. See the Japanese account of the attack in Oze, *Taikō-ki*, 428.

37. *SDZK*, 36; *PRL*, 250; *MSJSBM*, 2375; *MS*, 6194. Li Yousheng hailed from Li Rusong's hometown and had long served under him. *CPC*, 276.

38. Matsura, *Matsura Hōin seikan nikki*, 12–13; Oze, *Taikō-ki*, 429–31. The Matsura claimed rewards for 380 kills for their clan. Figures for the number of dead vary widely. Korean sources put the figures somewhere in the hundreds, perhaps 500–600 on each side. See *CXSL*, 141; and Zheng L., *Ming dai Zhong-Ri guanxi*, 601. Ming reports indicate 167 Japanese were killed as they retreated and that the allies captured 45 horses and 91 military implements, losing 264 dead and suffering 49 wounded. *FGYB*, 533–34. Kuwata Tadachika estimates 6,000 allied dead. *CNE*, 153.

39. *SDZK*, 36; *MTJ*, 2736; *CPC*, 278.

40. See, for example, Turnbull, *Samurai Sourcebook*, 247. Rai Sanyo, in *Nihon gaishi*, says the Japanese killed 10,000 men in the engagement. See Wang C., "Li Rusong zheng dong kao," 347. This figure is given in *SI*, 595. It is repeated in Turnbull, *Samurai*, 214.

41. Kuno, *Japanese Expansion*, 1:164; *MS*, 8358; *WKSL*, 491.

42. *ZDSJ*, 898; *CPC*, 2.

43. Zhu, "Ming dai yuan Chao," 157–58; *CPC*, 280–81; *BOC*, 167–68; *FGYB*, 457; *IWSC*, 1:136. The Ming estimated that they had only 16,000 horses left by this time. *FGYB*, 556. Officials requested from China medicine to combat the spread of disease among the men. Ibid., 454–55. Climatological

charts for Korea can be found in Wang C., "Li Rusong zheng dong kao," 349. Modern Chinese historian Wang Xiangrong sees Song's caution and meticulous concern for logistics to be his greatest contributions to the war effort. *Zhong-Ri guanxi wenxian lunkao*, 270–78. For a more thorough discussion of various interpretations of the Battle of Pyŏkchegwan and the reasons for the temporary Ming retreat, see Wang C., "Li Rusong zheng dong kao," 351–65.

44. *ZDSJ*, 895–96; Li Guangtao, *Chaoxian (Renchen Wohuo) Yanjiu*, 102. On cavalry engagements during the war, see Suh, "Cavalry Engagements." The debate over tactics is summarized in Wang C., "Li Rusong zheng dong kao," 363. Also see *MS*, 6194. Wang Chongwu charges Song Yingchang in particular with overstating the capabilities of Japanese weaponry to his superiors in China because he wanted a peace settlement. "Li Rusong zheng dong kao," 365.

45. Li Guangtao, *Chaoxian (Renchen Wohuo) Yanjiu*, 108. Li wrote of the southern troops, "They feared regulations but they did not fear the enemy." Ibid., 112. On the Korean appreciation of southern Chinese troops, see *YM*, 30–31.

46. Li Guangtao, *Chaoxian (Renchen Wohuo) Yanjiu*, 103. *CBR*, 390; *CMN*, 174–75; *CXSL*, 172. Luo earned quite a reputation among the Koreans both for his bravery and for the colorful red outfits of his Zhejiang troops, which were said to have inspired great fear in the Japanese. Li Guangtao, "Chaoxian renchen Wohuo yu Li Rusong," 290–92.

47. Li Guangtao, *Chaoxian (Renchen Wohuo) Yanjiu*, 102–103; *CBR*, 382, 384; *CXSL*, 172. Song himself complained about shortages in supplies, including firearms. *FGYB*, 507.

48. *CPC*, 281; *SMR*, 1:158. The Ming claimed they had already spent more than 1 million liang of silver. *IWSC*, 1:167.

49. *SMR*, 1:158–59.

50. *IWSC*, 1:157, 173–77; *SMR*, 1:159; *FGYB*, 354–55 (from earlier in the year).

51. *FGYB*, 424, 426; *NC*, 7:329–30; *IWSC*, 1:163–64.

52. "Kiyomasa Korai jin oboegaki," 302–303; *CNE*, 271–72.

53. *FGYB*, 471–72. On these figures, see *CNE*, 234–36; and Chinju National Museum, *Imjin Waeran*, 15.

54. *SDZK*, 36–37; *PRL*, 251; *MS*, 6194; *FGYB*, 499–500, 512. Samuel Hawley doubts the veracity of Zha's raid. *Imjin War*, 322–23.

55. *YI*, 278, 280; *YM*, 13.

56. There are reproductions of this weapon in Seoul and at the Chinju National Museum. See the illustration in Turnbull, *Samurai Invasion*, 149.

57. *SI*, 599–600; *NC*, 7:334; *CPC*, 284–85; *CNE*, 154.

58. *BOC*, 170–71; *NC*, 7:335.

59. *NC*, 7:335; *MSJSBM*, 2376; *GQ*, 4699. Kitajima Manji estimates that prior to the burning of the grain stores, the Japanese had two months' supplies. *Hideyoshi no Chōsen shinryaku*, 55.

60. Kitajima, *Hideyoshi no Chōsen shinryaku*, 56; "Kiyomasa Korai jin oboegaki," 306. Katō himself also admitted that supplies were an issue. Ibid., 309–12.

61. *CPC*, 297, 301. For descriptions of the bizarre disagreement over etiquette, see ibid., 298–99; and *BOC*, 177–78.

62. *FGYB*, 568–69, 594–97; Oze, *Taikō-ki*, 409–10; *CS*, 1, 50b. The translation closely follows that of W. J. Boot's forthcoming manuscript.

63. *SDZK*, 38; *CBR*, 380; *SI*, 613; *CPC*, 289. This had been stipulated in the talks, however. The corpses of men and mounts were burned that evening by allied troops to prevent the spread of disease. *CBR*, 398–99.

64. *CPC*, 303, 304.

65. *CPC*, 305, 306; *FGYB*, 417, 629. Some Koreans suspected Li Rusong of coming to an agreement with the Japanese that allowed them to withdraw. *CBR*, 383, 400. Qian Shizhen reported skirmishing, however. *ZDSJ*, 898. Yu Sŏngnyong maintained that Li pulled back after the initial chase and let the Japanese get away, infuriating Song Yingchang.

66. *FGYB*, 657; *YM*, 6–7; *SMR*, 1:160.

67. *FGYB*, 667–74, 681, 708–709; *SMR*, 1:162.

68. *CPC*, 285, 296–97; *FGYB*, 637–38.

69. *SMR*, 1:153; *SI*, 604; *CNE*, 88–89. For a study of these castles, see Ōta, "Gunbu ni yoru Bunroku-Keichō no eki no jōkaku kenkyū." For a comparative look at Japanese castles and their defenses, see Parker, *Military Revolution*, 142–42. On Korean fortresses, see Cha, "Notable Characteristics of Korean Fortresses"; and Bacon, "Fortresses of Kyonggido."

70. These figures and garrison locations come from Kitajima, *Chōsen nichinichiki*, 246–48. They pertain to the summer of 1593 but would change after the sack of Chinju. For charts on the amounts of each item in a typical garrison, see Turnbull, *Samurai Invasion*, 165. His charts are derived from *CNE*, 95.

71. *CNE*, 156; *SI*, 606; *CMN*, 178; *SMR*, 1:188.

72. *SI*, 626, 628, 630; *CPC*, 316.

73. *NC*, 7:347; *CNE*, 158, 159; Oze, *Taikō-ki*, 402.

74. *CNE*, 290; *CPC*, 316; *NC*, 7:354.

75. *NC*, 7:354; *SI*, 631–32; *CXSL*, 281.

76. *CPC*, 317–18; Turnbull, *Samurai Invasion*, 159.

77. *SI*, 632–34; *CBR*, 401; *CMN*, 183. For the Japanese perspective of the sack of Chinju, see Kitajima, *Chōsen nichinichiki*, 248–52.

78. Jung, "Mobilization of Women's Sexuality." For the story of Nongae, see Chinju National Museum, *Imjin Waeran*, 150–55. Visitors today can visit the shrine at Chinju and see the rock from which she allegedly jumped.

79. *CPC*, 321; *NC*, 8:4–5; *NC*, 7:351–52; *SMR*, 1:201.

80. Swope, "Deceit, Disguise, and Dependence," 770. Sources vary on the exact date of the princes' return to Korean hands. Ming records fix the date at August 18, but Korean accounts suggest an earlier date. See Song Yingchang's letter of congratulations in *FGYB*, 794–95. Hawley states that the princes were released to keep the talks alive. *Imjin War*, 369.

81. Kitajima, *Chōsen nichinichiki*, 251; *NC*, 7:345–46, 351; *MS*, 276; *CNE*, 91. On their distrust of Shen, see *CXSL*, 271, 282.

82. *SMR*, 1:190, 192–93.

83. *FGYB*, 733–34, 767, 768, 774. Soldiers received extra pay for distance traveled and duration of stay. For the rates of pay, as well as rewards for battle exploits, see ibid., 836–40.

84. Ibid., 797. For details on these troop dispensations and their commanders, see ibid., 800–801.

85. *SMR*, 1:180, 265–67; *IWSC*, 1:182–84.

86. *CS*, 1, 63a. Supposedly, Li met Shen Weijing on his way home and chided him for bringing treasures to the robbers. Ibid., 63b–64a.

87. *NC*, 8:9–10; *FGYB*, 803, 893–96; *YM*, 18–19.

88. *NC*, 8:16–17, 21–22, 24; Yi W., *Yi Sanguk ilgi*, 650.

89. *NC*, 8:26–27, 32; *SMR*, 1:267–71.

90. *SMR*, 1:206, 235–36; *IWSC*, 1:209, 212.

91. *CNE*, 95. For a table of the major fortresses and their commanders, see ibid., 93–94. Also see Turnbull, *Samurai Invasion*, 164. A *monme* equals 3.75 grams.

92. Cory, "Father Gregorio des Cespedes," 11.

93. *IWSC*, 1:214–17; Kang H., *Kan'yōroku*. On the transmission of Korean people and culture to Japan, particularly during the second offensive of 1597–98, see Kim Hong-kyu, *Hideyoshi mimizuka yonhyaku nen*, 119–40.

94. *FGYB*, 961–64.

95. Ibid., 1008–11, 1024–27; *CPC*, 324–25, 348; Wang Xiangrong, *Zhong-Ri guanxi wenxian lunkao*, 282–88.

96. *FGYB*, 1083; *CPC*, 324; *SMR*, 1:248. For an exhaustive list of the rewards and promotions granted to Ming participants, see *FGYB*, 1098–1130. On the distribution of food to Korean commoners, see *CMN*, 187.

97. *CPC*, 344.

98. Ibid., 352, 353; *IWSC*, 1:318–19.

99. *CPC*, 333–37, 358–59, 368; *IWSC*, 1:320–21.

100. *IWSC*, 1:193–95, 234, 338–39.

101. Ibid., 332, 348–54.

102. Parker, *Military Revolution*, 80. On logistical difficulties faced by European armies in the early sixteenth century, see ibid., 64–81; and Fissel, *English Warfare*, 5–8, 34–40.

103. Parker, *Military Revolution*, 56–58; B. Hall, *Weapons and Warfare in Renaissance Europe*, 228–29.

104. *FGYB*, 1024, 1057.

5. CAUGHT BETWEEN THE DRAGON AND THE RISING SUN

1. *SI*, 608.

2. There are several variations on these demands in the sources. See, for example, Berry, *Hideyoshi*, 214–15; Cao, *Wanli huangdi da zhuan*, 265–66; and *SI*, 607–608. A full translation of the terms as dictated by Hideyoshi is in Kuno, *Japanese Expansion*, 1:327–32.

3. Kim cited in Li Guangtao, *Wanli ershisan nian feng Riben*, 156. For a discussion of Hideyoshi's position as laid out in the *Chōsen seibatsuki*, see Nakamura Tokugoro, "Ni-Min kōwa haretsu shi temmatsu," 972–77. On Katō as a man of action, see *STS*, 12b.

4. Li Guangtao, *Wanli ershisan nian feng Riben*, 3; *STS*, 12a.

5. This passage cited in Li Guangtao, *Wanli ershisan nian feng Riben*, 13.

6. Fan S., *Wanli zhuan*, 239; *DMB*, 731.

7. *CBR*, 393; *SI*, 609–10. On Shen's agreement with Konishi, see *MSG*, 5:26. On Hideyoshi's supposed desire for investiture, see *YM*, 16–17.

8. Song M., *Jiuyue qianji*, 5b; *WKSL*, 494.

9. Wang C., "Li Rusong zheng dong kao," 367; *WKSL*, 496–97.

10. *MTJ*, 2742; Shen cited in Wang C., "Li Rusong zheng dong kao," 373.

11. *CNE*, 161; *PRL*, 257; *CPC*, 313. The gifts sent to the Japanese included a gazetteer of the Ming empire, a book of official Ming laws and regulations, and the *Seven Military Classics*. *PRL*, 258.

12. Oze, *Taikō-ki*, 436–38.Some sources put the departure date a week earlier. See, for example, *CNE*, 161. The Chinese mission to Nagoya and the exchange between them and the Japanese is covered in Zheng L., *Ming dai Zhong-Ri guanxi*, 619–21.

13. Oze, *Taikō-ki*, 437, 448–50; *SI*, 617. Also see Zheng L., *Ming dai Zhong-Ri guanxi*, 622–23. On the matter of the Koreans being at fault, see *IC*, 116–18. For Hideyoshi's demands, see Oze, *Taikō-ki*, 448–50.

14. Oze, *Taikō-ki*, 444.

15. *MSJSBM*, 2376; *SDZK*, 38. On Ming concerns about the continued presence of Japanese troops at Pusan, see *FGYB*, 765–66.

16. *NC*, 8:35, 51.

17. *MSJSBM*, 2376; *WKSL*, 502; Zhu, "Ming dai yuan Chao," 157.

18. Li Guangtao, *Wanli ershisan nian feng Riben*, 67–68; *CXSL*, 257–65; *CNE*, 162; Wang C., "Liu Ting zheng dong kao," 140. Some Japanese accounts have Shen and Konishi arriving in early July, which would indicate that they were back in Korea when the massacre at Chinju took place. See, for example, *CNE*, 161. Mao Ruizheng says the mission returned on July 18, but this is a mistake given the fact that the massacre at Chinju is said to have occurred while the envoys were in Japan. See *CBR*, 400–401; *SDZK*, 40; and *ZDSJ*, 899. When questioned by Li Rusong about the massacre at Chinju, two Japanese commanders allegedly just kowtowed and said nothing. *WKSL*, 502.

19. *IC*, 107–108.

20. *CXSL*, 309–15; *MTJ*, 2745; *IC*, 109. The figure of 50,000 liang a month may be high, for other sources state that the Ming estimated it could keep 16,000 troops in Korea at a cost of about 100,000 liang for the year. But that annual estimate may assume that the Koreans would be paying for part of their upkeep. See *WLDC*, 789; and *SDZK*, 41.

21. *CBR*, 455. These military reforms are discussed in Palais, *Confucian Statecraft and Korean Institutions*, 84–89. Also see Kim Hong-kyu, *Hideyoshi mimizuka yonhyaku nen*, 109–203.

22. *IC*, 111, 121.

23. Ibid., 108; Li Guangtao, *Wanli ershisan nian feng Riben*, 69; *NC*, 8:51.

24. *IC*, 108–109; Li Guangtao, *Wanli ershisan nian feng Riben*, 161–71. Also see *SMR*, 2:10–13.

25. Hideyoshi's concern for his infant heir (and thus his legacy) dominated the rest of his life. It was the major reason why he himself never went to Korea, and it certainly affected his judgment in political and military affairs. On Hideyori, see Berry, *Hideyoshi*, 217–23.

26. *GQ*, 4709; *WKSL*, 500, 504; *MS*, 8293; *GQ*, 4704; Li Guangtao, *Wanli ershisan nian feng Riben*, 30. Wanli's belief that the Japanese were afraid of Ming military strength was possibly based on a report from Song Yingchang. *WKSL*, 500–501; *FGYB*, 878–79. Another source questions the letter's veracity. See *CHJ*, 283. An account of the Ming envoys' experience in Japan as related to Yi Sunsin is in *IC*, 116–18.

27. Konishi Joan reached Liaoyang in May 1594. *WKSL*, 518. In addition to the enormous costs involved, the Ming were also concerned about possible troop mutinies if the men were forced to remain in Korea. On the hardships suffered by Korean commoners, see *FGBYB*, 869–71.

28. *SMR*, 1:398.

29. *ZDSJ*, 900; *MS*, 276; *MTJ*, 2745; *GQ*, 4717. Li Rusong was honored by the Koreans, who eventually erected a statue of him in Pyongyang. He was made grand guardian of the heir apparent and received a salary increase of 100 shi of grain per year. Song Yingchang was made vice minister of war of the left. *GQ*, 4718; *MSG*, 5:26. On Gu's advocating the total withdrawal of Ming troops and his desire for peace, see *MS*, 6392.

30. *WKSL*, 507. The text of Wanli's letter is in *GQ*, 4711.

31. *GQ*, 4709–11; Fan S., *Wanli zhuan*, 241. This version of Song's memorial comes from *SI*, 615–16. Also see *MSJSBM*, 2376; *MS*, 8293; and *GQ*, 4703. The passage is also cited in Zhuan Q., *Zhongguo gu waijiao shiliao huibian*, 1416–17.

32. *SI*, 647–48; *MSJSBM*, 2376; *CXSL*, 348–50. A biography of He can be found in *DMB*, 507–509. The full extent of the disagreements within both the Ming and the Korean courts are covered in Li Guangtao, *Wanli ershisan nian feng Riben*, 77–124.

33. *WKSL*, 512; *SI*, 650.

34. Li Guangtao, *Chaoxian (Renchen Wohuo) Yanjiu*, 140–41; *SI*, 648. On the taking of slaves and other Japanese atrocities, see Kim Hong-kyu, *Hideyoshi mimizuka yonhyaku nen*, 124–40; and Kim Pong-hyon, *Hideyoshi no Chōsen*, 389–404. Escaped slaves were an important source of information on conditions within the Japanese camps. See, for example, *IC*, 174–79.

35. *GQ*, 4722, 4724; *WKSL*, 515.

36. *WKSL*, 516. This edict is translated in Kuno, *Japanese Expansion*, 1:334–35. Also see Li Guangtao, *Wanli ershisan nian feng Riben*, 124–28.

37. *WKSL*, 519–20; *SI*, 656–57. Some troops were stationed along the Yalu, and Wanli approved a proposal for the repair of coastal fortifications and integrated land- and naval-training operations. *WKSL*, 525–26. On Ming deliberations, see Cao, *Wanli huangdi da zhuan*, 267.

38. *HMJSWB*, 25:245–52. In another memorial submitted during the second invasion of Korea, Zhang asked that if the Japanese wanted trade with China so badly, why did they keep attacking Korea, for this was certainly not the way to gain access to Chinese products. Ibid., 265–66.

39. Shi was also suspicious of the Japanese and would not dare make a final decision. *SI*, 663. For more on bureaucratic strife at this time, see *GQ*, 4715–16; and *WLDC*, 738–62.

40. *WKSL*, 528–29; *MHY*, 1135. The Koreans were enthusiastic backers of these efforts. *CXSL*, 452–53.

41. *MS*, 8294; *MTJ*, 2753. Defense expenditures for Jizhen, which had been just 15,000 liang annually at the beginning of the Ming era, by this time exceeded 1.3 million liang per year. *WLDC*, 765, 777.

42. *MS*, 8294; *WLDC*, 867–68; *MSJSBM*, 2376.

43. *IWSC*, 2:5–8. For example, when Guo Shi, an official in the Ministry of Justice, submitted a memorial opposing the resumption of tributary relations, Wanli immediately issued an imperial decree making him a commoner, adding that anyone who stood in the way of the resumption of tributary relations and fabricated words to delude people would suffer a similar fate. Fan S., *Wanli zhuan*, 242. Also see *WLDC*, 828–29.

44. *SI*, 664; Wang C., "Liu Ting zheng dong," 138–39.

45. *CBR*, 406; *NC*, 8:49–51, 57.

46. *STS*, 1a, 4a–4b; *NC*, 8:55, 78–85.

47. *STS*, 5b, 6b, 8b.

48. Ibid., 17a–18a, 20a–23a, 25a.

49. Ibid., 27b–28a, 29a–31b.

50. *CPC*, 405–409; 410.

51. Ibid., 411–12.

52. *NC*, 8:66, 67, 71.

53. Ibid., 60, 62.

54. *GQ*, 4726; *MTJ*, 2753–54; *WLDC*, 919. Liu Ting was accused of trying to bribe a censor to get a better reward for his service in Korea. Some officials recommended that he not be reappointed to high position, but they were overruled by Wanli. Ibid., 880.

55. *FGYB*, 1170; *CPC*, 403; Li Guangtao, *Wanli ershisan nian feng Riben*, 127–28; *PRL*, 264; *CBR*, 408–409; *WLDC*, 877. The presentation of documents was scheduled for January 29 but was moved up. Other sources indicate the investiture decision was not reached until the end of the second lunar month. See, for example, *CPC*, 390.

56. *IWSC*, 2:10–15.

57. Ibid., 17, 22–23.

58. *WKSL*, 534–37; *CS*, 1, 70a–75a; *SI*, 665; *PRL*, 262; *CXSL*, 517; Li Guangtao, *Wanli ershisan nian feng Riben*, 148–51; *FGYB*, 1172. Konishi's experiences in Beijing and his audiences with the Ming court are also described in *MSL*, 5172–5209. The Japanese perspective is found in Kitajima, *Chōsen nichinichiki*, 273–77.

59. Li Guangtao, *Wanli ershisan nian feng Riben*, 150; *CS*, 1, 74b. The statement regarding the emperor is false. Konishi Joan is referring to Nobunaga's removal of Ashikaga Yoshiaki from the post of shogun in 1573. For more on this, see J. Hall et al., eds., *Japan before Tokugawa*, 155–73.

60. *FGYB*, 1166–68, 1174–77.

61. *CPC*, 373–77, 395.

62. *IWSC*, 2:51–55, 68–70, 129, 132.

63. Ibid., 76–82, 142; Hur N., "Politicking or Being Politicked," esp. 329–33. The upkeep for the Zhejiang troops was estimated at 11,381 liang per month plus rations.

64. *IWSC*, 2:67, 104.

65. Ibid., 98–99, 103; *CPC*, 379. The Ming also sent goods and supplies for the Koreans to perform sacrifices for their war dead and to erect memorials in Pyongyang, Kaesŏng, and Pyŏkchegwan, possibly to soothe bruised feelings but also to remind their allies of the price already paid. Ibid., 422.

66. *CPC*, 381, 383, 398–99.

67. *FGYB*, 1188–93; Li Guangtao, *Chaoxian (Renchen Wohuo) Yanjiu*, 133.

68. This translation is abridged and adapted from Kuno, *Japanese Expansion*, 1:337–39. A photograph of the document is found in Zheng L., *Ming dai Zhong-Ri guanxi*, 632. For excerpts, see also *GQ*, 4745–46; and Fan S., *Wanli zhuan*, 242–44. The original is held in the Osaka City Museum.

69. Li Guangtao, *Chaoxian (Renchen Wohuo) Yanjiu*, 133; *SI*, 667; *STS*, 39b.

70. *FGYB*, 1182–83, 1188. Illustrations of these items can be found in Zheng L., *Ming dai Zhong-Ri guanxi*, 632–33. Also see Li Guangtao, *Wanli ershisan nian feng Riben*, 128–29.

71. *GQ*, 4743; *SMR*, 1:463; *NC*, 8:87.

72. *CPC*, 429–30; *SMR*, 2:43; *CBR*, 409; *SMR*, 1:481, 482; *GQ*, 4756.

73. *SMR*, 1:440–41; Li Guangtao, *Wanli ershisan nian feng Riben*, 187. The full exchange between the envoys is found in ibid., 184–90.

74. *CPC*, 435.

75. Translated in Kuno, *Japanese Expansion*, 1:333.

76. Kitajima, *Hideyoshi no Chōsen shinryaku*, 66; Cory, "Father Gregorio des Cespedes," 44.

77. Hawley, *Imjin War*, 392; Kitajima, *Hideyoshi no Chōsen shinryaku*, 66–67; *SMR*, 1:287–90.

78. *SMR*, 1:521; *CNE*, 166; *IWSC*, 2:196; *WKSL*, 549. Also see *WLDC*, 932.

79. *IWSC*, 2:259, 260–62.

80. Ibid., 276; *SMR*, 2:85. On Hideyoshi's mental state and final decline, see Berry, *Hideyoshi*, 226–36.

81. *WKSL*, 557; He B. et al., *Ming Shenzong yu Ming Dingling*, 109. Also see *GQ*, 4766–67.

82. *CPC*, 435; *NC*, 8:97; *WKSL*, 558–59; *WLDC*, 953. Also see *GQ*, 4771; and *SI*, 679. This version of the story is supported in *CHJ*, 284. Some sources relate that Li took some servants with him. See *CBR*, 410; and *WKSL*, 565.

83. According to Gu Yingtai, the woman in question was the wife of Sō Yoshitoshi and the daughter of Konishi Yukinaga. *MSJSBM*, 2377. Another source simply states that Li had improper relations with one of the ladies in the Japanese entourage. *MTJ*, 2764. Also see *CNE*, 167. Li Guangtao confirms the story about the woman in question being Sō's wife and Konishi's daughter. *Wanli ershisan nian feng Riben*, 219–21, 358–59. Some versions of the story maintain that the incident took place on Tsushima, though how Li then got back to Korea is unclear. See, for example, He B. et al., *Ming Shenzong yu Ming Dingling*, 110.

84. Yi W., *Yi Sanguk ilgi*, 650; *PRL*, 275; *WLDC*, 953.

85. He B. et al., *Ming Shenzong yu Ming Dingling*, 110; *CPC*, 442–43.

86. *WKSL*, 562–63; *WLDC*, 950–51. Also see *CPC*, 438 (which includes a poem about the event).

87. *PRL*, 277; *SI*, 679–80.

88. Yue enumerated three disgraces (*ru*), four shames (*chi*), five regrets (*hen*), five cases of inflicting hardship (*nan*) on the state, and five endangerments (*wei*), or tactical errors. All these charges are in *WKSL*, 574–76.

89. *MSJSBM*, 2377; *GQ*, 4772; *WKSL*, 574–75. On Cao Xuecheng, see *MTJ*, 2764; *GQ*, 4772–74; and *MSJSBM*, 2377.

90. *WLDC*, 964–65; *WKSL*, 563–64.

91. *WKSL*, 580, 592; *CPC*, 455. Also on July 10, Li Zongcheng was imprisoned. *GQ*, 4780.

92. *SI*, 682; *CPC*, 466, 475. Ŏ Hŭimun posited that the earthquake was divine retribution for Hideyoshi's actions. *SMR*, 2:85.

93. *SI*, 683; *WLDC*, 1039; *CPC*, 478.

94. *CPC*, 481–88.

95. These episodes and the letter itself are discussed in *SI*, 684–87. Also see Li Guangtao, *Wanli ershisan nian feng Riben*, 224.

96. *SI*, 689; Li Guangtao, *Wanli ershisan nian feng Riben*, 221.

97. *SI*, 689–90.

98. Ibid., 690–91; *PRL*, 281.

99. *CBR*, 412; *CPC*, 477–78; *MS*, 8295. For the Japanese perspective on the investiture ceremony, see Chōsen Shi Henshukai, *Chōsen shi*, 10:628–31. Also see *CHJ*, 284–85. For an alternative version of Hideyoshi's reaction, see *MTJ*, 2769.

100. Berry, *Hideyoshi*, 216–17, 232.

101. Li Guangtao, *Wanli ershisan nian feng Riben*, 361; *WKSL*, 596; Zhu, "Ming dai yuan Chao," 160. Concerning the importance of sending royal envoys to Japan in Hideyoshi's eyes, see Li Guangtao, *Wanli ershisan nian feng Riben*, 374–75. Sun Kuang believed that war could still be averted if the Koreans would just send a prince recognizing Hideyoshi's status. *GQ*, 4785. In a Japanese letter explaining the reasons for the second invasion, Korea's refusal to acknowledge Hideyoshi's superiority was foremost on the list of transgressions. *PRL*, 282–83.

102. Zhu, "Ming dai yuan Chao," 159, 160; *CMN*, 196–97. On Hideyoshi's personal reasons for the second invasion, see, for example, the exchange between Hideyoshi and Frois quoted in Berry, *Hideyoshi*, 216.

103. *WLDC*, 1041; *GQ*, 4786. Also see *MSG*, 5:27.

104. *WLDC*, 1042; *MS*, 279, 8295; *SDZK*, 46. Shi was cast into jail immediately and his family was exiled to the wastelands. He eventually died in prison in the ninth lunar month of 1599. *MSG*, 5:27; *WLDC*, 1064. Xing Jie (1540–1621) was a native of Shandong and earned his *jinshi* degree in 1571.

105. *SI*, 691–92, 693; Hwang Sin's report, *NC*, 8:118–19.

106. *CPC*, 507–10, 511.

107. *CBR*, 412–15. See also the next chapter.

108. *SI*, 702–703.

109. Zhu, "Ming dai yuan Chao," 161.

6. BACK INTO THE GATES OF HELL

1. *CNE*, 175; *IWSC*, 2:327–28.

2. *IWSC*, 2:338–39; *NC*, 8:122, 123.

3. *IWSC*, 2:343–44, 45; *WLDC*, 1030. On the Japanese battle array and initial arrival in Korea, see *CS*, 5, 12b–21a; and *CNE*, 170–71. On Hideyoshi's plans, see ibid.

4. *IWSC*, 2:345–46.

5. *CNE*, 171; *CXSL*, 997; *IWSC*, 2:347–48, 349.

6. For the full text, see *CXSL*, 998–99.

7. On the personal nature of the invasion's goals, see, for example, Hawley, *Imjin War*, 441–42. For the invasion as an attempt to seize the southern provinces of Korea, see Kitajima, *Hideyoshi no Chosen shinryaku*, 74; and Nakao, *Chōsen tsushinshi to Jinshin waran*, 80.

8. Hawley, *Imjin War*, 441–42.

9. *IWSC*, 2:359, 362–74, 378–79. On Qing policies, see Dai, "Qing State, Merchants, and the Military Labor." On the European adoption of such trading practices, see Parker, *Military Revolution*, 80–81.

10. For a complete list of the Ming commanders selected for Korea, along with brief career notes, see *CPC*, 519–24. For the deployment plans, see *IWSC*, 2:423–32.

11. *IWSC*, 3:6, 12–13. The full text of the conference is in ibid., 3–64.

12. *WKSL*, 601; *IWSC*, 3:15, 21.

13. *IWSC*, 3:24–33; *CPC*, 512–18, 519.Regarding Shen's role in ruining the peace talks, see Arano, "Chōsen tsushinshi no shumatsu Shin Ikan 'Kaiyūroku ni yosete.'"

14. *IWSC*, 3:33–34, 39–40; Miller, "State Versus Society," chap. 3 (esp. 258–96). For a narrative account of the eunuch "mining" activities, see *MSJSBM*, 2386–90.

15. The nominal commanders of Japanese forces were fifteen-year-old Kobayakawa Hideaki, a nephew of Hideyoshi and adopted son of Kobayakawa Takakage; twenty-three-year-old Ukita Hideie; and eighteen-year-old Mōri Hidemoto, but they do not appear to have played important roles in either the fighting or the decision making. On the sending of tiger skins to Hideyoshi, see "Kiyomasa Korai jin oboegaki," 321.

16. Naito, "So Keinen to *Chōsen nichnichiki*," 161. For critical analysis and evaluation of Keinen's diary, see Elison, "Priest Keinen"; and Naito, "So Keinen no *Chōsen nichinichiki* ni tsuite." For information on the history of the work and its author, see Naito, "So Keinen to *Chōsen nichinichiki*," 155–60.

17. *CHJ*, 293; Zheng L., *Ming dai Zhong-Ri guanxi*, 634; Maske. See also the next chapter.

18. Turnbull, *Samurai Sourcebook*, 245; Murdoch, *History of Japan Vol. II*, 356–58; *IWSC*, 3:68. For copies of the communications between Hideyoshi and his commanders pertaining to the taking of noses, see Kitajima, *Hideyoshi no Chōsen shinryaku*, 82–83. The Mimizuka is discussed in depth in Kim Hong-kyu, *Hideyoshi mimizuka yonhyaku nen*, 141–78. For its historical evolution and significance, see Nakao, *Chōsen tsushinshi to Jinshin waeran*, chap. 3.

19. *IWSC*, 3:122. According to a report by Liu Ting, this suggested that the Japanese were serious about attacking China as well as Korea.

20. For Kwŏn's report, see *IWSC*, 3:66. For the higher figure, see *PRL*, 288; and *SDZK*, 48. The total number of Japanese mobilized for the second invasion

was around the same as that for the first: 141,490 plus reserves. A battle array of the initial force can be found in Kim Pong-hyon, *Hideyoshi no Chōsen*, 331–32. Also see *SI*, 700. The total number of Chinese mobilized for the second campaign in Korea has been estimated at perhaps 120,000. See Li Guangtao, *Chaoxian (Renchen Wohuo) Yanjiu*, 184–85. Ming projections called for raising 8 million piculs (533,320 tons) of grain to support these troops. See Cao, *Wanli huangdi da zhuan*, 272. Special funds were also designated for military physicians, no doubt in response to the disease encountered in the previous campaign. See *IWSC*, 3:47. Also see *CS*, 5, 22a–23b; and *IWSC*, 3:42–43.

21. *IWSC*, 3:87–100; *NC*, 8:127–28.

22. *IWSC*, 3:110–11, 133; *CS*, 5, 9a–10b. See the Japanese account in *CS*, 5, 11a–12a.

23. *NI*, 254; *CXSL*, 1969; *SMR*, 2:136–37; *CPC*, 531. While Yu Sŏngnyong stood up for Yi Sunsin, other officials disliked Yi, charging that the admiral secretly boasted of his achievements and had sometimes retreated in battle. Li Guangtao, *Chaoxian (Renchen Wohuo) Yanjiu*, 187–88; *NC*, 8:120–24; *CXSL*, 906. On the rivalry between Yi and Wŏn, see Niderost, "Yi Sun Sin and Won Kyun." Yi was permitted to stop by Asan and mourn his mother's death as he took up his new post. *CPC*, 531.

24. *PRL*, 295.

25. *CS*, 6; Li Guangtao, "Ming ren yuan Han yu Jishan da jie," 1–3. On these annexation concerns, see *SMR*, 2:195; and *CXSL*, 947–50.

26. *IWSC*, 3:114–16; *SI*, 699–700; *PRL*, 300.

27. *CPC*, 524; *SDZK*, 48. Xing Jie reached Liaodong about the same time, though it is unclear whether or not he and Ma were together. Some sources maintain Xing did not reach Seoul until that fall, but this seems questionable given the number of orders he issued concerning matters in Korea itself. See *MSJSBM*, 2377; and *SI*, 733.

28. *NC*, 8:133; *CPC*, 527. Liu boasted that he would capture Konishi Yukinaga himself. *SI*, 704.

29. *PRL*, 303.

30. *IWSC*, 3:151, 163. Yang Hao and other Chinese leaders also repeatedly pressed the Koreans to adopt a monetary economy and open more mines, though to no avail. Palais, *Confucian Statecraft and Korean Institutions*, 857.

31. *IWSC*, 3:171.

32. *SI*, 704; *NC*, 8:137; *MSJSBM*, 2377; *CPC*, 538–39; *IWSC*, 3:222–24; *SDZK*, 52; *PRL*, 309–10. Sources differ as to exactly when and where Shen was arrested. Some say he was not apprehended until he returned to China, while others state that he helped the Japanese for awhile before being captured. Xia Xie says Shen led 200 men to Pusan but was apprehended by Yang Yuan, who took him to Ma Gui's camp. *MTJ*, 2774. Gu Yingtai states that both Shi Xing and Shen were ordered arrested and interrogated by Wanli after being impeached by Yang Fangheng. *MSJSBM*, 2377. Regardless, most agree that Shi was arrested in March 1597. Shen and Shi were both sentenced to death in the ninth month of 1597. *MTJ*, 2778. Shi's family was banished to a malarial district in perpetuity. *WLDC*, 1064. Shen's wife and children would later be enslaved after his execution. Shen D., *Wanli yehuo bian*, 440–41.

33. *CPC*, 532–33.

34. *NC*, 8:135; *CPC*, 532–33.

35. *NC*, 8:136–37; *IWSC*, 3:181–83; *CPC*, 537; *CXSL*, 1044; *CNE*, 304; *NI*, 295–96. Katō's exploits are described in *SI*, 710–13. Also see E. Park, *Between Dreams and Reality*, 195–200. There are slight variations on Wŏn's story, including one in which he was killed as he reached shore after a naval engagement. See Li Guangtao, *Chaoxian (Renchen Wohuo) Yanjiu*, 195–96; and E. Park, *Between Dreams and Reality*, 195–200. Some Japanese sources suggest the two sides fought at night, not in the morning. See, for example, *CNE*, 304. Japan's victories are discussed further in *CXSL*, 1020–22.

36. *SI*, 714; *IWSC*, 3:217. At the same time the Japanese approached Namwŏn, another large force was advancing toward Kyŏngju and Taegu. On the Japanese advance, see Kitajima, *Toyotomi Hideyoshi*, 190–91.

37. *CPC*, 528; *NC*, 8:140.

38. *CPC*, 547–48. For a map showing the position of Japanese units around Namwŏn, see Kitajima, *Toyotomi Hideyoshi*, 192.

39. *NC*, 8:145.

40. *CXSL*, 1062; *SI*, 719.

41. *NC*, 8:143; Li Guangtao, *Chaoxian (Renchen Wohuo) Yanjiu*, 207.

42. *NC*, 8:144; Matsura, *Matsura Hōin seikan nikki*, 15–16. The Matsura would be credited with killing twenty-seven officers and 121 soldiers.

43. *CBR*, 424–25, 426; *CPC*, 547; *PRL*, 315; *SI*, 721. Also see *SDZK*, 52; and Turnbull, *Samurai Sourcebook*, 248–49. Gu Yingtai states that Yang stood up in his tent as soon as he heard the Japanese attack and simply fled for his life. *MSJSBM*, 2377. Some speculated that Yang was allowed to escape so that he could bring word of the sack of Namwŏn north and spread fear of the invaders.

44. Matsura, *Matsura Hōin seikan nikki*, 16; *SI*, 721–22; *PRL*, 316; Keinen, *Chōsen nichinichiki*, 17–18; Yamamoto, *Shimazu kokushi*, 21, 5a; Naito, "So Keinen to *Chōsen nichinichiki*," 165. Concerning Japanese chronicles of Namwŏn, see Turnbull, *Samurai Invasion*, 192–94. Yang was later executed by order of Wanli. *CS*, 6, 15a–19a.

45. *CXSL*, 1040; *NC*, 8:148. On Korean concerns in the aftermath of the debacle at Namwŏn as the Japanese were advancing, see *CXSL*, 1044–46.

46. *CXSL*, 1049; *IWSC*, 3:247–50.

47. *PRL*, 327; *SI*, 723; *MS*, 8296; *SDZK*, 52; *MSJSBM*, 2377; *IWSC*, 3:272–74. A similar statement is attributed to Yang Hao. See *CNE*, 179. This statement is somewhat puzzling in that over the course of the next year, Xing generally maintained a tough stance and on a number of occasions refused to listen to Japanese entreaties. The *Ming shi* records that Xing and the Koreans continued to negotiate secretly while outwardly preparing for battle. *MS*, 8296–97.

48. *IWSC*, 3:289–91, 303–306 (Xing's memorial). On the general distress in Chŏlla, see Yu Sagyŏng, *Yug'yudang ilgi*. The diary is unpaginated.

49. For the text of the memorial, see *HMJSWB*, 25:254–65.

50. Ibid., 259; *WKSL*, 620; *MS*, 6405. At the time of his appointment, Chen was drilling troops at Shanhaiguan.

51. Consider, for example, the British preference for "martial races" like the Sikhs in their imperial army.

52. *HMJSWB*, 25:265; *WKSL*, 610; *WLDC*, 1063.

53. *WKSL*, 612; Li Guangtao, *Chaoxian (Renchen Wohuo) Yanjiu*, 161. Some Korean officials did flee the capital. *SMR*, 2:225. Reportedly, others returned after Yang Hao arrived in the city.

54. *CXSL*, 953–58.

55. *CPC*, 542–43; *CNE*, 191.

56. *NC*, 8:148–49; *IWSC*, 3:404–10.

57. Reportedly, Sŏnjo himself greeted Yang when he reached the capital. Yang apologized for his failure to hold back the Japanese, to which the king replied that he was not to blame. *CXSL*, 1062. Nonetheless, Yang would be publicly executed outside Seoul's great south gate the following year for his failure. *CXSL*, 1371.

58. *CPC*, 550–51; *NC*, 8:150–51. Also see Zhang X. and Liu, *Zhongguo gudai zhanzheng tongjian*, 804; and Li Guangtao, "Ming ren yuan Han yu Jishan da jie," 5–6. Li relies on Korean sources.

59. *NC*, 8:151; *CNE*, 306.

60. *SI*, 725; *CXSL*, 1071,1091.

61. *SDZK*, 53.

62. Li Guangtao, "Ming ren yuan Han yu Jishan da jie," 9–11; *CNE*, 194; *SI*, 727–29. A Korean report estimated 173 Japanese dead. *IWSC*, 3:355. Also see a Japanese account of the battle in *CS*, 7, 11a–12a.

63. He B. et al., *Ming Shenzong yu Ming Dingling*, 114; Zhang X. and Liu, *Zhongguo gudai zhanzheng tongjian*, 804.

64. *MSG*, 5:28; Park Y., *Admiral Yi*, 207. Kawaguchi Choju states that the people of Seoul were disquieted when Jie Sheng arrived "with false reports of a great victory." The army, though, believed Jie and took heart from the news. *SI*, 729. He Baoshan and his coauthors state that Shen, who had theretofore been helping the invaders, delivered this letter personally to Konishi. Shen had recently been captured by the Ming and forced to deceive the Japanese. *Ming Shenzong yu Ming Dingling*, 114. Another version relates that Shen wrote the letter. See *MTJ*, 2778; and *MSJSBM*, 2377. Zhuge Yuansheng is in agreement on Shen's connivance with the Japanese, charging that he had informed them of allied plans and positions prior to his arrest by Yang Yuan. When his residence was searched, investigators found Japanese swords, uniforms, and other items. *PRL*, 310–11.

65. He B. et al., *Ming Shenzong yu Ming Dingling*, 113; *CPC*, 552; *SMR*, 2:232–33. Zhuge Yuansheng observes that Chiksan crushed Japanese morale and saved the city of Seoul, even though casualties were not high and the Ming had not yet brought their full strength to bear. *PRL*, 334.

66. Park Y., *Admiral Yi*, 202; *CPC*, 546; *IWSC*, 3:190–91; Li Guangtao, "Ming ren yuan Han yu Jishan da jie," 12–13. On Yi's reappointment, see Park Y., *Admiral Yi*, 200–204.

67. Park Y., *Admiral Yi*, 213. See Yi's account of Myŏngyang in *NI*, 314–15. Korean sources maintain that Yi had but twelve ships under his command in this battle, but this is almost certainly mythology. See, for example, *CBR*, 427. Other Korean sources put the fleets closer to parity in numbers. See, for example, Li Guangtao, "Ming ren yuan Han yu Jishan da jie," 13. On the "Miracle at Myŏngyang," see Park Y., *Admiral Yi*, 211–14; and *IWSC*, 4:33–35.

68. *IWSC*, 3:412–31, 4:3–5.
69. Li Guangtao, "Ming ren yuan Han yu Jishan da jie," 5 (from *Ming shilu*, 25th year of Wanli, 3rd month); *SI*, 725. For a biography of Yang, see *MS*, 6685–88. On Korean perceptions of Yang, see Ledyard, "Confucianism and War," 86–91, 112–13.
70. *IWSC*, 4:43, 46. The full memorial can be found in ibid., 39–50.
71. Ibid., 22–23; *SMR*, 2:249.
72. *IWSC*, 3:396–97, 4:51–52, 55.
73. *CS*, 7, 15a–16a; *NC*, 8:153. For accounts of the hardships experienced by Koreans, see Keinen, *Chōsen nichinichiki*, 43–49. Also see Kitajima, *Hideyoshi no Chōsen shinryaku*, 89–90.
74. *NC*, 8:167, 172; *WKSL*, 622–23.
75. *IWSC*, 4:60–63, 80–81.
76. Turnbull, *Samurai*, 220.
77. *IWSC*, 4:84, 98, 143, 145–48; *PRL*, 344.
78. *PRL*, 335–37; *IWSC*, 4:129. On the effectiveness of the righteous armies during the second invasion, see Kim Pong-hyon, *Hideyoshi no Chōsen*, 401–28.
79. *CPC*, 557–58. On ceremonies prior to marching, see *CXSL*, 1134.
80. Li Guangtao, "Yang Hao Weishan zhi yi," 545; *CNE*, 310; *SI*, 736; *MSJSBM*, 2377; *CPC*, 558–59. In some accounts the Chinese claimed to have killed as many as 3,000 in this ambush.
81. *CNE*, 171, 308; Keinen, *Chōsen nichinichiki*, 69–73; Elison, "Priest Keinen," 34–37. Also see Oze, *Taikō-ki*, 418. Oze gives a figure of 500,000 allied forces.
82. *MSJSBM*, 2378; *CNE*, 311; Turnbull, *Samurai Invasion*, 210; Oze, *Taikō-ki*, 418; *SI*, 739.
83. *Taiko-ki*, 418; *CS*, 8, 7a–10a, 10b–16b; *SDZK*, 54; *CXSL*, 1162; *CNE*, 313.
84. *CXSL*, 1163–64; *CPC*, 560–61; *CS*, 8, 13b–15a.
85. Li Guangtao, "Yang Hao Weishan zhi yi," 553; *CPC*, 561; *CXSL*, 1165.
86. *CXSL*, 1167–68; *SI*, 744.
87. Li Guangtao, "Yang Hao Weishan zhi yi," 547; *CXSL*, 1972; *CPC*, 567.
88. Yi Tŏkhyŏng maintained that 800 were killed in battle and 3,000 more wounded, 1,000 of whom died later. Ding Yingtai reported 4,800 dead and 6,000 dead and wounded, which could mean either 4,800 dead and 1,200 wounded or 4,800 dead and 6,000 wounded, some of whom later died. Ledyard, "Confucianism and War," 93; *CXSL*, 1420. Sin Kyŏng gives a figure of 1,400 killed and 3,000 wounded. *CPC*, 569. Yet another source gives casualties as a mere 3,700. *CXSL*, 1170–71. The *Taikō-ki*, in its typically exaggerated fashion, presents a figure of 60,000–70,000 killed, maintaining that this proved the superiority of Japanese warriors once more as well their divine blessing. Oze, *Taikō-ki*, 421. Another Japanese account of the siege can be found in *CS*, 8, 1a–21a.
89. *CS*, 8, 17a–18a; *CXSL*, 1172. The commander in question was reportedly Lu Jizhong, though this may well be an error. *MSJSBM*, 2378. Other sources credit Wu and Mao with covering the retreat. *MTJ*, 2780; *MS*, 6686. Still other sources credit Li Fangchun. See, for example, Li Guangtao, "Ding Yingtai yu Yang Hao," 159. Also see *SMR*, 2:267.
90. *CXSL*, 1165, 1167; *CPC*, 561; Li Guangtao, "Yang Hao Weishan zhi yi," 554; *SI*, 740.

91. *WKSL*, 630; *CXSL*, 1197. Xing's report reached Wanli on March 11, 1598. Ledyard, "Confucianism and War," 86.

92. *CXSL*, 1203. On these exchanges, see ibid., 1216–18.

93. *WKSL*, 632.

94. *MS*, 8297; *WKSL*, 626; *GQ*, 4805. Ding's report was presented on July 6, 1598. Ledyard, "Confucianism and War," 87. Yang supposedly reined in Chinese forces under Chen Yin just as they were about to exploit a breach in the Japanese defenses because Yang wanted Li Rumei to get the honor and rewards for the victory. *MTJ*, 2780.

95. Ledyard, "Confucianism and War," 90–91; *CXSL*, 1332; *SMR*, 2:274.

96. *MS*, 8298. For a lengthier examination of Yang and the siege of Ulsan within the context of Ming political history, see Swope, "War and Remembrance."

97. *CXSL*, 1221; Li Guangtao, "Ding Yingtai yu Yang Hao," 139; Ledyard, "Confucianism and War," 87. Ding's charges themselves are in *CXSL*, 1286.

98. Ledyard, "Confucianism and War," 89; Li Guangtao, "Ding Yingtai yu Yang Hao," 141. The original is in *CXSL*, 1292–93.

99. Ledyard, "Confucianism and War," 89; Li Guangtao, "Ding Yingtai yu Yang Hao," 143; *IWSC*, 4:176–82. The original text of the court conference is in *CXSL*, 1293–96.

100. Cited in Li Guangtao, "Ding Yingtai yu Yang Hao," 150–51 (excerpted from *Shenzong shilu*, juan 323), 155–56. Also see *WLDC*, 1135–37.

101. Ledyard, "Confucianism and War," 90, 91; *CXSL*, 1330.

102. Ledyard, "Confucianism and War," 93; *CXSL*, 1343–45. For a lengthier discussion and translation of Ding's charges against the Koreans, see *CXSL*, 1351–53; and Ledyard, "Confucianism and War," 95.

103. Ledyard, "Confucianism and War," 104. The notice was passed to the king on October 26, 1598. *CXSL*, 1363.

104. Ledyard, "Confucianism and War," 109; *CXSL*, 1393, 1429.

105. Li Guangtao, "Yang Hao Weishan zhi yi," 555–58; *CXSL*, 1174–76, 1198; *MTJ*, 2781–82; *IWSC*, 4:214–28. On the death of Li Rusong and his epitaph, see *GQ*, 4810–11.

106. *CBR*, 429; *IC*, 234. Koreans maintained that Chen was haughty and arrogant but was overawed by the righteous bearing of Yi Sunsin. *IC*, 232–33. Korean sources are in direct contradiction to Chinese sources, which refer to Yi as Chen's assistant. While this was probably not the case, Chen certainly played a larger role than claimed by Koreans, if for no other reason than because the Chinese navy was larger than that of Korea. Park Yune-hee criticizes Chen as a vainglorious bully. *Admiral Yi*, 229.

107. *SI*, 749. This quote is taken from *Nihon gaishi* as cited in Li Guangtao, *Ming-Qing dang'an*, 828.

108. Li Guangtao, *Ming-Qing dang'an*, 828, 831; *CXSL*, 18. For one version of Hideyoshi's discussions with his commanders, see "Kiyomasa Korai jin oboegaki," 327–28. On the Japanese generals' desire to withdraw and their recommendation to Hideyoshi, see Park Y., *Admiral Yi*, 227–28.

109. On the withdrawal decision by Hideyoshi, see *CNE*, 174. For the traditional interpretation, see Kitajima, *Hideyoshi no Chōsen shinryaku*, 92–94. Kitajima also relates a story about the Japanese agreeing to peace if the Koreans

sent honey, pharmaceuticals, and tiger skins in apology. On Hideyoshi's death saving the allies, see, for example, *MS*, 8358. A line in the *Ming shi* states that after seven years of battle and hundreds of thousands of taels of silver spent and tens of thousands of lives lost, the calamity was ended by the death of Hideyoshi. This passage is unsurprisingly a favorite of nationalistic Japanese scholar Yoshi Kuno. See *Japanese Expansion*, 1:340–41.

110. Yi C., "Korean Envoys and Japan," 26; *CNE*, 174–75.

111. Stramigioli, "Hideyoshi's Expansionist Policy," 100.

112. Kuno, *Japanese Expansion*, 1:174.

113. *MTJ*, 2787. This is a mistake. According to his biographer, Hideyoshi died at Fushimi Castle on September 18, 1598. Berry, *Hideyoshi*, 235. This date is also given in *SI*, 753. Also see *CS*, 9, 13b.

114. Li Guangtao, *Ming-Qing dang'an*, 831; *CNE*, 174; Berry, *Hideyoshi*, 234–35; *CPC*, 583; *IWSC*, 4:170–72; *SMR*, 2:293–303; *NC*, 8:186–88. It was also around this time too that Yang Yuan was executed, his head afterward suspended outside the walls of Seoul. *NC*, 8:200.

115. *CNE*, 202.

116. *SMR*, 2:293–96, 317, 319–20; *NC*, 8:185.

117. *NC*, 8:197–98; *IWSC*, 4:315–21. A complete list of troop figures and commanders can be found in *NC*, 8:183; and *IWSC*, 4:198–214. The troop estimates of 142,700 might be a bit high, though. For communications on the delivery of military supplies and provisions, see *IWSC*, 4:249–82.

118. *MS*, 6201; *SMR*, 2:341–42; *CS*, 9, 25b. Despite their personal animosity, Katō agreed to help Konishi return home, their common bond as samurai overriding other concerns. "Kiyomasa Korai jin oboegaki," 330.

119. Li Guangtao, *Chaoxian (Renchen Wohuo) Yanjiu*, 260; Yamamoto, *Shimazu kokushi*, 21, 5b–6a. Some Japanese records claim that 200,000 troops attacked Sachŏn, a figure that must represent the total number of allied troops in Korea at the time. See *CNE*, 316; and *CPC*, 603. The Japanese artwork mentioned is reproduced in Turnbull, *Samurai Sourcebook*, 250. Turnbull, however, inflates the number of allied troops present to some 36,000 men, presumably in an attempt to substantiate the claims made in the Shimazu chronicles that they took 33,700 noses in this battle.

120. *PRL*, 366; *CPC*, 626, 627; Yi Hyŏngsŏk, *Imjin chŏllansa*, 1560.

121. Yi Hyŏngsŏk, *Imjin chŏllansa*, 1561; *NC*, 8:198; *CS*, 9, 8a–8b; *CNE*, 316.

122. Yi Hyŏngsŏk, *Imjin chŏllansa*, 1560.

123. Li Guangtao, *Chaoxian (Renchen Wohuo) Yanjiu*, 261.

124. *NC*, 8:203; Turnbull, *Samurai Invasion*, 220; *MSJSBM*, 2378. On Peng accidentally setting off the Japanese magazines, see, for example, *SDZK*, 57; and *PRL*, 371. Dong Yiyuan's biography states that the Japanese set off the explosion on purpose. *MS*, 6214. Also see the Korean account, which blames Mao's subordinates, in *CXSL*, 1375–76. The Japanese version can be found in *SI*, 757–60.

125. *MSJSBM*, 2378; *CS*, 9, 11b–12a; Yamamoto, *Shimazu kokushi*, 21, 8b–12a; *SI*, 760; *PRL*, 372. The Japanese recovered 12,000 piculs (800 tons) of provisions. Yi Hyŏngsŏk, *Imjin chŏllansa*, 1560; *NC*, 8:203. Dong was demoted three grades in rank. *SDZK*, 57.

126. Li Guangtao, *Chaoxian (Renchen Wohuo) Yanjiu*, 262; *PRL*, 381.

127. *NC*, 8:194; *MSJSBM*, 2378; *SI*, 752. After Kŏjedo, Chen proclaimed to Yi, "You are truly a shield for your king."

128. *CBR*, 437–38; *CS*, 9, 26b–27a; Park Y., *Admiral Yi*, 237; *IWSC*, 4:343; *NC*, 8:203; Matsura, *Matsura Hōin seikan nikki*, 20–21. Park repeats the story that Admiral Chen was also bribed by Konishi, but Yi convinced him to renege on the deal. Park Y., *Admiral Yi*, 237–40. Kawaguchi Choju states that Liu signed a ten-day truce with Konishi that provided for the uncontested withdrawal of Japanese forces. *SI*, 763.

129. *CPC*, 627; *NC*, 8:205–206.

130. *SDZK*, 56; *IWSC*, 4:352; *DMB*, 171; *NC*, 8:207; *CPC*, 627, 630; Li Guangtao, *Chaoxian (Renchen Wohuo) Yanjiu*, 266–74.

131. *CPC*, 635; *NC*, 8:208–209; *NI*, 342–43. It is interesting to note that while Yi Sunsin reports that the Japanese dispatched numerous gift-bearing envoys to negotiate with Chen, he never suggests that the admiral was moved by their presents.

132. *MS*, 6412.

133. *CPC*, 641, 642; *IC*, 239–41; *BOC*, 227–28.

134. *MS*, 6405; *CBR*, 434–35; Li Guangtao, "Ming ren yuan Han yu Chen Lin jiangong," 6; *SI*, 769; *NC*, 8:210; *CXSL*, 1454–55.

135. Wang C., "Liu Ting zheng dong," 143; *CXSL*, 1373, 1394, 1414–15. Also see *MSJSBM*, 2378; and *CPC*, 638. For a Japanese account of the battle and escape, see Matsura, *Matsura Hōin seikan nikki*, 22–24.

136. *PRL*, 393–94; Zhuan Z. et al., *Zhongguo junshi shi*, 405; Kuno, *Japanese Expansion*, 1:173.

137. *MSJSBM*, 2378; *MTJ*, 2794. Gu Yingtai is quite critical of these actions, calling it a case of loyal ministers being punished as the venal were rewarded. *MSJSBM*, 2379; *MTJ*, 2795. Tan Qian, though, agrees with Grand Secretary Shen Yiguan, who argued at the time that since the Japanese were defeated, there was no reason to pursue lengthy investigations. *GQ*, 4829–30.

138. Li Guangtao, "Ming ren yuan Han yu Chen Lin jiangong," 7.

139. The dazzling array of ships possessed by the late Ming navy are described in *WBZ*, 4762–4821. Also see Needham et al., *Science and Civilisation*, vol. 5, pt. 7, 408–29. Zheng Liangsheng finds that lucrative foreign trade provided the Ming with the finances necessary to successfully pursue the Three Great Campaigns. *Ming dai Zhong-Ri guanxi*, 640.

140. *IWSC*, 4:361–62, 365–81.

7. AFTERMATH AND LEGACIES

1. Kuba, "Jūroku seikimatsu," esp., 33–37, 47; *SDZK*, 59.

2. *IWSC*, 4:404–406, 410–12; *CPC*, 645–46. Wanli's Decree of Merit for Service in Korea was issued in the ninth month of 1599. For details on who received which honors, see ibid., 705–10.

3. *CPC*, 647; *IWSC*, 4:425–32. Sŏnjo's complete letter can be found in ibid., 413–23.

4. Ledyard, "Confucianism and War," 82; Mason, 131–32. The altar (including a map), other memorials, and sacrificial services to Wanli and Ming

generals are discussed in detail in Li Guangtao, *Ming-Qing dang'an*, 835–48. Chong is an ultraconservative Confucian scholar, so his views should not be taken as indicative of the mainstream opinion in Korea. Contemporary Koreans are far more likely to remember the heroics of Yi Sunsin and little else.

5. *WKSL*, 654; *MSJSBM*, 2378; *CPC*, 710. A total of 2,248 Japanese were captured during the invasion. Also see *CPC*, 694–95.

6. *CPC*, 658, 685–86; *MS*, 281. Zhuge Yuansheng estimates that the war in Korea cost 8 million taels of silver. *PRL*, 383. Li Guangtao gives a figure of 8,830,000 taels, and Mao Ruizheng estimates the campaign cost 10 million taels, with 4 million paid by Korea. Li Guangtao, *Ming-Qing dang'an*, 827; *SDZK*, 59–60.

7. *IWSC*, 4:432–36, 441; *MS*, 8299; *WKSL*, 667–68, 669; *CPC*, 713. For the text of the Ming proclamation, see *WKSL*, 664–65. Also see Cao, *Wanli huangdi da zhuan*, 274–76; and *WKSL*, 652. Later Sŏnjo asked for an additional 8,000 naval troops to help patrol the coasts. *WKSL*, 654–56. A Korean source indicates that 15,000 Ming troops were left behind. *CPC*, 646. Sŏnjo ordered his Ministry of Revenue to handle the matter of feeding the Ming troops. Some suggested that the Chinese should feed them. *IWSC*, 4:455–59. Wanli sent a letter to Sŏnjo in 1602 praising Korean improvements in defense and preparedness.

8. *CPC*, 683–85; *IWSC*, 4:443–51; *SMR*, 2:405–406.

9. Kang H., *Kan'yōroku*; Hawley, *Imjin War*, 496–99; Kim Ha-tai, "Transmission of Neo-Confucianism," 85, 86–92; E. Kang, *Diplomacy and Ideology*, 108. Elison estimates that about 50,000–60,000 Korean POWs were taken to Japan. "Inseparable Trinity," 293. Also see Hawley, *Imjin War*, 564.

10. Kim Ha-tai, "Transmission of Neo-Confucianism," 93–96; E. Kang, *Diplomacy and Ideology*, 114.

11. Nakamura H., "Chōsengun no horyo ni natta Fukuda Kanyuki," 324–26; Maske, "Origins of Takatori Ware"; Turnbull, *Samurai Invasion*, 231; Hawley, *Imjin War*, 499. On Korean abductees to Japan, also see Naito Shumpo, "Bunroku-Keichō no eki ni okeru Chōsenjin no sakkan mondai ni tsuite"; and Yonetani, "Repatriation of Korean Captives."

12. Hawley, *Imjin War*, 564; Zheng L., *Ming dai Zhong-Ri guanxi*, 638–40; *SMR*, 2:374, 447.

13. Postwar reform efforts are masterfully discussed in Palais, *Confucian Statecraft and Korean Institutions*. On the military issues, see E. Park, *Between Dreams and Reality*.

14. *SMR*, 2:405, 461; *CPC*, 717; *NC*, 8:302, 311. The issues of inadequate resources and infrastructure are discussed in Palais, *Confucian Statecraft and Korean Institutions*, 92–114. Some argue that Dutch castaways also contributed to the spread of modern firearms in Korea, though it is difficult to estimate their real influence, which was most likely a postwar development. See, for example, Shin D., "Oranda jin hyōryūmin."

15. *NC*, 8:217. For a lengthier discussion of post-Hideyoshi normalization of foreign relations, see Toby, *State and Diplomacy*, 23–52. Also see E. Kang, *Diplomacy and Ideology*, 136–66; and Lee G., "Keichō." Regarding Tsushima, see, for example, *CMN*, 215–16.

16. *NC*, 8:226–33; Kobata and Matsuda, *Ryukyuan Relations*, 31.

17. *CPC*, 723; Kitajima, *Hideyoshi no Chōsen shinryaku*, 99; Kuno, *Japanese Expansion*, 2:274; *NC*, 8:266–98, 307–12; *STS*, 57b–63b. For a full treatment of the repatriations, see Naito, *Bunroku keichō no eki ni okeru hiryonin no kenkyū*. Some Koreans fled Japan and landed in China, from whence they were sent home. *NC*, 8:219.

18. Kitajima, *Hideyoshi no Chōsen shinryaku*, 100; Toby, *State and Diplomacy*, 30–31; Yamagata, "Japanese-Korean Relations," 5–7; E. Kang, *Diplomacy and Ideology*, 146; *NC*, 8:405. The convoluted language of these exchanges and the agreement eventually reached is discussed in Kuno, *Japanese Expansion*, 2:281–82. Also see *STS*, 54b–65a, for Genso's involvement in these talks.

19. Toby, *State and Diplomacy*, 39–41; Kang E., *Diplomacy and Ideology*, 118–25; J. Lewis, *Frontier Contact*, 10, 27; *CHJ*, 299; Ryang, "Korean-Japanese Relations," 442–44; Yi C., "Korean Envoys and Japan," 31. On the evolution of the "Japan House," see J. Lewis, *Frontier Contact*.

20. Toby, *State and Diplomacy*, 45–52; Toby, "Contesting the Centre," 359.

21. Toby, "Contesting the Centre," 349.

22. Haboush and Deuchler, *Culture and the State in Late Chosŏn Korea*, 50–51, 69; Haboush, "Dead Bodies in the Postwar Discourse."

23. Kitajima, *Hideyoshi no Chōsen shinryaku*, 1; Ōta, "Gunbu ni yoru Bunroku-Keichō no eki no jōkaku kenkyū," 35–39, 40. On the *Seikan ron* issue, see E. Kang, *Diplomacy and Ideology*, 9; and Conroy, *Japanese Seizure of Korea*.

24. Ōta, "Gunbu ni yoru Bunroku-Keichō no eki no jōkaku kenkyū," 41, 42–43; Kim Tae-chun, "Yi Sun-sin's Fame in Japan," 94–95, 106–107. Incidentally, some studies, such as that of Ikeuchi Hiroshi mentioned in the introduction, were suspended due to difficulties associated with the war.

25. I am reminded of a presentation given at the University of Michigan in 1999 in which a Korean scholar of literature discussed literary representations of the Japanese invasion. He spent virtually all his time denigrating the "feudal" Yi dynasty and its craven king, at times almost working himself into a rage. All his evidence seemed to be based on folk tales and popular literature. When asked about specific events and historical documents pertaining to the war, he knew nothing, though that is probably more a function of the way the war is remembered in Korea than a reflection on his methods. For a folk-tale version of the war, see Peter Lee's *Record of a Black Dragon Year*.

26. Contentions that the Chinese wanted to secure their own border are more understandable. For an immediate postwar suggestion of this rationale, see *CMN*, 224.

27. *CHJ*, 290; *CHC 8*, 299; Hur N., "International Context," 707. Clark also cites the drain on Ming treasuries.

28. Black, *War in the Early Modern World*, 10. On the expansion of the Ming state, see L. Shin, *Making of the Chinese State*.

29. He B. et al., *Ming Shenzong yu Ming Dingling*, 118.

30. R. Huang, *Taxation and Finance*, 303.

31. Parker, *Military Revolution*, 62. For information on Ming military costs, see R. Huang, *Taxation and Finance*, 290–94.

32. Fan S., *Wanli zhuan*, 247; He B. et al., *Ming Shenzong yu Ming Dingling*, 119.

33. See, for example, Sansom, *History of Japan*, 360. This interpretation is part of Japan's national myth, as evidenced by a conversation I had with a Japanese man on a bullet train in the spring of 2000. When I told him about my research, he responded, "It is funny that Japan, such a little country, always defeats China in every war."

34. On the significance of these naval developments in Europe, see McNeill, *Pursuit of Power*, 100–102; and Cipolla, *Guns, Sails, and Empires*, 21–89. For a discussion of the use of naval artillery outside of Europe in the early modern era, see ibid., 90–131.

35. McNeill, *Pursuit of Power*, 125; Parker, *Military Revolution*, 150–51. For a complete illustrated translation of this work, see Sang H. Kim, *Muye Dobo Tongji*. Li Rusong's sword form is found in ibid., 223–32.

36. This also refers to the fact that the war began during the year of the dragon and continued through the year of the serpent.

BIBLIOGRAPHY

Adolphson, Mikael S. *The Teeth and Claws of the Buddha: Monastic Warriors and Sōhei in Japanese History*. Honolulu: University of Hawaii Press, 2007.

———. *The Gates of Power: Monks, Courtiers, and Warriors in Premodern Japan*. Honolulu: University of Hawaii Press, 2000.

An Pangjun. *Ubŏng yasa pyŏllok*. Seoul: Asea munhwasa, 1996.

Antony, Robert J. *Like Froth Floating on the Sea: The World of Pirates and Seafarers in Late Imperial South China*. Berkeley: University of California Press, 2003.

Aoyogi, Nanmei, et al., eds. *Senjin no shiruseru Hō taikō seikan senki*. Seoul: Chōsen kenkyūkai, 1913.

Arano Yasunori. *Kinsei Nihon to Higashi Ajia*. Tokyo: Tokyo daigaku shuppankai, 1988.

———. "Chōsen tsūshinshi no shūmatsu—Shin Ikan *Kaiyūroku ni yosete*." *Rekishi hyōron* 355 (November 1979): 63–74.

Arima Seiho. *Chōsen no eki suigunshi*. Tokyo: Umito sorasha, 1942.

Arnesen, Peter J. *The Medieval Japanese Daimyo*. New Haven: Yale University Press, 1979.

Asami Masaichi. "Kyokai shiryō o toshite mita Cho Kenjo no Shikawa shihai." *Shigaku* 59.2–3 (1990): 49–91.

Aston, W. G. "Hideyoshi's Invasion of Korea." *Transactions of the Asiatic Society of Japan* 6 (1878): 227–45; 9 (1881): 87–93, 213–22; and 11 (1883): 117–25.

Atwell, William S. "Ming Observers of Ming Decline: Some Chinese Views on the 'Seventeenth Century Crisis' in Comparative Perspective." *Journal of the Royal Asiatic Society of Great Britain and Ireland* 2 (1988): 316–48.

———. "Some Observations on the Seventeenth Century Crisis in China and Japan." *Journal of Asian Studies* 45.2 (February 1986): 223–44.

———. "International Bullion Flows and the Chinese Economy." *Past and Present* 95 (May 1982): 68–90.

———. "Notes on Silver, Foreign Trade, and the Late Ming Economy." *Ch'ing shih wen-t'i* 3.8 (December 1977): 1–33.

———. "From Education to Politics: The Fu She." In *The Unfolding of Neo-Confucianism,* edited by W. T. DeBary, 333–67. New York: Columbia University Press, 1975.

Austin, Audrey. "Admiral Yi Sun-sin: National Hero." *Korean Culture* 9.2 (Summer 1988): 4–15.

Bachrach, Bernard S. "Medieval Siege Warfare: A Reconnaissance." *Journal of Military History* 58.1 (January 1994): 119–33.

Bachrach, David S. "The Military Administration of England: The Royal Artillery (1216–1272)." *Journal of Military History* 68.4 (October 2004): 1083–1104.

Bacon, Wilbur, trans. "Record of Reprimands and Admonitions (*Chingbirok*) by Yu Songnyong." *Transactions of the Korea Branch of the Royal Asiatic Society* 47 (1972): 9–24.

———. "Fortresses of Kyonggido." *Transactions of the Korea Branch of the Royal Asiatic Society* 37 (1961): 1–64.

Bak, Hae-ill. "A Short Note on the Ironclad Turtle Boats of Admiral Yi Sun-sin." *Korea Journal* 17.1 (January 1977): 34–39.

Ballard, G. A. *The Influence of the Sea on the Political History of Japan.* Westport, Conn.: Greenwood, 1973.

Barfield, Thomas J. *The Perilous Frontier: Nomadic Empires and China, 221 BC to AD 1757.* Cambridge, Mass.: Blackwell, 1992.

Barr, Allan H. "The Wanli Context of the Courtesan's Jewel Box Story." *Harvard Journal of Asiatic Studies* 57.1 (1997): 107–42.

Batten Bruce. *Gateway to Japan: Hakata in War and Peace, 500–1300.* Honolulu: University of Hawaii Press, 2006.

———. "Frontiers and Boundaries of Pre-modern Japan." *Journal of Historical Geography* 25 (1999): 166–82.

Bendian bianzebu, eds. *Zhang Juzheng dazhuan.* Taibei: Taiwan kaiming shudian, 1968.

Berry, Mary Elizabeth. *The Culture of Civil War in Kyoto.* Berkeley: University of California Press, 1994.

———. *Hideyoshi.* Cambridge, Mass.: Harvard University Press, 1982.

Black, Jeremy, ed. *War in the Early Modern World.* London: UCL, 1999.

Boot, W. J. "Chōsen Seibatsu: The Japanese View." In Chung Doo-hee, *Transnational History of the "Imjin Waeran,"* 283–312.

Boots, J. L. "Korean Weapons and Armor." *Transactions of the Korea Branch of the Royal Asiatic Society* 23.2 (1934): 1–37.

Boscara, Adriana, trans. and ed. *101 Letters of Hideyoshi: The Private Correspondence of Toyotomi Hideyoshi.* Tokyo: Sophia University Press, 1975.

Boxer, C. R., ed. *South China in the Sixteenth Century.* London: Hakluyt Society, 1953.

———. *The Christian Century in Japan, 1549–1650.* Berkeley: University of California Press, 1951.

———. "Notes on Early European Military Influence in Japan." *Transactions of the Asiatic Society of Japan,* 2nd ser., 8 (1931): 67–93.

Bradbury, Jim. *The Medieval Siege.* Woodbridge, UK: Boydell, 1992.

Brook, Timothy. "Japan in the Late Ming: The View from Shanghai." In Fogel, *Sagacious Monks and Bloodthirsty Warriors,* 42–62.

Brown, Delmer C. "The Impact of Firearms on Japanese Warfare, 1543–1598." *Far Eastern Quarterly* 7.3 (May 1948): 236–53.

Cao Guoqing. *Wanli huangdi da zhuan.* Shenyang: Liaoning jiaoyu chubanshe, 1994.

Cha Yong-geol. "Notable Characteristics of Korean Fortresses." *Koreana* 19.1 (Spring 2005): 14–17.

Chan, Albert. *The Glory and Fall of the Ming Dynasty.* Norman: University of Oklahoma Press, 1982.

Chang, Chun-shu, and Shelley Hsueh-lun Chang. *Redefining History: Ghosts, Spirits, and Human Society in Pu Songling's World.* Ann Arbor: University of Michigan Press, 1998.

———. *Crisis and Transformation: Society, Culture, and Modernity in Li Yü's World.* Ann Arbor: University of Michigan Press, 1992.

Chang Hak-keon. "Condition of a Battlefield and a Variation of the Turtle-boat's Shape." *Kunsa* [Military History] 51.4 (2004): 45–77.

Chang, Shelley Hsueh-lun. *History & Legend: Ideas and Images in the Ming Historical Novels.* Ann Arbor: University of Michigan Press, 1990.

Chase, Kenneth. *Firearms: A Global History to 1700.* Cambridge: Cambridge University Press, 2003.

Chen Baoliang. "Ming dai de minbing yu xiangbing." *Zhongguo shi yanjiu* (1994.1): 82–92.

Chen Gaohua and Qian Haihao, eds. *Zhongguo junshi zhidu shi.* Zhengzhou: Daxiang chubanshe, 1997.

Chen Zilong et al., comps. *Huang Ming jingshi wenbian.* 30 vols. 1638. Taibei: Guolian tushu chuban youxian gongsi, 1964.

Chinju National Museum. *Imgin Waeran* (catalogue). Chinju: National Museum, 1998.

Cho Hŏn. *Chungbŏng chip.* Ca. 1593. Vol. 54 in *Han'guk munchi ch'onggan.* 220 vols. Seoul: Kyŏngon munhwasa, 1990.

Cho Inbok. *Firearms of Ancient Korea.* Seoul: Institute of Korea National Defense History, 1974.

Cho Kyŏngdal. *Pansan sego; Pan'gok nanjung ilgi.* Ca. 1600. Seoul: Asea munhwasa, 1987.

Cho Kyŏngnam. *Nanjung chamnok.* 2 vols. Ca. 1618. Vols. 7–8 of Han et al., *Imjin waeran saryŏ ch'ongso.*

Cho Ungnok. *Chukkye ilgi.* 2 vols. 1590s. Seoul: Kuksa pyŏnchan wiwonhoe, 1992.

Ch'o Wŏnnae. *Hŏnam ŭibyong kangching sa.* Sunchŏn: Sunchŏn University Museum, 2001.

———. *Imnan ŭibyŏng Kim Ch'ŏnil yon'gu: Purok kŏnjae chip chŏnjae.* Seoul: Hangmunsa, 1982.

Choe Kwan. *Bunroku keichō no eki: Bungaku no kizamareta senso: Imjin chongyu waeran.* Tokyo: Kōdansha, 1994.

Choe Yŏnghŭi. *Imjin waeran chung ui sahoe tongt'ae: Uibyŏng ul chungsim uro.* Seoul: Han'guk yŏnguwŏn, 1975.

Choe Yŏnghŭi et al., comps. *Imjin waeran kwa Ich'i taech'ŏp*. Taejŏn: Ch'ungnam taehakgyo, 1999.

Choi, Byonghyon, trans. *The Book of Corrections: Reflections on the National Crisis during the Japanese Invasion of Korea, 1592–1598*. Berkeley: University of California Press, 2003.

Choi Suk. "Factional Struggle in the Yi Dynasty of Korea, 1575–1725." *Koreana Quarterly* 7.1 (Spring 1965): 60–91.

Chŏlla Province Imjin History Society. *Hŏnam chibang imjin waeran saryo chip*. 4 vols. Kwangju: South Chŏlla Province, 1990–92.

Chŏng Kyŏngdal. *Pansan sego; Pan'gok nanjung ilgi*. Ca. 1600. Seoul: Asea munhwasa, 1987.

Chŏng Tak. *Longwan wen jian lu* [*Yongman mun'gyŏnnok*]. 1590s. In *Zhong-Han guanxi shiliao xuanji* vol. 6. Taibei: Guiting chubanshe, 1980.

———. *Nakp'o yongsa ilgi*. 1592–93. Pusan: Pusan taehakgyo, 1962.

Chŏng Yagyong. *Imjin waeran kwa Pyŏngja horan*. Ca. 1800. Seoul: Hyŏndae sirkhasa, 2001.

Chōsen Shi Henshukai. *Chōsen shi*. 22 vols. Seoul: Chōsen insatsu kabushiki kaisha, 1938.

Chung Doo-hee, ed. *A Transnational History of the "Imjin Waeran": East Asian Dimension*. Seoul: Sogang University, 2006.

Chung Hae-eun. "Chosŏn's Early Experience with Short-arm Weapons during the Imjin War and the Publication of the *Muyae Jaebo*." *Kunsa* [Military History] 51.4 (2004): 151–83.

Cipolla, Carlo M. *Guns, Sails, and Empires: Technological Innovation and the Early Phases of European Expansion 1400–1700*. New York: Minerva, 1965.

Clark, Donald N. "Sino-Korean Tributary Relations under the Ming." In Mote and Twitchett, *Cambridge History of China Volume 8*, 272–300.

Conlan, Thomas Donald. *State of War: The Violent Order of Fourteenth-Century Japan*. Ann Arbor: University of Michigan Center for Japanese Studies Press, 2003.

Conroy, Hilary. *The Japanese Seizure of Korea: 1868–1910: A Study of Realism and Idealism in International Relations*. Philadelphia: University of Pennsylvania Press, 1960.

Cooper, Michael, trans. and ed. *This Island of Japon: Joao Rodrugues' Account of 16th-Century Japan*. Tokyo: Kodansha, 1973.

———. *They Came to Japan: An Anthology of European Reports on Japan, 1543–1650*. Berkeley: University of California Press, 1965.

Cory, Ralph. "Some Notes on Father Gregorio des Cespedes, Korea's First European Visitor." *Transactions of the Korea Branch of the Royal Asiatic Society* 27 (1937): 1–55.

Crawford, Robert B. "Chang Chü-cheng's Confucian Legalism." In DeBary et al., *Self and Society in Ming Thought*, 367–413.

———. "Chang Chü-cheng's Life and Thought, 1525–1582." Ph.D. diss., University of Washington, 1961.

Crossley, Pamela Kyle. *A Translucent Mirror: History and Identity in Qing Imperial Ideology*. Berkeley: University of California Press, 1999.

———. *The Manchus*. Cambridge, Mass.: Blackwell, 1997.

Dai Yingcong. "The Qing State, Merchants, and the Military Labor Force in the Jinchuan Campaigns." *Late Imperial China* 22.2 (December 2002): 35–90.

Dardess, John W. *Blood and History in China: The Donglin Faction and Its Repression, 1620–1627.* Honolulu: University of Hawaii Press, 2002.

DeBary, William Theodore. *Waiting for the Dawn: A Plan for the Prince Huang Tsung-hsi's Ming-i-tai-fang lu.* New York: Columbia University Press, 1993.

DeBary, William Theodore, et al., eds. *Self and Society in Ming Thought.* New York: Columbia University Press, 1970.

DeVries, Kelly. *Medieval Military Technology.* Peterborough, Ont.: Broadview, 1992.

Diamond, Norma. "Defining the Miao: Ming, Qing, and Contemporary Views." In *Cultural Encounters on China's Ethnic Frontiers,* edited by Stevan Harrell, 92–116. Seattle: University of Washington Press, 1995.

———. "The Miao and Poison: Interactions on China's Southwest Frontier." *Ethnology* 27 (1988): 1–25.

Di Cosmo, Nicola. "Did Guns Matter? Firearms and the Qing Formation." In Struve, *Qing Formation,* 121–66.

Dreyer, Edward L. *Early Ming China: A Political History, 1355–1435.* Stanford, Calif.: Stanford University Press, 1982.

Duncan, John B. "The Hideyoshi Invasions: Popular Memories and Ethnic Consciousness." In Chung Doo-hee, *Transnational History of the "Imjin Waeran,"* 253–64.

Eikenberg, Karl W. "The Imjin World." *Military Review* 68.2 (1988): 74–82.

Elison, George [Jurgis Elisonas]. "The Inseparable Trinity: Japan's Relations with China and Korea." In Hall, *Cambridge History of Japan,* 235–300.

———. "The Priest Keinen and His Account of the Campaign in Korea, 1597–1598: An Introduction." In *Nihon Kyoikushi ronsō: Motoyama Yukihiko Kyoju taikan kinen rombunshu,* edited by Motoyama Yukihiko Kyoju taikan kinen rombunshu henshu iinkai, 25–41. Kyoto: Sibunkaku, 1988.

———. *Deus Destroyed: The Image of Christianity in Early Modern Japan.* Cambridge, Mass.: Harvard University Press, 1973.

Elison, George, and Bardwell L. Smith, eds. *Warlords, Artists, and Commoners: Japan in the Sixteenth Century.* Honolulu: University of Hawaii Press, 1981.

Elleman, Bruce A. *Modern Chinese Warfare, 1795–1989.* New York: Routledge, 2001.

Elliott, Mark C. *The Manchu Way: The Eight Banners and Ethnic Identity in Late Imperial China.* Stanford, Calif.: Stanford University Press, 2001.

Elman, Benjamin A. *A Cultural History of Civil Examinations in Late Imperial China.* Berkeley: University of California Press, 2000.

———. "Imperial Politics and Confucian Societies in Late Imperial China: The Hanlin and Donglin Academies." *Modern China* 15.4 (October 1989): 379–418.

Endō Shūsaku. *Tetsu no kubikase: Konishi Yukinaga den.* Tokyo: Chūo kōronsha, 1977.

Engels, Donald W. *Alexander the Great and the Logistics of the Macedonian Army.* Berkeley: University of California Press, 1978.

Fairbank, John King, ed. *The Chinese World Order: Traditional China's Foreign Relations.* Cambridge, Mass.: Harvard University Press, 1968.

———. *Chinese Thought and Institutions*. Chicago: University of Chicago Press, 1957.

Fairbank, John King, and Edwin O. Reischauer. *China: Tradition and Transformation*. Boston: Houghton Mifflin, 1989.

Fan Shuzhi. *Quan yu xue: Ming diguo guanchang zhengzhi*. Beijing: Zhonghua shuju, 2004.

———. *Wan Ming shi*. 2 vols. Shanghai: Fudan daxue chubanshe, 2003.

———. *Wanli zhuan*. Beijing: Renmin chubanshe, 1993.

Fan Zhongyi. *Qi Jiguang zhuan*. Beijing: Zhonghua shuju, 2003.

———. "Ming dai junshi sixiang jianlun." *Ming-Qing shi* 24.1 (1997): 37–50.

———. "Ming dai haifang shu lue." *Lishi yanjiu* 3 (1990): 44–54.

Fan Zhongyi and Tong Xigang. *Ming dai wokou shilue*. Beijing: Zhonghua shuju, 2004.

Fang, Zhiyuan. "Ming dai de xunfu zhidu." *Zhongguo shi yanjiu* (1988.3): 87–98.

Farmer, Edward. *Early Ming Government: The Evolution of Dual Capitals*. Cambridge, Mass.: Harvard University Press, 1976.

———. *Zhu Yuanzhang and Early Ming Legislation: The Reordering of Chinese Society Following the Era of Mongol Rule*. Leiden: E. J. Brill, 1995.

Farris, William Wayne. *Heavenly Warriors: The Evolution of Japan's Military, 500–1300*. Cambridge, Mass.: Harvard University Press, 1995.

Finch, Michael C. E. "Civilian Life during the Japanese Invasions and Occupation of Korea (1592–98): Study on *Swaemirok* [Record of a Wandering Refugee] by Ŏ Hŭimun (1539–1603)." *Proceedings of the Association for Korean Studies in Europe Biennial Conference: University of Sheffield* (July 2005): 55–61.

Fissel, Mark Charles. *English Warfare, 1511–1642*. London: Routledge, 2001.

Fitzpatrick, Merrilyn. "Local Interests and the Anti-pirate Administration in China's South-east, 1555–1565." *Ch'ing shih wen-t'i* 4 (December 1979):1–50.

———. "Building Town Walls in Seven Districts of Northern Chekiang, 1553–1566." *Papers on Far Eastern History* 17 (1978): 15–51.

Flynn, Dennis O., and Arturo Giraldez. "Born with a 'Silver Spoon': The Origin of World Trade in 1571." *Journal of World History* 6.2 (Fall 1995): 201–21.

Fogel, Joshua A., ed. *Sagacious Monks and Bloodthirsty Warriors: Chinese Views of Japan during the Ming-Qing Period*. Norwalk, Conn.: Eastbridge, 2002.

Franke, Wolfgang. *An Introduction to the Sources of Ming History*. Kuala Lumpur: University of Malaya Press, 1968.

Friday, Karl F. *Samurai, Warfare, and the State in Early Medieval Japan*. New York: Routledge, 2004.

———. *Hired Swords: The Rise of Private Warrior Power in Early Japan*. Stanford, Calif.: Stanford University Press, 1992.

Fujii Nobuo. *Ri Sunshin oboegaki*. Tokyo: Furukawa shobō, 1982.

Fujiki Hisashi. *Toyotomi heiwarei to sengoku shakai*. Tokyo: Tokyo daigaku shuppankai, 1988.

———. *Oda, Toyotomi seiken*. Tokyo: Shōgakukan, 1975.

Fujiki Hisashi and Kitajima Manji, eds. *Shokuhō seiken*. Vol. 6 in *Ronshū Nihon rekishi*. Tokyo: Yūseidō, 1974.

Fujiki Hisashi and George Elison. "The Political Posture of Oda Nobunaga." In Hall et al., *Japan before Tokugawa,* 149–93.

Gao Rui, ed. *Zhongguo junshi shilue.* Vol. 2. Beijing: Junshi kexue chubanshe, 1992.

Gernet, Jacques. *A History of Chinese Civilization.* Cambridge: Cambridge University Press, 1982.

Goodrich, L. C., and Fang Chao-ying, eds. *Dictionary of Ming Biography.* 2 vols. New York: Columbia University Press, 1976.

Graff, David A. *Medieval Chinese Warfare.* London: Routledge, 2002.

Graff, David A., and Robin Higham, eds. *A Military History of China.* Boulder: Westview, 2002.

Grossberg, Kenneth A. *Japan's Renaissance: The Politics of the Muromachi Bakufu.* Cambridge, Mass.: Harvard University Press, 1981.

Grousset, Rene. *The Empire of the Steppes: A History of Central Asia.* Trans. by Naomi Walford. New Brunswick, N.J.: Rutgers University Press, 1994.

Gu Yingtai. *Ming shi jishi benmo.* 1658. Reprited in *Lidai jishi benmo.* 2 vols. Beijing: Zhonghua shuju, 1997.

Guan Wenfa and Yan Guangwen. *Ming dai zhengzhi zhidu yanjiu.* Beijing: Zhongguo shehui kexue chubanshe, 1995.

Guo Nugui et al. *Zhongguo junshi shi, Vol.4: Bing fa.* Beijing: Jiefangjun chubanshe, 1988.

Ha Young-whee. "Reinterpreting the Past: The Battle of the Hwawang Fortress." In Chung Doo-hee, *Transnational History of the "Imjin Waeran,"* 265–82.

Haboush, Jahyun Kim. "Dead Bodies in the Postwar Discourse of Seventeenth-Century Korea: Subversion and Literary Production in the Private Sector." *Journal of Asian Studies* 62.2 (May 2003): 415–42.

Haboush, Jahyun Kim, and Martina Deuchler, eds. *Culture and the State in Late Chosŏn Korea.* Cambridge, Mass.: Harvard University Press, 1999.

Hall, Bert S. *Weapons and Warfare in Renaissance Europe.* Baltimore: Johns Hopkins University Press, 1997.

Hall, John Whitney, ed. *The Cambridge History of Japan Volume 4: Early Modern Japan.* Cambridge: Cambridge University Press, 1991.

———. "Hideyoshi's Domestic Policies." In Hall et al., *Japan before Tokugawa,* 194–223.

———. *Government and Local Power in Japan: 500–1700.* Princeton: Princeton Uuniversity Press, 1966.

Hall, John Whitney, et al., eds. *Japan before Tokugawa: Political Consolidation and Economic Growth, 1500–1650.* Princeton: Princeton University Press, 1981.

Han Myŏnggi. "An Evaluation of the Activities of the Ming Forces during the Imjin Waewran." In Chung Doo-hee, *Transnational History of the "Imjin Waeran,"* 391–408.

———. *Kwanghae Kun: T'agwŏrhan oegyo chŏngch'aek ŭl p'yŏlch'in kunju.* Seoul: Yŏksa pip'yongsa, 2000.

———. *Imjin Waeran kwa Han-Chung kwan'gye.* Seoul: Yŏksa pip'yongsa, 1999.

Han Myŏnggi et al., comps. *Imjin waeran saryŏ ch'ongso.* 31 vols. Chinju: Chinju National Museum, 2000–2002.

Hanawa Hokiichi, comp. *Zoku gunsho ruijū.* 33 vols. Tokyo: Zoku gunsho ruijū kansei-kai, 1923–28.

Harada Tanezuma. *Chōsen no eki monogatari.* Tokyo: Yuzankaku shuppan, 1971.

Hawley, Samuel. *The Imjin War: Japan's Sixteenth-Century Invasion of Korea and Attempt to Conquer China.* Seoul: Royal Asiatic Society, Korea Branch, 2005.

Hayashi Maiko. "Ri shi Chōsen ōchō ni okeru taigai shisetsu no deshi ni tsuite." *Shisen* 89 (January 1999): 16–24.

Hazard, Benjamin H. "The Formative Years of the Wakō, 1223–1263." *Monumenta Nipponica* 22.3 (1967): 260–77.

He Baoshan, Han Qihua, and He Dichen. *Ming Shenzong yu Ming Dingling.* Beijing: Beijing Yanshan chubanshe, 1998.

———. *Wanli huangdi—Zhu Yijun.* Beijing: Beijing Yanshan chubanshe, 1990.

He Zhiqing and Wang Xiaowei. *Zhongguo bing zhi shi.* Taibei: Zhongguo wenhua shi congshu, 1997.

Heijdra, Martin. "The Socioeconomic Development of Rural China during the Ming." In Mote and Twitchett, *Cambridge History of China Volume 8,* 417–578.

Hŏnam changŭi dong sa rok. 1600s. Chinju: Chinju National Museum Archives. Manuscript.

Hōri Kyōan. *Chōsen seibatsuki.* 1659. East Asian Library, University of California–Berkeley. Manuscript (microfilm).

Hu Yuewei, Tao Bochu, and Qian Facheng. *Wanli wangchao.* Chengdu: Sichuan wenyi chubanshe, 2002.

Huai Xiaofeng. *Shiliu shiji Zhongguo de zhengzhi fengyun.* Hong Kong: Shangwu yinshuguan, 1988.

Huang K'uan-chung. "Mountain Fortress Defence: The Experience of the Southern Song and Korea in Resisting the Mongol Invasions." In Van de Ven, *Warfare in Chinese History,* 222–51.

Huang, Ray. *1587: A Year of No Significance.* New Haven: Yale University Press, 1981.

———. "The Liao-tung Campaign of 1619." *Oriens Extremus* 28.1 (1981): 30–54.

———. *Taxation and Government Finance in Sixteenth Century Ming China.* London: Cambridge University Press, 1974.

———. "Military Expenditures in Sixteenth Century Ming China." *Oriens Extremus* 17 (1970): 39–62.

Huang Yuezhi. *Zunyi fuzhi.* 2 vols. 1841. Taibei: Chengwen chubanshe, 1968.

Hucker, Charles O. *A Dictionary of Official Titles in Imperial China.* Stanford, Calif.: Stanford University Press, 1985.

———. *The Ming Dynasty: Its Origins and Evolving Institutions.* Ann Arbor: University of Michigan Press, 1971.

———. *Two Studies on Ming History.* Ann Arbor: University of Michigan Press, 1971.

———, ed. *Chinese Government in Ming Times: Seven Studies.* New York: Columbia University Press, 1969.

————. *The Censorial System of Ming China.* Stanford, Calif.: Stanford University Press, 1966.

————. *The Traditional Chinese State in Ming Times.* Tucson: University of Arizona Press, 1961.

Hughes, Lindsey. *Russia in the Age of Peter the Great.* New Haven: Yale University Press, 1998.

Hummel, Arthur O., ed. *Eminent Chinese of the Ch'ing Period.* 2 vols. Washington, D.C.: Library of Congress, 1943.

Hur Kyoung-jin. "Town Walls Create a Safe Haven for the Populace." *Koreana* 19.1 (Spring 2005): 24–31.

Hur Namlin. "Politicking or Being Politicked: Wartime Governance in Chosŏn Korea." In Chung Doo-hee, *Transnational History of the "Imjin Waeran,"* 327–42.

————. "The International Context of Toyotomi Hideyoshi's Invasion of Korea in 1592: A Clash between Chinese Culturalism and Japanese Militarism." *Korea Observer* 28.4 (Winter 1997): 687–707.

Hwang Chŏnguk, et al. *Chich'ŏn chip; Oum yugo; Ch'ungmugong ch'ŏnsŏ; Ch'ŏng'uk chip.* Ca. 1600. Vol. 1 in Yi U., *Imjin waeran kwan'gye.*

Hyujŏng. *Ki'am chip.* 1590s. Seoul: Kyujanggak Archives. Manuscript.

Ike Susumu. *Tenka tōitsu to Chōsen shinryaku.* Tokyo: Yoshikawa kōbunkan, 2003.

Ikeuchi Hiroshi. *Bunroku keichō no eki.* Tokyo: Tōyō bunko, 1936.

Ishihara Michihiro. "Bunroku-keichō waeran to Seki Keimitsu no shimpō." *Chōsen gakuhō* 37–38 (January 1966): 143–71.

————. *Bunroku keichō no eki.* Tokyo: Hanawa shobō, 1963.

Iwai Shigeki. "Junana seiki no Chugoku henkyo shakai." In Ono, *Minmatsu Shinsho,* 625–59.

Iwanami kōza Nihon rekishi. 26 vols. Tokyo: Iwanami shoten, 1975–77.

Jansen, Marius B., ed. *Warrior Rule in Japan.* Cambridge: Cambridge University Press, 1995.

————. *China in the Tokugawa World.* Cambridge, Mass.: Harvard University Press, 1992.

Jeon, Sang-woon. *Science and Technology in Korea: Traditional Instruments and Techniques.* Cambridge, Mass.: MIT Press, 1974.

Jho Sung-do. *Yi Sun-shin: A National Hero of Korea.* Chinhae: Choongmookong Society, 1970.

Ji Deyuan, ed. *Zhongguo junshi zhidu shi: Junshi fazhi juan.* Zhengzhou: Daxiang chubanshe, 1997.

Jiang Fen. *Ming shi jishi.* Ca. 1640s (postscript, 1790). Fenghuang: Jiangsu guangling guji keyinshe, 1990.

Jiang Jin. "Heresy and Persecution in Late Imperial China: Reinterpreting the Case of Li Zhi." *Late Imperial China* 22.2 (December 2001): 1–34.

Jiang Weiguo et al., comps. *Zhongguo lidai zhanzheng shi.* 18 vols. Taibei: Liming wenhua shiye, 1980.

Jin Runcheng. *Ming chao zongdu xunfu xia qu yanjiu.* Tianjin: Tianjin guji chubanshe, 1996.

Johnston, Alastair Iain. *Cultural Realism: Strategic Culture and Grand Strategy in Chinese History.* Princeton: Princeton University Press, 1995.

Jones, Richard L. C. "Fortifications and Sieges in Western Europe, c. 800–1450." In Keen, *Medieval Warfare,* 163–85.

Jung Ji-young. "The Mobilization of Women's Sexuality in the Shadow of War: Reinvention of 'Nongae' in the Post–Korean War Era." In Chung-doo Hee, *Transnational History of the "Imjin Waeran,"* 27–48.

Kaeuper, Richard W. *Chivalry and Violence in Medieval Europe.* Oxford: Oxford University Press, 2001.

Kamigaito Ken'ichi. *Kukyonam shuppei: Hideyoshi no Bunroku keichō no eki.* Tokyo: Fukutake shōten, 1989.

Kang, Etsuko Hae-jin. *Diplomacy and Ideology in Japanese-Korean Relations: From the Fifteenth to the Eighteenth Century.* New York: St. Martin's, 1997.

Kang Hang. *Kan'yōroku: Chōsen jusha no Nihon yokuriyūki.* Ca. 1638. Tokyo: Heibonsha, 1984.

Kang Sung-moon. "Strategy and Tactics of Kim Simin in the Glorious Chinju Campaign." *Kunsa* [Military History] 51.4 (2004): 185–217.

Katano Tsugio. *Ri Sunshin to Hideyoshi: Bunroku keichō no kaisen.* Tokyo: Seibundō shinkōsha, 1983.

Kawaguchi Choju. *Seikan iryaku.* 1831. In Wu Fengpei et al., *Renchen zhi yi shiliao huiji,* 2:471–774.

Kazui Tashiro. "Foreign Relations during the Edo Period: *Sakoku* Reexamined." Translated by Susan Downing Videen. *Journal of Japanese Studies* 8.2 (1982): 283–306.

Keen, Maurice., ed. *Medieval Warfare: A History.* Oxford: Oxford University Press, 1999.

———. "The Changing Scene: Guns, Gunpowder, and Permanent Armies." In Keen, *Medieval Warfare,* 273–92.

Keinen. *Chōsen nichinichiki o yomu: Shinshuso ga mita Hideyoshi no Chōsen shinryaku.* 1598. Kyoto: Hozokan, 2000.

Kemuyama Sentarō. *Seikanran jissō: Chōsen Ri Shunshin den: Bunroku seikan suishi shimatsu.* Tokyo: Ryūkei shosha, 1996.

Kierman, Frank A., Jr., and John K. Fairbank, eds. *Chinese Ways in Warfare.* Cambridge, Mass.: Harvard University Press, 1974.

Kikuchi Kasugaro, Tsurumine Shigenobu, and Hashimoto Sadahide. *Ehon Chōsen seibatsu ki.* 20 vols. Edo: Mankyukaku, 1853.

Kim Dong-uk. "Suwon Hwaseong Fortress: Monument to Korea's Architectural Expertise." *Koreana* 19.1 (Spring 2005): 8–13.

Kim Ha-tai. "The Transmission of Neo-Confucianism to Japan by Kang Hang, a Prisoner of War." *Transactions of the Korea Branch of the Royal Asiatic Society* 37 (1961): 83–103.

Kim Hong-kyu, ed. *Hideyoshi mimizuka yonhyaku nen: Toyotomi seiken no Chōsen jimmin no tatakai.* Tokyo: Yazukaku shuppansha, 1998.

Kim, Kichung. "Resistance, Abduction, and Survival: The Documentary Literature of the Imjin War (1592–8)." *Korean Culture* 20.3 (Fall 1999): 20–29.

Kim Pong-hyon. *Hideyoshi no Chōsen shinryaku to gihei toso.* Tokyo: Sairyusha, 1995.

Kim Pyŏng-dong. *Mimizuka: Hideyoshi no hanakiri mimikiri o megutte.* Tokyo: Sowasha, 1994.

Kim, Samuel Dukhae. "The Korean Monk-Soldiers in the Imjin Wars: An Analysis of Buddhist Resistance to the Hideyoshi Invasion, 1592–1598." Ph.D. diss., Columbia University, 1978.

Kim, Sang H., trans. *Muye Dobo Tongji: The Comprehensive Illustrated Manual of Martial Arts of Ancient Korea.* Hartford, Conn.: Turtle, 2000.

Kim Sŏngil. *Haech'arok.* Ca. 1600. Vol. 1 in *Haehang ch'ongjae.* Seoul: Minjŏk munhwa ch'ujinhae, 1982.

Kim Tae-chun. "Admiral Yi Sun-sin's Fame in Japan." *Journal of Social Sciences and Humanities* 47 (June 1978): 93–107.

Kitajima Manji. *Hideyoshi no Chōsen shinryaku.* Tokyo: Yoshikawa kōbunkan, 2002.

———. *Jinshin Waeran to Hideyoshi, Shimazu, Ri Shunshin.* Tokyo: Azekura shobō, 2002.

———. *Toyotomi Hideyoshi no Chōsen shinryaku.* Tokyo: Yoshikawa kōbunkan, 1995.

———. *Toyotomi seiken no taigai ninshiki to Chōsen shinryaku.* Tokyo: Azekura shobo, 1990.

———. "Toyotomi seiken no dai niji Chōsen shinryaku to daimyo ryōkoku no taiō." In Tanaka, *Nihon zenkindai,* 101–43.

———. "Toyotomi seiken no taigai ninshiki." In Nagahara, *Chūsei kinsei no kokka to shakai,* 23–39.

———. *Chōsen nichinichiki, Korai nikki: Hideyoshi no Chōsen shinryaku to sono rekishiteki kokuhatsu.* Tokyo: Sōshiete, 1982.

"Kiyomasa Korai jin oboegaki." In Kokusho kankōkai, *Zokuzoku gunsho ruijū,* 4:293–331.

Ko Kyŏngmyong. *Chonggirok.* 1592. Kumsong: Im Song-hon, 1688.

Kobata Atsushi and Matsuda Mitsugu. *Ryukyuan Relations with Korea and South Sea Countries: An Annotated Translation of Documents in the Rekidai Hoan.* Kyoto: Kobata Atsushi, 1969.

Kokusho kankōkai. *Zokuzoku gunsho ruijū.* 17 vols. Reprint, Tokyo: Zoku gunsho ruijū kanseikai, 1969–70.

Korean-Japanese Cultural Studies Institute, comp. *Kyŏngnamdo waesŏng chi.* Pusan: Pusan University Press, 1961.

Kristof, Nicholas D. "Japan, Korea, and 1597: A Year That Lives in Infamy." *New York Times,* Sept. 14, 1997.

Kuba Takashi. "Jūroku seikimatsu Nihon shiki teppō no Min-Cho he no dempa: Banreki Chōsen no eki kara Banshū Yo Ōryo no ran he." *Toyo Gakuhō* 84.1 (June 2002): 33–54.

Kuno, Yoshi S. *Japanese Expansion on the Asiatic Continent.* 2 vols. Berkeley: University of California Press, 1937–40.

Kusudo Yoshiaki. *Seisho busho no seisei ruten: Toyotomi Hideyoshi no Chōsen shuppei to Naito Joan.* Tokyo: Kōdansha, 2000.

Kuwata Tadachika. *Toyotomi Hideyoshi no hassōryoku to chibō.* Tokyo: Kōsaidō shuppansha, 1982.

———. *Toyotomi Hideyoshi.* Tokyo: Chosakushū, 1979.

——. *Toyotomi Hideyoshi kenkyū.* Tokyo: Kadokawa shoten, 1975.

——, ed. *Taikō shiryō-shū.* Tokyo: Shinjimbutsu ōraisha, 1971.

——. *Taikōki no kenkyū.* Tokyo: Tokuma shoten, 1965.

Kuwata Tadachika and Yamaoka Shohachi, eds. *Chōsen no eki. (Nihon no senshi, vol. 5).* Tokyo: Tokuma shōten, 1965.

Kwak Chaeu. *Mang'u sonsaeng munchip.* Ca. 1600s. Seoul: National Library of Korea, 2005. Manuscript (accessed from electronic database).

——. *Changguirok.* Ca. 1600. Hyŏnpung: Kwanchalsa, 1854.

Kye, Seung B. "An Indirect Challenge to the Ming Order: Nurhaci's Approaches to Korea during the Imjin War, 1592–1598." In Chung Doo-hee, *Transnational History of the "Imjin Waeran,"* 423–51.

——. "In the Shadow of the Father: Court Opposition and the Reign of King Kwanghae in Early Seventeenth-Century Chosŏn Korea." Ph.D. diss., University of Washington, 2006.

Lamers, Jeroen. *Japonius Tyrannus: The Japanese Warlord Oda Nobunaga Reconsidered.* Leiden: Hotei, 2000.

Ledyard, Gari. "Confucianism and War: The Korean Security Crisis of 1598." *Journal of Korean Studies* 6 (1988–89): 81–120.

——. "Korean Travelers to China over Four Hundred Years: 1488–1887." *Occasional Papers on Korea* 2 (1974): 1–42.

Lee Chan et al. *Seoul, Her History and Culture.* Seoul: Seoul Metropolitan Government, 1992.

Lee Chong-young, ed. *Imjin Changch'o: Admiral Yi Sun-sin's Memorials to Court.* Translated by Ha Tae-hung. Seoul: Yonsei University Press, 1981.

Lee Gye-hwang. "Keichō no eki ato no kokusai kankei etsu wa kōshō ni okeru Nihon-Chōsen-Min no dōkō." *Shirin* 76.6 (November 1993): 74–107.

Lee Hyoun-jong. "Military Aid of the Ryukyus and Other Southern Asian Nations to Korea during the Hideyoshi Invasion." *Journal of Social Sciences and Humanities* 46 (December 1977): 13–24.

Lee, Ki-baik. *A New History of Korea.* Translated by Edward W. Wagner with Edward J. Shultz. Cambridge, Mass.: Harvard University Press, 1984.

Lee Min-woong. "The Activities of the Chosŏn Naval Forces during the Imjin Waeran." In Chung Doo-hee, *Transnational History of the "Imjin Waeran,"* 343–64.

——. "A Comparison among Chosŏn-Ming-Japan's Strategy Tactics in Sea Engagements of the Imjin Waeran." *Kunsa* [Military History] 51.4 (2004): 79–108.

Lee, Peter H. *The Record of the Black Dragon Year.* Honolulu: University of Hawaii Press, 2000.

Lei Haizong and Lin Tongqi. *Zhongguo wenhua yu Zhongguo di bing.* Reprint; Changsha: Yuelu shushe, 1989.

Lewis, James B. *Frontier Contact between Chosŏn Korea and Tokugawa Japan.* New York: RoutledgeCurzon, 2003.

Lewis, Mark Edward. *Sanctioned Violence in Early China.* Albany: State University of New York Press, 1990.

Li Du. *Ming dai huangquan zhengzhi yanjiu.* Beijing: Zhongguo kexue shehui chubanshe, 2004.

Li Guangbi. *Ming chao shilue.* Wuhan: Hubei renmin chubanshe, 1957.

Li Guangtao. *Ming-Qing dang'an lunwen ji.* Taibei: Lianjing chuban shiye gongsi, 1986.

——. "Ding Yingtai yu Yang Hao—Chaoxian renchen Wohuo luncong zhi yi." *Lishi yuyan yanjiusuo jikan* 53 (1982): 129–66.

——. *Chaoxian (Renchen Wohuo) Yanjiu.* Taibei: Zhongyang yanjiu yuan lishi yuyan yanjiusuo, 1972.

——. "Ming ren yuan Han yu Jishan da jie." *Lishi yuyan yanjiusuo jikan* 43 (1971): 1–14.

——. *Ming-Qing shi lun ji.* 2 vols. Taibei: Taiwan shangwu yinshuguan, 1971.

——, comp. *Chaoxian "Renchen Wohuo" shi liao.* 5 vols. Taibei: Zhongyang yanjiu yuan lishi yuyan yanjiusuo, 1970.

——. "Ming ren yuan Han yu Chen Lin jiangong." *Zhong Hua wenhua fuxing yuekan* 30 (1970): 5–7.

——. "Ming ren yuan Han yu Yang Hao Weishan zhi yi." *Lishi yuyan yanjiusuo jikan* 41 (1969): 545–66.

——. *Wanli ershisan nian feng Riben guo wang Fengchen Xiuji kao.* Taibei: Zhongyang yanjiuyuan lishi yuyan yanjiusuo, 1967.

——. "Chaoxian renchen Wohuo yu Li Rusong zhi dong zheng." *Lishi yuyan yanjiusuo jikan* 22 (1950): 267–98.

Li Hualong. *Ping Bo quan shu.* 1601. In *Congshu jicheng,* no. 3982–88, edited by Wang Yunwu. Changsha: Shangwu yinshuguan, 1937.

Li Xinda, ed. *Zhongguo junshi zhidu shi: Wu guan zhidu juan.* Zhengzhou: Da xiang chubanshe, 1997.

Li Yingfa. "Mingmo dui hongyi pao de yinjin yu fazhan." *Xinan shifan daxue xuebao* (1991.1): 45–50.

Liang Fangzhong. "Ming dai zhi min bing." *Ming shi yanjiu luncong* 1 (June 1982): 243–76.

Liang Miaotai. "Ming dai jiubian de junshu." *Zhongguo shi yanjiu* 73.1 (1997): 147–57.

Lieberman, Victor B. *Burmese Administrative Cycles: Anarchy and Conquest, c.1580–1760.* Princeton: Princeton University Press, 1984.

Liew Foon Ming. *The Treatises on Military Affairs of the Ming Dynasty.* 2 vols. Hamburg: Gesellschaft fûr nature und Völkerlande ostasiens, 1998.

——. "The Luchuan-Pingmian Campaigns (1436–1449) in the Light of Official Chinese Historiography." *Oriens Extremus* 39.2 (1996): 162–203.

Lin Shuxun et al., eds. *Shaozhou fuzhi.* 1874. Vol. 2 in *Zhongguo fangzhi congshu.* Taibei: Chengwen chubanshe, 1966.

Liu Shaoxiang, ed. *Zhongguo junshi zhidu shi: Junshu zuzhi tizhi bianzhi juan.* Zhengzhou: Da xiang chubanshe, 1997.

Liu Shaoxiang and Wang Xiaowei. *Lidai bingzhi qian shuo.* Beijing: Jiefang jun chubanshe, 1986.

Liu Zehua, ed. *Zhongguo zhengzhi sixiang shi (Sui, Tang, Yuan, Ming, Qing juan).* Hangzhou: Zhejiang renmin chubanshe, 1996.

Lo Jung-pang. "Policy Formation and Decision-Making on Issues Respecting Peace and War." In Hucker, *Chinese Government in Ming Times,* 41–72.

Lo, Winston W. "The Self-image of the Chinese Military in Historical Perspective." *Journal of Asian History* 31.1 (1997): 1–24.

Long Wenbin. *Ming huiyao.* 2 vols. 1887. Taibei: Shijie shuju, 1960.

Lorge, Peter, ed. *The International Library of Essays in Military History: Warfare in China to 1600.* Aldershot: Ashgate, 2005.

———. *War, Politics, and Society in Early Modern China, 900–1795.* London: Routledge, 2005.

Lu Zhongli. *Liang yuan zouyi.* 1600s. Vol. 4.1 of *Ming-Qing shiliao huibian,* compiled by Shen Yunlong. Taibei: Wenhai chubanshe, 1967.

Luo Lixin. "Ming dai jingying zhi xingcheng yu shuaibei." *Ming shi yanjiu zhuankan* 6 (June 1983): 1–36.

Lynn, John A., ed. *Feeding Mars: Logistics in Western Warfare from the Middle Ages to the Present.* Boulder: Westview, 1993.

———, ed. *Tools of War: Instruments, Ideas, and Institutions of Warfare, 1445–1871.* Urbana: University of Illinois Press, 1990.

Mallett, Michael. "Mercenaries." In Keen, *Medieval Warfare,* 209–29.

Mao Ruizheng. *Wanli san da zheng kao.* 1621. Vol. 58 of *Ming-Qing shiliao huibian,* compiled by Shen Yunlong. Taibei: Wenhai chubanshe, 1971.

Mao Yuanyi. *Wubei zhi.* 22 vols. 1621. Taibei: Huashi chubanshe, 1987.

Marumo Takeshige. "Chōsenjin yokuryū ni kansuru shiryō." In Fujiki and Kitajima, *Shokuhō seiken,* 329–37.

Maske, Andrew. "The Continental Origins of Takatori Ware: The Introduction of Korean Potters and Technology to Japan through the Invasions of 1592–1598." *Transactions of the Asiatic Society of Japan,* 4th ser., 9 (1994): 43–61.

Mason, David A. "The *Sam Hwangje Paehyang* (Sacrificial Ceremony for Three Emperors): Korea's Link to the Ming Dynasty." *Korea Journal* 31.3 (Autumn 1991): 117–36.

Mass, Jeffrey P., and William B. Hauser, eds. *The Bakufu in Japanese History.* Stanford, Calif.: Stanford University Press, 1985.

Matsuda Kiichi. *Hideyoshi to Bunroku no eki: Furoisu "Nihon shi" yori.* Tokyo: Chūō koronsha, 1974.

Matsumoto Yoshishige. *Hō taikō seikan hiroku.* Tokyo: Seikansha, 1894.

Matsura Hiroshi, comp. *Matsura Hōin seikan nikki shō.* Abridged ed. Tokyo: Yoshikawa han shichiya, 1894.

McCormack, Gavan. "Reflections on Modern Japanese History in the Context of the Concept of Genocide." In *The Specter of Genocide: Mass Murder in Historical Perspective,* edited by Robert Gellately and Ben Kiernan, 265–88. Cambridge: Cambridge University Press, 2003.

McNeill, William. *The Pursuit of Power: Technology, Armed Force, and Society since AD 1000.* Chicago: University of Chicago Press, 1982.

Mei Guozhen. *Xi zheng ji.* 2 vols. 1592 (preface, 1638). Facsimile reprint, Tokyo: Tokyo daigaku, 1973.

Meng Sen et al. *Ming dai bian fang.* Vol. 6 in *Ming shi luncong,* edited by Bao Zunpeng. Taibei: Taiwan xuesheng shuju, 1968.

Meskill, John. *Gentlemanly Interests and Wealth on the Yangtze Delta.* Ann Arbor: Association for Asian Studies, 1994.

———. *Academies in Ming China: A Historical Essay.* Ann Arbor: Association for Asian Studies, 1985.

Miki Haruo. *Konishi Yukinaga to Shin Ikei: Bunroku no eki Fushimi jishin soshite Keichō no eki.* Tokyo: Nihon toshokan kankokai, 1997.

Miki Seiichirō. "Kampaku gaikō taisei no tokushitsu o megutte." In Tanaka, *Nihon zenkindai,* 72–99.

——. "Chōsen eki ni okeru gunyaku taikei ni tsuite." *Shigaku zasshi* 75.2 (February 1966): 129–54.

Miller, Harry S. "Newly Discovered Source Sheds Light on Late Ming Faction: Reading Li Sancai's *Fu Huai Xiao Cao.*" *Ming Studies* 47 (Spring 2003): 126–40.

——. "State Versus Society in Late Imperial China, 1572–1644." Ph.D. diss., Columbia University, 2001.

Millinger, James Ferguson. "Ch'i Chi-kuang: A Ming Military Official as Viewed by his Contemporary Civilian Officials." *Oriens Extremus* 20.1 (1973): 103–17.

——. "Ch'i Chi-kuang, Chinese Military Official: A Study of Civil Military Roles and Relations in the Career of a Sixteenth-Century Warrior, Reformer, and Hero." Ph.D. diss., Yale University, 1968.

Miyamoto Musashi. *The Book of Five Rings.* Translated by Thomas Cleary. Boston: Shambhala, 1994.

Moloughney, Brian, and Xia Weizhong. "Silver and the Fall of the Ming: A Reassessment." *Papers on Far Eastern History* 40 (September 1989): 51–78.

Mori Katsumi. "The Beginnings of Overseas Advance of Japanese Merchant Ships." *Acta Asiatica* 23 (1972): 1–24.

——. "International Relations between the 10th and 16th Century and the Development of Japanese International Consciousness." *Acta Asiatica* 2 (1961): 69–93.

Morillo, Stephen. "Guns and Government: A Comparative Study of Europe and Japan." *Journal of World History* 6.1 (Spring 1995): 75–106.

Mote, Frederick W. *Imperial China, 900–1800.* Cambridge, Mass.: Harvard University Press, 1999.

Mote, Frederick W., and Denis Twitchett, eds. *The Cambridge History of China, Volume 8: The Ming Dynasty, 1368–1644, Part II.* Cambridge: Cambridge University Press, 1998.

——. *The Cambridge History of China, Volume 7: The Ming Dynasty, 1368–1644, Part I.* Cambridge: Cambridge University Press, 1988.

Mungello, D. E. *The Great Encounter of China and the West, 1500–1800.* Lanham, Md.: Rowman and Littlefield, 1999.

Murai Shōsuke. *Chūsei wajinden.* Tokyo: Iwanami shoten, 1993.

Murakami Tsuneo. *Kan Han: Jukyo o tsutaeta ryoshu no sokuseki.* Tokyo: Akashi shoten, 1999.

Murdoch, James. *A History of Japan Vol. II: During the Century of Early Foreign Intercourse(1542–1651).* London: Kegan Paul, Trench, and Trubner, 1925.

Naito Shumpo. *Bunroku keichō no eki ni okeru hiryonin no kenkyū.* Tokyo: Tokyo daigaku shūppansha, 1976.

——. "Sō Keinen no Chōsen nichinichiki ni tsuite." *Chōsen gakuhō* 35 (May 1965): 155–67.

———. "Bunroku Keichō no eki ni okeru hiryo Chōsenjin no sakkan mondai ni tsuite: Chōsen shiryo ni yoru." Pt. 3. *Chōsen gakuhō* 34 (January 1965): 74–140.

———. "Bunroku Keichō no eki ni okeru hiryo Chōsenjin no sakkan mondai ni tsuite: Chōsen shiryo ni yoru." Pt. 2. *Chōsen gakuhō* 33 (October 1964): 48–103.

Nagahara Keiji and Yamamura Kozo. "Shaping the Process of Unification: Technological Process in Sixteenth- and Seventeenth-Century Japan." *Journal of Japanese Studies* 14.1 (1988): 77–109.

Nagahara Keiji et al., eds. *Chūsei kinsei no kokka to shakai.* Tokyo: Tokyo daigaku shuppankai, 1986.

Nakamura Hidetaka. "Chōsengun no horyo ni natta Fukuda Kanyuki no kyōjutsu." In Fujiki and Kitajima, *Shokuhō seiken,* 324–28.

———. "Torigai sensō ni okeru Toyotomi Hideyoshi no mokuteki." In Fujiki and Kitajima, *Shokuhō seiken,* 277–305.

———. *Nihon to Chōsen.* Tokyo: Shibundō, 1966.

———. *Nissen kankeishi no kenkyū.* 3 vols. Tokyo: Yoshikawa kōbunkan, 1965–69.

Nakamura Tadashi. "Chōsen no eki to Kyushu." In Fujiki and Kitajima, *Shokuhō seiken,* 262–76.

Nakamura Tokugoro. "Ni-Min kōwa haretsu shi temmatsu." *Shigaku zasshi* 8.10 (October 1897): 957–83.

Nakano Hitoshi. *Toyotomi seiken no taigai shinryaku to Taika kenchi.* Tokyo: Azekura shobo, 1996.

Nakao Hiroshi. *Chōsen tsushinshi to Jinshin waran: Nitcho kankei shiron.* Tokyo: Akashi shōten, 2000.

Nakura Tetsuzō. "Hideyoshi no Chōsen shinryaku to shinkoku-bakuhanseishihai ideorogii keisei no ichi zentei to shite." *Rekishi hyōron* 314 (1976): 29–35.

Nazakato, Norimoto. *Hideyoshi no Chōsen shinko to minshu bunroku no eki (Imujin ueran): Nihon minshu no kuno to Chōsen minshu no teiko.* 2 vols. Tokyo: Bunken shūppansha, 1993.

Needham, Joseph, et al. *Science and Civilisation in China Volume 5, Part 6: Chemistry and Chemical Technology: Military Technology; Missiles and Sieges.* Cambridge: Cambridge University Press, 1994.

———. *Science and Civilisation in China Volume 5, Part 7: Chemistry and Chemical Technology: Military Technology; The Gunpowder Epic.* Cambridge: Cambridge University Press, 1986.

Neves, Jaime Ramalhete. "The Portuguese in the Im-Jim War?" *Review of Culture* 18 (1994): 20–24.

Niderost, Eric. "Yi Sun Sin and Won Kyun: The Rivalry That Decided the Fate of a Nation." *Korean Culture* 22.4 (Winter 2001): 10–19.

Nishijima Sadao. *Nihon rekishi no kokuksai kankyō.* Tokyo: Tokyo daigaku shuppankai, 1985.

Noguchi Kakuchu. *Yakimono to tsurugi: Hideyoshi no Chōsen shuppei to toko dai torai.* Tokyo: Kōdansha, 1980.

Nukii Masayuki. *Toyotomi seiken no kaigai shinryaku to Chōsen gihei kenkyū.* Tokyo: Aoki shōten, 1996.

———. *Hideyoshi to tatakatta Chōsen busho.* Tokyo: Rokko shuppan, 1992.

Ŏ Hŭimun. *Swaemirok.* 2 vols. Ca. 1601. Seoul: National History Institute, 1962.

Okano Masako. "Banreki niju nen Neige heihen." In Ono, *Minmatsu Shinsho,* 587–623.

———. "Minmatsu Hashu ni okeru Yō Ōryo no ran ni tsuite." *Tōhōgaku* 41 (March 1971): 63–75.

Okuyama Norio. "Mindai junbu seido no hensen." *Tōyōshi kenkyū* 45.2 (September 1986): 55–80.

Ono Kazuko, ed. *Minmatsu Shinsho no shakai to bunka.* Kyoto: Kyoto daigaku jimbun gaku kenkyūsho, 1996.

———. ed. *Min-Shin jidai no seiji to shakai.* Kyoto: Kyoto daigaku jinbun kagaku kenkyūsho, 1986.

———. "'Banreki teisho' to 'Banreki shosho.'" *Tōyōshi kenkyū* 39.4 (March 1981): 33–52.

Ooms, Herman. *Tokugawa Ideology: Early Constructs, 1570–1680.* Princeton: Princeton University Press, 1985.

Osa Masanori. "Keitetsu Genso ni tsuite-ichi gaikō sō no shutsuji to hōkei." *Chōsen gakuhō* 29 (1963): 135–47.

Osaka Castle Museum. *Hideyoshi and Osaka Castle: A Look into Its History and Mystery.* Osaka: Osaka Castle Museum, 1988.

Osawa Akihiro. "Minmatsu shukyo teki hanran no ichi kosatsu." *Tōyōshi kenkyū* 44.1 (June 1985): 45–76.

Ōta Hideharu. "Gunbu ni yoru Bunroku-Keichō no eki no jōkaku kenkyu." *Gunji shigaku* 38.2 (September 2002): 35–48.

Oze Hoan. *Taikō-ki.* Ca. 1625. Tokyo: Iwanami shoten, 1996.

Pak Tongnyang. *Kijae chapki.* 1590s. Seoul: National Library of Korea, 2005. Manuscript (accessed via electronic database).

Palais, James B. *Confucian Statecraft and Korean Institutions: Yu Hyŏnggwŏn and the Late Chosŏn Dynasty.* Seattle: University of Washington Press, 1996.

Park, Eugene Y. *Between Dreams and Reality: The Military Examination in Late Chosŏn Korea.* Cambridge, Mass.: Harvard University Press, 2007.

———. "Military Examination Graduates in Sixteenth-Century Korea: Political Upheaval, Social Change, and Security Crisis." *Journal of Asian History* 35.1 (2001): 1–57.

Park Jae-gwang. "A Study on the Fire Weapons of Chosŏn, Ming, and Japan in the Imjin Waeran." *Kunsa* [Military History] 51.4 (2004): 109–49.

Park Yune-hee. *Admiral Yi Sun-shin and His Turtleboat Armada.* Seoul: Hanjin Publishing, 1978.

Parker, Geoffrey. "The Limits to Revolutions in Military Affairs: Maurice of Nassau, the Battle of Nieuwpoort (1600) and the Legacy." *The Journal of Military History* 71.2 (April 2007): 331–72.

———. *The Grand Strategy of Philip II.* New Haven: Yale University Press, 1998.

———. *The Military Revolution: Military Innovation and the Rise of the West 1500–1800.* 2nd ed. Cambridge: Cambridge University Press, 1996.

———, ed. *The Cambridge Illustrated History of Warfare: The Triumph of the West.* Cambridge: Cambridge University Press, 1995.

Perdue, Peter C. *China Marches West: The Qing Conquest of Central Eurasia.* Cambridge, Mass.: Harvard University Press, 2005.

Perrin, Noel S. *Giving up the Gun: Japan's Reversion to the Sword, 1543–1879.* Boston: David R. Godine, 1979.

Qi Jiguang. *Jixiao xinshu.* 1562. Taibei: Wuzhou chubanshe, 2000.

Qian Jibo. *Ming jian.* 2 vols. Taibei: Qiming shuju, 1959.

Qian Shizhen. *Zheng dong shiji.* Ca.1598. In *Congshu jicheng xubian,* vol. 23. Shanghai: Shanghai shudian, 1994.

Qian Yiben, comp. *Wanli dichao.* 3 vols. Ca. 1617. Taibei: Zhengzhong shuju, 1982.

Qu Jiusi. *Zuben Wanli wu gong lu.* 5 vols. 1612. Taibei: Yiwen shuguan, 1980.

Rai Sanyo. *Nihon gaishi.* 2 vols. 1827. Taibei: Guangwen shuju, 1982.

Rawski, Evelyn S. *The Last Emperors: A Social History of Qing Imperial Institutions.* Berkeley: University of California Press, 1998.

Reid, Anthony. *Southeast Asia in the Age of Commerce, 1450–1680. Volume One: The Lands below the Winds.* New Haven: Yale University Press, 1988.

———. *Southeast Asia in the Age of Commerce, 1450–1680. Volume Two: Expansion and Crisis.* New Haven: Yale University Press, 1993.

Ricci, Matteo. *China in the Sixteenth Century: The Journals of Matthew Ricci, 1583–1610.* Translated by Louis J. Gallagher. New York: Random House, 1953.

Robinson, David M., ed. *Culture, Courtiers, and Competition: The Ming Court (1368–1644).* Cambridge, Mass.: Harvard University Asia Center, 2008.

———. "Disturbing Images: Rebellion, Usurpation, and Rulership in Early Sixteenth-Century East Asia—Korean Writings on Emperor Wuzong." *The Journal of Korean Studies* 9.1 (Fall 2004): 97–127.

———. *Bandits, Eunuchs, and the Son of Heaven: Rebellion and the Economy of Violence in Mid-Ming China.* Honolulu: University of Hawaii Press, 2001.

———. "Korean Lobbying at the Ming Court: King Chungjong's Usurpation of 1506: A Research Note." *Ming Studies* 41 (1999): 37–53.

Robinson, Kenneth R. "An Island's Place in History: Tsushima in Japan and in Chosŏn, 1392–1592." *Korean Studies* 30 (2006): 40–66.

———. "Centering the King of Chosŏn: Aspects of Korean Maritime Diplomacy, 1392–1592." *Journal of Asian Studies* 59.1 (February 2000): 109–25.

———. "The Imposter Branch of the Hatekeyama Family and Japanese-Chosŏn Court Relations, 1455–1580s." *Asian Cultural Studies* 25 (1999): 67–88.

———. "Policies of Practicality: The Chosŏn Court's Regulation of Contact with Japanese and Jurchens, 1392–1580s." Ph.D. diss., University of Hawaii, 1997.

———. "The Tsushima Governor and the Regulation of Contact with Chosŏn in the Fifteenth and Sixteenth Centuries." *Korean Studies* 20 (1996): 23–50.

———. "From Raiders to Traders: Border Security and Border Control in Early Chosŏn." *Korean Studies* 16 (1992): 94–115.

Rogers, Clifford J., ed. *The Military Revolution Debate.* Boulder: Westview, 1995.

Rossabi, Morris. "The Ming and Inner Asia." In Mote and Twitchett, *Cambridge History of China Volume 8,* 221–71.

———. "The Tea and Horse Trade with Inner Asia during the Ming." *Journal of Asian History* 4.2 (1970): 136–68.

Ryang, Key S. "The Korean-Japanese Relations in the Seventeenth Century." *Korea Observer* 13.4 (Winter 1982): 434–50.

Sadler, A. L. "The Naval Campaign in the Korean War of Hideyoshi (1592–1598)." *Transactions of the Asiatic Society of Japan*, 2nd ser., 14 (June 1937): 179–208.

Sanbō honbu, comp. *Nihon senshi: Chōsen no eki.* Reprint, Tokyo: Murata shoten, 1978.

Sansom, George. *A History of Japan, 1334–1615.* Stanford, Calif.: Stanford University Press, 1994.

Sasama Yoshihiko. *Jidai kōshō Nihon kassen zuten.* Tokyo: Yuzankaku, 1997.

Sato Fumitoshi. "Dozoku Riseizan no ran ni tsuite Minmatsu kahoku nomin hanran no ichi keitai." *Toyo Gakūho* 53.3–4 (1971): 117–63.

Satow, E. "The Korean Potters in Satsuma." *Transactions of the Asiatic Society of Japan* 6.2 (1878): 193–203.

Sawyer, Ralph D. *Fire and Water: The Art of Incendiary and Aquatic Warfare in China.* Boulder: Westview, 2004.

———, trans. *One Hundred Unorthodox Strategies: Battle and Tactics of Chinese Warfare.* Boulder: Westview, 1996.

———. *The Seven Military Classics of Ancient China.* Boulder: Westview, 1993.

Selby, Stephen. *Chinese Archery.* Hong Kong: Hong Kong University Press, 2000.

Serruys, Henry. "Towers in the Northern Frontier Defenses of the Ming." *Ming Studies* 14 (1982): 9–76.

———. "Sino-Mongol Relations during the Ming III: Trade Relations: The Horse Fairs (1400–1600)." *Melanges Chinois et bouddhiques* 17 (1973–75): 9–275.

———. *Sino-Mongol Relations during the Ming II: The Tribute System and Diplomatic Missions (1400–1600).* Vol. 14 of *Melanges Chinois et Bouddhiques.* Brussels: Institut Belge des hautes etudes Chinoises, 1967.

———. "Four Documents Relating to the Sino-Mongol Peace of 1570–1571." *Monumenta Serica* 19 (1960): 1–66.

———. *Genealogical Tables of the Descendants of Dayan-Qan.* The Hague: Mouton, 1958.

Shahar, Meir. *The Shaolin Monastery: History, Religion, and the Chinese Martial Arts.* Honolulu: University of Hawaii Press, 2008.

Shen Defu. *Wanli yehuo bian.* 3 vols. 1619. Beijing: Zhonghua shuju, 1980.

Shen Guoyuan. *Huang Ming congxin lu.* 1627. Yangzhou: Jiangsu guangling guji keyinshe, 1987.

Shin Dongkyu. "Oranda jin hyōryūmin to Chōsen no seiyō shiki heiki no kaihatsu." *Shi'en* 61.1 (November 2000): 54–70.

Shin Leo K. *The Making of the Chinese State: Ethnicity and Expansion on the Ming Borderlands.* New York: Cambridge University Press, 2006.

Shore, David H. "Last Court of Ming China: The Reign of the Yung-li Emperor in the South, 1647–1662." Ph.D. diss., Princeton University, 1976.

Showalter, Dennis. "Caste, Skill, and Training: The Evolution of Cohesion in European Armies from the Middle Ages to the Sixteenth Century." *The Journal of Military History* 57.3 (July 1993): 407–30.

Shultz, Edward J. *Generals and Scholars: Military Rule in Medieval Korea.* Honolulu: University of Hawaii Press, 2000.

Sim Nosung, comp. *Paerim*. 10 vols. Ca. 1800. Seoul: T'amgudang, 1969–70.

Sin Hum. *Sangch'on ko*. Vols. 71–72 in *Han'guk munchip ch'onggan*. 220 vols. Seoul: Kyŏngin munhwasa, 1990.

———. *Sangch'on Sŏnsaeng chip*. 1636. Berkeley: University of California, 1972. Manuscript (microfilm).

Sin Kisu. *Jusha Kan Han to Nihon: Jukyo o Nihon ni tsutaeta Chōsenjin*. Tokyo: Akashi shōten, 1991.

Sin Kyŏng. *Zaizao fanbang zhi [Chaejo pŏnbang chi]*. 2 vols. Ca. 1693. Taibei: Guiting chubanshe, 1980.

So Kwan-wai. *Japanese Piracy in Ming China during the Sixteenth Century*. East Lansing: Michigan State University Press, 1975.

Sohn Pow-key, ed. *Nanjung Ilgi: War Diary of Admiral Yi Sun-sin*. Translated by Ha Tae-hung. Seoul: Yonsei University Press, 1977.

Song Maocheng. *Jiuyue qianji*. Ca. 1612. Facsimile reprint, Kyoto: Kyoto daigaku, 1973.

Song Yingchang. *Jinglue fuguo yaobian*. 2 vols. 1590s. Taibei: Taiwan xuesheng shuju, 1986.

———. *Song jinglue shu*. Ca. 1594. In *Zhong-Han guanxi shiliao xuanji vol. 6*. Taibei: Guiting chubanshe, 1980.

Souryi, Pierre Francois. *The World turned Upside Down: Medieval Japanese Society*. Translated by Kate Roth. New York: Columbia University Press, 2001.

Spence, Jonathan D., and John E. Wills, eds. *From Ming to Ch'ing: Conquest Region and Continuity in Seventeenth Century China*. New Haven: Yale University Press, 1979.

Stramigioli, Giuliana. "Hideyoshi's Expansionist Policy on the Asiatic Mainland." *Transactions of the Asiatic Society of Japan*, 3rd ser. (December 1954): 74–116.

Strauss, Barry. "Korea's Legendary Admiral." *Military History Quarterly* 17.4 (Summer 2005): 52–61.

Struve, Lynn A., ed. *The Qing Formation in World-Historical Time*. Cambridge, Mass.: Harvard University Press, 2004.

———. *The Ming-Qing Conflict, 1619–1683: A Historiography and Source Guide*. Ann Arbor: Association for Asian Studies, 1998.

———, ed. and trans. *Voices from the Ming-Qing Cataclysm: China in Tiger's Jaws*. Princeton: Princeton University Press, 1993.

———. *The Southern Ming: 1644–1662*. New Haven: Yale University Press, 1984.

Suganuma, Unryu. "Sino-Liuqiu and Japanese-Liuqiu Relations in Early Modern Times." *Journal of Asian History* 31.1 (1997): 47–60.

Suh In-han. "Cavalry Engagements Involving the Allied Forces of Chosŏn and Chinese Ming Troops." *Kunsa* [Military History] 51.4 (2004): 1–43.

Sun Laichen. "Ming China and Korea, c. 1368–1600: With Special Reference to Gunpowder Technology." Unpublished conference paper presented at the International Conference on Asian Studies, 2004.

———. "Qi Jiguang and the Japanese Invasion of Korea (1592–1598)." Unpublished paper presented at the Annual Meeting of the Association for Asian Studies, 2004.

———. "Military Technology Transfers from Ming China and the Emergence of Northern Mainland Southeast Asia (c. 1390–1527)." *Journal of Southeast Asian Studies* 34.3 (October 2003): 495–517.

———. "Ming–Southeast Asian Overland Interactions, 1368–1644." Ph.D. diss., University of Michigan, 2000.

Sun Wenliang. *Ming-Qing renwu*. Shanghai: Shanghai renmin chubanshe, 1991.

Sung Ying-hsing. *Chinese Technology in the Seventeenth Century: T'ien kung k'ai-wu*. Translated by E-tu Zen Sun and Shiou-chuan Sun. Mineola, N.Y.: Dover, 1997.

Susser, Bernard. "The Toyotomi Regime and the Daimyo." In Mass and Hauser, *Bakufu in Japanese History*, 129–52.

Suzuki Chusei. *Chugokushi ni okeru kakumei to shukyo*. Tokyo: Tokyo daigaku shuppankai, 1974.

Suzuki Ryōichi. *Toyotomi Hideyoshi*. Tokyo: Iwanami shoten, 1954.

Swope, Kenneth M. "Cutting Dwarf Pirates Down to Size: Amphibious Warfare in Sixteenth-Century East Asia." Forthcoming in Selected Papers of the 2007 Naval History Symposium, Annapolis, Md.

———. "Bestowing the Double-edged Sword: Wanli as Supreme Military Commander." In Robinson, *Culture, Courtiers, and Competition*, 61–115.

———. "War and Remembrance: Yang Hao and the Siege of Ulsan of 1598." *Journal of Asian History* 42.2 (December 2008): 165–95.

———. "Approaches to the Imjin War." *Journal of Korean Studies* 12.1 (Fall 2007): 154–61.

———. "Protecting the Dragon's Teeth: Reasons for Ming China's Intervention." In Chung Doo-hee, *Transnational History of the "Imjin Waeran*," 365–90.

———. "Beyond Turtleboats: Siege Accounts from Hideyoshi's Second Invasion of Korea, 1597–1598." *Sungkyun Journal of East Asian Studies* 6.2 (October 2006): 177–206.

———. "Crouching Tigers, Secret Weapons: Military Technology Employed during the Sino-Japanese-Korean War, 1592–1598." *The Journal of Military History* 69.1 (January 2005): 11–43.

———, ed. *The International Library of Essays in Military History: Warfare in China since 1600*. Aldershot, U.K.: Ashgate, 2005.

———. "A Few Good Men: The Li Family and China's Northern Frontier in the Late Ming." *Ming Studies* 49 (2004): 34–81.

———. "Turning the Tide: The Strategic and Psychological Significance of the Liberation of Pyongyang in 1593." *War and Society* 21.2 (October 2003): 1–22.

———. "All Men Are Not Brothers: Ethnic Identity and Dynastic Loyalty in the Ningxia Mutiny of 1592." *Late Imperial China* 24.1 (June 2003): 79–129.

———. "Deceit, Disguise, and Dependence: China, Japan, and the Future of the Tributary System, 1592–1596." *The International History Review* 24.4 (December 2002): 757–82.

———. "The Three Great Campaigns of the Wanli Emperor, 1592–1600: Court, Military, and Society in Late Sixteenth-Century China." Ph.D. diss., University of Michigan, 2001.

————. "Civil-Military Coordination in the Bozhou Campaign of the Wanli Era." *War and Society* 18.2 (October 2000): 49–70.

Takagi Hiroshi. "Toyotomi Hideyoshi in Modern Japan." In Chung Doo-hee, *Transnational History of the "Imjin Waeran,"* 243–52.

Takagi, Shōsaku. "Hideyoshi's Peace and the Transformation of the Bushi Class—the Dissolution of the Autonomy of the Medieval Bushi." *Acta Asiatica* 49 (1985): 46–77.

Takayanagi Mitsutoshi. *Sengoku jinmei jiten.* Tokyo: Yoshikawa kobunkan, 1973.

Tamura Jitsuzō. "Mindai no hoppen bōei taisei." In *Mindai Man-Mō shi kenkyū* edited by Tamura Jitsuzō, 73–161. Kyoto: Kyoto daigaku, 1963.

Tamura Jōji. *Konishi Yukinaga.* Tokyo: Chūō shuppansha, 1978.

Tan Qian, ed. *Guoque.* 10 vols. 1653. Taibei: Dingwen shuju, 1978.

Tan Qixiang, ed. *Zhongguo lishi ditu ji.* Vol. 7 of Yuan-Ming. Shanghai: Ditu chubanshe, 1991.

Tanaka Takeo, ed. *Nihon zenkindai no kokka to taigai kankei.* Tokyo: Yoshikawa kobunkan, 1987.

Tanaka Yoshinari. *Toyotomi jidaishi.* Reprint, Tokyo: Kōdansha, 1980.

Taniguchi Kikuo. "Minmatsu hokuhen boei ni okeru saisochi ni tsuite." In Ono, *Minmatsu Shinsho,* 1–26.

————. "Peasant Rebellions in the Late Ming." *Acta Asiatica* 38 (March 1980): 54–68.

Tashiro Kazui. "Foreign Relations during the Edo Period: *Sakoku* Reexamined." *Journal of Japanese Studies* 8.2 (Summer 1982): 283–306.

Taylor, Romeyn. *The Guard System of the Ming Dynasty: Its Original Organization and Its Decline.* Chicago: University of Chicago, 1953.

————. "Yüan Origins of the *Wei-so* System." In Hucker, *Chinese Government in Ming Times,* 23–40.

Tien Chen-ya. *Chinese Military Theory: Ancient and Modern.* Oakville, N.Y.: Mosaic, 1992.

Tilly, Charles. *Coercion, Capital, and European States, 990–1990.* London: Basil Blackwell, 1990.

Toby, Ronald P. "Contesting the Centre: International Sources of Japanese National Identity." *The International History Review* 7.3 (August 1985): 347–63.

————. *State and Diplomacy in Early Modern Japan: Asia in the Development of the Tokugawa Bakufu.* Stanford, Calif.: Stanford University Press, 1984.

Tokutomi Iichirō. *Toyotomi Hideyoshi: Toyotomi shi jidai.* Tokyo: Kōdansha, 1981.

Tokyo daigaku shiryō hensanjo, comp. *Hō taikō Shinseki shū.* 3 vols. Tokyo: Tokyo daigaku shuppan kai, 1938.

Tong Chao, ed. *Zhongguo junshi zhidu shi: Houqin zhidu juan.* Zhengzhou: Da xiang chubanshe, 1997.

Tong, James. *Disorder under Heaven: Collective Violence in the Ming Dynasty.* Stanford, Calif.: Stanford University Press, 1991.

Totman, Conrad. *Early Modern Japan.* Berkeley: University of California Press, 1993.

Tsai, Shih-shan Henry. *Perpetual Happiness: The Ming Emperor Yongle.* Seattle: University of Washington Press, 2001.

———. *The Eunuchs in the Ming Dynasty.* Albany: State University of New York Press, 1996.

Tsunoda Ryusaku, William Theodore de Bary, and Donald Keene, comps. *Sources of Japanese Tradition.* New York: Columbia University Press, 1960.

Tsuruta Kei. "The Establishment and Characteristics of the 'Tsushima Gate.'" *Acta Asiatica* 67 (1994): 30–48.

Turnbull, Stephen. *The Samurai and the Sacred.* Oxford: Osprey, 2006.

———. *Ninja: The True Story of Japan's Secret Warrior Cult.* London: Caxton, 2003.

———. *Samurai Invasion: Japan's Korean War, 1592–1598.* London: Cassell, 2002.

———. *The Samurai Sourcebook.* London: Cassell, 2000.

———. *Samurai Warfare.* London: Arms and Armour, 1997.

———. *The Samurai: A Military History.* Surrey: Japan Library, 1996.

Udagawa Takehisa. *Higashi Ajia heiki kōryūshi no kenkyū: Jūgo kara jūnana seiki ni okeru heiki no juyō to denpa.* Tokyo: Yoshikawa kōbunkan, 1993.

———. *Teppō denrai: heiki ga kataru kinsei no taryō.* Tokyo: Chūō kōronsha, 1990.

Underwood, Horace H. "Korean Boats and Ships." *Transactions of the Korea Branch of the Royal Asiatic Society* 23 (1934): 1–99.

Van de Ven, Hans, ed. *Warfare in Chinese History.* Leiden, U.K.: Brill, 2000.

Von Glahn, Richard. *Fountain of Fortune: Money and Monetary Policy in China, 1000–1700.* Berkeley: University of California Press, 1996.

Von Verschuer, Charlotte. "Japan's Foreign Relations, 1200–1392 A.D.: Translation from *Zenrin kokuhôki.*" *Monumenta Nipponica* 57.4 (2002): 413–45.

Wade, Geoff. "The *Ming shi-lu* as a Source for Thai History—Fourteenth to Seventeenth Centuries." *Journal of Southeast Asian Studies* 31.2 (September 2000): 249–94.

Wakeman, Frederic, Jr. "China and the Seventeenth-Century Crisis." *Late Imperial China* 7.1 (June 1986): 1–26.

———. *The Great Enterprise: The Manchu Reconstruction of Imperial Order in Seventeenth Century China.* 2 vols. Berkeley: University of California Press, 1985.

Wakita Osamu. "The Emergence of the State in Sixteenth-Century Japan: From Oda to Tokugawa." *Journal of Japanese Studies* 8.2 (Summer 1982): 343–67.

Wakita Osamu and James L. McClain. "The Commercial and Urban Policies of Oda Nobunaga and Toyotomi Hideyoshi." In Hall et al., *Japan before Tokugawa,* 224–47.

Waldron, Arthur. *The Great Wall of China: From History to Myth.* Cambridge: Cambridge University Press, 1992.

Waley-Cohen, Joanna. *The Culture of War in China: Empire and the Military under the Qing Dynasty.* London: I. B. Tauris, 2006.

———. "Civil-Military Relations in Imperial China: Introduction." *War and Society* 18.2 (October 2000): 1–8.

Walker, Brett L. "Foreign Affairs and Frontiers in Early Modern Japan: A Historiographical Essay." *Early Modern Japan* 10.2 (Fall 2002): 44–62.

Walker, Hugh D. "The Yi-Ming Rapprochment: Sino-Korean Foreign Relations, 1392–1592." Ph.D. diss., University of California, 1971.

Wang Chongwu. "Li Rusong zheng dong kao." *Lishi yuyan yanjiusuo jikan* 14 (1948): 343–74.

———. "Liu Ting zheng dong kao." *Lishi yuyan yanjiusuo jikan* 16 (1947): 137–49.

Wang Hongxu, comp. *Ming shigao.* 7 vols. 1723. Taibei: Wenhai chubanshe, 1962.

Wang Li. "Ming dai yingbing zhi chutan." *Beijing shifan daxue xuebao* (1991.2): 85–93.

Wang Qi. *Sancai tuhui.* 3 vols. 1610. Shanghai: Shanghai guji chubanshe, 1988.

Wang Tianyou and Xu Daling, eds. *Ming chao shiliu di.* Beijing: Zijincheng chubanshe, 1991.

Wang,Xiangrong. *Zhong-Ri guanxi wenxian lunkao.* Beijing: Yuelu shushe, 1985.

Wang Xiaowei, ed. *Zhongguo junshi zhidu shi: Bingyi zhidu juan.* Zhengzhou: Daxiang chubanshe, 1997.

Wang Yi-t'ung. *Official Relations between China and Japan, 1368–1549.* Cambridge, Mass.: Harvard University Press, 1953.

Wang Yong. "Realistic and Fantastic Images of 'Dwarf Pirates': The Evolution of Ming Dynasty Perceptions of the Japanese." In Fogel, *Sagacious Monks and Bloodthirsty Warriors,* 17–41.

Wang Yuquan. *Ming dai de juntian.* Beijing: Zhonghua shuju, 1965.

Watanabe Takeshi, ed. *Hideyoshi to Momoyama bunka.* Osaka: Osaka Castle Museum, 1997.

Watanabe Yosuke. *Hō taikō no shiteki seikatsu.* Tokyo: Kōdansha, 1980.

Weems, Clarence Norwood, ed. *Hulbert's History of Korea.* 2 vols. New York: Hillary House, 1962.

Whitmore, John K. "Vietnam and the Monetary Flow of Eastern Asia, Thirteenth to Eighteenth Centuries." In *Precious Metals in the Later Mediaeval and Early Modern Worlds,* edited by John F. Richards, 363–93. Durham, N.C.: Carolina Academic Press, 1983.

Wolters, O. W. "Ayudhya and the Rearward Part of the World." *Journal of the Royal Asiatic Society of Great Britain and Ireland* 3–4 (1968): 166–78.

Wu Fengpei et al., comps. *Renchen zhi yi shiliao huiji.* 2 vols. Beijing: Quanguo tushuguan wenxian suowei fuzhi zhongxin chubanshe, 1990.

Wu Han, comp. *Chaoxian Li chao shilu zhong de Zhongguo shiliao.* 12 vols. Beijing: Zhonghua shuju, 1980.

Wu Yanhong. *Ming dai chongjun yanjiu.* Beijing: Shehui kexue wenxian chubanshe, 2003.

Xia Xie. *Ming tongjian.* 5 vols. Ca. 1870. Taibei: Xinan shuju, 1982.

Xu Xianyao. "Ming dai de goujun." *Ming shi yanjiu zhuankan* 6 (June 1983): 133–92.

Yamagata I. "Japanese-Korean Relations after the Japanese Invasion of Korea in the 16th Century." *Transactions of the Korea Branch of the Royal Asiatic Society* 4.2 (1913): 1–11.

Yamamoto Masayoshi. *Shimazu kokushi.* 10 vols. Tokyo: Seikyō kappan insatsujo, 1905.

Yanigada Toshio. "Bunroku Keichō no Eki to kirisitan senkyōshi." *Shigaku* 52.1 (1982): 19–39.

Yang Hsien-yi and Gladys Yangs, trans. *The Courtesan's Jewel Box: Chinese Stories of the Xth–XVIIth Centuries.* Peking: Foreign Languages Press, 1957.

Yang Hu. *Ming dai Liaodong dusi.* Zhengzhou: Zhengzhou guji chubanshe, 1988.

Yang Shaoxian and Mo Junqing. *Ming dai minzu shi.* Chengdu: Sichuan minzu chubanshe, 1996.

Yao Guangxiao et al., comps. *Ming shilu.* 133 vols. plus 21 vols. of appendices. Taibei: Zhongyang yanjiuyuan lishi yuyan yanjiusuo, 1962–66.

Yi Chin-hui. "Korean Envoys and Japan: Korean-Japanese Relations in the 17th to 19th Centuries." *Korea Journal* 25.12 (December 1985): 24–35.

Yi Homin et al. *Obong chip; Injae chip.* Vol. 3 in Yi U., *Imjin waeran kwan'gye.*

Yi Hyŏngsŏk. *Imjin chŏllansa.* 3 vols. Seoul: Sinhyonsilsa, 1974.

Yi Kae-hwang. *Bunroku keichō no eki to Higashi Ajia.* Kyoto: Rinsen shōten, 1997.

Yi No. *Yŏngsa ilgi.* 1592–93. Seoul: Ŭlyu munhwasa, 1974.

Yi Sanhae et al. *Agye yugo: Ilsong chip; Sogyong chip; Yuch'on chip.* Ca. 1600. Vol. 2 in Yi U., *Imjin waeran kwan'gye.*

Yi T'akyŏng. *Chŏngmannok.* Ŭisŏng: Ŭisŏngkun, 2002.

Yi Usong, et al., comps. *Imjin waeran kwan'gye munhon ch'onggan.* Ca. 1600. 3 vols. Seoul: Asea munhwasa, 1984.

Yi Wŏn'ik. *Yi Sanguk ilgi.* 1620s. In vol. 6 of *Paerim,* compiled by Sim Nosung. Ca. 1800. Seoul: T'amgudang, 1969.

Yonetani, Hitoshi. "Repatriation of Korean Captives from the Hideyoshi Invasion." In Chung Doo-hee, *Transnational History of the "Imjin Waeran,"* 313–26.

Yoshio Hiroshi. "Minmatsu Yo Shimasa no chi-iki boei an ni tsuite." *Tōyōshi kenkyū* 45.4 (March 1987): 1–24.

Yoshioka Shinichi. "Bunroku-Keichō no eki ni okeru kaki ni tsuite no kenkyū." *Chōsen gakuho* 108 (July 1983): 71–109.

Yu Jae-chun. "Mountain Fortresses: The Front Line of National Defense." *Koreana* 19.1 (Spring 2005): 18–23.

Yu Sagyŏng. *Yug'yudang ilgi.* 1597–1605. Seoul: National Library of Korea, 1972.

Yu Sŏngnyong. *Chingbirok.* Ca. 1600 (published 1695). In Wu Fengpei et al., *Renchen zhi yi shiliao huiyi,* 2:257–470.

Yu Yanfang. *Chaonu yicuo.* Ca. 1620. Facsimile reprint, Nanjing: Nanjing daxue, 1928.

Yu Zhijia. *Ming dai junhu shi xi zhidu.* Taibei: Taibei xuesheng shuju, 1987.

Yuan Suiren. "Lun Zhang Juzheng gaige de lishi jiejian." *Zhongguo shi yanjiu* (1994.2): 50–58.

Yujŏng. *Sam taesa wangpu ch'al chop.* 1590s. Seoul: Kyujanggak Archives. Manuscript.

———. *Songun Taesa Punch'ung sŏnallok.* 1739. Berkeley: University of California, 1972. Manuscript (microfilm).

Yun, Peter I. "Rethinking the Tribute System: Korean States and Northeast Asian Interstate Relations, 600–1600." Ph.D. diss., University of California, Los Angeles, 1998.

Zhang Haiying. *Zhang Juzheng gaige yu Shanxi Wanli qingzhang yanjiu.* Taiyuan: Shanxi renmin chubanshe, 1993.

Zhang Jincheng, comp. *Qianlong Ningxia fuzhi.* 2 vols. 1780. Yinchuan: Ningxia renmin chubanshe, 1992.

Zhang Juzheng. *Zhang Wenzhong gong quanji.* 1500s. Taibei: Taiwan shangwu yinshuguan, 1968.

Zhang Tingyu et al., comps. *Ming shi.* 12 vols. 1739. Taibei: Dingwen shuju, 1994.

Zhang Xiaosheng and Liu Wenyan, eds. *Zhongguo gudai zhanzheng tongjian.* 2 vols. Beijing: Changcheng chubanshe, 1988.

Zhao, Jie. "A Decade of Considerable Significance: Late-Ming Factionalism in the Making, 1583–1593." *T'oung Pao* 88 (2002): 112–50.

Zhao Shizhen. *Shenqi pu.* 1598–99. Kyoto University Library. Facsimile manuscript.

Zheng Liangsheng, ed. *Ming dai Wokou shiliao.* 5 vols. Taibei: Wenshizhe chubanshe, 1987.

———. *Ming dai Zhong-Ri guanxi yanjiu.* Taibei: Wenshizhe chubanshe, 1985.

Zheng Ruozeng. *Chouhai tubian.* 1562 (attr. Hu Zongxian, 1624). Lilly Library, Indiana University. Facsimile reprint.

Zhi Yingrui. *Ping xi guanjian.* 1592. Facsimile reprint of Naikaku Bunko edition in *Shan ben shu ying.* Vol. 70. Kyoto: Kyoto daigaku, 1970.

Zhong Kan, ed. *Ningxia gudai lishi jinian.* Yinchuan: Ningxia renmin chubanshe, 1988.

Zhong Kan, Chen Mingyou, and Wu Zhongli. *Ningxia shi hua.* Yinchuan: Ningxia renmin chubanshe, 1988.

Zhu Yafei. "Ming dai yuan Chao zhanzheng heyi wenti xin tan." *Zhongguo shi yanjiu* (1995.2): 155–64.

Zhuan Qixue, comp. *Zhongguo gu waijiao shiliao huibian.* 2 vols. Taibei: Guoli bianzeguan Zhonghua congshu bianshen weiyuanhui, 1980.

Zhuan Zhongxia et al. *Zhongguo junshi shi, Vol. 2 Supplement: Lidai zhanzheng nianbiao.* Beijing: Jiefangjun chubanshe, 1986.

Zhuge Yuansheng. *Liang chao ping rang lu.* 1606. Taibei: Taiwan xuesheng shuju, 1969.

INDEX

References to illustrations appear in italic type.

Aboriginal troops, with Ming, 147, 245–46. *See also* Frontier policy, Ming

Agriculture, 146, 201, 209, 288. *See also* Supply *entries*

Akechi Mitsuhide, 51

Altan Khan, 25

Andong, 259

Angolpo area battles, 115–16, 120, 228

An Hongkuk, 238, 240

Anju, 113

Archers, overview: Japan, 76, 77; Korea, 74, 83; Ming China, 79. *See also* Weapons *entries*

Armor, 75, 76, 77, 249

Arquebus guns, overview, 52, 75–76, *84*, 163, 284. *See also* Weapons *entries*

Asahi Shimbun, 4

Asano Nagayoshi, 257, 266

Ashikaga Yoshimitsu, 47, 54, 321*n*14

Atrocities, 4–5, 175–76, 233–34

Bai Sai, 256

Baishi Pass, 206

Banditry, 202–203

Batten, Bruce, 315*n*12, 316*n*13

Berry, Mary Elizabeth, 64, 222–23

Boats. *See* Naval *entries*

Bo Cheng'en, 27, 33

Bounties. *See* Rewards

Bows. *See* Archers, overview

Bozhou conflict, 34–39, 206, 276, 284

Buddhism, 49. *See also* Monks

Bureaucracy myth, Ming military establishment, 16–17

Bushugtu, 32

Cambridge History of China, 294

Cambridge History of Japan, 294

Cannons, overview: Japan, 52, 76, 77, 322*n*24; Korea, 74–75; Ming China, 78, *85*. *See also* Weapons *entries*

Cao Guoqing, 16

Cao Xibin, 268

Toby, Ronald, 292
Tōdō Takatora, 90, 115, 239, 240, 242, 287
Toksan Castle, 141
Tokugawa Ieyasu, 105, 225–26, 290–91, 292
Tongnae fortress, 91
Tongyŏng, 4
Trade relations: investiture debate, 182; in peace talks, 132, 151, 188, 189–91, 198, 201; and piracy, 276; postwar, 289–92; prewar, 44, 47–48, 321n14, 352n138; treaty terms, 208, 223–24; as war incentive, 60, 63, 66, 207, 324n55, 324n57, 325n65. *See also* Tributary system
Training documents, Ming military, 18–19
Treaty of Kiyu, 291
Tributary system: importance of, 184, 187–88; military support, 121, 123, 150; in peace talks, 190–91, 192; prewar Korea-China, 43–47; treaty terms, 211–13. *See also* Trade relations
Troop statistics, Japan, before first invasion, 62, 67–68, 325n67
Troop statistics, Japan, during first offensive: castle retreats, 172–73; Chenju Island, 180; Chinju attack, 173, 174; Ch'ungju battle, 95; depletion of, 141, 167, 333n142; Hamgyŏng defense, 135, 159; Pyŏkchegwan battle, 161; Pyongyang, 149, 330n96, 335n23; rumored numbers, 137, 149, 336n30; Seoul, 149, 167; totals, 5, 160; withdrawal phase, 180
Troop statistics, Japan, during second offensive: Hwangsŏk fortress, 247; invasion force, 229, 240, 345n20; rumored numbers, 234; Seoul advance, 247; totals, 5; Ulsan, 256, 258–59, 268; and withdrawal decision, 266
Troop statistics, Korea: before invasion, 72; during peace talks, 209

Troop statistics, Korea, during first offensive: Chinju, 140, 174; Ch'ungju battle, 92, 95, 135; guerrilla operations, 108; Haengju fortress defense, 168; Kimhae, 90–91; Pusan defense, 89, 90; Pyongyang, 158; Seoul defense, 97; Tongnae fortress, 91; totals, 5; ŭiju defense, 141; Yong'in battle, 106
Troop statistics, Korea, during second offensive: Chiksan battle, 248; Chungchŏng province, 240; Kyŏngsang, 237, 247; Myŏngyang battle, 251; naval forces, 254; at remobilization, 228; Sachŏn, 351n119; totals, 5; Ulsan seige, 255
Troop statistics, Ming: frontier conflicts, 13, 39; during peace talks, 196, 203; postwar occupation, 284
Troop statistics, Ming, during first offensive: arrivals in Korea, 123–24, 147–48, 150, 330n95, 334n1; coastal defense, 144, 145; Hamgyŏng, 159; Han River crossing, 171; Kaesŏng defense, 161; mobilization planning, 123, 125, 128, 130–31, 138, 142, 146, 165, 333n154; rumored numbers, 332n135; Seoul liberation, 152; Shen's promises, 132; Tianjin defense, 128, 145; totals, 5, 8; withdrawal planning, 177–78
Troop statistics, Ming, during second offensive: Chiksan battle, 248; final advance, 268; mobilization period, 231, 234, 236, 237, 246, 345n20; reinforcements, 250; Sachŏn, 351n119; Sunchŏn battle, 271; totals, 5, 8; Ulsan seige, 255
Tsushima, 46, 47, 56, 89, 289–91, 321n12
Turnbull, Stephen, 69, 351n119
Turtleboats, 75, 118–19, *281*, 330n84
Turtle carts, 174